Learning ActionScript 3.0

A Beginner's Guide

Rich Shupe with Zevan Rosser

O'REILLY®

Beijing · Cambridge · Farnham · Köln · Sebastopol · Taipei · Tokyo

Learning ActionScript 3.0
A Beginner's Guide
by Rich Shupe, with Zevan Rosser

Published by O'Reilly Media, Inc., 1005 Gravenstein Highway North, Sebastopol, CA 95472.

O'Reilly Media books may be purchased for educational, business, or sales promotional use. Online editions are also available for most titles (*safari.oreilly.com*). For more information, contact our corporate/institutional sales department: 800-998-9938 or *corporate@oreilly.com*.

Editor: Robyn Thomas

Production Editor: Michele Filshie

Copy Editor: Jill Steinberg

Technical Reviewer: Matthew Roberts

Proofreader: Linda Seifert

Interior Designer: Ron Bilodeau

Cover Designer: Mark Paglietti

Indexer: Joy Dean Lee

Print History:

December 2007:   First edition.

RepKover. This book uses RepKover™, a durable and flexible lay-flat binding.

ISBN: 978-0-596-52787-7   [11/09]
[F]

Adobe Developer Library, a copublishing partnership between O'Reilly Media Inc. and Adobe Systems, Inc., is the authoritative resource for developers using Adobe technologies. These comprehensive resources offer learning solutions to help developers create cutting-edge interactive web applications that can reach virtually anyone on any platform.

With top-quality books and innovative online resources covering the latest tools for rich-Internet application development, the *Adobe Developer Library* delivers expert training, straight from the source. Topics include ActionScript, Adobe Flex®, Adobe Flash®, and Adobe Acrobat® software.

Get the latest news about books, online resources, and more at *adobedeveloperlibrary.com*.

CONTENTS

PREFACE

When deciding if the book in your hands will be a good resource for your library, it might help you to know why we, the authors, wrote *this* particular book. We are both developers who use Flash extensively in our everyday work, but we are also teachers. Collectively, we have taught thousands of students at multiple universities, training facilities, and conferences, and yet we share one significant common experience. We were consistently told that no feature-rich ActionScript book satisfied this beginner audience.

At first we were surprised at how truly overwhelming this sentiment was, but then we realized that we didn't have enough information to form an opinion. We didn't use beginner resources in our work and had only our own curriculum to go on. So, we started to research how we could fill this void and provide a book to our students that would really help them beyond the classroom. We talked with a lot of students, user groups, and instructors and began to sketch out a book that we thought would put what we learned into practice.

When ActionScript 3.0 was released, the interested audience grew dramatically. Reactions ranged from excitement to uncertainty to fear, as the ActionScript 3.0 learning curve became apparent. Talk of the Flash Platform splintering into Flex ("developer") and Flash ("designer") camps left many designers and beginner programmers more uncertain than ever about their futures. When Flash CS3 Professional was released, the need for a guiding resource didn't dissipate (and, in many cases, increased), and we knew it was time to develop the book you hold in your hands.

We hope this book will help Flash users of all kinds—from curious to intimidated, from eager to experienced—embrace the power and performance of ActionScript 3.0. We hope these pages will ease the transition from whatever prior version, if any, of ActionScript might have been in use, to the biggest architectural change to the language since its inception.

Who This Book Is For

This book is aimed at Flash designers and developers coming to ActionScript 3.0 for the first time, as well as beginner programmers looking to brush up on their ActionScript 3.0 knowledge. Although we feel this volume covers the basics fairly well, both a familiarity with the Flash interface and a small amount of scripting experience is assumed.

We believe we've explained the material herein clearly and concisely enough for any reader to get started, so even if you are new to programming, we welcome you! However, if you have a few moments, we recommend that you skim Chapter 2 to see if you think we've provided enough core programming fundamentals to fill any gaps in your knowledge base. Throughout this book we cover relevant syntax with extensive comments, but the first two chapters serve as a foundation upon which the rest of the chapters are built.

Similarly, if you are a relatively experienced ActionScript 2.0 programmer, you may wish to glance at a few chapters of interest before deciding whether or not this book is for you. We highlight ActionScript 2.0-to-ActionScript 3.0 migration issues, but want you to be happy with the tone and straightforward approach we've adopted before you decide to rely on this book. We endeavor to teach the basic principles behind each chapter topic in a form, chapter number, and page count that is easily digested. In any case, take a moment to read through the next two sections to make sure this is the right book for you.

How This Book Is Organized

Unlike any other book on ActionScript 3.0 that we've seen, this book does not rely extensively on *object-oriented programming (OOP)* principles. If you are unfamiliar with this term, don't worry. You have the correct book in your hands, and you'll learn more with each successive chapter.

We demonstrate key chapter concepts using focused syntax that is executable within the timeline, and gradually introduce OOP concepts along the way. The first five chapters—including coverage of the new ActionScript 3.0 event model and means of displaying content (the display list)—do not introduce more than a modicum of content that is class- or OOP-related. Starting in Chapter 6, we provide increased object-oriented coverage, beginning with an OOP primer, and continuing for the remaining nine chapters with select class- or OOP-based applied examples.

If you're interested in immersing yourself in OOP examples from the outset, all of the main chapter examples are also available in class form in the downloadable source code. This not only provides a jumpstart for those with some OOP experience, but it also serves as a self-guided learning opportunity if you find yourself a bit ahead of the learning curve. Best of all, Flash CS3 Professional's new *Document Class* feature allows you to start using classes more quickly than ever before, allowing a class to serve as a kind of stand-in for the main timeline of any *.fla* file. All you have to do to use it is enter the name of the class in the Flash Property Inspector. (If you can't wait to learn more, jump to the section "The Document Class" in Chapter 1.)

Finally, we've designed an expanded project to go hand in hand with this book. Beginning with Chapter 7, the first chapter following our OOP primer, the downloadable source code features a class package for every chapter. The classes include handy utility methods and properties that will be used in the supplemental project. When you feel comfortable with the syntax of ActionScript 3.0, and the basic principles of object-oriented programming, you can reinforce what you've learned by building the project. The files are available from the book's companion website, which we'll talk about in just a moment.

What Is—and Isn't—In This Book

We've tried to design a book that covers as many ActionScript essentials as we could include, given its size and scope.

What's In

Part I: Getting Started

Part I begins with Chapter 1, discussing ActionScript 1.0, 2.0, and 3.0, and how the different versions are used in the Flash CS3 Professional application and Flash Player. It concludes with Chapter 2 looking at the building blocks that are ActionScript's language-neutral core fundamentals.

Part II: Graphics and Interaction

Chapter 3 leads off Part II, the largest section of the book, with explanations of the basic vocabulary of ActionScript: properties, methods, and events (including ActionScript 3.0's significantly different event model). Chapter 4 focuses on displaying content dynamically, Chapter 5 covers timeline control, and Chapter 6 introduces OOP. Chapter 7 discusses animating objects using ActionScript, and Chapters 8 and 9 explain drawing with code.

Part III: Text

Chapter 10 is the only chapter in Part III and focuses on text formatting, HTML support, and the use of cascading style sheets.

Part IV: Sound and Video

Chapter 11 opens Part IV with a discussion about sound. In addition to manipulating internal and external sounds, it touches on parsing of ID3 metadata and culminates with a sound visualization exercise, drawing a sound's waveform during live playback. Chapter 12 wraps up Part IV by demonstrating how to play video both with and without components, as well as how to subtitle your videos for accessibility and multilingual support.

Part V: Input/Output

Part V focuses on loading assets into Flash and sending data out to a server or another client. Chapter 13 covers loading SWF files, images, and URL-encoded data, as well as communicating between ActionScript 3.0 and ActionScript 1.0/2.0 loaded SWFs, and a brief discussion of security issues. Chapter 14 covers XML and the new standard for working with XML that makes the task as easy as working with other ActionScript objects, methods, and properties.

Part VI: Programming Design and Resources

We wrap up the book with Part VI. Chapter 15 takes a short look at programming methodologies, object-oriented design patterns, and resources for further learning.

What's Not

This book focuses on ActionScript 3.0, which applies to most segments of the Flash platform, but it is presented within a Flash CS3 Professional context. As such, it does not include coverage of Flex, AIR, Flash Media Server, or other evolving Flash platform technologies.

Further, while it does include coverage of object-oriented programming techniques, it does not address this material in great depth. For more information about this point, please see the previous section, "How This Book Is Organized."

As an entry-level text, this book has understandable constraints that limit the extent of coverage we can offer. Browsing through the Table of Contents should give you a pretty good idea of the topics we'll be featuring and, in some cases, the depth in which we will cover the material. However, there are a few notable areas of ActionScript that are not discussed at all due to their intermediate or advanced nature. These include database connectivity, regular expressions, programming for mobile devices, Web services, remoting, and creating your own components.

We don't claim that this is a reference book. If you're an experienced ActionScript programmer looking for a quick start with version 3.0 of the language, we recommend that you read the *ActionScript 3.0 Cookbook*, by Joey Lott, Keith Peters, and Darron Schall (O'Reilly). If you are looking for a comprehensive reference book, we recommend trying *Essential ActionScript 3.0* by Colin Moock (O'Reilly). Our book may serve as a useful companion to one of these titles, particularly if you are not an advanced user, but it is not a substitute for either.

Companion Website

All the exercises included in this book are available for download from the book's companion website, *http://www.LearningActionScript3.com*. Supplemental materials are also available, including additional exercises, self quizzes, extended examples, ongoing learning suggestions, an expanded resource list, reader comments, errata, and more. Various community resources will be added to the site, such as a forum in which we will participate. Both authors can be reached directly through this website.

Typographical Conventions Used In This Book

The following typographical conventions are used in this book:

Plain Text

> Indicates menu titles, menu options, menu buttons, and keyboard modifiers (such as Alt and Command).

Italic

> Indicates new terms, URLs, email addresses, filenames, file extensions, pathnames, and directories.

`Constant width`

> Indicates ActionScript code, text output from executing scripts, XML tags, HTML tags, and the contents of files.

`Constant width bold`

> Shows commands or other text that should be typed literally.

`Constant width italic`

> Shows text that should be replaced with user-supplied values.

NOTE

A note gives additional information, such as resources or a more detailed explanation.

WARNING

This box indicates a warning or caution.

Using Code Examples

This book is here to help you get your job done. In general, you may use the code in this book in your programs and documentation. You do not need to contact us for permission unless you're reproducing a significant portion of the code. For example, writing a program that uses several chunks of code from this book does not require permission. Selling or distributing a CD-ROM of examples from O'Reilly books does require permission. Answering a question by citing this book and quoting example code does not require permission. Incorporating a significant amount of example code from this book into your product's documentation does require permission.

We appreciate, but do not require, attribution. An attribution usually includes the title, author, publisher, and ISBN. For example: *Learning ActionScript 3.0* by Rich Shupe and Zevan Rosser. Copyright 2008 O'Reilly Media, Inc., 978-0596527877.

If you feel your use of code examples falls outside fair use or the permission given above, feel free to contact us at *permissions@oreilly.com*.

We'd Like to Hear from You

Please address comments and questions concerning this book to the publisher:

O'Reilly Media, Inc.

1005 Gravenstein Highway North

Sebastopol, CA 95472

(800) 998-9938 (in the United States or Canada)

(707) 829-0515 (international or local)

(707) 829-0104 (fax)

We have a web page for this book, where we list errata, examples, and any additional information. You can access this page at:

http://www.oreilly.com/catalog/9780596527877

To comment or ask technical questions about this book, send email to:

bookquestions@oreilly.com

For more information about our books, conferences, Resource Centers, and the O'Reilly Network, see our web site at:

http://www.oreilly.com

Acknowledgments

Rich and Zevan would like to give special thanks to their peerless O'Reilly team: Robyn Thomas, Steve Weiss, Michele Filshie, Matthew Roberts, Jill Steinberg, Joy Dean Lee, Ron Bilodeau, Phil Dangler, Linda Seifert, Mark Paglietti, Karen Montgomery, and Laurie Petrycki. This team of wonderful people bent over so far backwards for this book, we heard spines cracking all over the country. We couldn't have been in better hands. Extra special thanks go to Robyn for her endless patience and support.

Zevan would like to thank: Rich Shupe, The School of Visual Arts, Jesse Reznick and the creative team at SOM, Ann Oren, all of his students, and his family.

Rich would like to thank: Zevan Rosser, Jodi Rotondo, Sally Shupe, Steven Mattson Hayhurst, Thomas Yeh, Aaron Crouch, Anita Ramroop, and his family for helping make this book possible.

Rich would also like to show his appreciation for:

- Bruce Wands, Joe Dellinger, Russet Lederman, Mike Barron, Jaryd Lowder, Diane Field, The School of Visual Arts, and all his students.

- Lynda Weinmann, Bruce Heavin, Toby Malina, Christoph Weise, Kevin Skoglund, and everyone at FlashForward.

- Terry O'Donnell, Russell Jones, and DevX.com; Karen Schneider; Paul Kent, Kristen Margulis, and IDG; John Davey and Flash on the Beach; Dave Schroeder and Flashbelt; Susan Horowitz, William Morrison, and University of Hawaii's Outreach program.

- Mike Downey, Mike Chambers, Richard Galvan, Nivesh Rajbhandari, Mally Gardiner, Jeff Kamerer, Michael Ninness, John Nack, Pete Falco, and Adobe.

- Aral Balkan, Pete Barr-Watson, Brendan Dawes, Chris Georgenes, Mario Klingemann, Seb Lee-Delisle, André Michelle, Erik Natzke, Keith Peters, Tim Saguinsin, Grant Skinner, Craig Swann, Jared Tarbell, Carlos Ulloa, and no doubt others that I'm forgetting for support and/or inspiration.

- Welcome Mina! This book is for Sally and Claire.

About the Authors

Rich Shupe is the founder and president of FMA—a full-service multimedia development company and training facility in New York City. Rich teaches a variety of digital technologies in academic and commercial environments, and has frequently lectured on these topics at FlashForward, Flash on the Beach, Macworld, and other national and international events. He is currently on the faculty of New York's School of Visual Arts in the MFA Computer Art department. As a technical writer, Rich is a regular columnist at DevX.com and the author of multiple books, including *Flash 8: Projects for Learning Animation and Interactivity* (O'Reilly), *Flash CS3 Professional Video Training Book* (Lynda.com/Peachpit), and the *CS3 Web and Design Workflow Guides* (Adobe). He also presents video training for Lynda.com. Visit Rich's website at *http://www.fmaonline.com*.

Zevan Rosser is a freelance designer/programmer/consultant and computer artist. He teaches ActionScript and Flash animation at New York's School of Visual Arts in the Undergraduate and Continuing Education programs, and has acted as thesis advisor for a handful of masters students. He also teaches ActionScript and Flash at FMA in New York. When he's not working on commercial projects, he works on his personal site, *http//www.shapevent.com*.

Colophon

Our look is the result of reader comments, our own experimentation, and feedback from distribution channels. Distinctive covers complement our distinctive approach to technical topics, breathing personality and life into potentially dry subjects. The text font is Linotype Birka; the heading font is Adobe Myriad Pro.

GETTING STARTED

Part I starts this book off with a collection of basic overviews, spanning Chapters 1 and 2. It begins with a survey of ActionScript, providing a list of new feature highlights, a brief explanation of procedural versus object-oriented programming, and an important note about how this book is organized.

It concludes with a review of core language fundamentals, most of which remain consistent across all versions of ActionScript. The material at the outset of the book serves as an introduction to ActionScript for those new to the language, or as a refresher for those already familiar with it, and allows you to focus later on ActionScript 3.0-specific syntax.

CHAPTER 1

ACTIONSCRIPT OVERVIEW

While you likely know what ActionScript is and are eager to begin working with the new version, a brief overview of its development will give you some insight into its use—particularly related to Flash Player and how it handles different versions of ActionScript. This brief introductory chapter will give you a quick look at where ActionScript 3.0 fits into your workflow, and will cover:

- **What Is ActionScript 3.0?** It's to be expected that a new version of ActionScript will bring with it new features. However, this version has been written anew from the ground up and is even handled separately from previous versions of ActionScript at runtime. This intentional splintering of Flash Player affords significant performance increases, but also brings with it limitations as to how multiple versions of ActionScript interact.

- **The Flash Platform.** At the time of this writing, ActionScript 3.0 is the internal programming language of Flex and AIR (the Adobe Integrated Runtime application). Differences in compiling and environment-specific attributes prevent every file written in ActionScript 3.0 from working in every aspect of the Flash Platform, but the fundamentals—indeed the bulk—of the language is the same throughout.

- **Procedural Versus Object-Oriented Programming.** A great deal of attention has been focused on the object-oriented programming (OOP) capabilities of ActionScript 3.0, and the power and robustness of the language really shine in this area. However, you'll be happy to learn that a move to ActionScript 3.0 doesn't mean that you must become an expert at OOP. It is still possible to use a structured collection of functions, which characterize procedural programming, to author ActionScript 3.0 projects. In addition, using Flash CS3, it is still possible to code in the timeline, rather than coding exclusively with external classes. If you prefer object-oriented programming, enhancements to ActionScript 3.0's OOP infrastructure make it more robust and bring it more in line with the features of other important, OOP-based languages (such as Java) and make moving between such languages a bit easier.

- **The** Document **Class.** Object-oriented programming is not for everyone, but for those starting on this journey, Flash CS3 offers a simpler entrance to an OOP application by way of the **Document** class. An attribute of the Properties Inspector, you need only specify which external class is your starting point, and no timeline script is required.

- **Legacy Code Compatibility.** Because ActionScript 3.0 cannot co-mingle with previous versions of the language in the same file, developing projects that support older code is a challenge. We'll briefly introduce the issues involved, and discuss them in greater depth in a later chapter.

What Is ActionScript 3.0?

Although the new version of Flash's internal scripting language contains much that will be familiar to users of prior versions, it's probably best to think of ActionScript 3.0 as entirely new, for a few simple reasons. First, a few things are quite different, such as the event model and the way assets are displayed. Second, subtle changes run throughout the language and require some attention until they become second nature. These are usually small concerns, such as a slight change in the name of a property.

Most importantly, however, ActionScript 3.0 has been rewritten from the ground up and uses a different code base than prior versions of the language. This optimization provides relatively dramatic performance increases, but it means that ActionScript 3.0 code cannot be mixed with prior versions of the language in the same file.

The newness of this version, however, shouldn't intimidate you. It's true that the learning curve for ActionScript 3.0 is steeper than for prior versions, but that is usually a function of its robustness more than one of difficulty. Typically, there is an adjustment period during which users must occasionally adapt to a slightly new way of doing things.

To help you get over any possible trepidation, here's a look at some of the highlights of the new features of ActionScript 3.0. Keeping these benefits in mind may help make it easier to accept change, particularly when that change may initially seem tedious or overly complicated. Select new features include:

More detailed error reporting

ActionScript 3.0 requires strict data typing of variables, arguments, function returns, and so on. This data typing is discussed in Chapter 2, but it boils down to telling the compiler what kind of data you expect to be working with at any specific time. Data type checking was introduced in ActionScript 2.0 but was previously optional. The heightened data typing enforcement improves error checking and provides more information while coding to allow you to correct a problem. Further, ActionScript 3.0 now enforces static data typing at runtime. This improves data type reliability at runtime, and also improves performance and reduces memory usage because the data types are stored in machine code rather than having to be dynamically addressed at runtime.

Syntax improvements

Syntax issues have been unified and cleaned up throughout the language. For example, property names have been clarified in some cases, and have been made consistent by removing the occasional leading underscores, as you'll see in Chapter 3. Also, multiple, subtly different ways of approaching the same or similar tasks have been made consistent, such as when loading external assets (discussed in Chapter 13) or linking to a URL (as seen throughout the book).

New display architecture

The many previous methods to dynamically add something to the display environment are now consolidated. The new display list simplifies this process significantly and also makes it easier to change the visual stacking order, as well as parent, child, and sibling hierarchical relationships, of display objects. As a major change introduced by ActionScript 3.0, we discuss this at length in Chapter 4.

New event architecture

Still another example of improved consistency, all events are now fielded by event listeners—essentially listening for a specific event to occur, and then reacting accordingly. The new event model is also more powerful, allowing mouse and keyboard events to propagate through multiple objects in the display list. The event model is discussed in Chapter 3.

Improved XML handling

A formerly cumbersome process, working with complex XML documents is now a pleasure with ActionScript 3.0. Adopting the standard commonly referred to as E4X, ActionScript now treats XML objects in a much more intelligent and familiar manner. The new approach allows you to use the same dot syntax to string related objects together.

More text scripting options

New text-processing methods now allow for much finer control over text manipulation. You can now find the text of a particular line in a text field, the number of characters in that line, and the character at a specified point (such as under the mouse). You can also find the index in the text field of the first character in a paragraph, and even get the minimum-bounding rectangle surrounding any specific character. All these options not only make working with a text field easier, but also allow a tighter integration with the lines and characters in a field and their surrounding stage elements. Text is discussed in Chapter 10.

New regular expressions

Another boon to text handling is the new native support for regular expressions. Regular expressions are like text manipulation on steroids. Instead of manipulating only specific, known strings of characters, you can now manipulate text using wild cards, character types (numeric, alpha, punctuation, and so on), white space (spaces, tabs, returns), repeating characters, and more. A simple example of regular expression use can be found in Chapter 10.

More sound management options

ActionScript 3.0's new sound capabilities are among the most eye-catching changes to the language. On a practical level, they improve access to both individual sounds and to all sounds playing. Sounds are now placed into separate channels, making it easier to work with multiple individual sounds. Sounds are also funneled through a sound mixer for collective control. You can also now get the amplitude and frequency spectrum data from sounds during playback. Sound is discussed in Chapter 11.

New access to raw data

For more advanced needs, you can now access raw binary data at runtime. Individual bytes of data can be read during download, during sound playback, or during bitmap data manipulation, to name a few examples. These bytes can be stored in a large list and still be accessed quickly and efficiently. We'll show one example of this technique in Chapter 11 when discussing sound visualization.

New automatic scope management

In a programming language, the word *scope* is sometimes used to define the realm in which an object lives. A Flash asset, such as a movie clip, might be in one part of the Flash movie but not another. For example, a child movie clip might be nested inside one of two movie clips found in the main timeline. That nested movie clip exists within one clip but not the other. Its scope, therefore, is restricted to its parent. Programming structures have limited scope, as well, and the challenge is making sure you work within the correct scope when addressing those structures. ActionScript 3.0 greatly simplifies this by automatically tracking scope as you program.

Improved object-oriented programming

Object-oriented programming structures have also been improved in ActionScript 3.0 with the inclusion of sealed classes and new namespaces, among other things. We'll discuss aspects of OOP in this chapter, as well as in Chapter 6, and provide class-based examples throughout the book. New in ActionScript 3.0, all classes are sealed by default, allowing only those properties and methods defined at author time to exist in the class at runtime. If you do find the need to change classes at runtime—by adding properties, for example—you can still do so by making the classes dynamic. Additionally, namespaces, including the ability to define custom namespaces, allow finer control over classes and XML manipulation.

The Flash Platform

It's important to note that this book focuses primarily on developing ActionScript 3.0 applications using the Flash CS3 Professional integrated development environment (IDE). However, ActionScript 3.0 is the programming language for other Flash Platform applications, as well—notably Flex and AIR (the Adobe Integrated Runtime desktop delivery application).

NOTE

AIR projects can also include HTML, JavaScript, and PDF, but ActionScript 3.0 is a large part of its appeal and the language most relevant to this discussion.

This means that the scripting skills you develop in Flash CS3 will be largely applicable in other areas of the Flash Platform, extending your reach as a programmer. There are, however, some important differences to understand when examining the big picture of cross-application scripting. We'll give you just a few brief examples here to consider.

To start with, Flash and Flex have different compilers so there is no guarantee that your project will compile correctly in both applications. You can use Flex Builder (the Flex compiler) to compile code-only ActionScript SWFs without the Flex framework, and load them into Flash CS3-generated projects. You can also load Flash CS3-compiled SWFs into a Flex project. However, as soon as you depart from core language needs, things start to get sticky.

For example, Flex does not have the resources of the Flash IDE to create visual assets (such as movie clips) and, by the same token, Flash does not support the Embed tag used by Flex to include such assets. This means that the same code cannot always be used seamlessly when such custom visuals are required. Similarly, the component architecture is different, including a different format and a component set that do not match.

This issue with visual assets has been a hotly debated issue for a while, and progress is being made to smooth the waters a bit. Adobe released the Flex Component Kit for Flash CS3 to make it easier to use Flash to create Flex components. However, it will probably be a while before moving code to and from these applications will be a comfortable process, if it ever happens. At a brisker pace, however, AIR development is becoming more of a crossover affair. Adobe is continuing to work on AIR authoring workflows that originate in Flash CS3.

The thing to keep in mind is that the ActionScript 3.0 language skills you develop will ease your move between applications in the Flash Platform, even if you must work with different authoring tools or compilers to end up with a finished product.

The programming terms parent, child, sibling, ancestor, *and similar words and phrases mean much the same as they do when used to describe families. In ActionScript, parent-child relationships can occur in multiple ways.*

Movie clips for example, can be nested within each other. The upper- or outermost movie clip is sometimes referred to as the parent (there is even an ActionScript property called {parent}), while the clips nested inside are sometimes called children. Similarly, two movie clips at the same hierarchical level are siblings, and clips that are more than one parent up the chain of nested clips are called ancestors.

Both procedural and object-oriented programming also use these terms when a similar, family-like inheritance is implied. For example, when you create an instance of a class, as you will learn to do later, the instance is sometimes called a child object of that class. Conversely, an instance can usually invoke methods of its parent class. In general, if you liken these terms to their every day uses, referring to families, you will readily grasp their meanings.

Procedural Versus Object-Oriented Programming

Much discussion has been made over the pros and cons of procedural versus object-oriented programming. To touch briefly on this, here is a little background concerning the evolution of ActionScript. ActionScript started as a *sequential* programming language, meaning that scripting was limited to a linear sequence of instructions telling Flash what to do in a step-by-step manner. This approach to scripting was not terribly flexible and did not promote reuse.

As the language evolved, it became a *procedural* programming language. Like sequential programming, procedural programming relied on a step-by-step set of instructions but introduced a more structured, modular approach to scripting. *Procedures*, otherwise known as functions (or, sometimes, subroutines), could be executed again and again as needed from different parts of a project, without copying and pasting copies of the code into the ongoing sequence of instructions. This modularity promoted reuse, and made the code easier to edit and more efficient.

Scripters in search of an even greater degree of modularity and reuse gravitated toward *object-oriented* programming. OOP languages create programs that are a collection of objects. Objects are individual instances of *classes*—collections of code that are self-contained and do not materially alter or disrupt each other. Dividing code into small capsules, appropriately known as *encapsulation*, is one of the hallmarks of an OOP language. Another important feature of OOP is *inheritance*, or the ability to derive classes from parent classes, passing on specific characteristics from the parent.

A classic example of OOP structure, and specifically inheritance, defines a set of transportation vehicles. You might start with a generic **Vehicle** class that includes traits common to all vehicles, such as the basic physics of movement. You might then create three subclasses: **GroundVehicle**, **WaterVehicle**, and **AirVehicle**. These classes would alter or introduce traits specific to ground, water, and air travel, respectively, but not yet be complete enough to represent an actual vehicle. Further derived classes might be **Car** and **Motorcycle** (descending from **GroundVehicle**), **Boat**, and **Submarine** (descending from **WaterVehicle**), and **Plane** and **Helicopter** (descending from **AirVehicle**). Depending on the complexity of your system, you can carry on this process, creating individual models with individual settings for fuel consumption, friction, and so on.

As you can probably imagine, this approach to development adds additional power, flexibility, and prospects for reuse. These benefits, among others, sometimes position object-oriented programming as the best approach to a problem. However, there is a tendency among some programmers to believe that OOP is the best solution to all problems or, effectively, the only solution. This is a faulty assumption.

OOP is often best for very large projects, or for working with a team of programmers, but it can often be overkill for small projects. Additionally, for the uninitiated, it can significantly increase the learning curve, and distract from key topical concepts during your studies. In short, OOP is not always the best tool for the job. Procedural programming still has its place, and Flash CS3 allows you to explore and employ both programming paradigms.

This book attempts to introduce material using both procedural and OOP where appropriate. Using object-oriented practices is a fine goal, and one that we will encourage in this volume. However, we will try first to focus on the material central to each chapter, highlighting syntax and explaining how and why each topic should be addressed in code.

In general terms, we will focus on procedural programming prior to Chapter 6; this chapter serves as a transition chapter between procedural and OOP practices. After Chapter 6, the beginning of each chapter will focus on the topics being discussed, without intrusion by the surrounding OOP class structures. When appropriate, however, each chapter will end with an applied OOP example.

This is our preferred approach to presenting material for all possible users—in both procedural and OOP formats. It is our hope that, regardless of your skill and experience, you will home in on the topics at hand, and then work in the timeline, or in classes, based on your comfort level.

The Document Class

If you decide you would like to start thinking in OOP terms right away, we will show you how to easily take a step in that direction. Flash CS3 introduced a new feature that simplifies associating a main class, or application entry point with your FLA. It is called the *document class* and it does all the work of instantiating the class for you. This means you don't need any code in the timeline at all, and can edit all examples in Flash or the external text editor or development environment of your choice.

Let's start with a simulated chapter example that you might use in the timeline. It does nothing more than use the **trace()** method to place a word into the Output panel—an authoring-only panel that accepts text output from your file.

```
trace("Flash");
```

To create a document class, you're going to create a kind of wrapper that encloses the **trace()** method in the correct class syntax.

NOTE

If you don't plan to start using OOP until we roll it out in later chapters, feel free to skip this section as it will be repeated in Chapter 6. We will provide minimal explanation here just to get you going using the document class, and will explain this material in greater detail in later chapters throughout the book.

Create a new ActionScript file (rather than a new FLA document) and type the following document class shell:

```
1    package {
2
3        import flash.display.MovieClip;
4
5        public class Main extends MovieClip {
6
7            public function Main() {
8
9            }
10
11       }
12   }
```

The first line, along with the closing brace in line 12, defines the class's *package*. A package is a mandatory structure that ensures your class is known to the compiler. Next, you must import any classes that you need to use in your package.

A document class essentially serves as a shortcut for creating an instance of a movie clip or sprite (a new Flash object that is nothing more than a one-frame movie clip) and adding it to the display list so it can be displayed by Flash Player. (This is true even when there is nothing to display, as in this case. We will cover manipulating the display list in Chapter 4.)

All document classes must be derived from either the **MovieClip** or **Sprite** class. (Other custom classes that are not document classes do not need to be extended from **MovieClip** or **Sprite** if that is not appropriate.) This example uses **MovieClip** so you must import the **MovieClip** class, as seen in line 3.

Line 5, along with its closing brace on line 11, is the class definition. Its name (in this case, "Main") is arbitrary but, when naming it, you should follow a few basic rules and conventions. The name should be one word that does not already exist in ActionScript, it should start with an alpha character (rather than a number or other character), and it is typically capitalized. The class must be public, meaning that other classes can access the constructor, and it must extend **MovieClip** or **Sprite**, as described previously.

Line 7, along with its closing brace on line 9, is the class *constructor*. This is the main function that automatically runs when creating an instance of this class. It, too, must be public and must have the same name as the class. Other functions (if any) can, and must, have unique names. All that remains is to add the lone method required in this case. The constructor must trace "Flash" to the Output panel, so add the following to line 8:

```
7            public function Main() {
8                trace("Flash");
9            }
```

Once finished, you must save the file in the same directory as your FLA file for now. (Later on, you'll learn how to place your class files in other locations.) You must give the file the same name as the class, but add an *.as* extension.

Therefore, this file should be named *Main.as*. Now create a new FLA file, choosing ActionScript 3.0 as its programming language version, and save it in the same directory as your previously created class file. The name of the FLA is unimportant.

Finally, open the Properties Inspector and add the name of your document class, not the name of the document itself, in the Document Class field. In this case, type `Main` instead of `Main.as`, as seen in Figure 1-1.

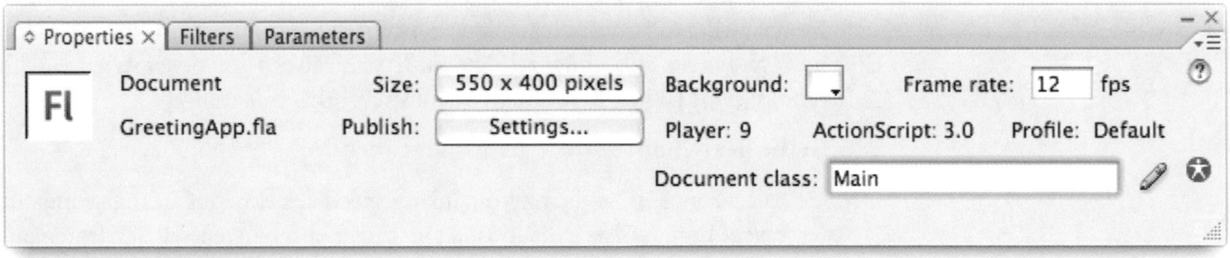

Figure 1-1. Adding a document class to your FLA

Now preview your file. Doing so will create an instance of the `Main` class (which extends `MovieClip` and, therefore, behaves like a movie clip) and add it to the display list. The class will trace "Flash" to the output panel, and your test application will be complete.

Hereafter, you can try any of our timeline code in a document class of your own. Initially, you probably won't know which classes to import or how to make any possible changes to variables or similar structures to conform to the class syntax. However, all the sample code will come with an accompanying class file for testing. You can use those files whenever you wish until you get used to the document class format.

Legacy Code Compatibility

I'd like to end this chapter with a small caveat. You cannot mix ActionScript 1.0 or 2.0 code with ActionScript 3.0 code in the same SWF. You are unlikely to do this if you're learning from scratch, but you may run into this situation if you attempt to update legacy projects by adding ActionScript 3.0 code.

If you ever have the need to run a discrete mixture of ActionScript 3.0 and a prior version of the language, such as showing a legacy file within a new demo interface shell, you can do so by loading a SWF. An ActionScript 3.0 file can load a SWF created in ActionScript 1.0 or 2.0, but it cannot access the older SWF's variables or functions. For all intents and purposes, the same is not true in reverse. An older SWF cannot load an ActionScript 3.0 SWF.

In Chapter 13, we will discuss how to communicate between these two discrete SWFs using a special process. For now, however, just remind yourself again that you cannot combine ActionScript 3.0 with older versions of the language in the same file.

What's Next?

Now that you know a little more about ActionScript 3.0 and the Flash Platform, it's time for a look at some of the fundamentals of the language. By reviewing version-independent concepts at the outset, we can focus on new syntax in subsequent chapters. If you have a lot of experience with ActionScript 1.0 or 2.0, you may wish to skim this material.

In the next chapter, we'll discuss:

- Basic concepts to bring you up to speed quickly, including using the `trace()` method as a diagnostic tool to see immediate feedback from your scripts

- Using variables to store data, including arrays and custom objects that allow you to easily manage more than one value, and data typing those values to improve error reporting

- Logical structures such as conditionals for decision making and loops for simplifying repetitive tasks

- Functions that can isolate code into convenient blocks that will be executed only when instructed

- Ways to address Flash objects with ActionScript, including using absolute and relative paths, and the shortcut identifier `this`

CORE LANGUAGE FUNDAMENTALS

It's true that ActionScript 3.0 is a complete rewrite of Flash's internal script-ing language, and it's also true that ActionScript 3.0 doesn't share the same runtime code base as prior versions of ActionScript. But that's all behind the scenes. The truth is, all versions of ActionScript to date share quite a bit in common.

This is not hard to understand, since ActionScript was based on a script-ing language standard (called ECMA-262) that grew from the success of JavaScript, and that ongoing versions of ActionScript are backward compat-ible to support legacy projects.

That is not to say that the language isn't growing. Certainly, each new version of ActionScript introduces a batch of newly supported features, as is true with the evolution of most programming languages. And, since the decision was made to write ActionScript 3.0 from the ground up, the opportunity presented itself to tidy up a few messy things that lingered from previous versions—namely, tightening up and requiring best practices that had been optional, and restructuring the event and display systems.

All of this progress, however, did not steamroll over the standard upon which ActionScript is based, and most of the language fundamentals remain intact. With the intention to focus on new ActionScript 3.0 options later on, we want to cover some of the more important fundamentals up-front. We do not intend to ignore these ideas throughout the rest of the book. However, because they are core fundamentals and are, therefore, used often, we hope to explain them in sufficient detail here and spend less time on them as we proceed.

If you're already comfortable with ActionScript and are reading this text for a head start learning version 3.0, you may want to skip, or at least skim, this chapter. It is by no means a comprehensive starter course. This book does not assume that you are well versed in any prior version of ActionScript, but its size and purpose requires that we assume a very basic understanding of general scripting concepts. If you haven't already, please look over the Preface for a good idea of who this book is for, as well as a few alternative references if you need more background information.

You can use this chapter, however, as a point of reference when an underlying programming concept needs further explanation. In these pages, we'll look at the following topics:

- **Miscellaneous Basics.** To identify some of the items and techniques used throughout this book that don't necessarily warrant a section for each, we'll start off with a few essentials.

- **Variables and Data Types.** Information must be stored in containers called variables if it is to be recalled for later use, and declaring which type of data will be stored in each variable can help Flash check for errors during development.

- **Conditionals.** Often, when a decision must be made in the course of a script's execution, a conditional is used to evaluate the outcome of a prescribed set of conditions. We'll look at the `if` and `switch` conditional forms.

- **Loops.** When you must execute an instruction multiple times, it is sometimes handy to do so within a loop structure. We'll look at the commonly used `for` loop structure, but also at alternatives to explicit loops, including frame and timer events.

- **Arrays.** While a basic variable can contain only a single value, it is frequently efficient, or even necessary, to store more than one value in a variable. Imagine a shopping list, with several items, written on a single piece of paper. The array is a data structure that allows you to store multiple values in a single variable.

- **Functions.** Functions are essential to just about any programming language, and allow you to execute code only when you are ready to do so, and reuse that code efficiently.

- **Custom Objects.** A custom object can be considered an advanced kind of variable that allows you to store lots of information, in a way that is easy and consistent to retrieve. Objects can also be very useful for simplifying the task of passing multiple optional values to a function.

- **this.** The `this` keyword is used as a shorthand reference, essentially meaning the object or scope in a script. This will become clearer in context, but understanding how the keyword works can save you much repetitive typing and reduce the need for more complex references in your scripts.

- **Absolute versus Relative Addresses.** ActionScript can reference addresses to its objects using absolute paths, such as starting from the root timeline and including every object between it and your destination, or relative paths, such as going up to a parent and down to a sibling, no matter where you are.

Again, this chapter is not meant to act as the only reference to bring you up to speed if you have absolutely no experience with ActionScript. It will likely serve the bulk of your needs but other basics—such as where scripts are stored in the Flash interface—have been omitted for space reasons.

As described in the Preface, for a starter book on the Flash interface, we recommend *Flash CS3 Professional, The Missing Manual*, published by O'Reilly, the publisher of this book. For a more complete ActionScript 3.0 resource, we heartily recommend the incomparable *Essential ActionScript 3.0* by Colin Moock, also published by O'Reilly. The latter is decidedly an intermediate to advanced reference but, at nearly three times the size of this volume, it is also substantially more comprehensive.

For the most part, this chapter, along with the context and supplemental explanations presented in subsequent chapters, should provide you with enough to understand the topics and to get the sample exercises working.

Miscellaneous Basics

Some basic topics probably don't require a section devoted to their discussion but should still be mentioned due to their use throughout the book. We'll include a few such examples here, just to get us started.

Execution order

In general, ActionScript executes in a top-to-bottom, left-to-right order— that is, each line executes one after another, working from left to right. Several things can change this order in subtle ways, but it's basically a reliable rule of thumb. For example, subroutines of one type or another can be called in the middle of a script, causing the execution order of the original script to pause while the remote routine is executed. When the subroutine has completed, the execution of the original script continues where it left off. These steps will be explained in context, in all scripts in this book.

Use of the semicolon(;)

The official use of the semicolon in ActionScript is to execute more than one instruction on a single line. This is rare in the average script, and we will look at this technique when discussing loops. However, the semicolon is also used to indicate the end of a line. This is not required, but it is recommended for clarity and to ease any possible transition into learning other languages in which the semicolon at the end of a line is required.

Evaluating an expression

It's helpful to note that you are usually not solving an equation when you see an expression with like values on the left and right of an equal sign. For example if you see something like $x = x + 1$, it is unlikely that you will be solving for the value of **x**. Instead, this line is assigning a new value to **x** by adding **1** to its previous value.

Use of the **trace** *command*

As a means of getting quick feedback in an example, or as a testing and debugging technique when writing scripts, it is very helpful to use the **trace** command. This instruction places any relevant text into the Output panel of the Flash interface. As such, this is an option that is available only at author-time, and has no use at runtime.

Variables and Data Types

Variables are best described as containers into which you place information for later recall. Imagine if you were unable to store any information for later use. You would not be able to compare values against previously described information (such as user names or passwords), your scripts would suffer performance lags due to repeated unnecessary calculations, and you wouldn't be able to carry any prior experiences through to the next possible implementation of a task. In general, you wouldn't be able to do anything that required data that your application had to "remember."

Variables make all this and more possible, and are relatively straightforward. In basic terms, you need only create a variable with a unique name, so it can be referenced separately from other variables and the ActionScript language itself, and then populate it with a value. A simple example is remembering the number 1 with the following:

```
myVariable = 1;
```

There are just a few rules and best practices to consider when naming variables. They must be one word, can only include alphanumeric characters along with the dollar sign ($) or underscore (_), should not start with a number, and should not already be a keyword or reserved word in ActionScript.

To help ensure that you are using variables appropriately, ActionScript will monitor them and warn you if you are trying to perform an illegal operation on them, or otherwise use them incorrectly. For example, if you try to perform a mathematical operation on a passage of text, Flash will issue a warning so you can correct the problem.

To do this, Flash must be told what you intend to store in each variable. This is accomplished by declaring the variable by preceding its first use with the **var** keyword, and citing the type of data to be stored therein by following the name of the variable with a colon (:) and data type. For instance, the previous example of remembering the number 1 should be written this way:

```
var myVariable:Number = 1;
```

There are several native data types including, but not limited to, those listed in Table 2-1:

Table 2-1. Variable types

Data type	Example	Description
Number	4.5	Any number, including floating point values (decimals)
int	-5	Any integer or whole number
uint	1	Unsigned integer or any non-negative whole number
String	"hello"	Text or a string of characters
Boolean	true	True or false
Array	[2, 9, 17]	More than one value in a single variable
Object	myObject	The basic structure of every ActionScript entity, but also a custom form that can be used to store multiple values as an alternative to **Array**.

There are also many dozens of additional data types that describe which class was used to populate the variable. (As discussed in Chapter 1, think of classes as external scripts that typically return information to your script and work as members of a larger team to create your application.) For example, the following line of code uses the **MovieClip** class (built into Flash) to create a movie clip at runtime:

```
var myMC:MovieClip = new MovieClip();
```

It is impractical to list every possible data type here, but we will reference data types frequently throughout the book, and it will soon become second nature to use them.

In previous versions of ActionScript, declaring and typing variables was optional. However, in ActionScript 3.0, this practice is required. This may seem cumbersome but, before long, this will become second nature, and you will come to appreciate the instant error checking and feedback this feature provides.

As we get further into the book, you'll learn that variables can apply to an entire scope (the realm in which the variable lives, such as Flash's main timeline, or a particular class) or be local to specific code structures. We will discuss this in context in the code examples.

NOTE

Throughout this book, the code examples are syntax-colored in the same way that the Flash interface colors scripts. This helps identify colored items as part of the ActionScript lexicon (such as keywords and identifiers) and makes it a bit easier to see comments (descriptive text passages that are not executed) and strings.

Conditionals

You will often have the need to make a decision in your script, choosing to do one thing under one circumstance, and another thing under a different circumstance. These situations are usually addressed by *conditionals*. Put simply, a test is created, asking whether a condition is met. If the condition is met, the test evaluates to **true**, and specific code is executed accordingly. If the condition is not met, either no further action is taken or an alternate set of code is executed.

if

The most common form of the conditional is the **if** statement. The statement's basic structure is the **if** keyword, followed by parentheses in which the conditional test resides, and braces in which the code resides that is executed when the statement evaluates to **true**. The first three lines in the following example establish a set of facts. The **if** statement evaluates the given facts. (This initial set of facts will be used for this and subsequent examples in this section.)

```
var a:Number = 1;
var b:String = "hello";
var c:Boolean = false;

if (a == 1) {
    trace("option a");
}
```

To evaluate the truth of the test inside the parentheses, conditionals often make use of *comparison* and *logical operators*. A comparison operator compares two values, such as equals (==), less than (<), and greater than or equal to (>=), to name a few.

A logical operator evaluates the logic of an expression. Included in this category are AND (**&&**), OR (**||**), and NOT (**!**). These allow you to ask if "this *and* that" are true, or if "this *or* that" is true, or if "this" is *not* true.

For example, the following would be false, because *both* conditions are not true. As a result, nothing would appear in the Output panel.

```
if (a == 1 && b == "goodbye") {
    trace("options a and b");
}
```

In this example, the test would evaluate to true, because *one* of the two conditions (the first) is true. As a result, "option a or b" would be traced.

```
if (a == 1 || b == "goodbye") {
    trace("option a or b");
}
```

Finally, the following would also evaluate to true, because the NOT operator correctly determines that **c** is not true. (Remember, that every **if** statement, at its core, is testing for truth.)

```
if (!c) {
    trace("not option c");
}
```

The NOT operator is also used as part of a comparison operator. When combined with a single equal sign, the pair means, "not equal to." Therefore, the following will fail because **a** does equal 1, and nothing will be traced.

```
if (a != 1) {
    trace("a does not equal 1");
}
```

Additional power can be added to the **if** statement by adding an unconditional alternative—that is, an alternative set of code is executed any time the main test fails, without a need for any additional evaluation. With the following new code added to the previous example, the last trace will occur.

```
if (a != 1) {
    trace("a does not equal 1");
} else {
    trace("a does equal 1");
}
```

Finally, the statement can be even more robust by adding a conditional alternative (or an additional test), to the structure. In this example, the second trace will occur.

```
if (a == 2) {
    trace("a does not equal 1");
} else if (a == 1) {
    trace("a does equal 1");
}
```

The **if** statement requires one **if**, only one optional **else** can be used, and any number of optional additional **else if** tests can be used. In all cases, however, only one result can come from the structure. Consider the following example, in which all three results could potentially execute—the first two because they are true, and the last because it is an unconditional alternative.

```
if (a == 1) {
    trace("option a");
} else if (b == "hello") {
    trace("option b");
} else {
    trace("option other");
}
```

In this case, only "option a" would appear in the Output panel because the first truth would exit the **if** structure. If you needed more than one execution to occur, you would need to use two or more conditionals. The following structure, for example, will trace twice by design.

```
if (a == 1) {
    trace("option a");
}
if (b == "hello") {
    trace("option b");
} else {
    trace("option other");
}
```

switch

An **if** statement can be as simple or as complex as needed. However, long **if** structures can be difficult to read and can sometimes better be expressed using the **switch** statement. In addition, the latter statement has a unique feature that lets you control which if *any* instructions are executed—even when a test evaluates to false.

Imagine an **if** statement asking if a variable is 1, **else if** it's 2, **else if** it's 3, **else if** it's 4, and so on. A test like that can become difficult to read quickly. An alternate structure appears as follows:

```
switch (a) {
    case 1 :
        trace("one");
        break;
    case 2 :
        trace("two");
        break;
    case 3 :
        trace("three");
        break;
    default :
        trace("other");
        break;
}
```

In this case, "one" would appear in the Output panel. The **switch** line contains the object or expression you want to test. Each case line offers a possible value. Following the colon are the instructions to execute upon a successful test, and each **break** line prevents any following instructions from executing. When not used, the next instructions in line will execute, even if that test is false.

For example, the following will place both "one" and "two" in the Output panel, even though **a** does not equal 2.

```
switch (a) {
    case 1 :
        trace("one");
    case 2 :
        trace("two");
        break;
}
```

This **break** feature does not exist with the **if** statement and, if used with care, makes **switch** an efficient alternative to a more complex series of multiple **if** statements. **Switch** statements must have one **switch** and one **case**, an optional unconditional alternative in the form of **default**, and an optional **break** for each **case** and **default**. The last **break** is not needed, but may be preferred for consistency.

Loops

It is quite common to execute many repetitive instructions in your scripts. However, including them line by line, one copy after another, is inefficient and difficult to edit and maintain. Wrapping repetitive tasks in an efficient structure is the role of *loops*. A programming loop is probably just what you think it is: Use it to go through the structure and then loop back to the start and do it again. There are a few kinds of loops, and the type you choose to use can help determine how many times your instructions are executed.

for Loop

The first type of loop structure we'll look at is the **for** loop. This loop executes its contents a finite number of times. For example, you may wish to create a grid of 25 movie clips or check to see which of 5 radio buttons has been selected. In our first example, we want to trace content to the Output panel three times.

To loop through a process effectively, you must first start with an initial value, such as 0, so you know you have not yet traced anything to the Output panel. The next step is to test to see whether you have exceeded your limit. The first time through, 0 does not exceed the limit of three times. The next step is to trace the content once, and the final step is to increment your initial value, registering that you've traced the desired content once. The process then starts over until, ultimately, you will exceed the limit of the loop. The syntax for a basic **for** loop is as follows:

NOTE

Note in each example loop the "official" use of the semicolon to execute more than one step in a single line.

```
for (var i:Number = 0; i < 3; i++) {
    trace("hello");
}
```

The first thing you may notice is the declaration and typing of the counter, **i**. This is a common technique because the **i** variable is often used only for counting and, therefore, is created on the spot and not used again. If you have already declared and typed the counter previously, that step can be omitted here. Next is the loop test. In this case, the counter variable must have a value that is less than 3. Finally, the double-plus sign (**++**) is equivalent to i = i + 1, or add 1 to the current value of **i**. The result is three occurrences of the word "hello" in the Output panel.

It is also possible to count down by reversing the values in steps 1 and 2, and then decrementing the counter:

```
for (var i:Number = 3; i > 0; i--) {
    trace("hello");
}
```

In other words, as long as the value of **i** is greater than 0, execute the loop, and subtract one from the counter each time. This is less common, and works in this case because the loop only traces a string. However, if you need to use the actual value of **i** inside the loop, that need may dictate whether you count up or down. For example, if you created 10 movie clips and called them **mc0**, **mc1**, **mc2**, and so on, it may be clearer to count up.

*Use **while** loops with caution until you are comfortable with them. It's very easy to accidentally write an infinite loop with no exit, which will cause your code to stop in its tracks. Do not try this code yourself, but here is a significantly simplified example of an infinite loop:*

```
var flag:Boolean = true;
while (flag) {
    trace("infinite loop");
}
```

As you can see from this example, the flag variable remains true and, therefore, the loop can never fail.

while Loop

The other kind of loop that you are likely to use is a **while** loop. Instead of executing its contents a finite number of times, it executes as long as something remains true. As an example, let's look at a very simple case of choosing a random number. Using the **Math** class's **random()** method, ActionScript chooses a random number between 0 and 1. So, let's say you wanted to choose a random number greater than or equal to 0.5. With essentially a 50-percent chance of choosing a desired number each time, you may end up with the wrong choice several times in a row. To be sure you get a qualifying number, you can add this to your script:

```
var num:Number = 0;
while (num < 0.5) {
    num = Math.random();
}
```

Starting with a default value of 0, **num** will be less than 0.5 the first time into the loop. A random number is then put into the **num** variable and, if it's less than 0.5, the loop will execute again. This will go on until a random number that is greater than 0.5 is chosen, thus exiting the loop.

A Loop Caveat

It's very important to understand that, although compact and convenient, loop structures are not always the best method to use to achieve an outcome. This is because loops are very processor intensive. Once a loop begins its process, nothing else will execute until the loop has been exited. For this reason, it may be wise to avoid **for** and **while** loops when interim visual updates are required.

In other words, when a loop serves as an initialization for a process that is updated only once upon its completion, such as creating the aforementioned grid of 25 movie clips, you are less likely to have a problem. The script enters the loop, 25 clips are created, the loop is completed, a frame update can then occur, and you see all 25 clips.

However, if you want each of the 25 clips to appear, one by one, those interim visual updates of the playhead cannot occur while the processor is consumed by the loop. In this situation, a loop that is achieved by other means—methods that do not interfere with the normal playhead updates—is desirable. Two such loops, frame and timer loops, are commonly used for this purpose. A frame loop is simply a repeating frame event, executing an instruction each time the playhead is updated. A timer loop is similar, but is not tied to the frame tempo. Instead, a timer event is triggered by an independent timer at a set frequency.

In both cases, the events occur in concert with any other events in the ordinary functioning of the file, so visual updates, as one example, can continue to occur. Both frame and timer loops will be explained, complete with examples, in the next chapter.

Arrays

Basic variables can contain only one value. If you set a variable to 1 and then set that same variable to 2 in the following line, the value would be reassigned, and the value of the variable would be 2.

However, there are times when you need one variable to contain more than one value. Think of a hypothetical set of groceries, including 50 items. The standard variable approach to this problem would be to define 50 variables and populate each with a grocery item. That is the equivalent of 50 pieces of paper, each with one grocery item written on its face. This is unwieldy and can only be created at author time—at which point the process is fixed—and you'd have to recall and manage all variable names every time you wanted to access the grocery items.

An array equivalent, however, is very much like how we handle this in real life. A list of 50 grocery items is written on one piece of paper. You can add to the list while at the store, cross each item off once it is acquired, and you only have to manage one piece of paper.

Creating an array is quite easy. You can prepopulate an array by setting a variable (typed as an **Array**) to a comma-separated list of items, surrounded by brackets. You can also create an empty array by using the **Array** class. Both techniques are illustrated here:

```
var myArray:Array = [1, 2, 3];
var yourArray:Array = new Array();
```

In both cases, you can add to, or remove from, the array at runtime. For example, you can add a value to an array using the **push()** method, which pushes the value into the array at the end. In short, a *method* is an action performed by an object—in this case adding something to the array—and will be discussed in detail in the next chapter. You can remove an item from the end of an array using the **pop()** method.

```
var myArray:Array = new Array();
myArray.push(1);
trace(myArray);
// 1 appears in the Output panel
myArray.push(2);
// the array now has two items: 1, 2
trace(myArray.pop());
// the pop() method removes the last item, displaying its value of 2
trace(myArray);
// the lone remaining item in the array, 1, is displayed
```

There are a dozen or so other array methods, allowing you to add to or remove from the front of an array, sort its contents, check for the position of a found item within the array, compare each value against a control value, and more.

NOTE

Both methods are added to the end of the **myArray** *variable with a dot separating the two. This is the syntax used to navigate the Flash document object model, and is sometimes referred to as dot syntax. Essentially, this system strings together a series of items, from biggest to smallest, and including only items relevant to the task at hand. In this case, the largest relevant item is the array itself and, below that is each method.*

Consider another example where you may wish to check the width of a movie clip that is inside another movie clip. The biggest item in this chain is the container movie clip, or parent. Let's call it **mc1**. *A reference to the child clip nested inside, called* **mc2** *in this example, follows, and the width property concludes the statement:*

```
mc1.mc2.width;
```

This dot syntax will be used in virtually every example for the rest of the book, and it will soon become quite easy to understand just what is referenced by each object along the way.

You can also add to or retrieve values from locations within the array, by using brackets and including the index, or position, of the array you need. To do so, you must understand that ActionScript uses zero-based arrays, which means that the first value is at position 0, the second is at position 1, the next at position 2, and so on. As an example, to retrieve the existing fifth value from an array, you must request the item at position 4.

```
var myArray:Array = ["a", "b", "c", "d", "e"];
trace(myArray[4]);
//"e" appears in the Output panel
```

There are other kinds of arrays, such as multidimensional arrays (arrays within arrays that can resemble database structures) and associative arrays (which store not only linear values, but also a linear *pair* of items—the value and a property name to describe that value), for example. However, due to space constraints, we've focused on the most common array type: the linear array. Any other uses of array structures will be highlighted in future chapters.

Functions

Functions are an indispensable part of programming in that they wrap code into blocks that can be executed only when needed. They also allow code blocks to be reused and edited efficiently, without having to copy, paste, and edit repeatedly. Without functions, all code would be executed in a linear progression from start to finish, and edits would require changes to every single occurrence of any repeated code.

Creating a basic function requires little more than surrounding the code you wish to trigger at will with a simple syntax that allows you to give the block a name. Triggering that function later requires only that you call the function by name. The following syntax shows a function that traces a string to the Output panel. The function is defined and then, to illustrate the process, immediately called. (In a real-world scenario, the function is usually called at some other time or from some other place, such as when the user clicks a button with the mouse.) The output is depicted in the comment that follows the function call.

```
function showMsg() {
    trace("hello");
}
showMsg();
//hello
```

If reusing code and executing code only when needed were the only advantage of functions, you'd already have a useful enhancement to linear execution of ActionScript, because it would allow you to group your code into subroutines that could be triggered at any time and in any order. However, you can do much more with functions to gain even greater power.

For example, assume you need to vary the purpose of the previous function slightly. Let's say you need to trace ten different messages. To do that without any new features, you'd have to create ten functions and vary the string that is sent to the Output panel in each function.

However, this can be more easily accomplished with the use of *arguments*, or very local variables that have life only within their own functions. By adding an argument to the function declaration, in this case the string argument `msg`, you can pass a value into that argument when you call the function. By using the argument in the body of the function, it takes on whatever value was sent in. In this example, the function no longer traces "hello" every time it is called. Instead, it traces whatever text is sent into its argument when the function is called. When using arguments, it is necessary to type the data coming in so Flash knows how to react and can issue any warnings needed to notify you of errors.

```
function showMsg(msg:String) {
    trace(msg);
}
showMsg("goodbye");
//goodbye
```

It is also possible to return a value from a function, increasing its usefulness. Having the ability to return a value to the script from which it was called means a function can vary its input *and* its output. Included below are examples to convert temperature values from Celsius to Fahrenheit and Fahrenheit to Celsius. In both cases, a value is sent into the function and a resulting calculation is returned to the script. The first example immediately traces the result, while the second example stores the value in a variable. This mimics real-life usage in that you can immediately act upon the returned value or store and process it at a later time.

```
function celToFar(cel:Number):Number {
    return (9 / 5) * cel + 32;
}
trace(celToFar(20));
//68

function farToCel(far:Number):Number {
    return (5 / 9) * (far - 32);
}
var celDeg:Number = farToCel(68);
trace(celDeg);
//20
```

Note that, when returning a value from a function, you should also declare the data type of the return value. This is achieved the same way as when applying other data types—with a colon followed by the type specific to that function—and this form is placed between the argument close parenthesis and the opening function brace. Once you get used to this practice, it is best to specify **void** as a return type when your function does not return a value.

Custom Objects

After just a short while working with ActionScript, you will realize that you are immersed neck-deep in objects. Most discrete entities in ActionScript are descendents of the Object class and tend to behave in a consistent manner. Central to this behavior is the ability for an object to have properties (which are essentially descriptive elements that contribute to the object's general characteristics, like width, location, rotation, and so on), methods (which are actions the object can perform), and even events (custom events that, like a mouse click or a key press, can trigger other processes in the course of working with a script).

You can also create custom objects and define your own properties, methods, and events. To demonstrate this, we'll create a custom object called plane, and give it properties for pitch, roll, and yaw. These properties are terms that describe rotation in 3D space. If you think of yourself seated in a plane, pitch is the angle of rotation that would cause the nose of the plane to go down or up. Roll is the angle of rotation that would cause the plane to spin along the length of the plane, keeping the nose facing forward as you spiral through flight. Finally, yaw is the angle of rotation that comes up perpendicularly through your seat on the plane, causing the plane to spin in a flat spin where the nose would no longer remain facing forward.

None of these terms—plane, pitch, roll, or yaw—are part of the ActionScript library. However, by creating a custom object, we will temporarily make them available to our scripts as if they were always there. The first step in this process is to create the object. Once created, we can add and populate properties:

```
var plane:Object = new Object();
plane.pitch = 0;
plane.roll = 5;
plane.yaw = 5;
```

These values would send the plane in a slow right-hand turn. They can be called up at any time, by querying the properties the same way they were created.

```
trace(plane.pitch);
//0
```

Creating a custom object to contain properties is a highly effective way of sending multiple optional parameters into a function. ActionScript 3.0 does not like having a variable number of arguments or values for those arguments. If you specify five arguments, it expects five parameters and will balk if you choose to omit any. If you plan your code ahead and plan to allow a series of optional parameters, it is easy to transmit an unknown number of parameter values through a fixed single argument that contains an object. You can then parse the values from this object inside the function, initializing the starting value of any specific properties that were omitted. Here is an example, using the previously created **plane** object:

```
function showPlaneStatus(obj:Object):void {
    trace(obj.pitch);
    trace(obj.roll);
    trace(obj.yaw);
}
showPlaneStatus(plane);
//0
//5
//5
```

this

Although a bit nebulous for some just starting with ActionScript, **this** can be your friend. It is essentially shorthand for "whichever object or scope you're working with now." *Scope* is the realm or space within which an object lives. For example, think of a movie clip inside Flash's main timeline. Each of these objects has a unique scope, so a variable or function defined inside the movie clip will not exist in the main timeline, and vice versa.

It is easiest to understand the usage of **this** in context, but here are a couple of examples to get you started. If, from the main timeline, you wanted to tell a movie clip called **mc** to go to frame 2, you might say:

```
this.mc.gotoAndStop(2);
```

Conversely, if you wanted to send the main timeline to frame 2, but do so from within the movie clip, you might say:

```
this.parent.mc.gotoAndStop(2);
```

In both cases, **this** is a reference point from which you start your path. It is common to drop the **this** keyword when going down from the current scope (as in the first example), but it is often required when going up to a higher scope (as in the second example). This is because Flash must understand what the parent is a parent *of* in order to start traversing through the hierarchy. Imagine a family reunion in which several extended family members, including cousins and multiple generations, are present, and you are looking for your mother, father, or grandparent. If you just said "parent," any number of parents might answer. If you, instead, said "my parent" or "my mother's parent," that would be specific enough to get you headed in the right direction.

NOTE

Depending on how you setup your file, it is often necessary to specifically declare what kind of parent you are referencing. For example, you may need to explicitly say the parent is a movie clip before you can work with its timeline. See "Casting a Display Object" in Chapter 4 for more information about this process.

Absolute versus Relative Addresses

Much like a computer operating system's directory, or the file structure of a web site, ActionScript refers to the address of its objects in a hierarchical fashion. You can reference an object address using an absolute or relative path. Absolute paths can be easy because you most likely know the exact path to any object starting from the main timeline. However, they are quite rigid and will break if you change the nested relationship of any of the referenced objects. Relative paths can be a bit harder to call to mind at any given moment, but they are quite flexible. Working from a movie clip and going up one level to its parent and down one level to a sibling will work from anywhere—be that in the root timeline, another movie clip, or nested even deeper—because the various stages aren't named.

Table 2-2 and Table 2-3 draw parallels to the operating system and web site analogies:

Table 2-2. Absolute (from main timeline to nested movie clip)

ActionScript	Windows OS	Mac OS	Web Site
`root.mc1.mc2`	*c:\folder1\folder2*	*Macintosh/folder1/folder2*	`http://www.domain.com/dir/dir`

Table 2-3. Relative (from a third movie clip, up to the root, and down to the child of a sibling)

ActionScript	Windows OS	Mac OS	Web Site
`this.parent.mc1.mc2`	..\folder1\folder2	../folder1/folder2	`../dir/dir`

What's Next?

Ideally, we've provided just enough background (or review) of key ActionScript fundamentals to now focus in on topical syntax. Although we won't entirely ignore basic elements within the scripts of future chapters, we will spend more time describing the collective goal of a script, and highlighting new issues introduced or updated by ActionScript 3.0.

Next, we start off the ActionScript 3.0-specific material with a look at the three essential building blocks of most ActionScript objects: properties, methods, and events—the latter being one of the most significantly changed elements of ActionScript, with the introduction of version 3.0.

In the next chapter, we'll discuss:

- The descriptive properties (such as width, height, location, alpha (opacity), rotation, and more) of each object that define its major characteristics

- The actions you may exert on objects, or that objects may take on other objects, in the form of methods

- The events issued by the user, or aspects of your program or environment, and, perhaps more directly, the *reactions* to those events

GRAPHICS AND INTERACTION

PART **II**

Part II represents the largest section of the book, spanning Chapter 3 through Chapter 9. This part covers many significant features that distinguish ActionScript 3.0 from prior versions. It focuses on graphics and interactions and includes the new event model and display list.

Chapter 3 is a discussion of properties, events, and methods—the items responsible for manipulating just about anything in Flash. Of particular importance is a section that describes a novel approach to handling events in ActionScript. Chapter 4 goes on to explain the display list, a great new way to display visual assets in Flash. Chapter 5 discusses timeline control, including various navigation techniques.

Chapter 6 marks an important transition in the book, as the remaining chapters focus more on object-oriented programming. Chapter 7 takes a look at various ways to animate graphics with ActionScript. Chapter 8 and 9 round out the presentation of graphics and interactivity with tutorials covering drawing with vectors and pixels. Included are demonstrations for creating vectors with ActionScript and manipulating a variety of bitmap properties in your projects.

PROPERTIES, METHODS, AND EVENTS

In addition to the core language fundamentals reviewed in the previous chapter, you will find that the majority of your scripts are written using properties, methods, and events. These are the basic building blocks of most scripted tasks and allow you to get and set characteristics of, issue instructions to, and react to input from, many Flash elements.

- **Properties.** Properties are somewhat akin to adjectives in that they describe the object being modified or queried. For example, you can check or set the width of a button. Most properties are read-write, in that you can both get and set their values. Some properties, however, are read-only, which means you can ask for, but not change, their values.

- **Methods.** Methods are a bit like verbs. They tell objects to do something, such as play and stop. In some cases, methods can be used to simplify the setting of properties. You might use a method called `setSize()`, for example, to simultaneously set the width and height of something. Other methods are more unique, such as `navigateToURL()`, which instructs a browser to display a web page.

- **Events.** Events are the catalysts that trigger the actions you write, setting properties and calling methods. For instance, a user might click the mouse button, which would then result in a mouse event. That event then causes a function to execute, performing the desired actions. *Event handlers* are the ActionScript middlemen that trap the events and actually call the functions. ActionScript 3.0 has unified event handling into a consistent system of what are called *event listeners*, which are set up to listen for the occurrence of a specific event and react accordingly.

In this chapter, you will build a utility that will demonstrate each of these ActionScript structures. By creating mouse and keyboard events, you will manipulate several common properties, as well as execute a few methods. The vast majority of ActionScript entities have properties, methods, and events. For clarity, we will focus primarily on the movie clip. Using the movie clip to centralize our discussion will make it easier for you to consult the Flash help system, online resources, and supplemental texts for additional information, as you look for other attributes to manipulate.

Inherited Attributes

One of the most important things to understand when consulting attributes is that ActionScript entities often share attributes in common with other entities. One reason for this is that they may be related in some way, such as being descendents from a common parent. In this case, the child inherits attributes from its parent. We introduced this concept a bit in Chapter 1 when we talked about classes. Consider the idea that a daughter, by virtue of being a different sex than her father, has several characteristics, or properties, that are distinct from her father. However, they also may share several characteristics in common, such as eye and hair color.

We will look at the sharing of attributes in greater depth throughout this book but, for now, all you need to know is that ActionScript reference materials are often organized by classes, and it would be redundant and cumbersome to list the same properties for every related class. Considering the movie clip, for example, every Flash element that can be displayed on stage—the movie clip among them—can have an x and a y coordinate, or location, on the stage. Listing these properties for every such item would eat up a lot of space and make the resource a bit harder to wade through.

To simplify things, the **x** and **y** properties are typically listed as inherited properties in the Flash help system. To view inherited properties, for example, in the Flash help system, just click the Show Inherited Public Properties link found immediately under the Public Properties header.

Properties

If you think of properties as ways of describing an object, they become second nature. Asking where a movie clip is, for example, or setting its width are both descriptive steps that both use properties.

In Chapter 2, we briefly discussed the object model and dot syntax that brings order and structure to ActionScript as well as many other scripting and programming languages. Referencing a property begins with an instance—let's call our square movie clip "box"—because you must decide which element you wish to query or change. If we consider a test file with only one movie clip in it, instantiated as "box," all that remains is referencing the property and either getting or setting its value.

To begin, we'll show you the syntax for making five changes to movie clip properties in the following table. Then, when we demonstrate how to handle events in the next section, we'll change these properties interactively. The following examples assume a movie clip of a square is on the stage, and has an instance name of "box." Figure 3-1 demonstrates the visual change made by each property. The light colored square is the original state when the movie clip is moved. (The **alpha** property shows only the final state.) The dashed stroke for the visible property is only to show that the box is not visible.

Table 3-1 represents six movie clip properties with sample syntax and notes regarding each property's unit of measure and possible sample range of values.

Table 3-1. Movie clip properties

Description	Property	Syntax for Setting Value	Units and/or Range
Location	x, y	`box.x = 100;` `box.y = 100;`	pixels
Scale (1)	scaleX, scaleY	`box.scaleX = 0.5;` `box.scaleY = 0.5;`	percent / 0-1
Scale (2)	width, height	`box.width = 72;` `box.height = 72;`	pixels
Rotation	rotation	`box.rotation = 45;`	degrees / 0-360
Transparency	alpha	`box.alpha = 0.5;`	percent / 0-1
Visibility	visible	`box.visible = false;`	Boolean

If you have experience with prior versions of ActionScript, you may notice a few changes in the property syntax. First, the properties do not begin with an underscore. This is a beneficial consistency introduced with ActionScript 3.0. Rather than varying property syntax, some with and some without leading underscores, no properties begin with the underscore character.

Second, some value ranges that used to be 0–100 are now 0–1. Examples include **scaleX**, **scaleY**, and **alpha**. Instead of using 50 to set a 50% value, specify 0.5.

Finally, the first scaling method uses properties **scaleX** and **scaleY**, rather than **_xscale** and **_yscale**, which are their AS1/AS2 equivalents. Typically, AS3 properties will cite the x and y version of a property as a suffix to make referencing the property easier.

Table 3-1 shows syntax for setting properties for the "box" movie clip. Querying the value of a property, also known as getting the property, is just as easy. For example, if you wanted to trace the box's alpha value, or store it in a variable, you could write either of the following:

```
trace(box.alpha);
var bAlpha:Number = box.alpha;
```

You can also use compound assignment operators—operators that simultaneously alter and assign values —to easily update the properties. The following code will add 20 degrees to the current value of the box's rotation.

```
box.rotation += 20;
```

box.x += 10;
box.y += 10;

box.scaleX = 0.5;
box.scaleY = 0.5;

box.rotation = 20;

box.alpha = 0.5;

box.visible = false;

Figure 3-1. Changes to five movie clip properties

Events

Events make the Flash world go 'round. They are responsible for setting your scripts in motion, causing them to execute. A button can be triggered by a mouse event, text fields react to keyboard events—even calling your own custom functions is a means of issuing a custom event.

Events come in many varieties. In addition to the obvious events like mouse and keyboard input, most ActionScript classes have their own events. For example, events are fired when watching a video, working with text, and resizing the stage. To take advantage of these events to drive your application, you need to be able to detect their occurrences.

In previous versions of ActionScript, there were a variety of ways to trap events. You could apply a script directly to a button, for example, and use the `on(Release)` approach. As the language matured, you could create event handlers and apply them remotely using instance names, using `myButton.onRelease` for example. Finally, you could use event listeners, primarily with components or custom objects.

In ActionScript 3.0, trapping events is simplified by relying on one approach for all event handling, which is to use event listeners regardless of the type of event or how it is used. The `EventDispatcher` class that "oversees" event listeners is not new, but it has been improved and is now responsible for handling the majority of events in AS3.

The `EventDispatcher` class allows you to listen for the occurrence of events by putting event listeners into service, clean up your code by removing unneeded listeners from service, and manually dispatching events when you need an event to occur at a specific time. You can also check to see whether an object has a listener already set up for a specific event, which we'll look at later when we talk about event propagation.

Using Event Listeners

The concept of event listeners is pretty simple. Imagine that you are in a lecture hall that holds 100 people. Only one person in the audience has been given instructions about how to respond when the lecturer asks a specific question. In this case, one person has been told to listen for a specific event, and to act on the instructions provided when this event occurs.

Now imagine that many more responses need to be planned. For example, when the lecturer takes the stage, the lights must be dimmed. When the lecturer clicks a hand-held beeping device, an audio/visual technician must advance to the next video in the presentation. When each video ends, the lecturer must react by introducing the next exhibit in the lecture. Finally, when an audience member raises a hand, an usher must bring a microphone to assist the audience member in asking his or her question.

These are all reactions to specific events that are occurring throughout the lecture. Some are planned and directed to a specific recipient—such as the beeping that triggers the technician to advance to the next video in the series. Others are unplanned, such as when, or even if, an audience member has a question. Yet each appropriate party in the mix has been told which event to listen for and how to react when that event occurs.

Creating an event listener, in its most basic form, is fairly straightforward. The nuances that make the process anything more than simple add power to the system and can be used to your advantage. The first main step is to identify the host of the listener—that is, who should be told to listen for a specific event. One easy-to-understand example is that a button should be told to listen for mouse events that might trigger its scripted behavior.

Once you have identified an element that should listen for an event, the next major step is choosing an event appropriate for that element. For example, it makes sense for a button to listen for a mouse event, but it makes less sense for the same button to listen for the end of a video or the resizing of the stage. It would be more appropriate for the video player to listen for the end of the video, and the stage to listen for any resize event. Each respective element could then act, or instruct others to act, when that event occurs—which is the third main step in setting up a listener.

To identify the instructions that must be executed when an event occurs, you simply need to write a function and tell the event listener to call that function when the event fires. That function uses an argument to receive information about the event that called it, allowing the function to use key bits of data during its execution.

To tie it all together, the **addEventListener()** method is used to identify the event and assign the function to be executed to the object that is supposed to be doing the listening. Let's go back to the button example in which the button should listen for a **mouse up** event. Let's say the button is called *rotate_right_btn*, and the function it should execute is **onRotateRight()**. The code would look something like this:

```
1    rotate_right_btn.addEventListener(MouseEvent.MOUSE_UP,
     onRotateRight);
2    function onRotateRight(evt:MouseEvent):void {
3        box.rotation += 20;
4    }
```

In line 1, you start with the button instance name and then add the **addEventListener()** method. The method requires two mandatory parameters. The first is the event for which you want to listen. Each event you are trying to trap, be it a built-in event or a custom event of your own making, originates in a class that defines that event. Built-in events are typically found in classes dedicated specifically to events, and the event itself is usually defined as a constant in that class. For example, the **MouseEvent** class contains constants that refer to mouse events like **mouse up** and **mouse down**. This example uses the **MOUSE_UP** constant to reference the **mouse up** event. Other examples include the **ENTER_FRAME** constant in the **Event** class, for simulating playhead updates, and the **KEY_UP** event in the **KeyboardEvent** class, for trapping user keyboard input. We'll look at both of these events later on in this chapter.

The second parameter is the function that should be called when the event is received. In this example, a reference to the **onRotateRight()** function, defined in lines 2 through 4, is specified. You will probably be familiar with the structure of the function from the discussion about functions in Chapter 2. To review, the function contents are defined by the braces. In this case, line 3 adds 20 degrees to the current rotation value of the movie clip "box." Also explained in Chapter 2, the *void* that follows the function name and parentheses indicates that no value is returned by the function.

What hasn't been fully explained is the argument of the function that receives that event. Unlike custom functions, the argument in listener functions is required. In the following code example, it is arbitrarily named **evt** and receives information about the event and element that triggered the event. If helpful, you can parse information from this argument for use in the function. The argument must be typed to the expected data. This will help you find errors if an incorrect event type is received. In this case, because we're listening for a MouseEvent, that is the data type used for the argument.

To illustrate this, let's look at another mouse event example. This time, however, we'll view multiple events, and parse information from the argument to show some of the benefits of this structure.

```
1  myMovieClip.addEventListener(MouseEvent.MOUSE_DOWN, onStartDrag);
2  myMovieClip.addEventListener(MouseEvent.MOUSE_UP, onStopDrag);
3  function onStartDrag(evt:MouseEvent):void {
4      evt.target.startDrag();
5  }
6  function onStopDrag(evt:MouseEvent):void {
7      evt.target.stopDrag();
8  }
```

In this example, two event listeners are assigned to a movie clip. One listens for a **mouse down** event, another listens for **mouse up**. They each invoke different functions. In both functions, however, the **target** property of the event, which is sought from the function argument, is used to identify which element received the mouse event. This allows the function in line 3 to start dragging the movie clip that was clicked and also allows the function in line 6 to stop dragging the movie clip that was clicked, both without specifying the movie clip by its instance name. This generic approach is very useful because it makes the function much more flexible. The function can act upon any appropriate item that is clicked and passed into its argument. In other words, the same function could start and stop dragging any movie clip to which the same listener was added.

In the accompanying source files, the *start_stop_drag.fla* file shows this by adding the following lines to the previous example:

```
9    myMovieClip2.addEventListener(MouseEvent.MOUSE_DOWN, onStartDrag);
10   myMovieClip2.addEventListener(MouseEvent.MOUSE_UP, onStopDrag);
```

A similar event property is currentTarget, which references the object to which the event listener is attached. When a listener is attached to a self-contained movie clip (as in the previous example), target and currentTarget are the same because you click on the object with the listener. However, you'll learn that events can pass from a parent clip down to any child clips within. When the listener is attached to the parent, and you click on the child, target will still refer to the child, but currentTarget will refer to the parent. You'll learn more about this later, but the file *start_stop_drag_currentTarget.fla* demonstrates this idea.

Using Mouse Events to Control Properties

Now we can combine the syntax we've covered in the "Properties" and "Events" sections to set up interactive control over properties. In the *chapter03* directory of the accompanying source code for this book, you'll find a file called *props_events.fla*. It contains nothing more than the example movie clip "box" and two buttons in the library that will be used repeatedly to change the five properties discussed earlier. The movie clip contains numbers to show which of its frames is visible, and the instance name of each button reflects its purpose. Included are *move_up_btn*, *scale_down_btn*, *rotate_right_btn*, *fade_up_btn*, and *toggle_visibility_btn*, among others. Figure 3-2 shows the layout of the file.

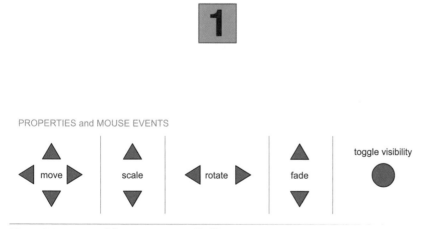

Figure 3-2. Layout of the props_events.fla *file*

Starting with movement, we need to define one or more functions to update the location of the movie clip. There are two common approaches to this task. The first is to create one function for all movement that uses a conditional to decide how to react to each event. We'll demonstrate that when we discuss keyboard events. For now, we'll use the simpler direct approach of defining a separate basic function for each type of movement as shown in Example 3-1.

Example 3-1. props_events.fla

```
1   function onMoveLeft(evt:MouseEvent):void {
2       box.x -= 20;
3   }
4   function onMoveRight(evt:MouseEvent):void {
5       box.x += 20;
6   }
7   function onMoveUp(evt:MouseEvent):void {
8       box.y -= 20;
9   }
10  function onMoveDown(evt:MouseEvent):void {
11      box.y += 20;
12  }
```

Once the functions are defined, all you have to do is add the listeners to the appropriate buttons.

```
13  move_left_btn.addEventListener(MouseEvent.MOUSE_UP, onMoveLeft);
14  move_right_btn.addEventListener(MouseEvent.MOUSE_UP, onMoveRight);
15  move_up_btn.addEventListener(MouseEvent.MOUSE_UP, onMoveUp);
16  move_down_btn.addEventListener(MouseEvent.MOUSE_UP, onMoveDown);
```

This simple process is then repeated for each of the buttons on stage. The remaining script collects the aforementioned properties and event listeners to complete the demo pictured in Figure 3-2.

```
17  scale_up_btn.addEventListener(MouseEvent.MOUSE_UP, onScaleUp);
18  scale_down_btn.addEventListener(MouseEvent.MOUSE_UP, onScaleDown);
19
20  rotate_left_btn.addEventListener(MouseEvent.MOUSE_UP, onRotateLeft);
21  rotate_right_btn.addEventListener(MouseEvent.MOUSE_UP,
    onRotateRight);
22
23  fade_in_btn.addEventListener(MouseEvent.MOUSE_UP, onFadeIn);
24  fade_out_btn.addEventListener(MouseEvent.MOUSE_UP, onFadeOut);
26
27  toggle_visible_btn.addEventListener(MouseEvent.MOUSE_UP,
    onToggleVisible);
28
29  function onScaleUp(evt:MouseEvent):void {
30      box.scaleX += 0.2;
31      box.scaleY += 0.2;
32  }
33  function onScaleDown(evt:MouseEvent):void {
34      box.scaleX -= 0.2;
35      box.scaleY -= 0.2;
36  }
37
38  function onRotateLeft(evt:MouseEvent):void {
39      box.rotation -= 20;
40  }
```

```
41
42   function onRotateRight(evt:MouseEvent):void {
43       box.rotation += 20;
44   }
45
46   function onFadeIn(evt:MouseEvent):void {
47       box.alpha += 0.2;
48   }
49   function onFadeOut(evt:MouseEvent):void {
50       box.alpha -= 0.2;
51   }
52
53   function onToggleVisible(evt:MouseEvent):void {
54       box.visible = !box.visible;
55   }
```

Methods

Methods, the verbs of the ActionScript language, instruct their respective objects to take action. For example, you can tell a movie clip to stop playing by using its **stop()** method. Like properties, methods appear consistently in the dot syntax that is the foundation of ActionScript, following the object calling the method. For example, if the movie clip "box" in the main timeline issues the **stop()** method, the syntax would appear like this:

```
box.stop();
```

Also like properties, most ActionScript classes have specific methods, and many inherit methods from ancestor classes. In addition, like properties, you can further define your own methods by writing functions in your own custom classes. For the following demonstration, we'll again focus on the movie clip from the prior example. This time, however, we'll introduce another event class and show you how to control your movie clips with the keyboard.

Using Keyboard Events to Call Methods

Trapping keyboard events is very similar to trapping mouse events, with one significant exception: The target of the event listener is not frequently the object you wish to manipulate. When working with text, the text field being manipulated may, indeed, serve well as the target of the keyboard events. When controlling movie clips, however, the stage itself is often a useful, centralized recipient of the keyboard events.

Adding an event listener to the stage means that you can process all key events with a single listener, and then isolate only the desired key events with a conditional, issuing instructions accordingly. To simplify the syntax of this last segment of our demonstration script, we'll use the *switch* form of conditional statements. The **switch** statement, reviewed in Chapter 2, is simply a more easily readable **if/else-if** conditional structure.

We'll start by adding the listener to the stage. In this case, we'll be looking for the **key down** event, which is specified using a constant like all predefined events, but this time it is part of the **KeyboardEvent** class. When the event is heard, our listener will call the **onKeyPressed()** function.

```
1    stage.addEventListener(KeyboardEvent.KEY_DOWN, onKeyPressed);
```

Next, we define the **onKeyPressed()** function, being sure to type the incoming argument value as **KeyboardEvent**. Finally, we parse the **keyCode** property from the incoming event information now stored in the **evt** argument. The **keyCode** is a unique number assigned to each key and allows you to determine which key was pressed.

One **keyCode** value is assigned to each key, so this value can't be used directly for case-sensitive key checking—that is, uppercase "S" has the same **keyCode** as lowercase "s." If you need to analyze case sensitivity, use **charCode**, which does have unique values for each case.

To specify each key, we'll use constants defined in the **Keyboard** class, rather than having to remember each numeric **keyCode** value. This makes it easier to reference the Enter/Return key as **Keyboard.ENTER**, the left arrow key as **Keyboard.LEFT**, and so on.

We'll use five keys to call five methods. When each desired key is pressed, it will execute the appropriate method, and then break out of the switch statement. We'll also add a default state that will trace the keyCode of any other key pressed. The final script segment looks like this:

```
2    function onKeyPressed(evt:KeyboardEvent):void {
3        switch (evt.keyCode) {
4            case Keyboard.ENTER:
5                box.play();
6                break;
7            case Keyboard.BACKSPACE:
8                box.stop();
9                break;
10           case Keyboard.LEFT:
11               box.prevFrame();
12               break;
13           case Keyboard.RIGHT:
14               box.nextFrame();
15               break;
16           case Keyboard.SPACE:
17               box.gotoAndStop(3);
18               break;
19           default:
20               trace("keyCode:", evt.keyCode);
21       }
22   }
```

The first four methods are basic movie clip navigation options: playing, stopping, or sending the movie clip to the previous or next frame in its timeline. The last method sends the movie clip to its third frame and then stops its playback. We'll look at these and other navigation options in greater detail in Chapter 5 when we discuss timeline control.

WARNING

Depending on your setup, many key events will not function properly in Flash when using the Control>Test Movie command. This is probably not an error but, instead, a result of Flash Player using keyboard shortcuts just like the Flash application does. To test your key events, simply use the Control>Disable Keyboard Shortcuts menu command to disable keyboard shortcuts in the Player (that is, after invoking Test Movie). Be sure to reenable the shortcuts, or you won't be able to use cmd+W (Mac) or Ctrl+W (Windows) to close the window, or use other familiar shortcuts. Alternatively, you can test the movie in a browser.

This code can be seen in the *methods_events.fla* file in the accompanying source code, as well as the combined file, *props_methods_events.fla*, which includes both the properties and methods examples in this chapter.

Event Propagation

So far in this chapter, we've been working with objects in the *display list*. We'll explain the display list in greater detail in the next chapter but, in essence, the display list contains all visual objects in your file. It includes the stage, any loaded SWFs, and any shapes, buttons, movie clips, and so on, down to the most deeply nested clip.

Objects in the display list are part of a special event flow often referred to as *event propagation*. When the target of certain events, including mouse and key events, is in the display list, the event is not dispatched directly to the event target. Instead, it is dispatched to the display list, and the event propagates from the top of the list down to the event target, and then bubbles (works its way) back up through the display list again.

Consider two movie clips (mc2 and mc3) within a movie clip (mc1) that is on the stage. Next, imagine that the target of the event is the nested movie clip, mc2. When the desired event occurs, it is not dispatched directly to mc2, but rather to the display list. First, the stage receives the event, then any relevant loaded SWFs (including the root timeline, in this example), then the parent movie clip, mc1, and then the target of the event, mc2. After the event is received by the target, it then propagates back up through the display list to mc2, root, and stage. Figure 3-3 depicts the process, showing a mouse event dispatched to the top of the display list, the stage, making its way through the root timeline and parent movie clip until it reaches the event target, and then bubbling back up through the display list again.

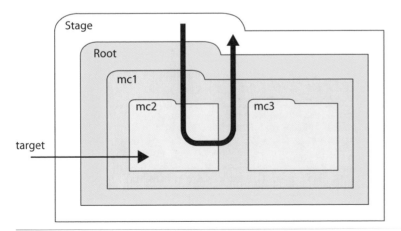

Figure 3-3. Event propagation process

Event propagation can be used to great advantage with just a little bit of planning. For example, let's say both nested movie clips, mc2 and mc3, were designed to react to **mouse over** and **mouse out** events. Whenever the user rolled the mouse over one of the clips, it would change its **alpha** value to indicate interaction. In this case, you would normally have to attach a listener for each event to each movie clip. The code for such an example follows, and Figure 3-4 depicts the result, where each movie clip is represented by a folder: *folder0* and *folder1*. Example 3-2 shows the code in the sample file.

Example 3-2. event_propagation1.fla

```
1   folder0.addEventListener(MouseEvent.MOUSE_OVER, onFolderOver);
2   folder0.addEventListener(MouseEvent.MOUSE_OUT, onFolderOut);
3   folder1.addEventListener(MouseEvent.MOUSE_OVER, onFolderOver);
4   folder1.addEventListener(MouseEvent.MOUSE_OUT, onFolderOut);
5
6   function onFolderOver(evt:MouseEvent):void {
7       evt.target.alpha = 0.5;
8   }
9
10  function onFolderOut(evt:MouseEvent):void {
11      evt.target.alpha = 1;
12  }
```

Figure 3-4 represents the standard listener approach, in which listeners for **mouse over** and **mouse out** events are attached to both folders. As the mouse moves over a folder, the **alpha** value changes.

Figure 3-4. The effect of the changing alpha values using mouse over and mouse out events

Now imagine having to use the same approach for many folders, as seen in Figure 3-5. The code could get quite extensive with all those listeners for each folder. However, with event propagation, it is possible to attach the listener to the parent movie clip, *folder_group* (indicated by the dashed line). The event will cascade through the display list, and the common listener functions will simply parse the object that is the intended target. The code that follows is significantly simplified thanks to event propagation and can be seen in the source file *event_propagation2.fla*.

```
1   folder_group.addEventListener(MouseEvent.MOUSE_OVER, onFolderOver);
2   folder_group.addEventListener(MouseEvent.MOUSE_OUT, onFolderOut);
3
4   function onFolderOver(evt:MouseEvent):void {
5       evt.target.alpha = 0.5;
6   }
7
8   function onFolderOut(evt:MouseEvent):void {
9       evt.target.alpha = 1;
10  }
```

NOTE

To see another example of the difference between the target *and* currentTarget *event properties, change* target *in lines 5 and 9, to* currentTarget *in the code at right. Because the listener is attached to the parent movie clip, which contains all the folders,* currentTarget *causes the parent clip to fade affecting all its children. Used judiciously, these properties could be used to highlight a single folder, or all folders as a group.*

Looking at Figure 3-5 again, the folders are numbered left to right, top to bottom, starting with 0. Imagine moving your mouse over *folder0*. The target of the event dispatched to the display list will be *folder0*, it will propagate through the list until it reaches *folder0*, and then it will bubble back up. Similarly, if you mouse over *folder5* or *folder10*, the listener function will know which folder was the target by parsing the **target** property of the event, and the alpha value of the appropriate folder will be changed. Figure 3-5 simulates listeners attached not to each folder, but rather to the parent movie clip (represented by the dashed line) within which each folder resides. Due to event propagation, the **mouse over** and **mouse out** events automatically dispatched to the display list are thereafter received by every child of the target movie clip.

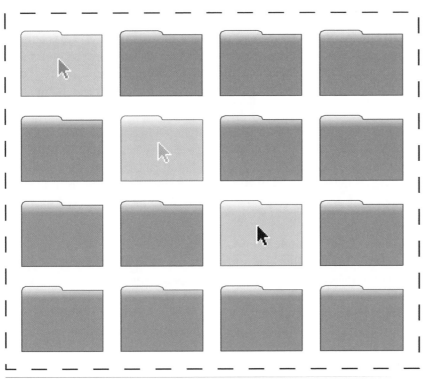

Figure 3-5. Using the parent movie clip to propagate events

Frame and Timer Events

We've been using mouse and keyboard events because you're almost certainly familiar with them to some degree, and they are ideally suited to this tutorial context. However, there are many, many events in the ActionScript language. While it's not possible to cover every one, we would like to round out the chapter with two other significant event types: *frame* and *timer*.

Frame Events

Frame events are not triggered by user input, the way mouse and keyboard events are. Instead, they occur naturally as the Flash file plays. Each time the playhead enters a frame, a frame script is executed. This means that frame

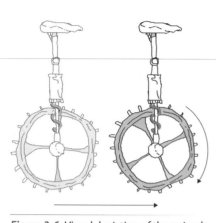

Figure 3-6. Visual depiction of the unicycle movements

This example also demonstrates a scripting shortcut aided by ActionScript. When specifying a rotation higher than 360 degrees, ActionScript will understand and use the correct value—that is, 360 degrees is one full rotation around a circle, bringing you back to degree 0 (720 degrees is twice around the circle and also equates to 0). Similarly, 370 degrees is equivalent to 10 degrees, as it is 10 degrees past degree 0, and so on. This allows you to set the rotation of the wheel movie clip to the x coordinate of the mouse, without worrying about moving past the 360-pixel point on the stage.

scripts execute only once for the life of the frame, making them an excellent location for seldom-executed tasks, such as initializations. In other words, for a frame script to execute more than once, the playhead must leave the frame and return—either because of an ActionScript navigation instruction, or a playback loop that returns the playhead to frame 1 when it reaches the end of the timeline.

However, using an event listener, you can listen for a recurring **enter frame** event that some display objects have, including the main timeline and the movie clips. An **enter frame** event is fired at the same pace as the document frame rate. For example, the default frame rate is 12 frames per second, so the default enter frame frequency is 12 times per second. Using the **enter frame** event allows your file to update frequently—a particularly handy thing for visual assets.

The *frame_events.fla* file in the accompanying source code demonstrates this event by updating the position of a unicycle every enter frame. It places the unicycle at the location of the mouse and, to further review your work with properties, rotates the child movie clip in which the wheel resides. Figure 3-6 visualizes the effect. As you move your mouse to the right on the stage, the unicycle will move to the right, and the wheel will rotate clockwise.

The code for this example follows. The first line adds an enter frame event listener to the main timeline, specifying the event using the **ENTER_FRAME** constant of the **Event** class. The function sets the unicycle's x coordinate and rotation to the x coordinate of the mouse. This code can be found in the source file *frame_events.fla*.

```
1   stage.addEventListener(Event.ENTER_FRAME, onFrameLoop);
2
3   function onFrameLoop(evt:Event):void {
4       cycle.x = mouseX;
5       cycle.wheel.rotation = mouseX;
6   }
```

Timer Events

An alternative to using enter frame events to trigger actions on a recurring basis is to use time-based events. Although it's among the most straightforward options, using the **enter frame** event exclusively for this purpose has disadvantages. For example, Flash Player can only reliably achieve moderate frame rates—somewhere between the default 12 frames per second and perhaps 18 to 35 fps on the high end. Your mileage may vary, but that's fairly accurate when averaging the CPU population at large. More importantly, the rate at which the enter frame fires is not always consistent.

On the other hand, time-based events are measured in milliseconds and, therefore, can fire more quickly. Further, time-based events don't vary from scenario to scenario, so they are more reliable and consistent.

Previous versions of ActionScript used the `setInterval()` method for ongoing recurring events and the `setTimeout()` method for finitely recurring events. ActionScript 3.0 wraps up these approaches neatly behind the scenes of the new `Timer` class, simplifying the process of using timers.

The first step in using the `Timer` class is to create an instance of the class:

```
var timer:Timer = new Timer(delay, repeatCount);
```

The class constructor takes two arguments. The first is mandatory and specifies the delay, in milliseconds, before the timer event is fired. The second is optional and is the number of times the event fires. Omitting the second argument will cause the event to fire infinitely, each time after the specified delay, similar to prior `setInterval()` implementations. Using a positive value, such as 1, will cause the event to fire that many times (again, after the specified delay), similar to prior `setTimeout()` implementations.

In the sample *timer_events.fla* in the accompanying source code, the timer event (specified as the constant `TIMER` in the `TimerEvent` class), occurs every second (1,000 milliseconds) and calls a function that adds rotation to a hand nested inside a watch movie clip. The code is quite simple, as shown in the following example:

```
1   var timer:Timer = new Timer(1000);
2   timer.addEventListener(TimerEvent.TIMER, onTimer);
3   timer.start();
4
5   function onTimer(evt:TimerEvent):void {
6       watch.hand.rotation +=6;
7   }
```

One important thing to note is line 3. The timer you instantiate does not start automatically the way prior intervals or timeouts started. This gives you greater flexibility and control over your timer events. You can also stop the timer using the `stop()` method, and reset the timer using the `reset()` method. The latter stops the timer and also resets the repeat count to zero. For example, if you specified that the timer call a function five times, but reset it after the third call, the timer would begin counting again from zero rather than picking up from three at the point when it was reset. Figure 3-7 depicts the code in the previous code sample. The hand on the stopwatch advances 5 degrees of rotation every second when a timer event calls a function.

NOTE

As described in Chapter 2, frame and timer loops, such as those seen in the previous examples, are often an attractive alternative to `for..loops` *because they allow additional updates to occur throughout the file. A code loop, such as a* `for..loop`, *is one of the most processor-intensive structures and will execute only the code inside the loop until the loop is finished. This means that other animation, sound or video updates, process progress reports, and so on, will all be halted while the loop is working.*

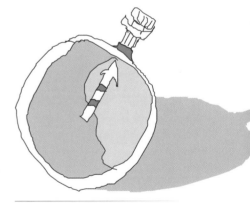

Figure 3-7. Use of the timer event in a stopwatch

Removing Event Listeners

While event listeners make most event handling easy to add and maintain, leaving them in place when unneeded can wreak havoc. From a logic standpoint, consider what could happen if you kept an unwanted listener in operation. Imagine a weeklong promotion for radio station 101 FM, which rewards customer number 101 who enters a store each day of that week. The manager of the store is set up to listen for "customer enter" events and, when customer 101 enters the store, oodles of prizes and cash are bestowed upon the lucky winner. Now imagine if you left that listener in place after the promo week was over. Oodles of prizes and cash would continue to be awarded at great, unexpected expense.

Unwanted events are not the only problem, however. Every listener created occupies a small amount of memory. Injudiciously creating many event listeners, without cleaning up after yourself, can result in a memory leak. Therefore, it's a good idea to remove listeners when you know they will no longer be needed.

To do so, you simply need to use the **removeEventListener()** method. By specifying the owner of the relevant event and the listener function that is triggered, you can remove that listener so it no longer reacts to future events. The **removeEventListener()** method requires two parameters: the event and function specified when the listener was created. Specifying the event *and* function is important because you may have multiple listeners set up for the same event.

Let's add to the previous example and remove the timer event listener when the rotation of the watch hand meets or exceeds 30 degrees of rotation. The new code is in bold.

```
1   var timer:Timer = new Timer(1000);
2   timer.addEventListener(TimerEvent.TIMER, onTimer);
3   timer.start();
4
5   function onTimer(evt:TimerEvent):void {
6       watch.hand.rotation +=6;
7           if (watch.hand.rotation >= 30) {
8               timer.removeEventListener(TimerEvent.TIMER, onTimer);
9           }
10  }
```

As discussed earlier, this can be accomplished using a repeat count in the timer, like this:

```
var timer:Timer = new Timer(1000, 5);
```

However, the point of the example is to show you how to remove the listener from your logic flow and, equally important, from memory, when it is no longer needed. We briefly discuss an additional scenario for removing listeners in the "Garbage Collection" sidebar but, in all cases, it's good practice to remove any listeners that you know you'll no longer need. This is demonstrated in the source file *removing_listeners.fla*.

Garbage Collection

Garbage collection is the method by which Flash Player purges from memory objects that you no longer need. Garbage collection and memory management typically are not topics you need to concern yourself with when just getting started with ActionScript 3.0. However, there are some intermediate coding practices that you can adopt relatively painlessly—even at the outset of your learning—that may prove to be useful habits in the long run. Garbage collection is such a practice.

We just want to scratch the surface of this subject, laying the groundwork for conventions that we'll use throughout the remainder of this book, and then refer you to additional resources for more information.

There are three optional parameters that you can add to the end of the **addEventListener()** method. Here is the syntax of the method, with which you are probably already partly familiar if you've read this chapter. The optional parameters we'll discuss are in bold.

```
eventTarget.addEventListener(EventType.EVENT_NAME,
    eventResponse, useCapture:Boolean,
    priority:int, weakReference:Boolean);
```

The first two optional parameters control when the listener function executes. You probably won't need to adjust these values, but here's a quick snapshot of their functionality so you can decide whether you want to explore them further.

The first optional parameter, **useCapture**, allows you to handle the listener event before it reaches its target (if set to **true**) or once the event has reached its target (if set to **false**) or is bubbling back up through the display list. The default (**false**) is to react to all events captured at or after the event reaches the target, and this is the configuration you will likely use most of the time.

The second optional parameter, **priority**, allows you to order the execution of multiple listeners set to respond to the same event in the same phase. This, too, is unlikely to be an issue, and the default parameter of **0** will serve you well in the vast majority of circumstances.

The third optional parameter, **weakReference**, is the option we want you to understand and start using. In a nutshell, this helps with memory management in the event that you're not careful about removing unneeded listeners.

Briefly, in ActionScript 3.0, memory management that you do not explicitly control is handled behind the scenes by the garbage collector. When you are no longer referencing an object in your application, it is marked for cleanup, and the garbage collector periodically sweeps through your application discarding unneeded items, freeing up memory along the way. However, if a reference to an object remains, the garbage collector can't know that the object should be purged from memory.

Try as we might to be good, it's not uncommon for developers to forget to remove event listeners in their code (see the section "Removing Event Listeners" in this chapter). However, a distant next-best thing is a weakly referenced listener. Simply put, weakly referenced listeners aren't supervised by the garbage collector and, therefore, don't have to be manually marked for removal. If only weak references to an object remain after you have finished using it, then the object is eligible for collection.

Using this option is very simple. All you need to do is change the **weakReference** setting of the **addEventListener()** method from its default value of **false**, to **true**. Because it's the third optional parameter, values for the first and second parameters must be included so Flash knows which parameter you are trying to set. You will rarely need to change those values, so you can use their aforementioned defaults (**false** for **useCapture** and **0** for **priority**).

So, our preference, and the convention we will use hereafter in this book, is to use the **addEventListener()** method with this syntax:

```
eventTarget.addEventListener(EventType.EVENT_NAME,
    eventResponse, false, 0, true);
```

If you get in the habit of using this syntax, you will be far less likely to run into memory management problems due to lax code maintenance. Remember, this is not a substitute for removing your unneeded listeners explicitly. However, it's a backup plan and a best practice that is easy to adopt.

Additional discussion of the event flow—including event phases, setting listener priority, stopping propagation along the way, manually dispatching events, and more—is featured on the companion web site. Flash developer Grant Skinner also wrote a helpful series of articles on resource management on his blog (*http://www.gskinner.com/blog*) that got us thinking about this in the first place. Finally, event flow is discussed in depth in Chapters 12 and 21 of our resource book of choice, *Essential ActionScript 3.0*.

What's Next?

This chapter has demonstrated ways to manipulate Flash objects but, in the case of our example movie clip, we have assumed that the movie clip already existed on the stage. This is an acceptable assumption for projects authored primarily using the timeline, but it is a limiting assumption. If all files are to be constrained by using only elements manually added to the stage at author time, and used only in the manner and order in which they were originally added, the files cannot be as dynamic as the ActionScript language allows.

Coming up, we'll talk more about the display list—an excellent means of managing visual assets. Understanding the basics of the display list is instrumental not only in dynamically adding elements at runtime, but also manipulating existing stage-bound objects to their fullest potential.

In the next chapter, we'll discuss:

- Adding new children to the display list

- Removing existing display list children

- Swapping depths of objects in the display list to change their visual stacking order dynamically

- Managing the hierarchical relationship of display list objects and how to change that relationship through reparenting

CHAPTER 4

THE DISPLAY LIST

One of the most dramatic changes introduced by ActionScript 3.0, particularly for designers accustomed to prior versions of ActionScript, is the way in which visual elements are added to an application at runtime. In prior versions of ActionScript, a separate approach was used to add most kinds of visual assets at runtime, requiring varied syntax. Management of those assets—particularly depth management—and creating and destroying objects, were also fairly restrictive and could be relatively involved depending on what you were trying to accomplish.

ActionScript 3.0 brings with it an entirely new way of handling visual assets. It's called the *display list*. It's a hierarchical list of all visual elements in your file. It includes common objects such as movie clips, but also objects such as shapes and sprites that either didn't previously exist or could not be created programmatically.

In this chapter, we'll look at the following topics:

- **The Sum of Its Parts.** Understanding the display list means understanding its parts. In addition to knowing the kinds of objects that can be part of the display list, it's also important to grasp the simple difference between display objects and display object containers.

- **Adding and Removing Children.** The best part of the display list is how easy and consistent it is to add objects to, and remove objects from, the list.

- **Managing Object Names, Positions, and Data Types.** In addition to adding and removing display objects, you will need to manipulate existing members of the display list. You will likely need to find an object, either by name or position in the list, or even identify an object's data type as a particular display object class.

- **Changing the Hierarchy.** It's also much easier than ever before to manage asset depths (z-order, or the visual stacking order controlled by ActionScript, rather than timeline layers), and to change the familial relationship of assets. Moving a child from one parent to another is a breeze.

- **A Dynamic Navigation Bar.** As a quick demonstration of using the display list, we'll show you how to dynamically generate a very simple navigation bar.

The Sum of Its Parts

If you start thinking about the display list by thinking about what you see in any given application, you're half-way home. In addition to contributing to the structure of the new event model, discussed in Chapter 3, the display list is responsible for maintaining the visual and spatial assets in your file. You will use the display list to create and destroy visual assets, to manage their coexistence, and manage how they interrelate.

Let's take a look at the contents of the display list of a simple file structure. Figure 4-1 shows that this file has a shape, a text element, and a movie clip, and inside the movie clip is a bitmap. Figure 4-2 shows the display list of the same structure.

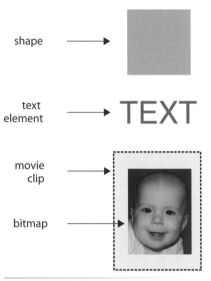

Figure 4-1. The visual layout of the simple file structure

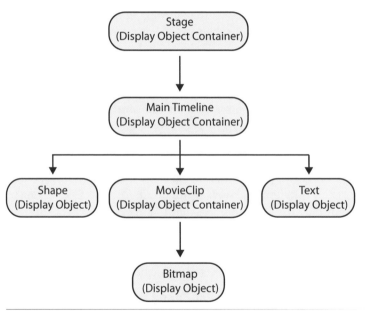

Figure 4-2. The display list of the sample file

At the top of the list is the stage. Although you can access the stage from many objects in the display list, it's easiest to think of the stage as the foundation on which everything is built. It also helps to think of the stage as the ultimate container within which all your visual assets reside at runtime. The container analogy will soon become central to this discussion. The stage contains everything.

Next is the main timeline, which is also referenced using the **root** display object instance variable. (See the sidebar, "_root versus root" for more information.) Like the stage, a Flash file requires one timeline within which all other assets are contained. Because of event propagation, it is common to use the main timeline as a location to add event listeners when writing scripts in the timeline. In that context, the main timeline is typically referenced using the **this** identifier, as in "this object being currently referenced within the context of the script." (For more information about event listeners and event propagation, see Chapter 3. For more information about **this**, see Chapter 2.)

Below the main timeline in the display list hierarchy are all the visual assets in the file. Included in the sample display list are the aforementioned shape, text, and movie clip assets, and inside the movie clip is the bitmap.

You may notice in Figure 4-2 that everything is subtitled as a display object or display object container. This is key to understanding and working with the display list effectively. It probably follows that everything in the display list is a display object. However, some display objects can contain other elements and therefore are also display object containers.

For example, a shape is a display object, as are bitmaps and videos. However, none of these items can have children, so the display list lineage ends there. A movie clip can have children, such as other movie clips, therein. Therefore, although a movie clip is a display object, it is also a display object container. This concept of display objects also possibly being containers is useful when traversing the display list, determining whether a display object has children, moving a child from one parent to another, and so on.

Display List Classes

In just a moment, we'll walk through a typical ActionScript display list that demonstrates the distinction between display objects and display object containers. First, however, take a look at the individual classes that contribute to the display list, as shown in Figure 4-3.

_root versus root

You may have heard you should avoid using the global **_root** variable in prior versions of ActionScript. That's because the value of the variable was subject to change. Before ActionScript 3.0, the **_root** variable referred to the timeline of the original host SWF no matter how many SWFs got loaded.

_root was the equivalent of an *absolute* address, like referring to an image in a web site as *http://www.yourdomain.com/image*, or a file on your computer as *C:\directory\file*, instead of a more flexible *relative* address such as "image" (or "../image," for example, if you needed to traverse directories first).

Because **_root** was an absolute address, if the file in which you used the global variable was loaded into another file, the variable was redefined to become the timeline doing the loading, rather than your original file. This was often not initially intended and would break many object path references that originated with **_root**.

In ActionScript 3.0, the display list changed that prevailing logic. **root** is now an instance variable of the display object, and doesn't always refer to the main timeline. It's relevant to the context in which it's used so it behaves more like a relative address and no longer changes just because your SWF is loaded into another SWF. The root of a movie clip in SWF A, is the same if it stands alone or is loaded into SWF B. The same goes for the root in SWF B, whether it stands alone or is loaded into SWF C, and so on.

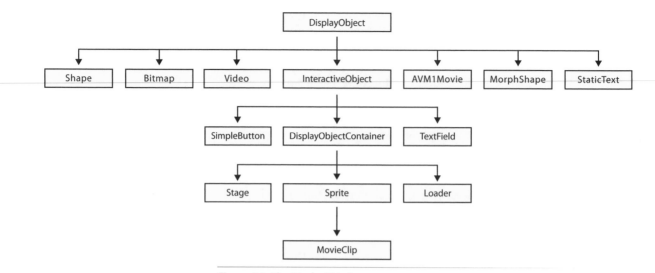

Figure 4-3. The DisplayList classes

We discussed classes in Chapter 1, and we'll be using them extensively as we delve deeper into the book. For now, however, and in this context, just think of these classes as objects that can be part of the display list. As you look through Figure 4-3, for instance, you'll recognize Shape, Bitmap, Video, and so on.

It is important to note, however, that, unlike Figure 4-2, this is not a hierarchical depiction of an actual display list. For example, it is possible for shapes, bitmaps, videos, and static text, among other items, to exist inside movie clips. Yet in the diagram in Figure 4-3, MovieClip appears to be lowest in the display list hierarchy, making this seem impossible in the traditional flowchart sense.

The key to this apparent dichotomy is that the display list classes originate with the **DisplayObject** class, and the flowchart shows the descendents of that class. Figure 4-3 is hierarchical, but it shows the possible objects that can be a part of *any* display object. Because a display object is anything that is, or can be, part of the display list, this flowchart is valid not only when examining the contents of the stage, but also when examining the contents of a movie clip, for example.

Here is a quick description of the classes in Figure 4-3, rearranged slightly for clarity of discussion.

DisplayObject

> Anything that can exist in the display list is a display object, and more specialized classes are derived from **DisplayObject**.

Shape

> This is a rectangle, ellipse, line, and so on, created with drawing tools. New to ActionScript 3.0, you can now create these at runtime.

Bitmap

This is an ActionScript bitmap created at runtime using the **BitmapData** class. Note that a standard JPG import does not create this kind of bitmap, but rather creates a shape. After creating a bitmap with this class, however, you can place an imported JPG into it for display.

Video

This is a video display object, the minimum required to play a video, rather than using a video component.

InteractiveObject

This class includes any display object the user can interact with using the mouse or keyboard. It is not used directly to manipulate the display list. Instead, you work with its descendents.

Skipping a bit, temporarily, and moving down a level:

SimpleButton

This class is used to create a button that's functionally equivalent to the buttons you probably have experience with in the authoring interface. However, in ActionScript 3.0, you can now create buttons on the fly by using other display objects for their up, over, down, and hit states.

TextField

This class includes dynamic and input text elements, controllable with ActionScript.

DisplayObjectContainer

This class is similar to **DisplayObject** in that it refers to multiple display object types. The difference here, however, is that this object can contain children. All display object containers are display objects, but only display objects that can have children are display object containers. For example, a video is a display object, but it cannot have children. A movie clip is a display object, and it can have children, so it's also a display object container. Usually, you will work directly with this class when traversing the display list, looking for children or ancestors. Usually, you will manipulate one or more of its descendent classes.

There are four kinds of display object containers:

Stage

Remember, the stage itself is part of the display list. This class demonstrates that any interactive object can reference the stage which, itself, is a display object container.

Sprite

New to ActionScript 3.0, a sprite is simply a movie clip without a timeline. Many ActionScript manipulations typically performed using movie clips only require one frame of the created movie clip's timeline. So, the size and administrative overhead of the timeline is unnecessary. As you become more accustomed to ActionScript 3.0, and begin to consider optimization more frequently, you may find yourself using sprites more than movie clips.

Loader

This class is used to load external assets destined for the display list, including bitmaps and other SWFs.

MovieClip

This is the movie clip you probably know and love, as a result of creating them in the authoring interface, via ActionScript, or both.

We left three items from the second tier for last, as you will probably use these classes the least often:

AVM1Movie

This class is for working with loaded SWFs created using ActionScript 1.0 or 2.0. AVM1, (which stands for ActionScript Virtual Machine 1) is reserved for SWFs that use ActionScript 1.0 and/or ActionScript 2.0, while AVM2 is used for SWFs that use ActionScript 3.0. Because Flash Player uses two discrete code bases, these virtual machines are not compatible. The **AVM1Movie** class provides a way of manipulating display properties of legacy SWFs, but does not facilitate communication between ActionScript 3.0 and older SWFs. This must be accomplished by other means, such as LocalConnections. We will discuss these other methods in Chapter 13.

MorphShape *and* StaticText

These two classes represent a shape tween and static text element, respectively, neither of which are controllable directly via ActionScript. However, they are part of the display classes because they inherit properties, methods, and events from their **DisplayObject** parent class. This makes it possible to rotate a static text element, for example.

Once you begin using the display list frequently—especially if you are familiar with the ActionScript 2.0 method of doing things—you will quickly become enamored with its power, flexibility, and simplicity. We will show you how to perform several common display list tasks in this chapter but, if you take one thing away from this initial discussion, it should be a basic understanding of display object versus display object container. To demonstrate this effectively, let's look at a short segment of code that traces requested content of the display list to the output window.

Displaying the Display List

It's sometimes useful, especially when you're creating many display objects with potentially complicated nested objects, to walk through the display list and analyze its contents. This little function, found in the companion source file *trace_display_list.fla* will trace the contents of any display object.

```
1    function showChildren(dispObj:*):void {
2        for (var i:int = 0; i < dispObj.numChildren; i++) {
3            var obj:DisplayObject = dispObj.getChildAt(i);
4            if (obj is DisplayObjectContainer) {
5                trace(obj.name, obj);
6                showChildren(obj);
7            } else {
8                trace(obj);
9            }
10       }
11   }
12
13   showChildren(stage);
```

NOTE

In the function described on this page, the argument may contain a display object or display object container, depending on which is passed in during the function call. For this reason, the asterisk identifier is used to indicate that the argument is untyped. By not checking the argument's data type at compile time, the function can process both DisplayObject and DisplayObjectContainer data types without the compiler generating an error.

Lines 1 and 11 define the function **showChildren()**, which requires as its argument the display object you wish to analyze. (See the adjacent note for more information on the use of the asterisk datatype.) Line 13 calls the function and, in this case, passes in the stage for analysis. In this example, the function will trace the contents of all children of the stage.

Lines 2 and 10 define a **for** loop, which will loop until there are no more children in the display object passed into the function. The number of loops is determined by the **numChildren** property, which returns the number of nested display objects in the object being analyzed. Each time through the loop, line 3 populates the **obj** variable with the next child in the display list using the **getChildAt()** method. This determines the child object at the level indicated by the loop counter (**i**). The first time through the loop, when **i** is 0, the first child will be returned. The second time, when **i** is 1, the second child will be returned, and so on.

Line 4 is what makes this function handy. It first checks to see whether the display object currently being analyzed is also a display object container. It does so by using the new **is** operator, which checks the data type of the object in question, comparing it against the **DisplayObjectContainer** type. This is important because if the display object is not a container, the walk through is over for that portion of the display list. The **if** statement will evaluate to **false**, jumping down to lines 7 and 8, and the object will be traced. The conditional then ends at line 9, and the code increments and goes through the loop again.

If the display object is also a container, it may have children, so the walk must continue down through that branch of the list. The **if** statement will evaluate to **true**, and the object (along with its name, in this case) is traced at line 5.

Finally, at line 6, *the function calls itself again.* passing in the object currently being inspected. This concept is called *recursion.* A function calling itself may seem redundant, but it can be very useful. In this case, each time the function is called, it receives a new display object to analyze, so the function reports the contents of that specific display object. The result is a complete walk-through of all display objects, no matter how many children each may have.

The showChildren() function in action

Take a look at the function in action. Figure 4-4 shows a sample file that will be analyzed. The rectangle and circle movie clips, with their instance names, are indicated in the figure. Within the rectangles, a shape gives the fill and stroke appearance. Inside the circles, a shape provides the fill and stroke and a static text element is added.

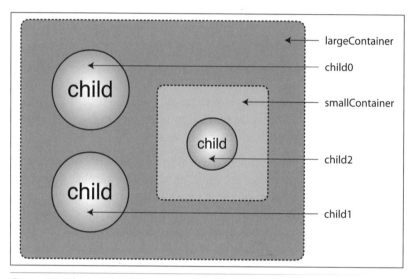

Figure 4-4. A look at the stage of trace_display_list.fla

When the function runs, the following is traced to the output window, showing all children of the stage. It lists display containers by name and object reference, and display objects by object reference alone.

```
root1 [object MainTimeline]
largeContainer [object largeContainer_1]
[object Shape]
smallContainer [object smallContainer_2]
[object Shape]
child2 [object MovieClip]
[object Shape]
[object StaticText]
child0 [object MovieClip]
[object Shape]
[object StaticText]
child1 [object MovieClip]
[object Shape]
[object StaticText]
```

You can improve the readability of the trace by adding indents to show the parent-child relationship of the traced objects. The following is seen in *trace_display_list2.fla* (bold lines are new or changed).

```
1    function showChildren(dispObj:*, indentLevel:Number):
     void {
2        for (var i:int = 0; i < dispObj.numChildren; i++) {
```

```
3          var obj:DisplayObject = dispObj.getChildAt(i);
4          if (obj is DisplayObjectContainer) {
5              trace(padIndent(indentLevel), obj.name, obj);
6              showChildren(obj, indentLevel + 1);
7          } else {
8              trace(padIndent(indentLevel) + obj);
9          }
10     }
11  }
12
13  showChildren(stage, 0);
14
15  function padIndent(indents:int):String {
16      var indent:String = "";
17      for (var i:Number = 0; i < indents; i++) {
18          indent += "    ";
19      }
20      return indent;
21  }
```

The function in lines 15 through 21 takes a desired indent level and returns four spaces for each indent specified. For example, the first child will have no indent, or an indent level of 0. Therefore, it will return four spaces zero times, for no indent effect. The first nested child will have an indent level of 1, so the function will return four spaces of indent. A child at a second tier of nesting will have an indent level of 2, so the function will return eight spaces of indent, and so on.

We can indicate the number of indents by passing a value into a second parameter in the main function, in the form of **indentLevel**, as seen in line 1. Now that this second parameter exists, we've changed the calls to the function, at lines 6 and 13, to add the indent value. The process begins at line 13 with an indent level of zero. Each recursive call, however, must be indented one more level, so line 6 adds 1 to the **indentLevel** argument each time the function is called.

Finally, lines 5 and 8 add the new spaces, for each level of indent, that are returned by the **padIndent()** function. The result, shown here, is a more human-readable output with the indents representing nested children.

```
root1 [object MainTimeline]
    largeContainer [object largeContainer_1]
        [object Shape]
        smallContainer [object smallContainer_2]
            [object Shape]
            child2 [object MovieClip]
                [object Shape]
                [object StaticText]
        child0 [object MovieClip]
            [object Shape]
            [object StaticText]
        child1 [object MovieClip]
            [object Shape]
            [object StaticText]
```

If you wish, you may also change the string returned from the **padIndent()** function to another number of spaces, or even another character such as a period.

Adding and Removing Children

The previous section described the parts of the display list, and how to analyze an existing list. But you'll also need to know how to add to, and remove from, the display list at runtime. In previous versions of ActionScript, you needed to rely on varying methods to add items to the stage. For example, you needed to use separate methods for creating a movie clip, placing a library movie clip on stage, or duplicating a movie clip. Using the ActionScript 3.0 display list, you only need one approach to create a movie clip. You will use `new MovieClip()`. Even adding a precreated movie clip from the library is consistent with this syntax, as you'll soon see.

Using addChild()

Adding a display object to the display list requires just two simple steps. The first is to create the object—in this case, an empty movie clip (that is, a movie clip created dynamically, but that currently has no content):

```
var mc:MovieClip = new MovieClip();
```

This literally creates the movie clip but does not display it. In order for the movie clip to display, you must add it to the display list using the **addChild()** method:

```
addChild(mc);
```

You can also specify a particular target for the movie clip, as long as that target is a display object container. (Remember, you can't add children to display objects like shapes, videos, text elements, and so on, because they are not display object containers.) So, if you instead wanted to add the **mc** movie clip nested inside another movie clip called **navBar**, you would change the second step to:

```
navBar.addChild(mc);
```

We've been using movie clips in our examples, but it's also as straightforward to add other display objects. Two simple examples include creating a sprite and a shape:

```
var sp:Sprite = new Sprite();
addChild(sp);
```

```
var sh:Shape = new Shape();
addChild(sh);
```

You don't even have to specify a depth (visible stacking order), because the display list automatically handles that for you. In fact, you can even use the same **addChild()** method for changing the depths of existing display objects, but we'll discuss depths in greater detail later in this chapter.

Adding Symbol Instances to the Display List

In the previous, simple examples, we've created display objects without content. In Chapter 8, we'll show you how to draw with code, so you can create content for these movie clips, relying solely on code for small file size and more dynamic control.

However, you will frequently find the need to use custom art in your files, and in those situations code-only solutions will not do. So, in this chapter, we're going to focus on dynamically adding movie clips that already exist in your library. In the accompanying source file, *addChild.fla*, you will find a unicycle in the library. To add this movie clip to the display list using ActionScript, you must set up the library symbol first.

In prior versions of ActionScript, there were two ways of doing this. The first approach was to assign the symbol a linkage identifier name. This was similar to an instance name for library symbols, in that you could reference the symbol by name using ActionScript. The second way was to assign a class to the movie clip so that it could be created when you created an instance of the class, and also have its own code to execute.

In ActionScript 3.0, these two approaches are unified. Rather than using the linkage identifier, you simply use a class name to reference a symbol in all cases. When you've written a class for the symbol, which we'll do in later chapters, the symbol will behave accordingly. However, when you just want to reference the symbol, Flash will automatically create an internal placeholder class for you, and use the class name to dynamically create the symbol when requested. This approach also allows you to easily add classes later while changing little or nothing in your file.

Figure 4-5. Accessing a symbol's linkage information

Continuing our movie clip example, to add a class name to a symbol, select the movie clip in your library, and then click the Symbol Properties button (it looks like an "i" at the bottom of the library) for access to all the symbol properties. Alternatively, you can focus only on the linkage information by choosing Linkage from the library menu, as seen in Figure 4-5.

In the resulting dialog, seen in Figure 4-6, click to enable the Export for ActionScript option, and add a name to the **Class** field. When you start working with classes, you will follow a few simple rules and conventions, one of which is to capitalize the first letter of your class name. This is a bit different from naming a variable, where you might choose to use a lowercase first letter, so it's a good idea to get into this practice now. In the *addChild.fla* source file, we've used the class name **Unicycle**.

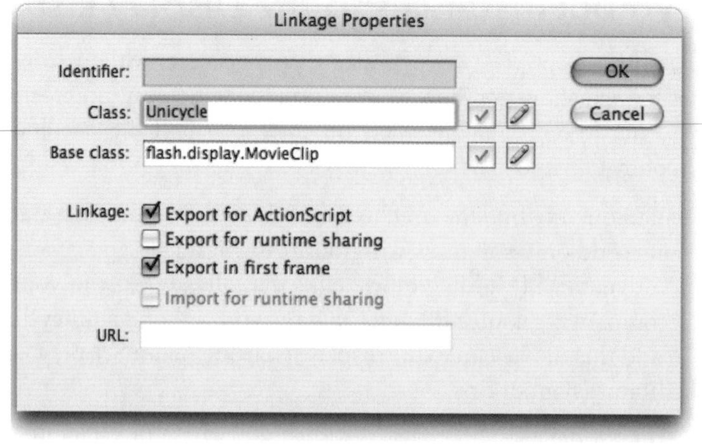

Figure 4-6. Entering a class name for a movie clip in the library Linkage Properties

You will also likely notice that Flash adds the **MovieClip** class (in this case) to the **Base** class field for you. This makes it possible to automatically access the properties, methods, and events available to the **MovieClip** class. For example, you can automatically manipulate the x and y coordinates of your new custom movie clip.

Now that you've given your movie clip a class name, you can create an instance of that custom movie clip class the same way you created an instance of the generic movie clip class. Instead of using **MovieClip()**, however, you will use **Unicycle()** to create the movie clip. The same call of the **addChild()** method is used to add the newly created movie clip to the display list, as seen in the following code. The code and required movie clip exist in the accompanying source file *addChild.fla*.

```
var cycle:MovieClip = new Unicycle();
addChild(cycle);
```

Using addChildAt()

The **addChild()** method adds the display object to the end of the display list, which places the object at the top-most z index. This makes it very easy to place items on top of all other items. However, it's also useful to be able to add a child at a specific position in the display list. For example, you may wish to insert an item into the middle of a vertical stack of display objects.

This example, found in the *addChildAt.fla* source file, adds a movie clip with the class name **Ball** to the *start* of the display list with every mouse click. The ultimate effect is that a new ball is added *below* the previous balls, and positioned up and to the right 10 pixels, every time the mouse is clicked.

```
1   var inc:int = 0;
2
3   stage.addEventListener(MouseEvent.CLICK, onClick, false, 0, true);
4
```

```
5    function onClick(evt:MouseEvent):void {
6        var ball:MovieClip = new Ball();
7        ball.x = ball.y = 100 + inc * 10;
8        addChildAt(ball, 0);
9        inc++;
10    }
```

Line 1 initializes a variable that will be incremented with each ball added. Line 3 adds an event listener to the stage, listening for a mouse click, so that any mouse click will trigger the listener's function. The function in lines 5 through 10 performs four basic tasks. In line 6, a new Ball movie clip is created.

Line 7 manipulates the x and y coordinates in a single instruction, setting **x** equal to **y**, which is equal to the value of an expression. This is handy when both **x** and **y** values are the same. In this case, the expression sets the new ball to **x** and **y** of 100 and adds a 10-pixel offset for each ball added. For example, when the first ball is added, **inc** is 0 so the additional pixel offset is 0*10 or 0. Then **inc** is incremented at the end of the function, in line 9. The next mouse click that calls the function will update the offset to 1*10 or 10 pixels for the second ball, 2*10 or 20 pixels offset for the third ball, and so on. Most importantly, line 8 adds the ball to the display list, but always at position 0, making sure the newest ball is always on the bottom.

NOTE

It is possible to manipulate display objects—such as setting properties or invoking methods—both before and after the object has been added to the display list. By doing this, you can create a display object, initialize its properties to your liking, but reserve adding it to the display list until it is needed. See the sidebar "Display Objects and References to Stage and Root" for a notable exception to this rule.

Display Objects and References to Stage and Root

It can be advantageous to manipulate display objects prior to adding them to the display list. For example, you may wish to change properties of an object over time, but prior to that object being visible or being capable of responding to events. If you added the object to the display list immediately, these changes may be seen or experienced by the end user.

Some display object properties or methods, however, may not be valid when the object is not part of the display list. Good examples of this scenario include the **root** and **stage** instances of any display object.

Once a display object is added to the display list, its **stage** and **root** properties are valid. However, if the object is not part of the display list, its **stage** property will always return **null**, and the **root** property will be valid only if the display object is already a child of another container in a loaded SWF.

Try the following example. You will see that, until the created movie clip is added to the display list, both its **stage** and **root** properties are **null**.

```
//create display object
var mc:MovieClip = new MovieClip();
// reference to stage and root return null
trace(mc.stage);
trace(mc.root);
//add the object to the display list
addChild(mc);
```

```
//references to stage and root return Stage and
    Main Timeline objects respectively
trace(mc.stage);
trace(mc.root);
```

Invalid **stage** and **root** properties can be a common problem if you don't plan ahead. For example, the following code tries to set the location of a movie clip to the center of the stage prior to adding the object to the display list. However, this will fail because querying the **stageWidth** property of the object's **stage** reference will not work until after adding the object to the display list.

```
var mc:MovieClip = new MovieClip();
mc.x = mc.stage.stageWidth / 2;
addChild(mc);
```

This problem can be corrected by transposing the last two lines of the script. It is also possible to work with the **stage** directly, as its own entry in the display list, as seen in the following snippet:

```
var mc:MovieClip = new MovieClip();
mc.x = stage.stageWidth / 2;
addChild(mc);
```

However, this is not always possible when using **root**, because the root of a display object is relative to the object itself. Keep this in mind if you get unexpected results, and check to make sure you are referencing these instance variables only after adding the object to the display list.

Removing Objects from the Display List and from Memory

It's equally important to know how to remove objects from the display list. The process for removing objects is nearly identical to the process for adding objects to the display list. To remove a specific display object from the display list, you can use the **removeChild()** method:

```
removeChild(ball);
```

Remove a display object at a specific level using **removeChildAt()**:

```
removeChildAt(0);
```

The following example is the reverse of the **addChildAt()** script discussed in the prior section. It starts by using a **for** loop to add 20 balls to the stage, positioning them with the same technique used in the prior script. (For more information on **for** loops, please review Chapter 2.) It then uses the event listener to *remove* the children with each click.

```
1    for (var inc:int = 0; inc < 20; inc++) {
2        var ball:MovieClip = new Ball();
3        ball.x = ball.y = 100 + inc * 10;
4        addChild(ball);
5    }
6
7    stage.addEventListener(MouseEvent.CLICK, onClick, false, 0, true);
8
9    function onClick(evt:MouseEvent):void {
10       removeChildAt(0);
11   }
```

Preventing out of bounds errors

The previous script works if something's in the display list. If after removing the last ball, you click the stage again, you're warned "the supplied index is out of bounds." That's because you're trying to remove a child from position 0 of the display list, when there's nothing in the display list at all.

To avoid this problem, you can first check to see whether there are any children in the display object container that you are trying to empty. Making sure that the number of children exceeds zero will prevent the aforementioned error from occurring. The following is an updated **onClick()** function, replacing lines 9-11 in the previous code, with the new conditional in bold. (For more information on conditionals, please review Chapter 2.)

```
9    function onClick(evt:MouseEvent):void {
10       if (numChildren > 0) {
11           removeChildAt(0);
12       }
13   }
```

NOTE

*If you ever want to use a **for** loop to remove many objects at once (everything in the display list, for example), it is easier to remove the objects from the bottom, as discussed here. This is because, as long as there is something in the display list, there will always be something in position 0, and you will avoid the index out of bounds error. For more information, consult Chapter 20 of Colin Moock's Essential ActionScript 3.0.*

Removing objects from memory

As we discussed when introducing event listeners in Chapter 3, it is important to remember that inadequate asset management can result in memory leaks. It is always a good idea to try to keep track of your objects and, when you are sure you will no longer need them, remove them from memory.

Keeping track of objects is particularly relevant when discussing the display list because it is easy to remove an object from the display list but forget to remove it from RAM. Doing so will cease displaying the object, but the object will still linger in memory. The following script, a simplification of the previous example, will both remove a movie clip from the display list and from RAM.

```
1    var ball:MovieClip = new Ball();
2    ball.x = ball.y = 100;
3    addChild(ball);
4
5    stage.addEventListener(MouseEvent.CLICK, onClick, false, 0, true);
6
7    function onClick(evt:MouseEvent):void {
8        this.removeChild(ball);
9        //ball removed from display list but still exists
10       trace(ball);
11       ball = null;
12       //ball now entirely removed
13       trace(ball);
14
15       stage.removeEventListener(MouseEvent.CLICK, onClick);
16   }
```

Lines 1 through 5 are derived from the previous example, creating and positioning the ball, adding it to the display list, and adding a mouse click listener to the stage. The first line of function content, line 8, removes the ball from the display list using the **removeChild()** method. Although it is no longer displayed, it is still around, as shown by line 10, which traces the object to the output panel. Line 11, however, sets the object to **null**, marking it for removal from memory—again, shown by tracing the object to the output panel in Line 13.

NOTE

As an added review of best practices, line 15 emphasizes the concept of removing event listeners covered in Chapter 3. This is a good example of this practice, since using a weak reference in the last parameter of the **addEventListener()** *method in line 5 is not reliable. Remember, weak references are a best practice backup plan, not a substitute for explicitly removing your unwanted listeners. For additional information, please review Chapter 3.*

Managing Object Names, Positions, and Data Types

As any display list grows, it inevitably becomes necessary to traverse its contents and work with individual display objects. This may require simple tasks such as identifying a display object by name or z index, or even by referencing existing display objects as a specific display list class.

Finding Children by Position and by Name

Many of the example scripts in this chapter demonstrate working with children that have previously been stored in a variable and that are already known to you. However, you will likely have the need to find children in the display list with little more to go on than their position or name.

Finding a child by position is consistent with adding or removing children at a specific location in the display list. Using the **getChildAt()** method, you can work with the first child of a container using this familiar syntax:

```
var dispObj:DisplayObject = getChildAt(0);
```

If you don't know the location of a child that you wish to manipulate, you can try to find it by name using its instance name. Assuming a child had an instance name of **circle**, you could store a reference to that child using this syntax:

```
var dispObj:DisplayObject = getChildByName("circle");
```

Finally, if you need to know the location of a display object in the display list, but have only its name, you can use the **getChildIndex()** method to accomplish your goal.

```
var dispObj:DisplayObject = getChildByName("circle");
var doIndex:int = getChildIndex(dispObj);
```

Casting a Display Object

Note that, in the preceding discussion, we used **DisplayObject** as the data type when retrieving a reference to a display object—rather than **MovieClip**, for example. This is because you may not know if the child is a movie clip, sprite, shape, and so on.

In fact, Flash may not even know the data type, such as when referencing a parent movie clip created using the Flash interface (rather than ActionScript), or even the main timeline. Without the data type information supplied in the ActionScript creation process, Flash sees only the parent timeline as a display object container.

To tell Flash the container in question is a movie clip, you can cast it as such—that is, you can change the data type of that object to **MovieClip**. For example, consider a movie clip created in the Flash interface that needs to tell its parent, the main timeline, to go to frame 20. A simple line of ActionScript is all that would ordinarily be required:

```
parent.gotoAndStop(20);
```

However, because Flash doesn't know that **gotoAndStop()** is a legal method of the display object container (the stage, for example, can't go to frame 20, and neither can a sprite), you will get the following error:

```
Call to a possibly undefined method gotoAndStop through a reference
    with static type flash.display:DisplayObjectContainer.
```

To tell Flash the method is legal for the main timeline, you need only state that the parent is of a data type that supports the method. In this case, the main timeline is a movie clip, so you can say:

```
MovieClip(parent).gotoAndStop(20);
```

This will prevent the error from occurring, and the movie clip will be able to successfully send the main timeline to frame 20.

Changing the Display List Hierarchy

In addition to the improved consistency over previous versions of ActionScript, when adding and removing visual assets at runtime, the display list also makes managing assets much easier. Particularly simplified are: changing the visual stacking order (depth management) and dynamically changing the familial relationship between visual assets (reparenting, or moving a display object from one parent to another).

Depth Management

Adding items to the display list does not require that you specify which level the new child should occupy, because all that is handled for you automatically. This also makes managing the depths of display objects much easier than ever before.

To begin with, you can simply use the **addChild()** or **addChildAt()** methods to alter the order of display list items. As we discussed, adding a child to a level below other elements using the **addChildAt()** method will automatically push the other element depths up a level. But you can also use the **addChild()** method on an object that *already* exists in the display list. This step will remove the object from its original position and move it to the top of stack, pushing the other elements down.

For example, consider the following code. Lines 1 through 6 use the standard approach of creating and adding movie clips to the display list, with the added step of giving each clip an instance name. Lines 7 and 8 display the results at this point and, as expected, **mc1**, or "clip1," is at level 0, and **mc2**, or "clip2," is at level 1.

```
1    var mc1:MovieClip = new MovieClip();
2    mc1.name = "clip1";
3    addChild(mc1);
4    var mc2:MovieClip = new MovieClip();
5    mc2.name = "clip2";
6    addChild(mc2);
7    trace(getChildAt(0).name);
8    trace(getChildAt(1).name);
```

However, if you add **mc1** to the display list again, it is moved from position 0 to the end of the list, and **mc2** gets pushed to position 0. This can be shown by adding these new lines to the script:

```
9    addChild(mc1);
10   trace(getChildAt(0).name);
11   trace(getChildAt(1).name);
```

There are three additional ways to set the z-order of objects that are already in the display list. The **swapChildren()** method will swap the locations of two known display objects. For example, adding the following line to the ongoing script will swap positions between mc1 and mc2, no matter where they are:

```
12   swapChildren(mc1, mc2);
```

If you don't already have references to the children, you can get them using the aforementioned **getChildByName()** method, or switch the children based on their current levels using the **swapChildrenAt()** method. Adding the following line to this simplified example will achieve this result, but this method will swap any two levels, even if they're not consecutive.

```
13   swapChildrenAt(0, 1);
```

Finally, you can specify a new index for any existing display object. The following new example, seen in the *setChildIndex.fla* source file, takes advantage of the event propagation discussed in Chapter 3 to automatically bring any display object that is rolled over with the mouse to the top of the visual stacking order.

```
1    addEventListener(MouseEvent.MOUSE_OVER, onBringToTop, false, 0,
     true);
2
3    function onBringToTop(evt:MouseEvent):void {
4        setChildIndex(MovieClip(evt.target), numChildren-1);
5    }
```

WARNING

Using prior versions of ActionScript, some developers specified depths known to be higher than any existing depth as a means of ensuring that an object would always be on top of all other objects. This is not possible in ActionScript 3.0. Specifying a level that is higher than the number of children in the display list will result in the "supplied index is out of bounds" error discussed in the prior section, "Preventing out of bounds errors."

This script accomplishes its task by setting the child's display list index to the highest level possible. The script first determines the number of children in the display object container (in this case, the main timeline) and then, because ActionScript arrays are zero-based (meaning the first item is item 0), it subtracts 1 to get the highest existing index in the display list. For example, if there are three items in the display list, their indices would be 0, 1, and 2. The number of children would be 3, and 3 minus 1 equals 2—the highest index in the list. Figure 4-7 illustrates.

By setting every item rolled over to the highest possible index, all other items are pushed back, popping the rolled-over item to the highest z index.

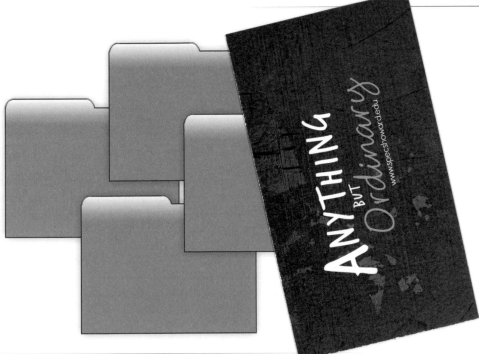

Figure 4-7. In setChildIndex.fla, *rolled-over items pop to the top*

Reparenting Children

Another task that is vastly simplified by the display list is moving a child from one parent to another. In the *reparenting.fla* source file, a moon can be moved to either of two night skies, just by clicking that sky (Figure 4-8). Both skies are also draggable, demonstrating that the moon will move with the night sky.

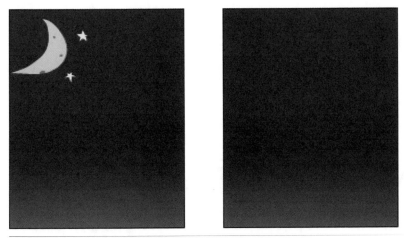

Figure 4-8. In reparenting.fla, *the moon and stars become a child of the clicked sky*

The script begins by adding the moon to the first sky (on the left) as its starting position. It then adds an event listener to the main timeline to allow any child that receives a **mouse down** event to call **onDrag()** and then, on **mouse up**, call **onDrop()**.

```
1    sky1.addChild(moon);
2
3    this.addEventListener(MouseEvent.MOUSE_DOWN, onDrag, false, 0,
     true);
4    this.addEventListener(MouseEvent.MOUSE_UP, onDrop, false, 0, true);
```

The **onDrag()** function starts by stopping its progress (by using the **return** keyword to leave the function) if the clicked item (the target of the **mouse down** event) is the moon itself. This prevents the circular error of trying to add a display object to itself.

This function then adds the moon to the sky that was clicked. This action removes the moon from its previous parent and adds it to the clicked item, therefore reparenting the moon. The function then enables dragging of the clicked item.

```
5    function onDrag(evt:MouseEvent):void {
6        if (evt.target == moon) { return; }
7        evt.target.addChild(moon);
8        evt.target.startDrag();
9    }
10
```

Finally, when the **mouse up** event is received, the **onDrop()** function disables dragging on the clicked item.

```
11   function onDrop(evt:MouseEvent):void {
12       evt.target.stopDrag();
13   }
```

As you can see, by using the **addChild()** method, you can move a display object from one parent container to another, resulting in the child inheriting all the relevant attributes of its new parent.

A Dynamic Navigation Bar

Now it's time to tie much of this together and create a dynamic navigation bar. This project will create a five-button navigation bar that will be centered on stage as shown in Figure 4-9. To simulate functionality, each button will trace its name to the Output panel when clicked.

Figure 4-9. A dynamically generated navigation bar

Here is the start of the script for the navigation bar:

```
1    var btnNum:int = 5;
2    var spacing:Number = 10;
3
4    var navBar:Sprite = new Sprite();
5    addChild(navBar);
```

The script begins at lines 1 and 2 by initializing the number of buttons used and the space in pixels between each button. It then creates a container for the buttons in line 4. This navigation bar doesn't need a timeline so, for added efficiency, a sprite will be used as the container rather than a movie clip. Next, line 5 adds the sprite to the display list.

```
6    var btn:SimpleButton;
7    for (var i:int = 0; i < btnNum; i++) {
8        btn = new Btn();
9        btn.name = "button" + i;
10       btn.x = spacing + i * (btn.width + spacing);
11       btn.y += 5;
12       btn.addEventListener(MouseEvent.CLICK, onTraceName, false, 0,
         true);
13       navBar.addChild(btn);
14   }
```

A **for** loop then creates the total number of buttons. Each time through the loop, a new button is created from a button symbol in the library with the linkage class of *Btn* (line 8). An instance name is assigned to the button, combining the string "button" and the loop counter value (line 9). Thus, the first button is called *button0*, the second is called *button1*, and so on.

The current button is positioned horizontally (line 10), offset by the spacing set in line 2, plus the width of the button and another spacing gap for each button in the loop. Therefore, the first button is positioned only 10 pixels to the right of the container's registration point (**spacing**, plus zero times the sum of the width of the button and **spacing**). The last button is positioned 10 pixels to the right of the container's registration point plus 4 times the width of the button and spacing. The vertical position is also set, moving the button down 5 pixels.

As the last instructions in the loop, a mouse click listener is added to the button, specifying the **onTraceName()** function to be called when the event is received (line 12), and the button is added to the **navBar** parent (line 13).

```
15   var bg:MovieClip = new NavBarBack();
16   bg.width = btnNum * (btn.width + spacing);
17   bg.width += spacing;
18   navBar.addChildAt(bg, 0);
```

Starting with line 15, a background is added to the **navBar**. Its width is set to the total number of buttons times the sum of the button width and **spacing**, plus a **spacing** gap to the right of the button. The background is then added to the **navBar** at position 0, ensuring that it's placed behind all the buttons.

```
19   navBar.x = (navBar.stage.stageWidth - navBar.width) / 2;
20   navBar.y = 20;
```

The finished **navBar** is then centered horizontally at an x coordinate determined by the width of the stage minus the width of the **navBar**, divided by 2 for a left and right margin. It is also positioned vertically at a y coordinate of 20 pixels.

```
21  function onTraceName(evt:MouseEvent):void {
22      trace(evt.target.name);
23  }
```

Finally, the **onTraceName()** function, identified in the event listener as the function to execute when the mouse click was received, traces the name of the clicked button.

This exercise demonstrates how to create a simulated navigation bar using the display list, when no assets previously existed on the stage. Later in the book, you will learn how to create the buttons and draw the background shape entirely with ActionScript, removing the need to precreate these assets as library symbols.

What's Next?

The display list is among the most important new introductions to ActionScript 3.0. It is worth the effort to explore the properties, methods, and events of the various display list classes—starting with the contents of this chapter, and then delving into the Flash help system, and additional resources, as you gain experience. Experimenting with the display list will show you that it is easy to use and, if you have experience with prior versions of ActionScript, you will soon find that it is much simpler and more consistent than equivalent methods in ActionScript 1.0 or ActionScript 2.0.

Next, we'll discuss timeline control. Regardless of whether you are creating lengthy linear animations or single-frame applications, you are likely to require some level of control over the main timeline or movie clips. ActionScript 3.0 offers a few new features for you to try out.

In the next chapter, we'll discuss:

- Controlling playback of your animations and applications by moving the playhead with ActionScript

- Using new ActionScript to parse frame label names from timelines and scenes

- Changing the frame rate of movie playback for the first time

CHAPTER 5

TIMELINE CONTROL

In this chapter, you'll learn some basic approaches to controlling timelines—both that of the main Flash movie and movie clips therein. We'll divide our focus into three main areas:

- **Playhead Movement.** Such as stopping and playing the file, and going to a specific frame.

- **Frame Labels.** Including improved playhead movement techniques without relying on frame numbers.

- **Frame Rates.** Changing the movie's frame rate, to increase or decrease animation speed during playback.

We'll also take a look at an undocumented feature that allows you to add frame scripts to movie clips at runtime. We'll lay some groundwork for our ongoing project and show you a demo on how to create a flexible structure for a Flash web site or application that will later evolve into our AS3 Lab interface.

Playhead Movement

One of the most basic ActionScript skills you need to embrace is the ability to navigate within your Flash movies. You will often use these skills to control the playback of movie clips nested within your main movies.

The code in this chapter is straightforward enough that you can create your own files to test the functionality. We'll cover the structural necessities for each file to make it easier for you to follow along using your own assets. In each section, we'll also cite the sample file we're using so you can consult that file if you prefer.

Let's start by covering the basic concept of stopping and starting playback of a movie or movie clip, and then add an initial jump to another frame. If you're creating your own file, be sure it has a linear animation in the main timeline, and that you have continuous access to four buttons that can trigger scripts. Alternatively, you can open the sample file *navigation_01.fla*.

IN THIS CHAPTER

Playhead Movement

Frame Labels

Frame Rate

A Simple Site or Application Structure

What's Next?

NOTE

We discussed movie clips in Chapters 3 and 4, so if you find the need for review, consult those chapters at will.

Figure 5-1 shows *navigation_01.fla*, which contains four timeline tweens of black circles. For added visual impact, the circles use the Invert blend mode to create an interesting optical illusion of rotating cylinders. We'll be starting and stopping playback at any point, as well as starting and stopping in a specific frame—frame one, in this example. Initially, we'll rely on frame numbers to specify where to start and stop.

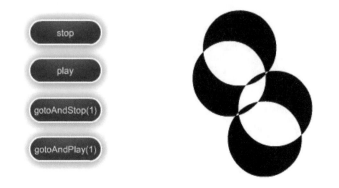

Figure 5-1. navigation_01.fla *demonstrates simple navigation.*

You've already seen the **stop()** action at work in a frame script as a passive means of halting playback at the end of an animation or, perhaps, to support a menu or similar single frame. Let's look at invoking the **stop()** action via user input, such as clicking a button.

In the first frame of the *actions* layer, you'll find the following code:

```
1   stopBtn.addEventListener(MouseEvent.CLICK, onStopClick, false, 0,
    true);
2
3   function onStopClick(evt:MouseEvent):void {
4       stop();
5   }
```

NOTE

If you don't know about event listeners or typed arguments, consult Chapter 3 for more information—paying particular attention to the sidebar, "Garbage Collection" on weak references. Lines 3 through 5 define the function called by the event listener.

This code does not introduce anything new, other than the aforementioned use of **stop()** as a method triggered by user interaction. Line 1 is an event listener added to a button named *stopBtn*. It uses a mouse click to call **onStopClick**.

The effect of this setup is to add to the *stopBtn* functionality for stopping the main movie. All playback of the main timeline will cease when the user clicks the button. Adding the bold lines to the script (shown in the following code) will allow you to restart playback. The code structure is similar to the previous example, but invokes the **play()** method on the *playBtn* instead. Using this pair of buttons, you can start and stop playback at any time without relocating the playback head in the process.

```
1   stopBtn.addEventListener(MouseEvent.CLICK, onStopClick, false, 0,
    true);
2   playBtn.addEventListener(MouseEvent.CLICK, onPlayClick, false, 0,
    true);
3
4   function onStopClick(evt:MouseEvent):void {
5       stop();
6   }
7   function onPlayClick(evt:MouseEvent):void {
8       play();
9   }
```

Using **stop()** and **play()** in this fashion is useful for controlling a linear animation, much in the same way a controller bar might control audio or video playback. However, it is less common in the case of menus or other navigation devices because typically you must jump to a specific point in your timeline before stopping or playing.

For example, you might have generic sections that could apply to any project, such as home (start), about (info), and help. If you were restricted to the use of **stop()** and **play()**, then you would be forced to play through one section to get to another.

Adding again to our script, the following content shown in bold adds a slight variation. The buttons in the new script function in similar ways but, instead of stopping in or playing from in the current frame, the new buttons go to a specified frame first. For example, if you had previously stopped playback in frame 20, triggering **play()** again would begin playback at frame 20. However, if you used **gotoAndPlay()** and specified frame 1 as a destination (as seen in the script that follows), you would resume playback at frame 1, rather than at frame 20. There are no structural differences in this code, so simply add the content shown in bold to your ongoing script.

```
1   stopBtn.addEventListener(MouseEvent.CLICK, onStopClick, false, 0,
    true);
2   playBtn.addEventListener(MouseEvent.CLICK, onPlayClick, false, 0,
    true);
3   gotoPlayBtn.addEventListener(MouseEvent.CLICK, onGotoPlayClick,
    false, 0, true);
4   gotoStopBtn.addEventListener(MouseEvent.CLICK, onGotoStopClick,
    false, 0, true);
5
6   function onStopClick(evt:MouseEvent):void {
7       stop();
8   }
9   function onPlayClick(evt:MouseEvent):void {
10      play();
11  }
12  function onGotoPlayClick(evt:MouseEvent):void {
13      gotoAndPlay(1);
14  }
15  function onGotoStopClick(evt:MouseEvent):void {
16      gotoAndStop(1);
17  }
```

Let's add two new properties to your script to add a nice level of diagnostic reporting to your playback. Using the **trace()** method to send text to the Output panel, you can query **totalFrames** to display how many frames are in your movie, and **currentFrame** to tell you which frame the playback head is displaying at the time the script is executed.

```
trace("This movie has " + totalFrames + " frames.");
trace(currentFrame);
```

The companion sample file, *navigation_02.fla*, demonstrates the use of these properties. It uses **totalFrames** at the start of playback, and **currentFrame** each time a button is clicked.

Frame Labels

Using frame numbers with **goto** methods has specific advantages, among them simplicity and use in numeric contexts (such as with a loop or other type of counter). However, frame numbers also have specific disadvantages. The most notable disadvantage is that edits made to your file after your script is written may result in a change to the frame sequence in your timeline.

For example, your help section may start at frame 100, but you may then insert or delete frames in a section of your timeline prior to that frame. This change may cause the help section to shift to a new frame, and your navigation script will no longer send the playback head to the help section.

One way around this problem is to use frame labels to mark the location of a specific segment of your timeline. As long as you shift content by inserting or deleting frames to all layers in your timeline—therefore, maintaining sync among your layers—a frame label will move with your content.

For example, if your help section, previously at frame 100, is also marked with a frame label called "help," adding 10 frames to all layers in your timeline will not only shift the help content, but will also shift the frame label used to identify its location. So, although you will still be navigating to the "help" frame label after the addition of frames, you will correctly navigate to frame 110.

This is a useful feature when you are relying heavily on timeline tweens for file structure or transitions (as we'll see in our demo site in a short while), or when you think you may be adding or deleting sections in your file. In fact, frame labels free you to simply rearrange your timeline if desired. The ability to go to a specific frame label, no matter where it is, means that you don't have to arrange your file linearly, and you are free to add last-minute changes to the end of your timeline without being concerned with remembering an odd sequence of frame numbers to jump to content.

The sample file, *frame_labels_01.fla*, demonstrates the use of frame labels instead of frame numbers when using a **goto** method. It also illustrates another important and useful concept, which is that you can use these methods to control the playback of movie clips as well as the main timeline.

Instead of controlling the playback of a linear animation, the sample file moves the playback head between the frames of a movie clip called "pages." This is a common technique for swapping content in a Flash structure because you can keep your main timeline simple, and jump the movie clip from frame to frame to reveal each new screen. Figure 5-2 displays the "page1" frame of the **pages** movie clip in *frame_labels_01.fla*, after jumping to the frame by specifying the frame label. The timeline inset shows the frame labels.

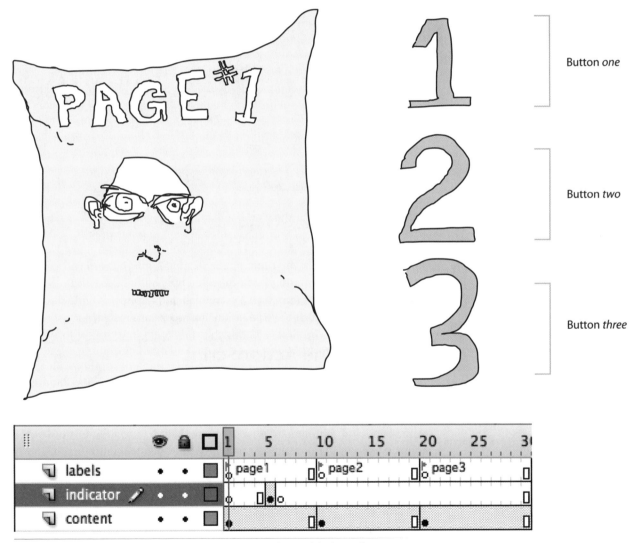

Figure 5-2. The "page1" frame of the pages movie clip in frame_labels_01.fla

The initial setup of this example requires that we prevent the movie clip from playing on its own, so we can exert the desired control over its playback. There are several ways to do this. The first, and perhaps most obvious approach, is to put a **stop()** action in the first frame of the movie clip. You will see this technique used often.

The second is to use the **stop()** method but to target the movie clip instead of the main timeline. To do this, precede the method with the object you wish to stop, as seen in line 1 of the following script. In this case, we are stopping the movie clip called *pages*.

We will look at a third method for stopping movie clips at the end of this chapter but, for now, let's focus on the simple changes this file introduces. In addition to stopping the *pages* movie clip in line 1, each button causes the movie clip to change frames in lines 8, 11, and 14.

```
1   pages.stop();
2
3   one.addEventListener(MouseEvent.CLICK, onOneClick, false, 0, true);
4   two.addEventListener(MouseEvent.CLICK, onTwoClick, false, 0, true);
5   three.addEventListener(MouseEvent.CLICK, onThreeClick, false, 0,
    true);
6
7   function onOneClick(evt:MouseEvent):void {
8       pages.gotoAndStop("page1");
9   }
10  function onTwoClick(evt:MouseEvent):void {
11      pages.gotoAndStop("page2");
12  }
13  function onThreeClick(evt:MouseEvent):void {
14      pages.gotoAndStop("page3");
15  }
```

NOTE

If you are unfamiliar with scenes, they are essentially a way of organizing very long timelines into smaller manageable chunks. At runtime, all scenes are treated as one giant timeline, and the playhead can move freely between scenes either automatically during linear playback, or with ActionScript.

We don't use scenes much in the work we do, but we have had students who rely on scenes to tell long stories through linear animation. Adding a new scene to a file effectively resets the interface to a new timeline, making it easier to work with the relevant frames without being distracted by prior or future scenes in your file. You can test individual scenes during development, rather than having to test your entire movie. This is very convenient when you want to test only the last of many scenes.

The code is essentially the same as the ActionScript you've seen before. To test the effectiveness of using frame labels, simply add or delete frames across all layers before one of the existing frame labels. Despite changing the frame count, you will find that the navigation still works as desired.

New Timeline ActionScript

ActionScript 3.0 provides a few new features relevant to timelines. The first is an associative array of all frame labels in a file called, appropriately, **labels**, and consisting of **name** and **frame** properties that provide the text of the frame label and the frame to which it is applied. In addition, you now have access to a **scenes** array that contains the name (**name**) and number of frames (**numFrames**) in each scene, as well as an array of all frame labels within each scene (again, called **labels**, this time as a child of the **scenes** array).

The sample file, *frame_labels_02.fla*, demonstrates several of these features, as well as illustrates a couple uses of the available frame label options. It uses the same *pages* movie clip as in the prior file but with adapted functionality and buttons. Figure 5-3 shows the direct navigation to a frame that is four frames ahead of a specified label.

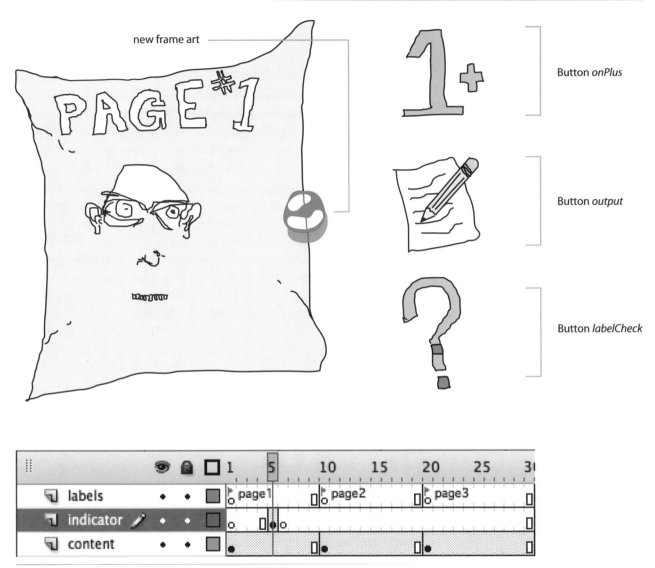

new frame art

Button *onPlus*

Button *output*

Button *labelCheck*

Figure 5-3. The **pages** *movie clip of* frame_labels_02.fla *showing how to query scene and frame information, as well as jump to relative frame addresses*

We're going to start by highlighting the functionality of the second button, *output*, that collects many of the features in one information dump to the Output panel. Looking at the following script, the first new item you will see is a main movie **stop()** action on line 1. This has been added because this file has a second scene to demonstrate the new **scenes** array and **currentScene** property.

```
1    stop();
2
3    pages.stop();
4
5    output.addEventListener(MouseEvent.CLICK, onOutputClick, false, 0,
     true);
6
7    function onOutputClick(evt:MouseEvent):void {
8        trace("The main movie has " + scenes.length + " scenes.");
9        trace("The current scene is '" + currentScene.name + "'.");
10       trace("It has " + currentScene.numFrames + " frame(s),");
11       trace("   and " + currentScene.labels.length + " label(s). ");
12       trace("The second scene's first label is '" +
         scenes[1].labels[0].name + "',");
13       trace("   which is in frame " + scenes[1].labels[0].frame +
         ".");
14       trace("Movie clip 'pages' has " + pages.currentLabels.length +
         " labels.");
15       trace("Its last label is '" + pages.currentLabels.length-1.name
         + "'.");
16   }
```

Lines 7 through 16 contain this button's goodies, tracing the number of scenes (line 8), the **name** and number of frames of the current scene (lines 9 and 10), and the total number of labels in the current scene. The script also traces the name and frame number of the first label of the second scene.

Finally, lines 14 and 15 look at the **currentLabels** array of a movie clip, getting the number of labels through the **length** property, and the name of the last label in the movie clip.

This series of trace commands offers a half dozen or so variants on the new scene and frame label features and should stimulate your imagination. Try to figure out interesting ways to make use of these properties. To get you started, we've provided two examples, included on the other two buttons.

Attached to the first button, **onePlus**, is a way of reaching a frame relative to a frame label. For instance, in a relatively rare circumstance you may want to revisit a section of your file, but without retriggering an initialization script found in the frame marked by your frame label. In that case, you may want to go to the "label frame plus one."

Perhaps more common is a uniformly structured file, such as a character animation cycle (walk, run, jump, duck, and so on), or an interface of drawers or tabs that slide in and out from off-stage. In these cases, each action might consist of the same number of frames. You may want to interrupt one sequence and jump to the same position in another sequence. Imagine, as an example, interrupting a timeline tween of an interface drawer sliding open, and wanting to jump to the same location in the timeline tween of the drawer sliding closed.

Not wanting to rely strictly on frame numbers, it helps to be able to start from a frame label and jump to a specific number of frames beyond that label. Adding to your ongoing script, look at the bold content that follows. Lines 8 through 10, as well as the listener on line 5, add functionality that sends the *pages* movie clip to a specific frame. That frame is determined first by the **getFrame()** function and then, in this case, adds four frames.

```
1   stop();
2
3   pages.stop();
4
5   onePlus.addEventListener(MouseEvent.CLICK, onOnePlusClick, false, 0,
    true);
6   output.addEventListener(MouseEvent.CLICK, onOutputClick, false, 0,
    true);
7
8   function onOnePlusClick(evt:MouseEvent):void {
9       pages.gotoAndStop(getFrame("page1", pages) + 4);
10  }
11
12  function onOutputClick(evt:MouseEvent):void {
13      trace("The main movie has " + scenes.length + " scenes.");
14      trace("The current scene is '" + currentScene.name + "'.");
15      trace("It has " + currentScene.numFrames + " frame(s),");
16      trace("  and " + currentScene.labels.length + " label(s). ");
17      trace("The second scene's first label is '" +
        scenes[1].labels[0].name + "',");
18      trace("  which is in frame " + scenes[1].labels[0].frame +
        ".");
19      trace("Movie clip 'pages' has " + pages.currentLabels.length +
        " labels.");
20      trace("Its last label is '" + pages.currentLabels.pop().name
        + "'.");
21  }
22
23  function getFrame(frLabel:String, mc:MovieClip):int {
24      for (var i:int = 0; i < mc.currentLabels.length; i++) {
25          if (mc.currentLabels[i].name == frLabel) {
26              return mc.currentLabels[i].frame;
27          }
28      }
29      return -1;
30  }
```

The aforementioned **getFrame()** function appears in lines 23 through 30. It defines the function to accept a String parameter containing the name of the original frame label, and the movie clip within which the label resides. It also types a return value as a signed integer so the compiler knows to expect a number from the function. The function then loops through all the labels in that movie clip, comparing the name of each label to the label desired. If a match is found, the frame in which the label resides is returned. If no match is found, a -1 is returned—a common technique to indicate no item was found in a zero-based array.

WARNING

A more feature-complete file would add error checking to the button function to look for a return value of -1, but for the sake of tutorial brevity, we will skip that step because we know the desired label exists in our sample file. Also, if you are unfamiliar with the function, loop, or conditional structures of this code, revisit Chapter 2 for review.

The desired result, in our sample file, is that the playhead jumps to frame 5 instead of frame 1 where the *page1* label resides. Another very similar option is to use these features to check whether a specific frame exists. This option can be used for navigation error checking, or simply to make sure you're working with the correct movie clip among many that may be available.

In a similar structure, lines 7, 24 through 26, and 37 through 44 define the button behavior. The workhorse of the bunch is the function **isFrameLabel()** defined in lines 37 through 44.

```
1    stop();
2
3    pages.stop();
4
5    onePlus.addEventListener(MouseEvent.CLICK, onOnePlusClick, false, 0,
     true);
6    output.addEventListener(MouseEvent.CLICK, onOutputClick, false, 0,
     true);
7    labelCheck.addEventListener(MouseEvent.CLICK, onLabelCheckClick,
     false, 0, true);
8
9    function onOnePlusClick(evt:MouseEvent):void {
10       pages.gotoAndStop(getFrame("page1", pages) + 4);
11   }
12
13   function onOutputClick(evt:MouseEvent):void {
14       trace("The main movie has " + scenes.length + " scenes.");
15       trace("The current scene is '" + currentScene.name + "'.");
16       trace("It has " + currentScene.numFrames + " frame(s),");
17       trace("  and " + currentScene.labels.length + " label(s).");
18       trace("The second scene's first label is '" +
         scenes[1].labels[0].name + "',");
19       trace("  which is in frame " + scenes[1].labels[0].frame +
         ".");
20       trace("Movie clip 'pages' has " + pages.currentLabels.length +
         " labels.");
21       trace("Its last label is '" + pages.currentLabels.length-1.
         name + "'.");
22   }
23
24   function onLabelCheckClick(evt:MouseEvent):void {
25       trace(isFrameLabel("page3", pages));
26   }
27
28   function getFrame(frLabel:String, mc:MovieClip):int {
29       for (var i:int = 0; i < mc.currentLabels.length; i++) {
30           if (mc.currentLabels[i].name == frLabel) {
31               return mc.currentLabels[i].frame;
32           }
33       }
34       return -1;
35   }
36
```

```
37  function isFrameLabel(frLabel:String, mc:MovieClip):Boolean {
38      for (var i:int = 0; i < mc.currentLabels.length; i++) {
39          if (mc.currentLabels[i].name == frLabel) {
40              return true;
41          }
42      }
43      return false;
44  }
```

Here, the functionality is nearly the same as the previous sample, except this function returns **true** if a queried frame label is found, or **false** if it is not found. In our sample file, the third button will trace **true** to the Output panel, because the *page3* frame label does exist in the *pages* movie clip. This subtle variant is just another simple example of how you might use the frame label and scene arrays and properties newly available in ActionScript 3.0.

Frame Rate

Also new to ActionScript 3.0 is the ability to dynamically change the frame rate at which your file plays at runtime. The default frame rate of a Flash movie is 12 frames per second, and it is quite common to adjust this to 15 or 18 frames per second and still achieve this accelerated rate in most browsers on most computers. Previously, whichever frame rate you chose used to be the frame rate you were stuck with for the life of your SWF. It is now possible to update the speed at which your file plays by changing the **frameRate** property of the *stage*, as demonstrated in the sample file *frame_rate.fla*.

NOTE

ActionScript 3.0 handles the stage and its children differently from prior versions of ActionScript. If you are not yet comfortable with these migration issues, review Chapters 3 and 4 for additional information.

Figure 5-4 demonstrates the runtime reassigning of frame rates.

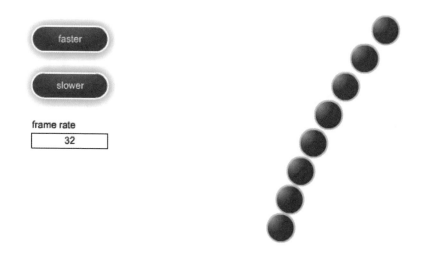

Figure 5-4. frame_rate.fla *with buttons on the left that increase and decrease the frame rate, which control the speed of the animation on the right*

The simple script increments or decrements the frame rate by 5 frames per second with each click of a button. You may also notice another simple example of error checking in the function used by the slower button, to prevent a frame rate of zero or below. Start the file and watch it run for a second or two at the default frame rate of 12 frames per second. Then, experiment with additional frame rates to see how they change the movie clip animation.

```
1   info.text = stage.frameRate;
2
3   faster.addEventListener(MouseEvent.CLICK, onFasterClick, false, 0,
    true);
4   slower.addEventListener(MouseEvent.CLICK, onSlowerClick, false, 0,
    true);
5
6   function onFasterClick(evt:MouseEvent):void {
7       stage.frameRate += 5;
8       info.text = stage.frameRate;
9   }
10  function onSlowerClick(evt:MouseEvent):void {
11      if (stage.frameRate > 5) {
12          stage.frameRate -= 5;
13      }
14      info.text = stage.frameRate;
15  }
```

The **frameRate** property requires little explanation, but its impact should not be underestimated. Other interactive environments have long been able to vary playback speed and this is a welcome change to ActionScript for many enthusiastic developers, especially animators. Be it for a *Matrix* parody or a sports game, slow mo has never been easier.

A Simple Site or Application Structure

As the final demo file in this chapter, we want to provide a very simple example of one of our most commonly requested uses of navigation to add visual interest. *demo_site.fla* shows how to design a basic site or application skeleton that gives you the freedom to combine your timeline animation skills with ActionScript coding.

This file intentionally uses detailed, and varied, timeline tweens—with inconsistent frame counts—to transition between three separate sections of this sample site or application. The idea is to take advantage of frame label navigation, but freely move from any section to any other section without concern of interrupting (or matching) the entrance or exit animations.

As you look through the sample file, you'll see that a virtual gamut of property manipulations add visual interest. Section 1 rotates in and skews out, section 2 bounces in and zooms out, and section 3 wipes in and fades out. Each section stops in the middle of the transitions to display its placeholder content. Moving unencumbered between any sections is achieved through a combination of the **play()** method and a variable.

Figure 5-5 shows a frame of *demo_site.fla*, which implements one of the most common requests for how variables can be used to create a very flexible screen-based site or application structure with animated transitions.

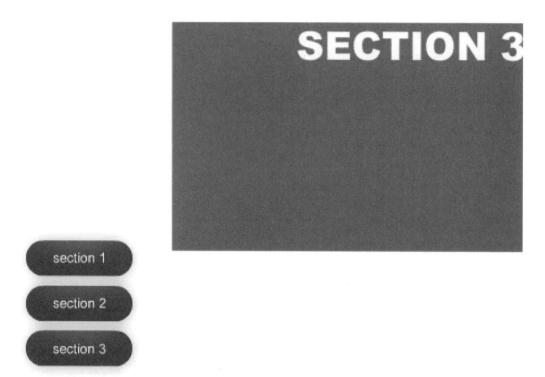

Figure 5-5. The file demo_site.fla *implements one of the most common requests from our beginner students.*

Line 1 of *demo_site.fla* initializes the **nextSection** variable, typing it as a string. We will store the destination frame label in this variable. Another frame script that executes during playback (which we'll look at in a moment) will use the **gotoAndPlay()** method to jump to the frame stored in this variable.

```
1   var nextSection:String = "";
2
3   section1.addEventListener(MouseEvent.CLICK, navigate, false, 0,
    true);
4   section2.addEventListener(MouseEvent.CLICK, navigate, false, 0,
    true);
5   section3.addEventListener(MouseEvent.CLICK, navigate, false, 0,
    true);
6
7   function navigate(evt:MouseEvent):void {
8       nextSection = evt.target.name;
9       play();
10  }
```

NOTE

*Chapter 3 discussed the use of the event argument in event listeners, and the ability to learn about the event trigger by querying its **target** property.*

The remainder of the script is similar to the previous examples, with one notable exception. Line 8 populates the **nextSection** variable using the name of the button that was clicked. Knowing that the **target** property can identify the button that was clicked, we can further query its **name** property and determine the name of the button. By naming buttons with names that match their destination frames, we can set up our file cleanly and efficiently. Clicking the **section1** button will take us to the corresponding *section1* frame label.

How, then, do we prevent the intro and outro animations from being interrupted or from overlapping? First, each button click populates the **nextSection** variable with the desired destination frame label. Then, instead of using **gotoAndPlay()**, we tell the file to **play()** until the frame script in the center of the section intro and outro animations tells the file to **stop()**.

```
//at end of section intro
stop();
```

This prevents repeated clicks from starting the intro animation of any given section over—a side effect of using **gotoAndPlay()**. In this case, however, triggering **play()** again will simply continue to play the file, rather than returning to the first frame of the sequence.

Having gone through the intro and stopped, the next click plays the outro of the current section and then hits the following script at the end of the outro animation:

```
//at end of section outtro
gotoAndPlay(nextSection);
```

This script is the last piece of the puzzle. It sends the playhead to the new section intro animation, stopping at the main-screen **stop()** action and repeating the sequence again. This structure allows you to be as creative as you want with timeline tweens and still move in and out of any section no matter how many frames each animation requires. Because you're using frame labels, you can easily change any sequence without having to adjust your scripts to update new frame numbers.

Undocumented: Adding Frame Scripts to Movie Clips at Runtime

To finish off our discussion of timelines, we want to show you an undocumented method for adding frame scripts to movie clips at runtime. As always, be careful using undocumented ActionScript, testing your implementation thoroughly and trying not to rely on its use for final production, if possible. In addition to making no warranties as to current reliability, there's no guarantee that future versions of Flash Player will support the technique.

To implement this feature, you need to create a movie clip with at least 10 frames, and no other ActionScript in the file. The sample file *addFrameScript.fla* demonstrates the feature. The method we will use is

```
<movieclip>.addFrameScript(<framenum>,<function>,
    ...rest);
```

Adding the method to a movie clip instance name, you can dictate that any function be called when the specified frame number is reached. The ellipsis followed by "rest" indicates this function will accept an unlimited number of comma-delimited arguments. In this case, the structure requires pairs of frame number, function, frame number, function, and so on. In the following example, only one frame script is added.

First, a function is defined to trace the word "ten" followed by a space and then the actual current frame of the movie clip (see Chapter 2 for more information about the this keyword).

```
function frameTen() {
    trace("ten " + mc.currentFrame);
}
mc.addFrameScript(9,frameTen);
```

Then the **addFrameScript()** method is used, specifying that the *frameTen* function be added to a frame indicated by the number 9. This, however, is not frame 9, as this parameter relies on the fact that ActionScript is a zero-based array language. Therefore, the first item is 0, the second item is 1, and so on. So, the 9 in this syntax specifies frame 10. (Again, for more information, see Chapter 2.)

When you run this file, the movie clip will animate and, when it reaches frame 10, will trace the following to the Output window:

```
ten 10
```

This is a significantly simplified example, but there could be many uses for this feature. One popular use could be adding a **stop()** action to movie clips. It is relatively trivial to stop a movie clip on its first frame by using

```
<instance>.stop()
```

as we did with the *pages* movie clip in this chapter. However, it requires a little more effort and is usually processor-intensive, such as a combination of a repeating event and a conditional to stop a movie clip on its last frame.

However, with this unsupported method, you could use something like the following:

```
function stopMC() {
    mc.stop();
}
mc.addFrameScript(mc.totalFrames-1, stopMC);
```

This instruction would add a script to the last frame of the movie clip (remember, this parameter is based on calling the first frame zero), which would then be executed only when that frame is reached.

Don't forget to use this unsupported method with caution, if at all, in any production files. Elsewhere, have fun and experiment!

What's Next?

By now you should have a relatively firm grasp of how to navigate timelines, be able to manipulate display objects (including their properties and methods), and understand the fundamentals of the AS3 event model. Up to this point, we've been focusing primarily on syntax and approaching each task using simple procedural programming techniques.

As you'll read in Chapter 6, you may find this sufficient for many of the projects you create. However, larger projects, and projects developed in a workgroup environment with multiple programmers, can significantly benefit from object-oriented programming (OOP) techniques. From this point on, we'll be using more and more OOP in our demos, and you will eventually end up with a final project that is built entirely using object-oriented programming.

In the next chapter, we'll introduce some basics of OOP, including:

- Using encapsulation and polymorphism
- Writing your first class
- Creating a sub-class that demonstrates inheritance
- Organizing your classes and packages

OOP

Object-oriented programming (OOP) is sometimes thought of as a problem-solving technique—a way of organizing your code into small, specific, easily digestible chunks (objects) to make project or application development more manageable. These objects are typically designed to be as self-contained as possible, but are also usually designed to play well with other objects. Choosing OOP as a programming methodology is a decision that is sometimes fairly obvious, such as when working with large projects or with a team of collaborating programmers. At other times, however, adopting OOP as a development strategy can be less obvious, and even debated.

The goal of this chapter is to give you a high-level view of object-oriented principles, as well as supporting examples, to help prepare you to make these decisions on a project-by-project basis. Each subsequent chapter in this book will continue to focus on syntax in concise, timeline-based exercises, but also make increasing use of classes. Ultimately, we hope you will continue your learning using the book's companion web site, where a cumulative project will collect much of what you've created along the way into a "lab" of experiments. The larger project will be OOP-based but also will contain exercises that you create using procedural techniques, exposing you to both authoring paradigms.

Knowing when to opt for an object-oriented model depends largely on understanding the benefits of OOP, among them:

- **Classes.** Classes are collections of related functions (called *methods*) and variables (called *properties*) gathered to facilitate one or more specific goals. They are the foundation of OOP, and we'll look at a few ways to use them.

- **Inheritance.** Inheritance is one of OOP's greatest sources of power, as it allows you to add functionality to an existing feature set without reinventing the wheel. This is known as *extending* an existing class to create a *subclass*, rather than originating a new class. Inheritance can save you time and labor, as well as improve project design.

- **Composition.** Inheritance isn't appropriate for every situation, and composition is often a useful alternative. Composition is a technique somewhat akin to collecting related classes, much like classes collect related functions and variables. The classes do not inherit characteristics from one another, but are made to work together in productive ways.

- **Encapsulation.** It's usually not a good idea to expose all aspects of a class to other classes or the surrounding application. Encapsulation isolates most elements of a class from the outside world, allowing only a select few elements, if any, to be seen by structures that use the class.

- **Polymorphism.** Polymorphism allows related classes to have methods that share the same name but that behave differently when invoked. By using polymorphism, you can reduce the number of methods that must be documented and learned, and, more importantly, make it easier to extend classes. New subclasses can use an existing method name but return a result appropriate to the new class.

It's important to understand that OOP is not appropriate for everyone, nor is it even appropriate for every situation. OOP can dramatically improve the development cycle of large projects, or projects to which more than one programmer can contribute. OOP can even be ideal for smaller projects that are particularly suited for object-based coding (such as some kinds of arcade games, as one generic example).

The common thread is that object-oriented programming benefits from economies of scale. The time, labor, and learning investments begin to pay off over time. Procedural programming is often more appropriate for small tasks and is sometimes less time consuming for smaller scale projects, resulting in code that is simpler to maintain.

You don't *need* to learn OOP to use ActionScript 3.0. The benefits and buzz of object-oriented programming, particularly the continuing swell of interest in design patterns, sometimes lead to almost fetishistic adherence to their principles, without context and at the cost of practicality.

The key to adopting any programming paradigm is finding the right tool for the job. It's certainly a good idea to learn OOP as soon as your schedule and skill set permits, simply because it gives you more options to choose from. Remember, however, that there is more than one way to create an interface. Before embracing your next significant project, try to set aside some time for planning, information architecture, and programming design. You may find that your goals will be more easily achieved by adopting an object-oriented approach. If your typical production schedule or project budget cannot allow the inevitable time and resource stumbles associated with attempting new challenges, try learning OOP through a series of fun experiments or artistic endeavors. You may find that the things you learn, the mistakes you make, and the epiphanies you experience will improve your next project.

Having said all that, we'll hit the high points in this introduction to object-oriented programming. This chapter is meant to be a transition between prior and future chapters. We will continue to introduce topics with basic, procedural, timeline-based demos that allow you to focus on the most relevant syntax, without the overhead of larger fully developed examples. However, we will make more frequent use of OOP techniques, particularly in applied examples at the end of the chapters, and even more so in the source code and enhanced learning available on the companion web site.

Classes

In Chapter 1, we discussed the three most common programming paradigms: sequential, procedural, and object-oriented. We described procedural programming as an improvement over sequential programming because, instead of being limited to a linear sequence of instructions, you can group related tasks together into procedures (or functions, in ActionScript).

Classes offer a similar improvement over procedural programming in that they collect related functions (called methods in classes), variables (called properties in classes), and other relevant items.

Classes are the foundation of object-based programming, and yet you have probably been working with them for some time. Even if you are new to programming, if you have followed this book through to this chapter, you already have some experience with classes but may not realize it. This is because most of what goes on behind the scenes in ActionScript is accomplished through the use of classes.

To start off with, Chapter 1 of this book gave you a quick peek at classes, and introduced the first use of the Document Class, which we'll cover again in just a moment. Beyond that, you learned how to manipulate events (using several event classes, including **EventDispatcher**, in Chapter 3), control how objects are displayed (using a large number of display classes, including **DisplayObjectContainer**, **DisplayObject**, and their numerous descendents in Chapter 4), and how to control navigation and timelines (with revisits to display classes as well as the **FrameLabel** class, among others in Chapter 5). Even in Chapter 2, when discussing basic language fundamentals, you learned aspects of the **Array** class and applicable data type classes.

If you're suddenly concerned that you've missed a lot of material, don't be. In part, that is the point. All of these examples make use of classes. You just may not be aware of it, or at least intimately conscious of it, because it's happening behind the proverbial curtain.

Take a look at the movie clip, for example. Throughout the preceding chapters, you've worked fairly extensively with movie clips. You've set numerous properties (such as **x**, **y**, **rotation**, **alpha**, and more), triggered methods (**play()**, **stop()**, and variants of **goto...()**, among them), and handled events (like **Event.ENTER_FRAME**). These are all uses of the **MovieClip** class. You even learned how to create a movie clip by creating an instance of the class—a fundamental step in working with classes:

```
var mc:MovieClip = new MovieClip();
```

So, with all that experience, what's the big deal about classes? A bit flippant perhaps, but not entirely off the mark. The fact is, you can apply that history to learning OOP. You may not have a lot of experience writing classes, but you do have some experience using them. In fact, it isn't until you begin working with custom classes that things begin to look new.

Custom Class Review

Start by revisiting the structure of the first custom class introduced in this book, all the way back in Chapter 1—a very basic use of Flash CS3's new *Document class*. A **Document** class eases you into OOP coding because it allows you to create a custom class that can be used as a type of timeline replacement, but it will be automatically instantiated by Flash. Using document classes is a great beginning way to create an organizational front end for additional classes that you may use later on.

You can review Chapter 1 for more information about the **Document** class, including how to reference it in Flash's Property Inspector. Here, however, we'd like to quickly review the formatting of the class, as you'll use this format for many classes in the future. Let's take a look at the following **Document** class.

```
1   package {
2
3       import flash.display.MovieClip;
4
5       public class Main extends MovieClip {
6
7           public function Main() {
8               trace("Flash");
9           }
10
11      }
12  }
```

Lines 1 and 12 wrap the class and any related items in a package. As you become more experienced using classes and packages, you can explore some of the features ActionScript 3.0 brings to package organization but, at this point, think of a package as nothing more than a wrapper for your class. You can place all your classes in the same directory as your *.fla* file, and they will be automatically found. Or, you can organize them in subdirectories, the path to which follows the **package** keyword. See the "Classpaths" section for more information.

Line 3 is a compiler directive that instructs the Flash compiler to include all the properties, methods, and events in the classes or packages listed when compiling your movie. Although this is needed only occasionally in the timeline, it is always required in external classes. As a rule of thumb, import everything you need in external classes.

Lines 5 and 11 declare the class. The first thing you may notice about this is the word **public** beginning the declaration. This is called a namespace and makes the class available to the rest of your project. We'll talk more about namespaces later when we discuss encapsulation. The next thing you may notice is the phrase **extends MovieClip** following the name of the class, **Main**. This means that all the events, methods, and properties of the **MovieClip** class will be available to this class, and is why the **MovieClip** class needed to be imported. We'll talk more about extending classes in the later section, "Inheritance."

Finally, lines 7 through 9 are the class constructor—the code invoked when an instance of the class is created. (In this case, it just traces the word "Flash" to the Output panel.) Just as you can create many instances of a symbol in the Flash timeline, you can create many instances of a class unless your class code specifically prohibits this. Although the **Document** class takes care of this for you automatically, you can also do this manually:

```
var main:Main = new Main();
```

Does all this look familiar? It should. This is the same format used to instantiate the vast majority of classes in ActionScript 3.0, including the recently cited example of creating a movie clip. So, you already have some of the skills required for working with custom classes, too!

Classpaths

You have a few choices when deciding where to place your external custom classes. Flash will automatically look for a class in the same directory as the *.fla* file making use of the class. This is the easiest way to handle external classes because any class in the same directory as your *.fla* file will automatically be found (meaning you don't have to import them), and it's easy to transport classes in your project by just moving the parent directory.

You can also organize your classes into directories, grouping classes of similar functionality together for easier management. To use a class in a specific subdirectory, you need to import the class, including the classpath. This technique includes Flash classes, as in the cited movie clip example, as well as your own custom classes. You can also import all classes in a package directory by using an asterisk as a wildcard. Here are examples of these techniques:

```
import flash.display.MovieClip;
import myapp.effects.Water;
import flash.events.*;
```

NOTE

We should reinforce from Chapter 1 that the name of an external class file must match the name of the class and constructor. In the class being discussed, the file must be called Main.as.

When writing classes, you must include the classpath in the package directive. Here is an example structure of a fictional **Water** class:

```
package myapp.effects {

    public class Water {

        public function Water() {
        }
    }
}
```

Finally, Flash needs to know where to find your class directories. Because Flash will automatically look in the same folder as your *.fla* file, you can put package directories as well as classes in this folder. However, this is impractical for classes that are not project-specific. If you intend to use or build libraries of classes, you will not want to duplicate these classes many times and keep them with your *.fla* files.

Instead, you can add a classpath to the list of paths Flash will search to find your classes. For example, Flash must know where to find the **flash.display. MovieClip** class just as much as it needs to know where to look for your custom classes. To add your own classpath to Flash, go to the ActionScript section of Flash's Preferences dialog, and choose which version of ActionScript you're working in, ActionScript 2.0 or ActionScript 3.0. Using the resulting dialog, seen in Figure 6-1, you can browse for the directory in which you will be maintaining your class libraries, and Flash will thereafter search in that directory when importing your classes.

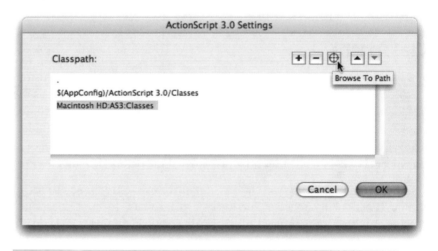

Figure 6-1. Adding your own classpath to Flash's ActionScript preferences

Inheritance

Among the most recognized benefits of an object-oriented programming model is *inheritance*. This means that you can create a new class, typically called a *subclass*, which can inherit attributes from the original class, also called the *parent*, *super*, or *ancestor* class. This is similar to the way you inherit characteristics from your parents. You share many things in common with a parent but also have several unique attributes. The same can be said of classes. Through inheritance, a class can acquire from its parent useful methods and properties, as well as add entirely new methods and properties.

The following script creates a class called **Box**, which is a subclass of **MovieClip**. As a result, it has access to all the properties, methods, and classes available to a movie clip, including the **x** property seen in line 22, and the **Graphics** class used in lines 13 through 16 to draw a blue box. We'll discuss drawing vectors with code in Chapter 8, but respectively, the script dictates a 1-pixel black line style, fills it with the color stored in the **color** variable, draws a box from point (0, 0) to point (100, 100), and ends the fill.

The **color** variable is declared in line 9. This is an example of a class property. It is defined within the class but outside the constructor so it can be available to the entire class. The declaration uses a **var** keyword and data type and is given a color value (navy blue). In this case, the **public** namespace also makes the variable available to code outside the class.

```
1   package {
2
3       import flash.display.MovieClip;
4       import flash.display.Graphics;
5       import flash.events.Event;
6
7       public class Box extends MovieClip {
8
9           public var color:uint = 0x000099;
10
11          public function Box() {
12              //draw a shape at runtime
13              this.graphics.lineStyle(1, 0x000000);
14              this.graphics.beginFill(color);
15              this.graphics.drawRect(0, 0, 100, 100);
16              this.graphics.endFill();
17
18              this.addEventListener(Event.ENTER_FRAME, onLoop, false,
                0, true);
19          }
20
21          public function onLoop(evt:Event):void {
22              this.x += 5;
23          }
24
25      }
26  }
```

The event listener created in line 18 calls the **onLoop()** function every enter frame and adds five pixels to the current x location of the class. The fact that this class extends **MovieClip** means that it is, in effect, a movie clip itself. Setting the x coordinate of the class is just like setting the x coordinate of a movie clip.

Creating an instance of this class is just like creating an instance of the **MovieClip** class. As discussed in the Classpaths section of this chapter, the Flash compiler must know where your class resides. The **Box** class does not include a path in its package declaration so, if you place this class into the same directory as your FLA, the compiler will find it. Therefore, all that is required is to create an instance using the **new** keyword. Finally, just like a movie clip, you must add the instance to the display list.

```
var myBox:Box = new Box();
addChild(myBox);
```

Having done this, an instance of the **Box** class will be created and added to the display list, and the drawn square will move across the stage at 5 pixels per enter frame.

Symbol Base Classes

We can take further advantage of inheriting from the **MovieClip** class by linking a class directly to a movie clip. You did this more than once in Chapter 4 when adding Library symbols to the display list. (See "Adding Symbol Instances to the Display List" in Chapter 4.) At that time, however, you had not created an external class to link up with the symbol instance, so you let Flash create a placeholder class just for the purpose of supporting runtime creation.

Now, you can make use of this link by providing Flash with an external custom class to execute when the symbol instance is created. In effect, adding the symbol to the display list, either manually within the timeline, or at runtime with ActionScript, is executing the constructor within the linked class.

The following example is the same as the previous script, but eliminates the runtime creation of the box. This is because you are linking this class directly to a movie clip in the Flash library so the visual comes from the library symbol.

```
1    package {
2
3        import flash.display.MovieClip;
4        import flash.events.Event;
5
6        public class Square extends MovieClip {
7
8            public function Square() {
9                this.addEventListener(Event.ENTER_FRAME, onLoop, false,
                     0, true);
10           }
11
```

```
12          private function onLoop(evt:Event):void {
13              this.x += 5;
14          }
15
16      }
17  }
```

A More Traditional Look at Inheritance

Now that you have a basic idea of how a custom class inherits the attributes of a movie clip, let's look at a more traditional example with a bit more substance. We described inheritance earlier by discussing how a child inherits from a parent. The same analogy can be made from other real-world scenarios. A **Dog** class might inherit from an **Animal** class, a **Ball** class might inherit from a **Toy** class, and a **Car** class might inherit from a **Vehicle** class. These are all classic examples of OOP methodologies. Examine a very simple execution of the Vehicle metaphor, for instance.

Whether a vehicle is a car or a truck—or even a plane or a boat, for that matter—it is still a vehicle and shares much in common with other vehicles. It makes sense, then, to create a class that contains basic methods and properties that are common to all vehicles. For simplicity, think about fuel availability (the number of gallons of fuel the vehicle has in its tank) and fuel efficiency (gas mileage, in miles per gallon, for our purposes). Also, a calculation based on that information could result in miles traveled and the resulting reduction in the amount of fuel.

NOTE

It is common practice to start class names, and therefore their file and constructor names, with a capital letter.

Vehicle class

Here is a basic class you can use to represent a generic vehicle. We'll call this class **Vehicle**, so the document name will be *Vehicle.as*, and the class will be saved in the same directory as your *.fla* file. This class created a vehicle and, when activated, increases the number of miles traveled and decrease the remaining gallons of gas after each enter frame event, tracing the result. You can see in the Output window how many miles the vehicle traveled before it ran out of gas.

The class has four public properties, including gas mileage, available fuel, and miles traveled, and a Boolean property called **_go**, which will be used to enable functionality when true, and disable functionality when false. All the properties and methods in the class are public so other classes can see them. We'll discuss that in further detail in a little while.

NOTE

It is common to precede class property names with an underscore, but this is not required.

The constructor does only two things. It sets the class properties for gas mileage and available fuel to the parameters passed in when the class was instantiated, and adds a listener to the vehicle that reacts to the enter frame event and calls the **onLoop()** method. It also includes default values for both parameters.

```
1    //Vehicle.as
2    package {
3
4        import flash.display.MovieClip;
5        import flash.events.Event;
6
7        public class Vehicle extends MovieClip {
8
9            public var _gasMileage:Number;
10           public var _fuelAvailable:Number;
11           public var _milesTraveled:Number = 0;
12           public var _go:Boolean;
13
14           public function Vehicle(mpg:Number=21, fuel:Number=18.5) {
15               _gasMileage = mpg;
16               _fuelAvailable = fuel;
17               this.addEventListener(Event.ENTER_FRAME, onLoop, false,
                     0, true);
18           }
```

When the **_go** property is true, the **onLoop()** method first decrements the **_fuelAvailable** property, increasing the **_milesTraveled** property by the value of the **_gasMileage** property. So, if a vehicle claims a gas mileage rating of 21 miles per gallon, after using 1 gallon of gas, the car will have traveled 21 miles.

Next, the method checks to see whether there's less than one gallon of gas remaining. If so, the listener is removed. If at least one gallon of gas remains, the vehicle object, miles it has traveled, and remaining fuel are traced to the output panel, and any MovieClip to which this class is associated will have its x coordinate set to the current number of miles traveled. The effect is that the movie clip moves across the stage by pixels that correspond to miles driven.

Finally, the **go()** method, when called from outside the class, sets the **_go** Boolean to **true** and allows the frame loop to work. This could be likened to starting the engine of the vehicle and driving. A more complex system might also provide a method for stopping the vehicle, as well as other features, but let's keep this example simple.

```
19           public function onLoop(evt:Event):void {
20               if (_go) {
21                   _fuelAvailable--;
22                   _milesTraveled += _gasMileage;
23                   if (_fuelAvailable < 1) {
24                       this.removeEventListener(Event.ENTER_FRAME,
                           onLoop);
25                   }
26                   trace(this, _milesTraveled, _fuelAvailable);
27                   this.x = _milesTraveled;
28               }
29           }
30
31           public function go():void {
32               _go = true;
```

```
33              }
34
35      }
36  }
```

Main Flash file

To see this class in action, you must first create an instance of the class in the main *.fla* file, passing in the desired gas mileage and available fuel. If desired, then add it to the display list to show any visual components of the class (which we'll get to later on). Finally, trigger the **go()** method of the class to start the tracing.

```
var vehicle:Vehicle = new Vehicle(21, 18);
addChild(vehicle);
vehicle.go();
```

The resulting trace output lists the **Vehicle** class instance, the accumulating miles traveled, and the decreasing fuel available. After several iterations (indicated by the ellipsis in the sample trace that follows), the trace stops and shows the final number of miles traveled and less than one gallon of gas remaining.

```
//output
[object Vehicle] 21 17
[object Vehicle] 42 16
[object Vehicle] 63 15
...
[object Vehicle] 336 2
[object Vehicle] 357 1
[object Vehicle] 378 0
```

That's fine if every vehicle you ever create is exactly the same kind of vehicle. However, the principle of inheritance allows you to subclass this **Vehicle** class, inheriting the generic attributes of **Vehicle**, but customizing it into individual kinds of vehicles, like car and truck, as in the following example.

The following two classes, **Car** and **Truck**, both extend **Vehicle**, so they inherit the properties and methods of **Vehicle**. Because the properties are inherited, they're not included in the subclasses. (Import directives must still be included.) Although both classes extend **Vehicle**, you can also add unique properties and methods to each class, customizing **Car** and **Truck**. For simplicity, we will add to each class a method to control an accessory—a sunroof for the car and a tailgate for the truck.

NOTE

*Neither the **Car** class nor the **Truck** class must import **Vehicle** because all three classes are in the same classpath.*

Car class

```
1    //Car.as
2    package {
3
4        import flash.display.MovieClip;
5        import flash.events.Event;
6
7        public class Car extends Vehicle {
8
9            public function Car(mpg:Number, fuel:Number) {
10               _gasMileage = mpg;
11               _fuelAvailable = fuel;
12           }
13
14           public function openSunroof():void {
15               trace(this, "opened sunroof");
16           }
17       }
18   }
```

Truck class

```
1    //Truck.as
2    package {
3
4        import flash.display.MovieClip;
5        import flash.events.Event;
6
7        public class Truck extends Vehicle {
8
9            public function Truck(mpg:Number, fuel:Number) {
10               _gasMileage = mpg;
11               _fuelAvailable = fuel;
12           }
13
14           public function lowerTailgate():void {
15               trace(this, "lowered tailgate");
16           }
17       }
18   }
```

Revised main Flash file

Now we can revisit the main Flash file and, instead of instantiating the **Vehicle** class, we can create instances of the **Car** and **Truck** classes. Following the example set forth in the prior section, we can create car and truck movie clips in the Flash file's library (perhaps with pictures of each vehicle type), and link the newly created classes to their associated movie clips. Because the **Vehicle** class extends **MovieClip**, and the x coordinate of **Vehicle** is updated, any subclass of the **Vehicle** class will also have its x coordinate updated.

So, set the **Car** instance (compact) and the **Truck** instance (pickup) to the same initial x value (lines 3 and 9), give each instance an appropriate gas mileage and fuel value through the class parameters (lines 2 and 8), and prepare to see which gets further on a tank of gas.

```
1    //host .fla file
2    var compact:Car = new Car(21, 18);
3    compact.x = 10;
4    compact.y = 10;
5    addChild(compact);
6    compact.openSunroof();
7
8    var pickup:Truck = new Truck(16, 23);
9    pickup.x = 10;
10   pickup.y = 100;
11   addChild(pickup);
12   pickup.lowerTailgate();
13
14   stage.addEventListener(MouseEvent.CLICK, onClick, false, 0, true);
15
16   function onClick(evt:MouseEvent):void {
17       compact.go();
18       pickup.go();
19   }
```

Before proceeding, trigger the custom methods of each instance once (lines 6 and 12) to show that they are now car and truck instead of generic vehicle. The resulting output will look like this:

```
[object Car] opened sunroof
[object Truck] lowered tailgate
```

When ready, click the stage to start the test run. The event listener in line 14 will trigger the **onClick()** method, driving the car and truck, and tracing a result similar to that of the **Vehicle**-only example to the Output panel. This time, however, you will be comparing the final miles traveled by the car and truck instances. Which will get the furthest on a tank of gas? The truck travels fewer miles per gallon but has a larger gas tank. Try it and see!

Composition

Although inheritance is a very common practice in object-oriented programming, it is not the only way for classes to work together. *Composition*, sometimes referred to as *aggregation*, is also appropriate in many circumstances. Composition says that an object can be composed of other objects, rather than descend from other objects. The best way to describe composition is by example, using a handy rule of thumb that asks "is a" or "has a."

Consider how to add tires to the vehicle example. You might be able to use inheritance ("is a"), but composition ("has a") might be better. A car "is a" vehicle, meaning inheritance will work well, but tires don't fit the "is a" vehicle or car or truck model. However, a car (and truck) "has a" set of tires, making this model suitable for composition. Composition makes it easier to switch out items of which a class is composed. If a car is extended from a vehicle, then you can't change that any more than you can change your blood relatives, parent, or child. However, if a car is composed of things, including tires, you can easily switch one set of tires for another.

Vehicle class

Let's start the composition example by adding a **_tires** property to the **Vehicle** class, as seen in line 13 of the class. This makes the property available to the **Car** and **Truck** classes.

```
1   //Vehicle.as
2   package {
3
4       import flash.display.MovieClip;
5       import flash.events.Event;
6
7       public class Vehicle extends MovieClip {
8
9           public var _gasMileage:Number;
10          public var _fuelAvailable:Number;
11          public var _milesTraveled:Number = 0;
12          public var _go:Boolean;
13          public var _tires:Tires;
14
15          public function Vehicle(mpg:Number=21, fuel:Number=18.5) {
16              _gasMileage = mpg;
17              _fuelAvailable = fuel;
18              this.addEventListener(Event.ENTER_FRAME, onLoop, false,
                    0, true);
19          }
20
21          public function onLoop(evt:Event):void {
22              if (_go) {
23                  _fuelAvailable--;
24                  _milesTraveled += _gasMileage;
25                  if (_fuelAvailable < 1) {
26                      this.removeEventListener(Event.ENTER_FRAME,
                            onLoop);
27                  }
28                  trace(this, _milesTraveled, _fuelAvailable);
29                  this.x = _milesTraveled;
30              }
31          }
32
33          public function go():void {
34              _go = true;
35          }
36
37      }
38  }
```

In both the **Car** and **Truck** classes, create an instance of a new **Tires** class, passing unique tire types into the constructor (lines 12 and 13 in both **Car** and **Truck** classes). In a real-world situation, the new class might affect the performance of a car or truck object. For example, using snow tires might reduce fuel efficiency, while upgrading to high-performance radials might improve mileage. In our simplified example, we'll just trace a string to simulate the use of the **Tires** class.

Pay close attention to how the final string is retrieved. The **type** property of the **tires** instance is queried, and this will be important when we explain how the **Tires** class works.

Car class

```
1    //Car.as
2    package {
3
4        import flash.display.MovieClip;
5        import flash.events.Event;
6
7        public class Car extends Vehicle {
8
9            public function Car(mpg:Number, fuel:Number) {
10               _gasMileage = mpg;
11               _fuelAvailable = fuel;
12               _tires = new Tires("highperformance");
13               trace(this + " has " + _tires.type + " tires");
14           }
15
16           public function openSunroof():void {
17               trace(this, "opened sunroof");
18           }
19       }
20   }
```

Truck class

```
1    //Truck.as
2    package {
3
4        import flash.display.MovieClip;
5        import flash.events.Event;
6
7        public class Truck extends Vehicle {
8
9            public function Truck(mpg:Number, fuel:Number) {
10               _gasMileage = mpg;
11               _fuelAvailable = fuel;
12               _tires = new Tires("snow");
13               trace(this + " has " + _tires.type + " tires");
14           }
15
16           public function lowerTailgate():void {
17               trace(this, "lowered tailgate");
18           }
19       }
20   }
```

New Tires class

This basic **Tires** class simulates an effect on the system by setting the type of tires applied, so the **Car** and **Truck** classes can trace its value. The important new technique here is in lines 22 through 24. You may recall that, in the **Car** and **Truck** classes, a **type** (without an underscore) property was queried. However, only a **type()** method exists. How does this work?

```
1    //Tires.as
2    package {
3
4        public class Tires {
5
6            public var _type:String;
7
8            public function Tires(type:String) {
9                //simulated functionality change based on tire type
10               switch (type) {
11                   case "snow" :
12                       _type = "storm-ready snow";
13                       break;
14                   case "highperformance" :
15                       _type = "high-performance radial";
16                       break;
17                   default :
18                       _type = "economical bias-ply";
19               }
20           }
21
22           public function get type():String {
23               return _type;
24           }
25       }
26   }
```

This is a demonstration of a special structure called a *getter*. A getter, and its companion *setter* (not used in this simplified example) treat a method like a property and automatically react based on how they are accessed. If no value is sent along with the call to the property-like method, as in the case of the **Car** and **Truck** classes, then ActionScript knows the current value is being requested. If a value is sent with the call, ActionScript knows to update the value with the new parameter. We'll show this process in greater detail in the next example, including a functional setter.

Main Flash file

No change is required to the main *.fla* file, but testing the file again will add a new element to the trace output. In addition to the use of the accessories (sunroof and tailgate) and the resulting miles traveled until fuel is depleted, the tires used will also be traced, as shown. (We'll leave it to you to see if the car or truck travels the farthest.)

```
[object Car] has high-performance radial tires
[object Car] opened sunroof
[object Truck] has storm-ready snow tires
[object Truck] lowered tailgate
[object Car] 21 17
[object Truck] 16 22
[object Car] 42 16
[object Truck] 32 21
...
```

Encapsulation

In the preceding examples, all class properties and methods were public. This is convenient in that it allows code outside the classes to see properties and methods inside classes. However, this is also dangerous because other elements of the application can change property values or execute methods, intentionally or even accidentally, when not desired.

The way to avoid this possible problem is through *encapsulation*. Put simply, encapsulation allows you to hide class properties and methods from other areas of your project but still allows you to manipulate them in a controlled fashion.

There are three additional namespaces, other than public, with specific purposes, but we're going to focus on one: private. Changing a property or method to private means that the item will be accessible only to elements of the same class.

For our purposes, the class and constructor must always be public so that any part of your project can create an instance of the class. (There are exceptions to this rule, but they are outside the scope of this overview.)

NOTE

For a more advanced look at namespaces, see Chapter 17 of Colin Moock's Essential ActionScript 3.0.

Vehicle class

The first thing we're going to do in this demonstration is make the properties in lines 9 through 13, and the method defined in line 21 in the code that follows, private. The **go()** method should remain public so it can easily be executed from other areas of your project.

However, now that the properties and **onLoop()** method are private, how can other parts of the file affect them? The answer is through the use of getters and setters. Lines 37 through 60 add a getter and setter pair for each of the private properties in the class. The idea behind this step is that the public face of the class, through getters and setters, can grant controlled access to private properties and methods, and you can process, redirect, or affect incoming requests and outgoing returns.

As discussed earlier, the get and set identifiers tell the respective methods to either return the current value or set a new value of a property, using the same syntax. They cause the instruction to be seen as a property, so you don't have to reference get or set or even use method syntax. All you need to do is set the property equal to a value, or request the value of the property. For example, the following syntax would change the gas mileage of an instantiated vehicle, followed by tracing the new gas mileage. As you can see, the syntax is the same, with the exception of the numerical value to the right of the equation that invokes the setter.

```
vehicle.gasMileage = 10;
trace(vehicle.gasMileage);
```

Here is the **Vehicle** class in its entirety:

```
1   //Vehicle.as
2   package {
3
4       import flash.display.MovieClip;
5       import flash.events.Event;
6
7       public class Vehicle extends MovieClip {
8
9           private var _gasMileage:Number;
10          private var _fuelAvailable:Number;
11          private var _milesTraveled:Number = 0;
12          private var _go:Boolean;
13          private var _tires:Tires;
14
15          public function Vehicle(mpg:Number=21, fuel:Number=18.5) {
16              _gasMileage = mpg;
17              _fuelAvailable = fuel;
18              this.addEventListener(Event.ENTER_FRAME, onLoop, false,
                    0, true);
19          }
20
21          private function onLoop(evt:Event):void {
22              if (_go) {
23                  _fuelAvailable--;
24                  _milesTraveled += _gasMileage;
25                  if (_fuelAvailable < 1) {
26                      this.removeEventListener(Event.ENTER_FRAME,
                            onLoop);
27                  }
28                  trace(this, _milesTraveled, _fuelAvailable);
29                  this.x = _milesTraveled;
30              }
31          }
32
33          public function go():void {
34              _go = true;
35          }
36
37          public function get gasMileage():Number {
38              return _gasMileage;
39          }
40
41          public function set gasMileage(mpg:Number):void {
42              _gasMileage = mpg;
43          }
44
45          public function get fuelAvailable():Number {
46              return _fuelAvailable;
47          }
48
49          public function set fuelAvailable(fuel:Number):void {
50              _fuelAvailable = fuel;
51          }
52
53          public function get milesTraveled():Number {
54              return _milesTraveled;
55          }
56
```

```
57        public function get tires():Tires {
58            return _tires;
59        }
60
61        public function set tires(tires:Tires):void {
62            _tires = tires;
63        }
64    }
65 }
```

Getters and setters are fine for simple queries and updates, but access issues are a little more direct within the constructor of a subclass. Remember that when **Car** and **Truck** instances were created, the constructor of these subclasses updated the **_gasMileage** and **_fuelAvailable** properties of the **Vehicle** class. However, if those properties are no longer public, this is no longer possible using the same techniques.

The best way to access private properties from a subclass (we'll look at issues of invoking methods in the next section, "Polymorphism") is to use the **super()** method to manipulate them in the super (parent) class.

In the **Car** and **Truck** constructors, the **super()** method (line 10 in both classes) sends the parameters received when instantiating the class up to the superclass, executing the constructor in **Vehicle**. Because **Vehicle** has access to its own private properties, the assignments are safely made in that private realm.

Car class

```
1  //Car.as
2  package {
3
4      import flash.display.MovieClip;
5      import flash.events.Event;
6
7      public class Car extends Vehicle {
8
9          public function Car(mpg:Number, fuel:Number) {
10             super(mpg, fuel);
11             var tires:Tires = new Tires("highperfomance");
12             trace(this + " has " + tires.type + " tires");
13         }
14
15         public function openSunroof():void {
16             trace(this, "opened sunroof");
17         }
18     }
19 }
```

Truck class

```
1    //Truck.as
2    package {
3
4        import flash.display.MovieClip;
5        import flash.events.Event;
6
7        public class Truck extends Vehicle {
8
9            public function Truck(mpg:Number, fuel:Number) {
10               super(mpg, fuel);
11               var tires:Tires = new Tires("snow");
12               trace(this + " has " + tires.type + " tires");
13           }
14
15           public function lowerTailgate():void {
16               trace(this, "lowered tailgate");
17           }
18       }
19   }
```

Tires class and main Flash file

No changes are required to either the **Tires** class or main *.fla* file, and no changes are made to the trace output when testing. However, the system is now more secure because other areas of the project can't inadvertently (or intentionally) change the private properties or execute the private methods.

Polymorphism

The last important concept of object-oriented programming that we want to discuss is *polymorphism*. This is the ability to execute methods of a subclass just like you would execute the same methods in its superclass. For example, you may have worked hard developing a robust vehicle class that includes steps necessary to move the vehicle. Having done so, it's less advantageous to use separate method names, perhaps "drive," "pilot," and "fly," to accomplish the same task of moving a car, boat, and plane.

Instead, a universal method name that would apply in all of these described scenarios, such as "move," would be preferable. This is referred to as *override polymorphism* because somewhat customized steps to move a car, boat, and plane each override the more general steps used to enable movement of a generic vehicle.

Another example to consider is the x coordinate of a display object. In Chapter 4, you learned that many display objects, like movie clip, sprite, and button, descend from the same parent. Much of their functionality overlaps, including the ability to set the x coordinate of each display object. Imagine, however, if you had to specify separate properties for each display type to accomplish this same goal. For example, imagine if you had to write "spriteX," "movieClipX," and "buttonX," instead of just **x**. Even though these display objects all have different data types, polymorphism allows you to use the same method to control a particular behavior of all the class instances.

To demonstrate this process effectively, let's begin by adding two methods to the **Vehicle** class we've been using throughout the chapter. The new methods can be seen in lines 33 through 39 in the following **Vehicle** class code, and include the generically named **useAccessory()** (as well as **changeGear()**, which we'll revisit when we discuss testing the file). In the **Vehicle** class, the accessory use is turning on lights, and both of the new methods are available to the **Car** and **Truck** subclasses because of inheritance.

Vehicle class

```
1    //Vehicle.as
2    package {
3
4        import flash.display.MovieClip;
5        import flash.events.Event;
6
7        public class Vehicle extends MovieClip {
8
9            private var _gasMileage:Number;
10           private var _fuelAvailable:Number;
11           private var _milesTraveled:Number = 0;
12           private var _go:Boolean;
13           private var _tires:Tires;
14
15           public function Vehicle(mpg:Number=21, fuel:Number=18.5) {
16               _gasMileage = mpg;
17               _fuelAvailable = fuel;
18               this.addEventListener(Event.ENTER_FRAME, onLoop, false,
                     0, true);
19           }
20
21           private function onLoop(evt:Event):void {
22               if (_go) {
23                   _fuelAvailable--;
24                   _milesTraveled += _gasMileage;
25                   if (_fuelAvailable < 1) {
26                       this.removeEventListener(Event.ENTER_FRAME,
                         onLoop);
27                   }
28                   trace(this, _milesTraveled, _fuelAvailable);
29                   this.x = _milesTraveled;
30               }
31           }
32
33           public function changeGear():void {
34               trace(this, "changed gear");
35           }
36
37           public function useAccessory():void {
38               trace(this, "vehicle lights turned on");
39           }
40
```

```
41          public function go():void {
42                  _go = true;
43          }
44
45          public function get gasMileage():Number {
46                  return _gasMileage;
47          }
48
49          public function set gasMileage(mpg:Number):void {
50                  _gasMileage = mpg;
51          }
52
53          public function get fuelAvailable():Number {
54                  return _fuelAvailable;
55          }
56
57          public function set fuelAvailable(fuel:Number):void {
58                  _fuelAvailable = fuel;
59          }
60
61          public function get milesTraveled():Number {
62                  return _milesTraveled;
63          }
64
65          public function get tires():Tires {
66                  return _tires;
67          }
68
69          public function set tires(tires:Tires):void {
70                  _tires = tires;
71          }
72      }
73  }
```

Car class

A public method also named **useAccessory()** is added to the **Car** class. Because this method also exists in the **Vehicle** superclass, this would ordinarily cause a conflict. So, the subclass must override the superclass, using the **override** keyword. This allows this **Car** class version of the method to execute instead of the method of the same name in the **Vehicle** class.

However, the desired purpose is the same in both classes: to use an accessory. Therefore, the **useAccessory()** method calls the existing **openSunroof()** method, performing the appropriate task based on the data type of **Car** instead of **Vehicle**.

```
1   //Car.as
2   package {
3
4       import flash.display.MovieClip;
5       import flash.events.Event;
6
7       public class Car extends Vehicle {
8
9           public function Car(mpg:Number, fuel:Number) {
10              super(mpg, fuel);
11              var tires:Tires = new Tires("highperformance");
12              trace(this + " has " + tires.type + " tires");
13          }
14
15          public function openSunroof():void {
16              trace(this, "opened sunroof");
17          }
18
19          override public function useAccessory():void {
20              openSunroof();
21          }
22      }
23  }
```

Truck class

In some cases when overriding, you may not want to entirely replace behavior that exists in the superclass. In those scenarios, you can execute the desired custom code in the overridden method but also call the same method in the superclass. This is accomplished by preceding the method name by the **super** identifier, as seen in line 21 of the **Truck** class.

```
1   //Truck.as
2   package {
3
4       import flash.display.MovieClip;
5       import flash.events.Event;
6
7       public class Truck extends Vehicle {
8
9           public function Truck(mpg:Number, fuel:Number) {
10              super(mpg, fuel);
11              var tires:Tires = new Tires("snow");
12              trace(this + " has " + tires.type + " tires");
13          }
14
15          public function lowerTailgate():void {
16              trace(this, "lowered tailgate");
17          }
18
19          override public function useAccessory():void {
20              lowerTailgate();
21              super.useAccessory();
22          }
23
24      }
25  }
```

Tires class and main Flash file

No change to the **Tires** class is required, but, to demonstrate the effect of polymorphism, we must add two method calls to the **Car** and **Truck** instances. Lines 6 and 7 execute **changeGear()** and **useAccessory()** in the **compact** car, and lines 13 and 14 execute the same methods in the **pickup** truck.

```
1   //host .fla file
2   var compact:Car = new Car(21, 18);
3   compact.x = 10;
4   compact.y = 10;
5   addChild(compact);
6   compact.changeGear();
7   compact.useAccessory();
8
9   var pickup:Truck = new Truck(16, 23);
10  pickup.x = 10;
11  pickup.y = 100;
12  addChild(pickup);
13  pickup.changeGear();
14  pickup.useAccessory();
15
16  stage.addEventListener(MouseEvent.CLICK, onClick, false, 0, true);
17
18  function onClick(evt:MouseEvent):void {
19      compact.go();
20      pickup.go();
21  }
```

An abbreviated output is seen here:

```
[object Car] has high-performance radial tires
[object Car] changed gear
[object Car] opened sunroof
[object Truck] has storm-ready snow tires
[object Truck] changed gear
[object Truck] lowered tailgate
[object Truck] turned on lights
[object Car] 21 17
[object Truck] 16 22
[object Car] 42 16
[object Truck] 32 21
...
```

The first and fourth lines come from the composition use of the **Tires** class, tracing the kinds of tires used by the car and truck, respectively. The second and fifth lines show the car and truck changing gears because of a straight-forward method call. The third line shows the car entirely overriding the **useAccessory()** method of the **Vehicle** superclass, tracing only that the sunroof was opened. The sixth and seventh line, however, show the truck over-riding the **useAccessory()** method to lower its tailgate, but also calling the same method in the superclass to turn on the lights.

Navigation Bar Revisited

Chapter 5 concluded with a simple navigation bar created using procedural programming techniques. We are now going to step through a new exercise to demonstrate one way to approach the same task using OOP. This exercise combines the use of standalone external classes with classes that are linked to movie clips in the main Flash file, *LAS3Lab.fla*.

This exercise is also the start of the navigation system for the book/companion web site collective project. In this chapter, you will use a basic array to create five main buttons. Later, in Chapter 14, you will add submenus to this system and load all the content dynamically through the use of XML.

The files and directories you create here will continue to be used and enhanced throughout the remainder of this book, so establishing a logical directory structure now will be very helpful. The main *.fla* file and document class should reside in the top level of a new directory. Adjacent to the main Flash file you will create two directories for classes: *com* for general packages that you may use in multiple projects, and *app* for classes specific to this project that you are less likely to reuse. For each class included in this section, the code will begin with a comment that describes where in this directory structure the class belongs.

The main *.fla* file requires two symbols in the library, included in the companion source:

MenuButtonMain

> In our example, this is a movie clip that looks like a tab. Each main menu button appears above a horizontal line to collectively form a navigation bar. Inside the tab movie clip is a text field, instantiated as `_label`, which contains the label of the button. The symbol's linkage information identifies as its class a class of the same name, but in its appropriate directory, making the class path `app.gui.MenuButtonMain`.

HLineThick

> This is simply a thick line, approximately 8 pixels tall and the width of your file. This serves as the horizontal plane on which the main menu buttons reside to form the navigation bar. There's no external class for this line, as it has no functionality. To create it dynamically, give it a linkage class of `app.gui.HLineThick`. The nice thing about presupposing a class name in this manner is that, if you ever want to add functionality to this asset, you can create a class in this location and perhaps avoid additional edits to the main *.fla* file.

Document class

The entry point to this project is the document class, **LAS3Main.as**. Lines 4 and 5 import the **Sprite** class and custom **NavigationBar** class, which you'll create in a moment. The remainder of the script is the class that extends **Sprite** and the class constructor. This navigation bar can feature a variable number of buttons, determined by the contents of an array seen in line 10. Line 11 creates an instance of the **NavigationBar** class, passing references to the document class and array into the **NavigationBar** constructor. Finally, line 12 adds the navigation bar to the display list.

```
1    //LAS3Main.as
2    package {
3
4        import flash.display.Sprite;
5        import app.gui.NavigationBar;
6
7        public class LAS3Main extends Sprite {
8
9            public function LAS3Main() {
10               var appData:Array = ["one", "two", "three", "four",
                     "five"];
11               var navBar:NavigationBar = new NavigationBar(this,
                     appData);
12               addChild(navBar);
13           }
14       }
15   }
```

NavigationBar

Next we need to create the **NavigationBar** class, which instantiates the main menu buttons. Line 2 adds a qualifying path to the package directive, showing the directory structure in which the file lives. Line 9 references the linkage class identifier, **HLineThick**, in the Flash file's library.

Lines 12 through 16 encompass the class constructor, receiving the document class and button array, during instantiation. The constructor populates two private properties, and then calls the **build()** method.

```
1    // app > gui > NavigationBar.as
2    package app.gui {
3
4        import flash.display.Sprite;
5
6        public class NavigationBar extends Sprite {
7
8            private var _app:Sprite;
9            private var _hline:HLineThick;
10           private var _navData:Array;
11
12           public function NavigationBar(app:Sprite, navData:Array) {
13               _app = app;
14               _navData = navData;
15               build();
16           }
```

Within the **build()** method, the process of creating the tab buttons begins with a **for** loop that executes as many times as there are buttons. The loop creates an instance of the **MenuButtonMain** class, passing the name of the button from the array into the constructor. It then positions the button horizontally (accounting for the width and spacing multiplied by the number of current buttons each time through the loop, plus a 20-pixel offset from the left edge). It also positions each button at a fixed **y** location. Each button is added to the display list in line 22.

Finally, the horizontal bar from the Flash library is added to the bottom of the menu buttons (lines 25 through 28) and, to prevent mouse feedback and event trapping, the mouse is disabled for the horizontal bar.

```
17          private function build():void {
18              for (var i:uint; i < _navData.length; i++) {
19                  var menuBtn:MenuButtonMain =
                    new MenuButtonMain(_navData[i]);
20                  menuBtn.x = 20 + (menuBtn.width + 2) * i;
21                  menuBtn.y = 75;
22                  addChild(menuBtn);
23              }
24
25              _hline = new HLineThick();
26              _hline.y = 100;
27              _hline.mouseEnabled = false;
28              addChild(_hline);
29          }
30      }
31  }
```

MenuButtonMain

Finally, we present the **MenuButtonMain** class, which creates the main menu button for each menu. The only thing noteworthy among the first 10 lines is the fact that **_label** is a public property. This is because it references the text field inside the button that resides in the library of your main Flash file.

The constructor receives the string for the button label and puts it into the text field, as seen in line 13. It then disables mouse activity in the text field, so the mouse can respond to the underlying button and update the cursor to a hand when rolling over the button. To enable the hand cursor, the movie clip is set to behave as a button by setting both the **buttonMode** and **useHandCursor** properties to **true**.

Finally, an event listener is added so that, when the button is clicked, it will trace its own label to demonstrate a simplified button behavior. The resulting navigation bar is shown in Figure 6-2.

```
1   // app > gui > MenuButtonMain.as
2   package app.gui {
3
4       import flash.display.Sprite;
5       import flash.text.TextField;
6       import flash.events.MouseEvent;
7
```

```
8        public class MenuButtonMain extends Sprite {
9
10           public var _label:TextField;
11
12           public function MenuButtonMain(labl:String) {
13               _label.text = labl;
14               _label.mouseEnabled = false;
15               buttonMode = true;
16               useHandCursor = true;
17               addEventListener(MouseEvent.CLICK, onClick, false, 0,
                     true);
18           }
19
20           private function onClick(evt:MouseEvent):void {
21               trace(_label.text);
22           }
23       }
24   }
```

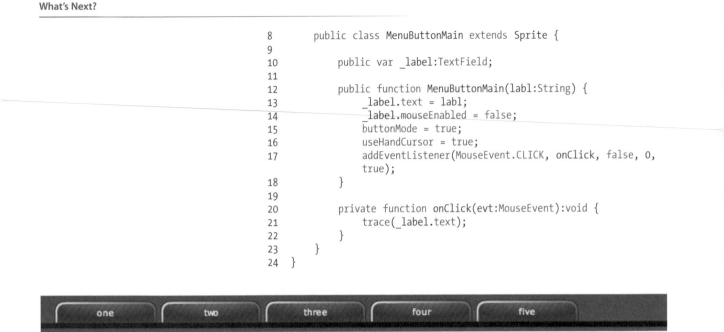

Figure 6-2. The finished navigation bar

What's Next?

Although we've only scratched the surface, this chapter presented some key concepts of object-oriented programming. As the chapter unfolded, and each section extended the vehicle/car/truck example, you addressed inheritance, added composition, improved data security with encapsulation, and simplified your method vocabulary with polymorphism. From a tutorial standpoint, the last set of files demonstrated basic best practices in all of these areas.

You also learned how to use classes as document classes and standalone classes that must be manually instantiated for each use. Finally, after getting a mere glimpse in Chapter 4, you learned how to link a class to a movie clip so the class would execute in tandem with the movie clip on the stage.

In the next chapter, we'll look at animating with ActionScript. You'll learn:

- Basic movement using the x- and y-coordinate system, velocity, and acceleration

- Light geometry and trigonometry, including circular movement, angle and distance calculation, and more

- Simplified physics, including gravity, friction, and springs

- ActionScript alternatives to timeline tweens, including easing

- Particle systems that put several of these principles into action while generating endless individual particles

CHAPTER 7

MOTION

From your very first experiment to the umpteenth time you've performed a familiar task, moving assets with code can be a gratifying experience. In addition to creating more dynamic work by freeing yourself from the permanency of the timeline, there is something very immediate and pleasing about controlling the motion of a symbol instance purely with ActionScript.

Because programming motion can cover a large number of concepts, we've chosen a few as the main focus areas for this subject. In each area, we offer what we call *simplified simulations*—that is, we do not maintain that our examples accurately reflect real-world scenarios. We won't be accounting for every possible force that can act on an object in each sample file. On the contrary, we try to present approaches to each topic that are simple enough to integrate into your projects with ease.

In addition to simplifying some topics, we also hope to show that math can be your friend. To some of you, this is a given, but to others, having to deal with numbers is an uphill journey. If you find yourself in the latter category, we hope to smooth over some of the smaller bumps that might be caused by a knee-jerk reaction to the need for math. Understanding just a few small applications of mathematical or scientific principles can really go a long way. You may even find yourself becoming comfortable with these principles and applying them even when there are other ways to accomplish a goal.

In this chapter, we'll look at the following topics:

- **Basic Movement.** We'll start with simple movement, updating x and y coordinates using constant velocities, and eventually adding acceleration.

- **Geometry and Trigonometry.** We'll then discuss three of the most basic principles of geometry and trigonometry. We'll show you how to determine the distance between two objects, and then how to animate objects in a circular path and point objects at a specific location.

- **Physics.** Friction, elasticity, and gravity add a bit of realism to animations, and you may be surprised how easy they are to simulate.

- **Programmatic Tweening.** Scripting movement entirely from scratch affords the greatest flexibility but also requires a fair amount of labor. Sometimes, a pre-written method or two can satisfy a basic need for motion. We'll demonstrate ActionScript's Tween class, and its occasional partner in crime, the Easing package.

- **Timeline Animation Recreations.** New to Flash CS3 is the ability to copy or export timeline tweens as XML and ActionScript. ActionScript 3.0's new Animator class can read that XML and recreate a timeline animation with ActionScript. We'll show you how to create a simple player for displaying such an animation.

- **Particle Systems.** We'll close out the chapter with an applied example covering much of what we've discussed herein, creating a simple particle system—a group of autonomous sprites that, taken collectively, simulate a complex material or environment, such as water, fireworks, or colonies of insects.

Basic Movement

When discussing scripted motion, a good place to begin is simple incrementing (increasing by a certain amount) or decrementing (decreasing by a certain amount) of x and y coordinates. Whether you realize it or not, you are probably used to working in a Cartesian coordinate system, where unique points are expressed on a single plane of two numbers, typically x and y. However, you are probably used to thinking about positive x values moving to the right and positive y values moving up, the way simple graphs are usually expressed.

The Flash coordinate system differs a bit from the typical coordinate system, in that the origin, or point (0, 0), is the upper-left corner of the stage, and y values increase when moving down. We will mention this again when it is directly applicable to an example, such as in Chapter 11 when you control sound volume with your mouse. However, if you try to remember this difference, you will probably have fewer surprises.

To increment or decrement a value, you simply add or subtract a unit from that value. Here are two example ways of doing this:

```
mc.x++;
mc.y--;

mc2.x += 10;
mc2.y -= 10;
```

The first example uses double plus signs to increment a movie clip's x coordinate by 1 and double minus signs to decrement its y coordinate by 1. If you need to add or subtract more than one unit, you can use a plus or minus sign followed by an equal sign to add the amount shown on the right side of the equation to the entity on the left side. The second example cited adds 10 pixels to the x coordinate and subtracts 10 pixels from the y coordinate. In both cases, because the amount added and subtracted is the same, these hypothetical movie clips will move up (subtracting y coordinate values moves a movie clip up) and to the right by 1 pixel in the first example, and move up and to the right 10 pixels in the second example.

As we start discussing speed, velocity, and acceleration, it might help to have a little background that you can relate to the code. Speed, or how fast an object is moving, is a *scalar* quantity. That means it is a value that can be expressed with a magnitude alone, such as 80 miles per hour. *Velocity* is the rate of change in movement, and is a vector quantity. It must be expressed with both a magnitude and a direction. In contrast to the definition of speed, velocity can be described as how fast in a particular direction, such as 80 miles per hour, South-South-East. *Acceleration* is also a vector quantity and is the rate of change in velocity.

These distinctions are subtle but helpful when it comes to getting from point a to point b. An easy way to remember each property is to think of your own movement. You can move very quickly, alternating one step forward and one step backward. This will give you speed but (from a simple way of looking at things) an overall velocity of 0. If you switch to always moving one step forward, you may move at the same speed but now have a constant velocity. If you increase your speed over time, while continuing to move forward, your velocity increases, giving you acceleration.

This is not terribly important if you just want to create a basic animation. However, as you begin to build more complex systems, it may help to understand what is required to meet your goals, and it may help you create more realistic simulations.

Velocity

Later on, we'll show you how to express a direction using an angle. For now, however, the direction of movement will be dictated by whether you increase or decrease x and y coordinates—that is, velocity is often implied in, or can be extrapolated from, simple code. For example, if you remember that positive x values move an object to the right, you can specify a velocity merely by incrementing an x coordinate.

Breaking out this change into a variable can make this clearer and easier to work with. For instance, if you think of always adding a velocity to a movie clip's position, you not only simplify your operator use, but you also need to add only a positive value to move in a positive direction, or add a negative value to move in a negative direction.

This code creates a ball from a library movie clip included in this lesson with the linkage identifier class **Ball**. It then adds 4 pixels to the ball's x and y coordinates each time the enter frame event occurs. This means the ball moves down and to the right, as depicted in multiple frames in Figure 7-1.

```
1    var ball:MovieClip = new Ball();
2    ball.x = ball.y = 100;
3    addChild(ball);
4
5    var xVel:Number = 4;
6    var yVel:Number = 4;
7
8    addEventListener(Event.ENTER_FRAME, onLoop, false, 0, true);
9    function onLoop(evt:Event):void {
10       ball.x += xVel;
11       ball.y += yVel;
12   }
```

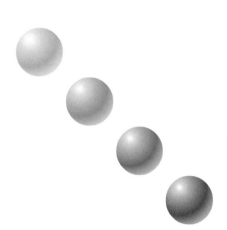

Figure 7-1. Simulated movement of a movie clip, at a constant velocity, down and to the right

Because the updated values are always 4 pixels, the ball is said to have a *constant velocity*. If you think of the **onLoop()** function executing once per second, the velocity would be 4 pixels per second, South-South-East. However, the function is executed every time the playhead enters the frame, so it's tied to the temp (frame rate). A frame rate of 20 frames per second (fps), therefore, would yield a velocity of 80 pixels (approximately one inch on a 72-pixel-per-inch monitor) per second. Let's see what happens if we vary the velocity over time.

Acceleration

Changing the velocity over time adds acceleration to an object. Consider the previous example of a constant velocity of 4 pixels down and to right. At 20 frames per second, this constant velocity (equivalent to 4 + 4 + 4 + 4, and so on) would take 3 seconds to move 240 pixels. However, if we accelerate the object 1 pixel per function execution, the changing velocity would look like 4 + 5 + 6 + 7 + 8, and so on. At that rate, using our 20 fps frame rate, the velocity would reach 23 pixels per iteration, and the ball would travel 270 pixels, in only one second. Acceleration is the compound interest of movement!

To realize this change, all you have to do is increment the velocity by the acceleration (rate of change of velocity) every time the function executes. Start with typed variables with initial values in lines 7 and 8, and then use them to increment the velocity in lines 15 and 16. This yields the effect of moving 4 pixels the first time, adding 1 to the velocity, moving 5 pixels the second time, adding 1, and so on.

```
1    var ball:MovieClip = new Ball();
2    ball.x = ball.y = 100;
3    addChild(ball);
4
5    var xVel:Number = 4;
6    var yVel:Number = 4;
7    var xAcc:Number = 1;
8    var yAcc:Number = 1;
```

```
 9
10   addEventListener(Event.ENTER_FRAME, onLoop, false, 0, true);
11   function onLoop(evt:Event):void {
12       ball.x += xVel;
13       ball.y += yVel;
14
15       xVel += xAcc;
16       yVel += yAcc;
17   }
```

The effect is a rapid acceleration of the ball along its set direction. Figure 7-2 illustrates this effect by depicting the increasing distance between ball positions.

The opposite of acceleration, deceleration can be simulated by decreasing the velocity. Later on, we'll use this technique, in part, to illustrate gravity, and we'll also look at a more sophisticated deceleration technique to simulate friction.

Figure 7-2. Acceleration increasing the velocity over time, simulated by increased movement in each frame

Geometry and Trigonometry

While many people find geometry and trigonometry intimidating, the small investment required to understand a few basic principles in these disciplines can pay large dividends. For example, what if you needed to find the distance between two points, or rotate one object around another? These small tasks are needed more often than you may think, and are easier to accomplish than you may realize.

Distance

Let's say you are programming a game in which a character must be pursued by an enemy and must exit through one of two doors to safety. However, the enemy is close enough that the character must choose the *nearest* exit to survive. The player controls the character, but you must make the game challenging enough for the enemy to catch the character if the player makes the wrong decision. To do that, the enemy must know which exit is closest.

To determine which of two objects (the doors) is closest to a given point (the enemy), you need only one formula called the Pythagorean theorem. Simplified, the theorem says that the length of the longest side of a right triangle is equal to the square root of the sum of the squares of the horizontal and vertical sides. For our needs, this can be determined by finding the differences between the two x values and two y values, and then checking the square root of the sum of those two squares. Figure 7-3 illustrates both descriptions.

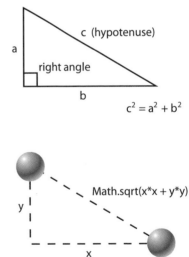

Figure 7-3. Calculating the distance between two points using geometry

To determine the distance between two points in ActionScript, you must calculate the difference between the x values of both points and multiply that difference by itself (squaring the value). Then do the same thing with the y values (squaring that difference, as well). Finally, following the Pythagorean theorem, use the Math object to return the square root of that sum.

```
function getDistance(x1:Number, y1:Number, x2:Number, y2:Number):
    Number {
    var dx:Number = x1 - x2;
    var dy:Number = y1 - y2;
    return Math.sqrt(dx * dx + dy * dy);
}
```

Here is an example usage of our **getDistance()** function, seen in the accompanying *distance2.fla* source file. It compares the distance between **ball0** and **ball1** to the distance between **ball0** and **ball2**:

```
var dist1 = getDistance(ball0.x, ball0.y, ball1.x, ball1.y);
var dist2 = getDistance(ball0.x, ball0.y, ball2.x, ball2.y);
if (dist1 < dist2) {
    trace("ball1 is closest to ball0");
} else {
    trace("ball2 is closest to ball0");
}
```

Movement Along an Angle

Earlier we discussed velocity as a vector quantity because it combined magnitude and direction. However, the direction in the previous example was determined by changing x and y coordinates. Unfortunately, such a direction is easily identifiable only when moving along simple paths, such as along the x or y axis. A much better way to indicate a direction is to specify an angle to follow.

Before we discuss angles and their different units of measure, it will help to understand how angles are indicated in the Flash coordinate system. As you might expect, angles are commonly referenced using degrees, but it's important to note that 0 degrees is along the x axis pointing to the right. The 360-degree circle then unfolds clockwise around the coordinate system. This means 90 degrees points down along the y axis, 180 degrees points left along the x axis, and so on. This is depicted in Figure 7-4.

Now that you have a correct point of reference, the next important concept to understand is that most of ActionScript, like most computer languages and mathematicians, does not use degrees as its preferred unit of measurement for angles. This is true for just about all common uses of angles, except for the **rotation** property of display objects and one or two somewhat more obscure items (such as a method of the **MatrixTransformer** class also used to rotate display objects). These entities use degrees as measure angles and to remain comfortable and familiar to users. The remainder of ActionScript uses *radians*: A *radian* is the angle of a circle defined by moving along the outside

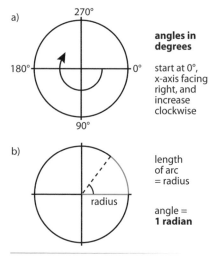

Figure 7-4. How Flash angles (a) and radians (b) are calculated

of the circle only for a distance as long as its radius, as seen in Figure 7-4. One radian is 180/PI degrees, which is approximately 57 degrees.

While some of that may prove helpful, or even interesting, for our purposes we don't need to memorize this information. Instead, all we need to do is remember that there is a formula handy for our conversion needs. Converting degrees to radians is accomplished by multiplying the original angle in degrees by (`Math.PI/180`). Conversely, radians can be converted to degrees by multiplying the original angle in radians by (`180/Math.PI`). In the upcoming example, we'll write a utility function for this purpose that we can use throughout the rest of our examples.

Now we're prepared to address the task at hand. We must send a movie clip off in a direction specified by an angle (direction) at a specific speed (magnitude). This will be the resulting velocity. This script starts by creating a movie clip and positioning it on stage at point (100, 100). It then specifies the speed and angle at which the movie clip will travel, and converts commonly used degrees to ActionScript-preferred radians using the utility function at the end of the script.

```
1    var ball:MovieClip = new Ball();
2    ball.x = ball.y = 100;
3    addChild(ball);
4
5    var speed:Number = 12;
6    var angle:Number = 45;
7    var radians:Number = deg2rad(angle);
```

With both a direction (angle) and magnitude (speed), the required velocities relative to the x and y axes can be determined. We accomplish this by using the **sine()** and **cosine()** methods of the **Math** class. Think of a triangle with one point at the origin of the x/y axes, as seen in Figure 7-5.

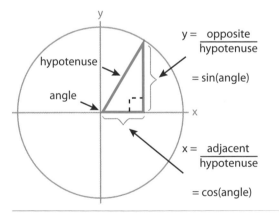

Figure 7-5. A point on a circle can be determined by using the cosine and sine of an angle, multiplied by a desired radius, to calculate the x and y values, respectively.

The sine of an angle is the length of the opposite side of the triangle divided by the length of the triangle's hypotenuse (which is the side opposite the triangle's right angle). The cosine of an angle is the length of the adjacent side of the triangle divided by the length of the triangle's hypotenuse. Therefore, the x component of the direction is determined by calculating the cosine of a specified angle, and the y component of the direction is determined by calculating the sine of the same angle. Multiply each value by the speed of the movement and you have a velocity vector.

```
8    var xVel:Number = Math.cos(radians) * speed;
9    var yVel:Number = Math.sin(radians) * speed;
```

All that remains is to add that change in velocity to the x and y coordinates of the ball and it's on the move.

```
10   addEventListener(Event.ENTER_FRAME, onLoop, false, 0, true);
11   function onLoop(evt:Event):void {
12       ball.x += xVel;
13       ball.y += yVel;
14   }
15
16   function deg2rad(deg:Number):Number {
17       return deg * (Math.PI / 180);
18   }
```

Circular Movement

Now that you know how to determine x and y coordinates from an angle, circular movement is a snap. For example, it will now be relatively trivial for you to move an object in a circle, the way a moon revolves around a planet. With circular movement, we are not interested in the velocity derived from direction and magnitude, because the ball in this example will not be traveling along that vector. Instead, we want to calculate the x and y coordinates of many consecutive angles. By plotting the sine and cosine of many angles, you can move the ball in a circle.

If you think of the sine and cosine values of various angles, this technique is easy to understand. (For simplicity, all angles will be discussed in degrees, but assume the calculations are performed with radians.) The values of both cosine and sine are always between -1 and 1. The x component, or cosine, of angle 0 is 1, and the y component, or sine, of angle 0 is 0. That describes point (1, 0), or straight out to the right. The cosine of 90 degrees is 0 and the sine of 90 is 1. That describes point (0, 1), or straight down.

This continues around the axes in a recognizable pattern. Remembering that we're discussing degrees but calculating in radians, the cosine and sine of 180 degrees are -1 and 0, respectively (point(-1, 0), straight to the left), and the cosine and sine of 270 degrees are 0 and 1, respectively (point(0, 1), straight up).

You have only two things you must still do to plot your movie clip along a circular path. Because all the values you're getting from your math functions are between -1 and 1, you must multiply these values by the desired radius of your circle. A calculated value of 1 times a radius of 150 equals 150, and multiplying -1 times 150 gives you -150. This describes a circle around the origin point of the axes, which spans from -150 to 150 in both horizontal and vertical directions.

Figure 7-6 illustrates these concepts in one graphic. Each color represents a different angle shown in degrees, with the x and y values expressed in both standard cosine and sine units (-1 to 1) and the result of multiplying that value by a desired radius of 150.

☐ deg = 50; rad = 50 * (Math.PI/180)
    x: Math.cos(rad) = 0.64; *0.64 * 150 = 96*
    y: Math.sin(rad) = 0.77; *0.77 * 150 = 114*

☐ deg = 140 °; rad = 140 * (Math.PI/180)
    x: Math.cos(rad) = -0.77; *-0.77 * 150 = -114*
    y: Math.sin(rad) = 0.64; *0.64 * 150 = 96*

☐ deg = 230 °; rad = 230 * (Math.PI/180)
    x: Math.cos(rad) = -0.64; *-0.64 * 150 = -96*
    y: Math.sin(rad) = -0.77; *-0.77 * 150 = -114*

☐ deg = 320 °; rad = 320 * (Math.PI/180)
    x: Math.cos(rad) = 0.77; *0.77 * 150 = 114*
    y: Math.sin(rad) = -0.64; *-0.64 * 150 = -96*

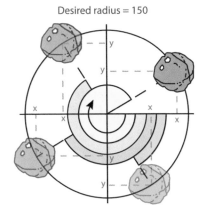

Desired radius = 150

Figure 7-6. Four angles rotating around a circle, expressed both in degrees and as x and y points on a circle with a radius of 150 pixels

Finally, you must position the circle wherever you want it on the stage. If you take no action, the object will rotate around the upper-left corner of the stage, or point(0, 0). This script centers the circle.

The first nine lines of the script initialize the important variables. Specified are a starting angle of 0, a circle radius of 150, an angle increment of 10, and a circle center that matches the center of the stage (its width and height divided by 2, respectively). Also created is the satellite that will be orbiting the center of the stage, derived from the **Asteroid** class. This uses the same technique you used to create the balls in the previous files, making a new display object from the linkage class of a library symbol, but you might need a little spice now, so an asteroid it is. To prevent a quick blink of the satellite at point(0,0), it is initially placed offstage in line 8 before becoming a part of the display list in line 9.

```
1    var angle:Number = 0;
2    var radius:Number = 150;
3    var angleChange:Number = 10;
4    var centerX:Number = stage.stageWidth/2;
5    var centerY:Number = stage.stageHeight/2;
6
7    var satellite:MovieClip = new Asteroid();
8    satellite.x = satellite.y = -200;
9    addChild(satellite);
```

The last part of the script is the frame loop and handy degree-to-radian conversion utility discussed earlier. The function begins by translating the specified angle from degrees to radians and determining the x (cosine) and y (sine) values that correspond to each angle. The function then multiplies each value by the desired radius and adds it to the origin point of the circle (in this case, center stage). After each plot, the angle is incremented (line 15) and then reset to an equivalent near-zero angle once it reaches or exceeds 360.

The angle value reset (line 16) is accomplished using the modulus operator, which simply determines the remainder after a division. For example, using the 10-degree increment in this example, 360 goes into 350 zero times, leaving a remainder of 340. However, 360 goes into 360 one time, leaving a remainder of 0. As a result, the angle is reset to 0, and you don't have to deal with angles like 370 or 380 degrees.

NOTE

The last step of the circular rotation script, resetting the angle on line 16, isn't wholly necessary because Flash will adjust angle values automatically. However, it's not a bad idea to understand what's going on in your scripts, in case you have to use a value for another purpose. Obviously, the fewer surprises you must face, the better.

```
10   addEventListener(Event.ENTER_FRAME, onLoop, false, 0, true);
11   function onLoop(evt:Event):void {
12       var radian:Number = deg2rad(angle);
13       satellite.x = centerX + radius * Math.cos(radian);
14       satellite.y = centerY + radius * Math.sin(radian);
15       angle += angleChange;
16       angle %= 360;
17   }
18
19   function deg2rad(deg:Number):Number {
20       return deg * (Math.PI / 180);
21   }
```

Rotation Toward an Object

Determining points on a circle when you start with an angle requires sine and cosine, as seen in the previous example. However, the opposite of that task requires a different trigonometric method. Determining an angle when starting with point data requires `atan2()`. This method of the `Math` class determines the angle between two points, based on two assumptions. The first is that the zero angle is on the right half of the x axis, and the second is that the angles increase moving counterclockwise from this zero point.

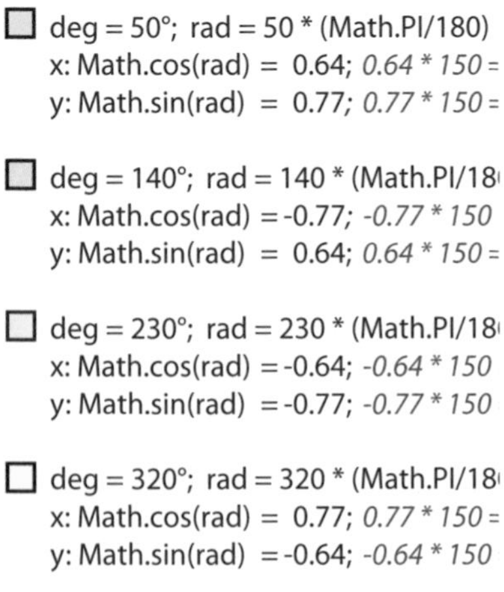

The `atan2()` method is especially useful when you want to use rotation to point something at another point. For instance, the next code example uses a frame event to continuously point a movie clip at the mouse location, no matter where the mouse is on the stage, as simulated in Figure 7-7.

There are two important issues to be aware of when using `atan2()`. The method always takes **y** point data as its first parameter (instead of **x**, which is more commonly placed in the first position), and the method returns its angle in radians, not degrees.

☐ deg = 50°; rad = 50 * (Math.PI/180)
 x: Math.cos(rad) = 0.64; *0.64 * 150 =*
 y: Math.sin(rad) = 0.77; *0.77 * 150 =*

☐ deg = 140°; rad = 140 * (Math.PI/18(
 x: Math.cos(rad) = -0.77; *-0.77 * 150*
 y: Math.sin(rad) = 0.64; *0.64 * 150 =*

☐ deg = 230°; rad = 230 * (Math.PI/18(
 x: Math.cos(rad) = -0.64; *-0.64 * 150*
 y: Math.sin(rad) = -0.77; *-0.77 * 150*

☐ deg = 320°; rad = 320 * (Math.PI/18(
 x: Math.cos(rad) = 0.77; *0.77 * 150 =*
 y: Math.sin(rad) = -0.64; *-0.64 * 150*

Figure 7-7. Using `atan2()`, *you can continuously point a movie clip at the mouse no matter where it is on the stage*

With that in mind, let's take a look at the script. It begins by creating a new instance of the **Hand** movie clip class from the library, placing it in the center of the stage, and adding it to the display list. The listener that follows in lines 6 through 9 then sets the rotation property of the resulting hand movie clip every time the playhead enters the frame. The angle is computed by the `getAngle()` function, after passing the location of the hand and mouse to the function.

```
1   var hand:MovieClip = new Hand();
2   hand.x = stage.stageWidth / 2;
3   hand.y = stage.stageHeight / 2;
4   addChild(hand);
5
6   addEventListener(Event.ENTER_FRAME, onLoop, false, 0, true);
7   function onLoop(evt:Event):void {
8       hand.rotation = getAngle(hand.x, hand.y, mouseX, mouseY);
9   }
```

The `atan2()` method in line 11 then subtracts the first location (the hand movie clip, which serves as the center of the circle), from the second location (in this case, think of the mouse as a point on a circle), to get its angle. However, remember that `atan2()` returns its angle value in radians, and you want to set the rotation of a movie clip, so degrees are required. Therefore, you must convert from radians to degrees using the `rad2deg()` function.

```
10  function getAngle(x1:Number, y1:Number, x2:Number, y2:Number):
    Number {
11      var radians:Number = Math.atan2(y2 - y1, x2 - x1);
12      return rad2deg(radians);
13  }
14
15  function rad2deg(rad:Number):Number {
16      return rad * (180 / Math.PI);
17  }
```

This example points one movie clip at the mouse, but the effect can be adapted in many ways. One obvious variant is to point a movie clip at another movie clip. Another visually interesting adjustment is to point many instances of a movie clip at the same object. A grid of such pointers, for example, looks interesting because each pointer rotates independently based on its location. Finally, the ultimate effect need not be visual. You can use this technique simply to track things, such as planning the trajectory of a projectile toward a target.

Physics

Adding physics to animations, games, and similar projects can really elevate them to another level of user enjoyment. The visual appearance and, in interactive scenarios, even the user experience, of a project are sometimes dramatically enhanced by surprisingly small code additions.

Although we're going to be discussing some basic physics principles in this section, it is initially more important to understand their effects than to focus minutely on the math and science behind them. For the scientifically minded, this should be viewed more as a matter of practicality than heresy. The formulas offered here are sometimes simplified, or even adapted, from their real-world counterparts for practical use or familiarity. Once you are comfortable with their uses, you can then refine their formulas, account for additional variables, and so on, to improve their realism. In short, it is often helpful to first simulate the simple orbit of a planet before considering the orbit's decay, the gravitational attraction of other bodies, and so on.

Gravity

Let's start off with a simple implementation of pseudo-physics that is based on an example used previously in this chapter. If you think about it, a basic Flash simulation of gravity requires little more than acceleration in the y direction, and requires only two small changes to the previous acceleration code. What do you think would happen if you added only 1 to the y velocity (meaning no change to the x velocity), and started out with a negative y value, as seen in the following code?

```
1   var ball:MovieClip = new Ball();
2   ball.x = ball.y = 100;
3   addChild(ball);
4
5   var xVel:Number = 4;
6   var yVel:Number = -10;
7   var yAcc:Number = 1;
8
9   addEventListener(Event.ENTER_FRAME, onLoop, false, 0, true);
10  function onLoop(evt:Event):void {
11      ball.x += xVel;
12      ball.y += yVel;
13
14      yVel += yAcc;
15  }
```

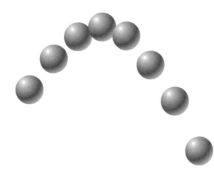

Figure 7-8. The effect of gravity on acceleration

NOTE

The role of the y acceleration in this discussion is important for future topics because it behaves as a coefficient of gravity. A coefficient is a modifier that alters a property of a system. It is often a multiplier, which we'll see in a little while, multiplying by a value less than 1 to reduce an effect, or by a value grater than 1 to exaggerate an effect. However, it can also add, subtract, or divide a value, as needed. If you altered the y acceleration value in the previous example to 2 or .5, it would be doubling or halving the amount of gravity applied, respectively.

This code would effectively simulate tossing a ball into the air. The ball would appear to rise initially because the y velocity is negative (remember that negative y is up in the Flash coordinate system). However, by adding a positive 1 in line 14, each time the function executes, the velocity decreases from -10 to -9 to -8, and so on, slowing the ball's ascent, just as if gravity were counteracting the upward force of the toss. Eventually, the y velocity reaches zero at the height of the toss, where the upward force and gravity reach equilibrium. Then the velocity changes to positive, continuing to increase by 1 each time. The value becomes 1, then 2, then 3, and so on, as the ball begins to accelerate downward due to the effect of gravity. Figure 7-8 shows the effect of the simulated gravity by depicting several frames of the animation at once. When a ball is tossed in the air, gravity slows its rate of ascent and then increases the rate at which it falls.

To continue your exploration of gravity, velocity, and acceleration, visit the book's companion web site. A file called *wall_bounce.fla* demonstrates all these concepts and adds several additional features. Included are conditionals to change the ball's direction when hitting a stage boundary, bounce behavior, and even a texture to simulate rotation during bouncing.

Friction

All other things being equal, if you slide a hockey puck along three surfaces—a street, a marble floor, and an ice rink—the puck will travel three different distances due to friction. Friction will be highest on the street, building up resistance to motion between the puck and the street surface, limiting the progress of the puck. Friction will be reduced on the marble surface, and lowest on the ice, allowing the puck to travel the farthest.

A simple way to add friction to an animation is to create a friction coefficient that gradually reduces velocity over time. To demonstrate this, we'll start with the example from the "Movement Along an Angle" section. You'll only need to do two things to add friction. First, create the coefficient variable, as seen in line 10, and then multiply the x and y velocities by this coefficient in lines 14 and 15. Remember that friction hinders movement, so you want to choose a friction value between 0 and 1. Depending on the application, you can vary the number. Perhaps you might use .97 for ice, .90 for marble, and .60 for asphalt.

```
1    var ball:MovieClip = new Ball();
2    ball.x = ball.y = 100;
3    addChild(ball);
4
5    var speed:Number = 12;
6    var angle:Number = 45;
7    var radians:Number = deg2rad(angle);
8    var xVel:Number = Math.cos(radians) * speed;
9    var yVel:Number = Math.sin(radians) * speed;
10   var frCoeff:Number = 0.95;
11
12   addEventListener(Event.ENTER_FRAME, onLoop, false, 0, true);
13   function onLoop(evt:Event):void {
14       xVel *= frCoeff;
15       yVel *= frCoeff;
16       ball.x += xVel;
17       ball.y += yVel;
18   }
19
20   function deg2rad(deg:Number):Number {
21       return deg * (Math.PI / 180);
22   }
```

NOTE

The effect of friction may be familiar to you as one kind of easing. Easing is so named because when used, an object appears to "ease in" to an animation, accelerating as the animation progresses, or "ease out" of an animation, decelerating as the animation finishes. We'll discuss several more elaborate easing equations already built in to ActionScript later in this chapter.

Zeno's Paradox

Another way to add friction to object movement is to use *Zeno's paradox*, which says that, when moving from one point to another, you never really reach your ultimate destination because you are dividing the remaining distance with every movement. If you divide the distance between point a and point b in half with every step, theoretically, you could never reach point b. Philosophy aside, this idea can be used to slow down an object as it approaches its destination, as illustrated in Figure 7-9.

Figure 7-9. Zeno's paradox, a simple way to depict friction or easing

This is especially handy when you simply want to add basic deceleration between two points and don't need a more elaborate system. The following example starts by creating a ball movie clip from the library, and then calls the **onLoop()** function every enter frame. **onLoop()** updates the movie clip's x and y coordinates separately by calling the **velFriction()** function, passing in the origin location, destination location, and number of times you want to divide the distance traveled.

```
1    var ball:MovieClip = new Ball();
2    ball.x = ball.y = 100;
3    addChild(ball);
4
5    addEventListener(Event.ENTER_FRAME, onLoop, false, 0, true);
6    function onLoop(evt:Event):void {
7        ball.x += velFriction(ball.x, mouseX, 8);
8        ball.y += velFriction(ball.y, mouseY, 8);
9    }
10
11   function velFriction(orig:Number, dest:Number, coeff:Number):
     Number {
12       return (dest - orig) / coeff;
13   }
```

The **velFriction()** function calculates the difference between the origin and destination point values and divides the result by the number of steps used to close the distance. Note that, despite the commonly stated form of Zeno's paradox, you do not always have to cut the distance in half using two steps. In fact, this is how you vary the animation's deceleration. Higher numbers require more time for the object to reach its destination, and lower numbers finish the animation more quickly. This value can be thought of as a friction coefficient.

Elasticity

Another property of physics that can liven up animations is elasticity. Elastic properties can be applied to spring simulations, of course, but can also be used as another easing method.

Elasticity is easily calculated using *Hooke's law*. Hooke's law says that the force exerted by a spring is linearly proportional to the distance it is stretched or compressed. It is expressed with the formula $F = -kx$. F is the resulting force, -k is a spring constant, indicating the strength of the spring, and x is the distance to which the spring is deformed. (Although not vital to this discussion, the equation is expressed as a negative because the force expressed by the spring, often called a restorative force, is not in the same direction as the force applied to the spring.)

The following example uses elasticity to settle a movie clip into each new location. The movie clip moves from a starting position to wherever the mouse is moved, bouncing around the destination until settled, as seen in Figure 7-10.

origin   2   4 5   3   1

Figure 7-10. A basic depiction of easing using Hooke's law of elasticity

The script starts by creating a movie clip and initializing x and y velocity variables. It then creates an enter frame listener that calls an elasticity function in lines 10 and 11 that determines both the x and y velocity, and increments the x and y positions of the ball over time. The elasticity function is called separately for x and y values, allowing greater flexibility in which property to affect. For example, to calculate the force of a spring in a cylinder, you might want to affect only the y value, rather than both x and y values. Passed to the function in lines 10 and 11 are the movie clip's starting and ending positions, the spring constant, a damping factor (both of which will be explained in a moment), and the current x and y velocities. Finally, the x and y locations of the movie clip are updated with the newly calculated velocities.

```
1    var ball:MovieClip = new Ball();
2    ball.x = ball.y = 100;
3    addChild(ball);
4
5    var xVel:Number = 0;
6    var yVel:Number = 0;
7
8    addEventListener(Event.ENTER_FRAME, onLoop, false, 0, true);
9    function onLoop(evt:Event):void {
10       xVel = velElastic(ball.x, mouseX, 0.14, 0.85, xVel);
11       yVel = velElastic(ball.y, mouseY, 0.14, 0.85, yVel);
12       ball.x += xVel;
13       ball.y += yVel;
14   }
```

All that remains is the elasticity calculation itself. The velocity with elasticity is calculated first by employing Hooke's law. The elastic force is determined in line 16 by multiplying the spring constant (the strength of the spring) by the distance between the starting point and the mouse location (the distance the fictional spring is stretched). This elasticity is compounded using the += operator so the value can vary with each new position of the movie clip and/or mouse. Because springs don't have infinite energy, the elastic force is dampened every time the function is called, exerting only 85 percent of the last force value on the current elasticity until the springiness is reduced to nothing.

```
15   function velElastic(orig:Number, dest:Number, springConst:Number,
     damp:Number, elas:Number):Number {
16       elas += -springConst * (orig - dest);
17       return elas *= damp;
18   }
```

Programmatic Tweening

When you need a relatively simple animation and don't want to spend time and effort coding it yourself, you may be able to use Flash's built-in **Tween** class. An example file called *as_tween.fla* can be found in the accompanying source code. The **Tween** class allows you to specify the compatible display object and property you wish to tween, the precreated easing function that will affect the property change, the beginning and finishing values of the property, the duration of the tween, and, finally, whether to use seconds or frames when evaluating the tween's duration. Here is a look at the class's constructor.

```
Tween(obj:Object, prop:String, func:Function, begin:Number, finish:
     Number, duration:Number, useSeconds:Boolean)
```

The following example creates a ball movie clip, places it at point (100, 100), and then creates the tween. It alters the x coordinate of the movie clip, using an elastic easing. It begins at position 100 and finishes at position 400, and it takes 3 seconds (indicated by the **true** value of the last parameter, *useSeconds*) to complete the tween.

```
1    import fl.transitions.Tween;
2    import fl.transitions.easing.*;
3
4    var ball:MovieClip = new Ball();
5    ball.x = ball.y = 100;
6    addChild(ball);
7
8    var ballXTween:Tween = new Tween(ball, "x", Elastic.easeOut, 100,
     400, 3, true);
```

NOTE

In this case, if the last parameter was **false***, the tween duration would be measured in frames. Considering a tempo of 20 frames per second, a frame equivalent of 3 seconds would be 60.*

Because a single tween instance controls a single property, it is possible, and even quite common, to create multiple tweens for the same object. Additional tweens don't even have to have values that keep pace with other related **Tween** class instances. For example, adding this new emphasized line (line 9) to the previous script will fade the opacity (**alpha**) of the **ball** movie clip from a value of 30 percent to 100 percent across the same 3 seconds, but in a linear process with no easing effect.

```
9    var ballAlphaTween:Tween = new Tween(ball, "alpha", None.easeOut,
     .3, 1, 3, true);
```

The **Tween** class has several additional properties, methods, and events for use by each instance of the class. Notable properties include the Booleans **isPlaying** and **looping** (indicating whether the animation is in progress and looping, respectively), and the Number **position**. The **position** property indicates the current value of the tweening property, so it refers to the current position of the *tween*, not the x/y position of the display object on stage—that is, the `ballAlphaTween` instance seen previously still reports the `position` variable, even though the alpha value of the movie clip is being tweened.

Available methods include several navigation options, which command the tween to stop, start, and resume playback, jump to the next, previous, first, and last frames of the animation, and play only until a specified point in the tween is reached. Events associated with the tween are fired when the animation is started, stopped, or resumed, when it loops or finishes, and even during the animation each time the screen is updated.

Select the easing class to use via the `fl.transitions.easing` package. Although specifying an easing class is required, one of the available options is **None**, so you don't have to apply an easing effect to your tween. The names and descriptions of available easing classes can be found in Table 7-1.

Table 7-1. Easing types found in the `fl.transitions.easing` *package*

Easing Class	Description
Back	Easing in begins by backing up and then moving toward the target. Easing out overshoots the target and backtracks to approach it.
Bounce	Bounces in with increasing speed, or out with decreasing speed.
Elastic	Undulates in an exponentially decaying sine wave, accelerating in and decelerating out.
None	Linear motion without easing.
Regular	Normal easing, like that found in the timeline's simple easing feature, accelerating in and decelerating out.
Strong	Emphasized easing, stronger than that found in the timeline's simple easing feature, but without additional effects. Accelerates in and decelerates out.

Each class has a minimum of three methods to cover easing in, easing out, and easing both in and out of the tween. All methods for each class support initial and final values of the property being animated, the duration of the easing, and the current time in the animation. Back also supports a value for the degree of overshoot beyond the target at the start and/or end of the animation, and Elastic adds support for the amplitude and period of the sine wave used to calculate the elasticity.

Timeline Animation Recreations

While this isn't entirely an ActionScript solution, we'd like to cover Flash CS3's new **Motion** and **Animator** classes. These classes, and their supporting players, make it possible to replay animations that have been created previously in the timeline. Scripting purists may be more interested in perfecting their ActionScript skills than relying on the timeline to originate animations.

However, this capability may be attractive to many Flash CS3 users, even coding curmudgeons, for two reasons.

First, it doesn't ultimately use the timeline but still makes it possible to reproduce complex animfations created there—including animations that might not be that easy to achieve strictly with ActionScript. Second, it offers a new path to improved designer-programmer collaboration. Designers can create timeline animations, and programmers can integrate that work into other projects without relying on the original timeline structure.

The foundation of this process exists in a feature called "Copy Motion as ActionScript 3.0." After creating a timeline tween, you can select the entire tween and then choose the Copy Motion as ActionScript 3.0 menu option from the Edit®Timeline menu. This copies to the clipboard all necessary information to recreate the tween with code. During the copy process, the feature prompts you for the tweened symbol's instance name with a convenient dialog—prepopulated if the instance name already exists.

Once the copy completes, you can paste the results in the Actions panel. All the ActionScript needed is included, and the motion is represented by XML information in the format required by the **Motion** class. A simple example, tweening a movie clip across the stage over 20 frames, follows:

```
1    import fl.motion.Animator;
2    var ball_xml:XML = <Motion duration="20" xmlns="fl.motion.*" xmlns:
     geom="flash.geom.*" xmlns:filters="flash.filters.*">
3        <source>
4            <Source frameRate="12" x="50" y="50" scaleX="1" scaleY="1"
                 rotation="0" elementType="movie clip" instanceName="ball"
                 symbolName="Ball">
5                <dimensions>
6                    <geom:Rectangle left="-10" top="-10" width="20"
                         height="20" />
7                </dimensions>
8                <transformationPoint>
9                    <geom:Point x="0.5" y="0.5" />
10               </transformationPoint>
11           </Source>
12       </source>
13
14       <Keyframe index="0">
15           <tweens>
16               <SimpleEase ease="0" />
17           </tweens>
18       </Keyframe>
19
20       <Keyframe index="19" x="450" />
21   </Motion>;
22
23   var ball_animator:Animator = new Animator(ball_xml, ball);
24   ball_animator.play();
```

Looking over the generated XML, you can pick out properties such as **duration**, **frameRate**, **x** and **y** coordinates, **scale**, and **rotation**. Also included are the display object type (movie clip), its instance name, and information about its dimensions, registration point, and transformation point. Finally, data about each keyframe is cited, including in which frame each resides, what kind of easing is used, and any information that has changed from keyframe to keyframe. In this case, only the x coordinate has been tweened, so the second keyframe itemizes only this property.

As you can see, everything you need to reproduce the tween is included in the XML, here stored in the variable **ball_xml**. The last two lines of this example include the instantiation of the **Animator** class, passing in the XML and target movie clip instance name. This class is responsible for playing back the animation, which occurs in line 24. To see the feature work, you can remove the tween from the timeline, place a movie clip with the same instance name on the stage, and test your movie.

This workflow is obviously not something you can carry over to runtime. However, you can do better. With the entire tween selected, you can use the Export Motion XML command found in the Commands menu. This saves the Motion XML only, without the ActionScript that accompanies the copy-paste workflow, into an external file. From there, you can build an Animator player all your own.

The following example reproduces a motion guide tween that traces the word "Flash" in script, with a ball movie clip. The original motion guide, which is the path the **Animator** class will retrace, can be seen in Figure 7-11. The figure shows two copies of the word because you later can use ActionScript to scale the animation, tracing the word at either size. The XML file needed to recreate this tween is quite long, so it cannot be reproduced here. However, the original file, *handwriting.fla*, is with the book's source code on the companion web site, and the animation has already been exported to *handwriting.xml* for easy download.

Figure 7-11. The motion guides used to create a tween that is recreated with the **Animator** *class*

This example creates a player that controls playback of the original animation in a new file. It requires nothing more than a movie clip to animate, and the Button component, which we'll use to create the controller buttons.

The first 10 lines of the script import the necessary classes, declare the needed variables, and create and position a ball movie clip from the library, but does not yet add it to the display list.

```
1    import fl.motion.*;
2    import flash.geom.*;
3    import fl.controls.Button;
4
5    var anim:Animator;
6    var isPaused:Boolean;
7    var isScaled:Boolean;
8
9    var ball:Sprite = new Ball();
10   ball.x = ball.y = 80;
```

The next segment covers the loading, and response thereto, of the external XML file. We'll cover this in greater detail in Chapter 13, but here's the essence of the matter. All URLs are handled consistently, passing through the **URLRequest** class. This class captures all HTML information, like MIME types, headers, and so on. In this case, we need only the URL file path to pass to the **URLLoader** class.

The information the **URLLoader** class loads can be text, raw binary data, or URL-encoded variables. In this case, the XML document is loaded as text. The event listener in line 13 reacts when this information has been completely loaded by calling the **xmlLoaded()** function.

```
11   var xml_url:URLRequest = new URLRequest("handwriting.xml");
12   var xml_loader:URLLoader = new URLLoader(xml_url);
13   xml_loader.addEventListener("complete", xmlLoaded, false, 0, true);
```

The **xmlLoaded()** function converts the loaded text to XML and instantiates the **Animator** class, passing both the XML and ball movie clip instance to the class. From this class, the **motion** object can provide information about the XML data that has been loaded. Because we know that the original tween includes color as well as position, we add line 17 to query the color in the first keyframe of that motion data, and set the initial color of the ball movie clip to that same color. This prevents the movie clip from appearing in its default color and then abruptly switching to the color of the first frame of the animation once it starts.

When these initializations are complete, it is safe to add the ball movie clip to the display list and, to round out the **xmlLoaded()** function, create another listener to react to the end of the animation. The listener's function, in lines 22 through 24, simply resets the name of a Play button, which we will discuss in the next code block.

```
14   function xmlLoaded(evt:Event):void {
15       var anim_xml:XML = XML(xml_loader.data);
16       anim = new Animator(anim_xml, ball);
```

```
17        ball.transform.colorTransform = anim.motion.keyframes[0].color;
18        addChild(ball);
19        anim.addEventListener(MotionEvent.MOTION_END, onMotionEnd,
          false, 0, true);
20    }
21
22    function onMotionEnd(evt:MotionEvent):void {
23        Button(getChildByName("Play")).label = "Play";
24    }
```

The following segment of ActionScript is responsible for creating all the buttons that will control the animation. The **createController()** function walks through a loop that creates as many buttons as are named in the array that is passed to it. Each time through the loop, an instance of the Button component is created and positioned, its width is adjusted, and its label and name are set to the string in the current index of the function array. Lastly, a mouse click listener is added to the array to trigger the function responsible for navigation, and the button is added to the display list. This process takes place five times, to match the five button names in the array passed to the function.

```
25    createController(["Play", "Pause", "Stop", "Next Frame", "Toggle
      Scale"]);
26
27    function createController(btns:Array):void {
28        for (var i:Number = 0; i<btns.length; i++) {
29            var btn:Button = new Button();
30            btn.x = 35 + i * 100;
31            btn.y = 350;
32            btn.width = 80;
33            btn.label = btns[i];
34            btn.name = btns[i];
35            btn.addEventListener(MouseEvent.CLICK, onNav, false, 0,
              true);
36            addChild(btn);
37        }
38    }
```

The last function in the script handles all the navigation for the animation. When a button is clicked, the listener calls this function, passing information about the event and, by extension, the button itself. Based on the name of the button, one of five blocks in a **switch** statement executes, invoking methods from the **Animator** class, as well as other tasks. If you are unfamiliar with the **switch** statement, please consult Chapter 2 for more information.

The Play button first confirms that the animation is not already playing and, if it is not playing, checks to see whether it's paused. If so, it resumes playback and clears the **isPaused** flag. If not, it plays the animation from the beginning. The Pause button pauses the animation and sets the **isPaused** flag. It also switches the label of the Play button to reflect the animation's paused status. The Stop button stops and rewinds the animation, clears the **isPaused** flag, and sets the label of the Play button back to "Play." The last playback control simply advances the animation to its next frame.

```
39   function onNav(evt:MouseEvent):void {
40       switch (evt.target.name) {
41           case "Play" :
42               if (!anim.isPlaying) {
43                   if (isPaused) {
44                       anim.resume();
45                       isPaused = false;
46                   } else {
47                       anim.play();
48                   }
49               }
50               break;
51           case "Pause" :
52               anim.pause();
53               isPaused = true;
54               Button(getChildByName("Play")).label = "Resume";
55               break;
56           case "Stop" :
57               anim.stop();
58               anim.rewind();
59               isPaused = false;
60               Button(getChildByName("Play")).label = "Play";
61               break;
62           case "Next Frame" :
63               anim.nextFrame();
64               break;
65           case "Toggle Scale" :
66               var m:Matrix = anim.positionMatrix = new Matrix();
67               var s:Number;
68               if (isScaled) {
69                   s = 1;
70                   isScaled = false;
71               } else {
72                   s = 0.5;
73                   isScaled = true;
74               };
75               MatrixTransformer.setScaleX(m, s);
76               MatrixTransformer.setScaleY(m, s);
77               break;
78       }
79   }
```

The final button in the controller just begins to hint at some of the most interesting things you can do to the preexisting animations. The **Animator** class has a property called the **positionMatrix** that allows you to alter the animation as a whole. It can be shifted, scaled, rotated, and/or skewed without otherwise distorting its appearance. The final controller button toggles the animation between full- and half-scale, the paths of which are both visible in Figure 7-11. If the animation is already scaled, the Toggle Scale button will toggle the scale value between full- and half-size, and set the **isScaled** flag accordingly. Finally, the code uses the static **MatrixTransformer** class—which automatically adjusts a matrix for you to reflect your desired changes—invoking the **setScaleX()** and **setScaleY()** methods to scale the entire animation.

With the ability not only to control, but also to easily transform, a potentially complex timeline tween entirely through ActionScript, the **Animator** class has a lot of potential for both utility and creativity. Many animations can be lovingly crafted and tweaked in the timeline and can be played back anywhere through code, again and again—even swapped and loaded from external sources at runtime. Entire libraries of highly portable animations can be created and stored in efficient XML formats. Even if you entirely focus on ActionScript, the **fl.motion** package, in which both the **Motion** and **Animator** classes reside, may be worth a look.

Particle Systems

Particle systems are a way of simulating complex objects or materials that are composed of many small particles, such as fluids, fireworks, explosions, fire, smoke, water, snow, and so on. Complex systems are achievable because individual particles are generated, each is given its own characteristics, and each behaves autonomously. Further, the particles themselves are typically easy to adjust, or even replace, making it possible to alter the appearance or functionality of the system relatively easily. These are also characteristics of object-oriented programming, so it's not surprising that particle systems are often written using this approach.

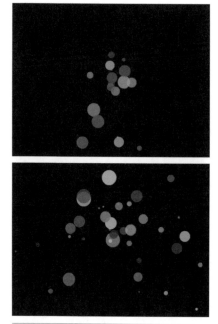

To end this chapter, we'd like to create a very simple particle system—using only two classes—which looks a little bit like a psychedelic water fountain. Color circles shoot up out of the "fountain" and then fall down under the effect of gravity. Figure 7-12 shows what the system looks like.

The entry point to the particle system is the document class **ParticleDemo**. After declaring variables to determine the point at which the particles will appear, all the class constructor does is add an enter frame event listener to the stage. Upon every enter frame event, the listener function creates a new instance of the **Particle** class, which creates a particle and adds it to the display list.

Figure 7-12. A particle system with a gravity setting of 2 and .2

```
1   package {
2
3       import flash.display.Sprite;
4       import flash.events.Event;
5
6       public class ParticleDemo extends Sprite {
7
8           private var emitterX:Number = stage.stageWidth / 2;
9           private var emitterY:Number = stage.stageHeight / 2;
10
11          public function ParticleDemo() {
12              stage.addEventListener(Event.ENTER_FRAME, onLoop,
                    false, 0, true);
13          }
14
```

```
15          private function onLoop(evt:Event):void {
16              var p:Particle = new Particle(emitterX,
17                                            emitterY,
18                                            Math.random() * 11 - 6,
19                                            Math.random()
20                                            1,
21                                            Math.random() * 0xFFFFFF);
22              addChild(p);
23          }
24      }
25  }
```

Five parameters pass to each class when its particle is created. The first two are the x and y coordinates of the particle emitter which dictate the origin location for each new particle. The next two parameters are randomly chosen values for the x and y velocities. The first value is for the x velocity, and is between -5 and 5. That's because the range of numbers is 0 to 11, but subtracting 6 offsets the selected value. The y velocity is between 0 and -20, so particles start by moving up. Next are a gravity value of 1 and a random color for each particle in the range of black (0x000000) to white (0xFFFFFF).

To see how the particle generator works, look within the **Particle** class. The first 13 lines cover the required setup, including importing the **display** and **geom** packages, and the **Event** class from the events package. Also included are the declaration of the position, velocity, and gravity variables that are private to this class.

```
1   package {
2
3       import flash.display.*;
4       import flash.geom.*
5       import flash.events.Event;
6
7       public class Particle extends Sprite {
8
9           private var _xpos:Number;
10          private var _ypos:Number;
11          private var _xvel:Number;
12          private var _yvel:Number;
13          private var _grav:Number;
```

First, the class constructor populates the private variables with the parameters passed in from the document class described earlier. Next, it creates a particle from the **Ball** class in the library and adds it to the display list. The constructor then sets four values: the particle's x and y position, opacity, and x and y scale. The same range-plus-offset technique used for x velocity when creating the particle is also used here for scale. This allows a scale range up to 200 percent, but guarantees a minimum scale of 10 percent.

```
14          public function Particle(xp:Number, yp:Number, xvel:Number,
            yvel:Number, grav:Number, col:uint) {
15              _xpos = xp;
16              _ypos = yp;
17              _xvel = xvel;
18              _yvel = yvel;
19              _grav = grav;
```

```
20
21              var ball:Sprite = new Ball();
22              addChild(ball);
23
24              x = _xpos;
25              y = _ypos;
26              alpha = 0.8;
27              scaleX = scaleY = Math.random() * 1.9 + .1;
28
29              var colorInfo:ColorTransform = ball.transform.
                colorTransform;
30              colorInfo.color = uint(col);
31              ball.transform.colorTransform = colorInfo;
32
33              addEventListener(Event.ENTER_FRAME, onRun, false, 0,
                true);
34          }
```

Lines 29 through 31 assign the particle's color by way of the **ColorTransform**
class. The first step in this process is to store the particle's default **colorTransform** information (which allows manipulation of the red, blue, green, and
alpha channels of the color), retrieved from the particle's **transform** object.
Next, line 30 changes the **color** property of the **colorTransform** to the new
color passed into the **col** argument.

However, that property prefers a **uint** data type (non-negative whole number) and the initial random color selection made when creating the particle
converted the color to a **Number** data type. Therefore, it's a good idea to cast
the number back to **uint** with the **uint()** data casting method. Finally, once
the color has been changed, update the particle's own **colorTransform** object
using the one in the variable you've been manipulating.

The last line of the constructor adds an enter frame listener to control the
particle's movement. It triggers the **onRun()** function, which follows. This
function uses the techniques discussed in the velocity and gravity examples
of this chapter, but adds one thing. A conditional determines whether the
next particle position is off the stage on the left, top, right, or bottom edge. If
so, the event listener is removed and the particle is removed from the display
list, ready for garbage collection.

```
35          private function onRun(evt:Event):void {
36              _yvel += _grav;
37              _xpos += _xvel;
38              _ypos += _yvel;
39              x = _xpos;
40              y = _ypos;
41
42              if (_xpos < 0 || _ypos < 0 || _xpos >
                stage.stageWidth || _ypos > stage.stageHeight) {
43                  removeEventListener(Event.ENTER_FRAME, onRun);
44                  parent.removeChild(this);
45              }
46          }
47      }
48  }
```

Particle systems are a lot of fun and can lead to many fruitful experiments. Run this system several times, modifying the values sent to the **Particle** class. Change the x and y velocities for a larger spread of particles, decrease the force of gravity to see what particle life is like on the moon, or even set the emitter location to the mouse location to move the system around.

Try to move some of the hard-coded properties, like **alpha**, **scaleX**, and **scaleY** into the argument list so they can be varied, too. As an example, we've created another version of this system for the book's companion web site that includes several new properties, including filter and blend mode settings that you'll learn about in the next chapter.

What's Next?

While this chapter details a variety of ActionScript animation techniques, it only begins to cover the subject of motion through code. However, the basic building blocks are here, and it's with these concepts (and related skills that grow from the ideas herein) that greater art and industry can be achieved.

Next on the to-do list is the ability to partially free yourself from the constraints of the Flash interface and approach code-only projects with a little more latitude. When working with visual assets, we've so far relied on symbols created within Flash and stored in the library of a SWF. We will continue to do that any time complex art warrants this practice, but we'll also begin to work with vectors and bitmaps created with code. In addition to giving you more freedom, this approach can also reduce file size and make your SWFs load faster.

In the next chapter, we'll discuss:

- Using the **Graphics** class to draw vectors to create assets on the fly without contributing to file size

- Calling methods of the **flash.geom** package to use rectangles and points in your scripts

- Using 9-slice scaling to achieve distortion-free symbol instance scaling

DRAWING WITH VECTORS

Drawing vectors with code brings with it special benefits. Included among them is the freedom to create assets on the fly, rather than be committed strictly to art drawn or imported at author-time. Related to this is the additional bonus of reduced file size, because assets are created at runtime rather than occupying space in your SWF. Smaller files mean your projects are delivered more quickly to the end user, and the experience is more enjoyable.

In this chapter, we'll focus on the first of two ways to create visual assets with code—drawing vectors. The next chapter will focus on creating and compositing bitmaps.

- **The Graphics class.** This class, casually referred to as the drawing API in its prior incarnation, contains methods for drawing vectors. You have control over stroke and fill attributes, and can move a virtual pen tool around choosing where to draw lines, curves, and shapes like circles and rectangles.

- **The Geometry package.** This utility package contains classes for creating points and rectangles, as well as transforming objects and their color, and creating matrices for complex simultaneous changes to rotation, scaling, and x and y translation. Using matrices, it's possible to achieve affects for which no properties exist, including skew and shear.

- **9-slice Scaling.** Through the use of a dynamically assignable rectangle, you can employ 9-slice scaling to prevent the sides and corners of a sprite or movie clip from distorting when scaled.

- **Applied Examples.** Combining what you'll learn in this chapter, you'll be able to create a simple color picker and a custom button class that can be reused from project to project.

The Graphics Class

You can use the **Graphics** class to define line and fill styles, and draw lines, curves, and shapes, similar to how you would by using the Flash interface. Before we get started with syntax-specific discussions, here's a quick word of advice. It is possible to draw vectors directly into the main timeline, but we recommend that you first create one or more display objects to serve as canvases for your drawings. This gives you much more flexibility and power when it comes to displaying list operations and effects.

For example, if you first create a canvas for a drawing, you can change its depth, assign it to a new parent, or change many display object properties to affect the appearance or functionality of the canvas. Similarly, as you'll learn in the next chapter, you can apply special effects and filters to a display object, which can't be applied directly to the stage.

All methods of the **Graphics** class must be called from the **graphics** property of the display object with which you are working. This is a departure from prior versions of ActionScript and something to watch for when migrating to ActionScript 3.0. As a shortcut, it is sometimes useful to create a reference to the canvas and graphics object into which you will be drawing. For example, the following code creates a sprite canvas and references its graphics object. (In these examples, *<method>* is a placeholder for syntax we are about to introduce.)

```
var sp:Sprite = new Sprite();
var g:Graphics = sp.graphics;
g.<method>;
```

Thereafter, you can call all methods of the **Graphics** class from the **g** reference. This is not a requirement, and we don't use this method universally throughout this chapter, but it's something to be aware of.

Another shortcut you may wish to explore is the use of the **with** statement. This statement allows you to affect many properties, and/or execute many methods, of a single object or reference without having to repeat that object or reference over and over again. For example, if you created a verbose name for an object reference, and used it repeatedly, it could become tedious rather quickly, making your code slightly less readable or harder to debug. Rather than introduce syntax prematurely, consider this general use pseudo-code for now:

```
var descriptiveSpriteName:Sprite = new Sprite();
descriptiveSpriteName.graphics.<method>;
descriptiveSpriteName.graphics.<method>;
//repeated method calls
descriptiveSpriteName.graphics.<method>;
descriptiveSpriteName.graphics.<method>;
```

The multiple references to the container's **graphics** object can be replaced by:

```
var descriptiveSpriteName:Sprite() = new Sprite();
with (descriptiveSpriteName.graphics) {
    <method>;
    <method>;
    //repeated method calls
    <method>;
    <method>;
}
```

Although not limited to use with the **Graphics** class, careless use of the **with** statement can lead to clarity issues in your code, most notably with scope. We will demonstrate its use along with other coding techniques but suggest that you limit your use of this structure to one object at a time. Think of its purpose as making it easier to address properties and methods of a single object, rather than for creating new objects or elements that may be children of multiple scopes.

Drawing Lines

The first step in drawing lines is to set a line style using the **lineStyle()** method. This is equivalent to setting several optional stroke properties in the Property Inspector of the Flash interface. The typical syntax is as follows:

```
1   var sp:Sprite = new Sprite();
2   addChild(sp);
3   var g:Graphics = sp.graphics;
4   g.lineStyle(2, 0x000000);
```

The first parameter represents line thickness in points, while the second is color in 0xRRGGBB hexadecimal format. When a color is not included, black is used as the default. When a line thickness of 0 is specified, a hairline thickness is used. If you don't want to use a line at all, you can omit the method, or call it with no parameters to clear any existing line style. Some of the optional parameters include the line alpha value, and which line cap style, joint styles, and miter limit value to use. All these properties share the same functionality as the same properties in the Flash Property Inspector.

The next step is to draw the actual line. Doing so is similar to you drawing a line on a piece of paper. Ordinarily, you don't start drawing a line from the upper-left corner of the paper to the first point of the line, and then on to the second point of the line, and so on. This is also true with the **Graphics** class. Typically, you begin by moving your virtual pen to the first point, just as you would in real life, and then continue to draw the line. Continuing our script, the following sequence will draw a line from point (150, 100) to point (400, 100):

```
5   g.moveTo(150, 100);
6   g.lineTo(400, 100);
```

To continue drawing straight lines, you can add more `lineTo()` methods. Each successive call will continue drawing the line from the previous location to the newly specified location. You can also change line styles at any time during the process. The following continuation of our script draws another line 20 pixels down, and then back to the left to the point at which we started. It then changes the line style from 2-pixel black to 4-pixel red, moves the pen to a new location 55 pixels below the prior line, and draws another line of the same length as the previously drawn horizontal lines.

```
7   g.lineTo(400, 120);
8   g.lineTo(150, 120);
9   g.lineStyle(4, 0xFF0000);
10  g.moveTo(150, 175);
11  g.lineTo(400, 175);
```

Drawing Curves

As you might imagine, you're not limited to drawing straight lines. You can also draw curves. The syntax for drawing a curve requires the addition of a point *through which* you will draw the curve. This is equivalent to creating a control point in a vector drawing program like Adobe Illustrator. Flash, however, uses the *quadratic* Bézier curve model, which uses one control point (often referred to as a handle) for both end points of a line segment, as opposed to the *cubic* Bézier model, which adds separate control handles for each point. A quadratic Bézier curve is illustrated in Figure 8-1, showing both end points and the control point through which the curve is drawn.

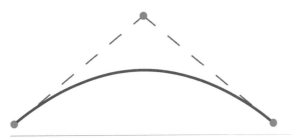

Figure 8-1. A quadratic Bézier curve with one control point for both end points of a line segment

The following code continues our script. It starts by switching to a 2-point blue line and moving the pen to point (150, 100). It then draws a curve that ends at point (400, 100) but is curved by a control point at point (275, 0).

```
12  g.lineStyle(2, 0x0000FF);
13  g.moveTo(150, 100);
14  g.curveTo(275, 0, 400, 100);
15  g.moveTo(0, 0);
```

The last line of this section is one way to prevent paths from closing or line style changes from affecting existing artwork. After your line is complete, move the pen to a new location. The use of point (0, 0) in this case is arbitrary, but it is as good a point as any.

It is also possible to draw simple shapes, including a circle and a rectangle, with or without rounded corners. To demonstrate this, we must first introduce how to style fills, including a dedicated method that is used to indicate that your drawing process is complete.

Adding Solid Fills

To add a solid-color fill to a drawing, you must use the **beginFill()** method. It accepts two parameters: color and alpha. Color is an unsigned integer and is typically specified in the 0xRRGGBB hexadecimal format, while alpha is a number in the percentage range of 0 to 1, with a default of 1 (100 percent).

After setting a fill style, you can continue drawing and then conclude with the **endFill()** method, which uses no parameters. The following code demonstrates fill styling and drawing a rectangle with the **lineTo()** method. It also demonstrates the use of the **with** statement, and the benefit of drawing into a dedicated canvas, allowing you to position the child anywhere on the stage.

```
16   var triangle:Sprite = new Sprite();
17   with (triangle.graphics) {
18       lineStyle(0);
19       beginFill(0xFF9900, 1);
20       moveTo(50, 0);
21       lineTo(100, 100);
22       lineTo(0, 100);
23       lineTo(50, 0);
24       endFill();
25   }
26   triangle.x = 50;
27   triangle.y = 250;
28   addChild(triangle);
```

> **NOTE**
>
> *For clarity and consistency, we've syntax-colored this example. Don't worry if your copy of Flash CS3 doesn't color the methods in the Actions panel or script document when using the* **with** *statement. Syntax coloring is partially determined by the object to which the method is attached. By moving the object from its adjoining method to the* **with** *statement, the syntax coloring engine doesn't know how to handle the code. Each method will, however, behave correctly.*

Drawing Shapes

Drawing one line segment at a time is not the only method for drawing shapes. It is also possible to draw primitive shapes using a trio of existing methods. The following code segment concludes our ongoing script by drawing three shapes, with varying fill colors and fill alpha values, into the same canvas. This code block demonstrates a few ideas.

Line 32 shows how to use a translucent stroke for a special effect. Note that, in lines 32 and 33, both the stroke and fill have an alpha value of 50 percent. The fill is red and the stroke is blue and 6-pixels thick. In Flash, strokes center on the edge to which they are applied, resulting in a 3-pixel overlap. The translucency of both stroke and fill result in a red circle with the appearance of a 3-pixel purple outline surrounded by a 3-pixel blue outline. Line 34 creates the circle itself, located at point (50, 50) within the **shapes** sprite, with a radius of 50 pixels.

```
29  var shapes:Sprite = new Sprite();
30  var gr:Graphics = shapes.graphics;
31
32  gr.lineStyle(6, 0x0000FF, 0.5);
33  gr.beginFill(0xFF0000, 0.5);
34  gr.drawCircle(50, 50, 50);
35  gr.endFill();
36
37  gr.lineStyle();
38  gr.beginFill(0x0000FF, 0.2);
39  gr.drawRect(125, 0, 100, 100);
40  gr.endFill();
41
42  gr.beginFill(0x0000FF, 0.5);
43  gr.drawRoundRect(250, 0, 100, 100, 50);
44  gr.endFill();
45
46  shapes.x = 150;
47  shapes.y = 250;
48  addChild(shapes);
```

Line 37 shows how to clear a previously existing line style. If you start out not wanting a stroke, it's easy to omit the method. If a stroke already exists, invoke the **lineStyle()** method with no parameters. A value of 0 creates a hairline stroke. Line 39 draws a rectangle using the **drawRect()** method, which accepts the x and y coordinates of the rectangle, followed by the width and height of the rectangle. The last shape method, **drawRoundRect()** in line 43, is the same as **drawRect()**, but adds a corner radius as its last parameter.

Figure 8-2 shows the appearance of all the accumulated script segments referenced so far. The collected script can be seen in *lines_curves_primitives.fla* in the accompanying source files.

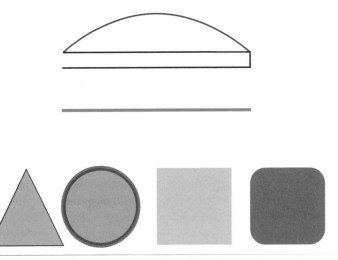

Figure 8-2. The culmination of several Graphics *class method calls*

Using Gradient Fills

If you want to fill a drawing or shape with a gradient rather than a solid color, style your fills using the **beginGradiantFill()** method, instead of **beginFill()**. We'll introduce a subset of available options for your first gradient, discussing the type of gradient, the colors and alpha values used, and the ratio of gradient dedicated to each color.

The gradient can be either linear (moving from left to right by default) or radial (moving from the epicenter of the gradient outward). The constants in the static **GradientType** class can be used to specify these values. The colors of the gradient are specified in an array, in the order in which they appear. Every color in the gradient can have an alpha value, and these are specified in a parallel array, matching the order of colors.

Finally, as in Flash's Color Mixer panel, you can weight any color by assigning to it a larger portion of the gradient—that is, a two-color gradient needn't be split 50/50 between the two colors. The weighting is expressed in a fashion similar to the manner used in the Color Mixer panel. You indicate a location for each color on a scale from 0 to 255. Thus, an equally weighted two-color gradient would place colors at either end of the scale. If you wanted to show more of the first color, you could push the first value higher, say to 100 (think of moving the color slider in the Color Mixer panel to the right). Decreasing the last value (think of moving its slider to the left) weights the last color more.

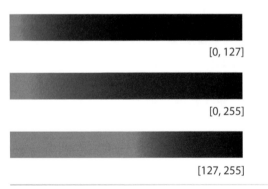

[0, 127]

[0, 255]

[127, 255]

Figure 8-3. Gradient color ratios

Let's take a look at these values in action. Line 1 of the following script specifies the use of a radial gradient. Lines 2 through 4 specify an equally weighted gradient from red to black, with all colors using an alpha value of 100 percent. Lines 5 through 7 then create a drawing canvas, use the **beginGradientFill()**

Figure 8-4. A radial gradient fill created with the Graphics *class*

method to pass in the specified gradient parameters, and draw a rectangle. Finally, the canvas is positioned and added to the display list in lines 8 and 9. Figure 8-4 shows the resulting shape created in this script.

```
1   var gradType:String = GradientType.RADIAL;
2   var colors:Array = [0xFF0000, 0x000000];
3   var alphas:Array = [1, 1];
4   var ratios:Array = [0, 255];
5   var canvas = new Sprite();
6   canvas.graphics.beginGradientFill(gradType, colors, alphas, ratios)
7   canvas.graphics.drawRect(0, 0, 100, 100);
8   canvas.x = canvas.y = 100;
9   addChild(canvas);
```

Wouldn't it be great if you could also position the gradient anywhere you wanted to or even rotate it, as the case of linear gradients? You will soon have the tools you need in the form of the Geometry package and its **Matrix** class. First, let's look at an applied example of drawing.

Simulating the Pencil Tool

A fine sample of interactive drawing can be found in simulating the functionality of the Flash Pencil tool. The process is outlined in the following script in the *pencil.fla* source file. Line 1 is a Boolean used to determine whether or not the pencil is drawing. Lines 3 and 4 set the line style and move the pencil to its first location, respectively. Line 6 attaches an event listener to the main timeline that triggers **onLoop()** every enter frame. Lines 7 and 8 attach listeners to the stage to respond to every mouse down and mouse up, calling their respective functions in lines 10 through 16 to toggle the **drawing** Boolean.

```
1   var drawing:Boolean = false;
2
3   this.graphics.lineStyle(1, 0x000000);
4   this.graphics.moveTo(mouseX, mouseY);
5
6   this.addEventListener(Event.ENTER_FRAME, onLoop, false, 0, true);
7   stage.addEventListener(MouseEvent.MOUSE_DOWN, onDown, false, 0,
    true);
8   stage.addEventListener(MouseEvent.MOUSE_UP, onUp, false, 0, true);
9
10  function onDown(evt:MouseEvent):void {
11      drawing = true;
12  }
13
14  function onUp(evt:MouseEvent):void {
15      drawing = false;
16  }
17
18  function onLoop(evt:Event):void {
19      if (drawing) {
20        this.graphics.lineTo(mouseX, mouseY);
21      } else {
22        this.graphics.moveTo(mouseX, mouseY);
23      }
24  }
```

Finally, the **onLoop()** function in lines 18 through 24 continuously draws lines to each new mouse location if **drawing** is **true** (meaning the mouse is down). If **drawing** is **false** (the mouse is up), the function moves the drawing point to the next mouse location so you can draw discreet lines at any time.

Add to this basic shape tools that call the **drawCircle()**, **drawRect()**, and **drawRoundRect()** methods, and you have a simple drawing application.

The Geometry Package

The **flash.geom** package is a handy set of utility classes that help create and manipulate points, rectangles, and data used to transform the appearance of objects. Here we'll focus on three of its classes: **Points**, **Rectanges**, and **Matrices**. We'll revisit the **Geometry** package later when discussing color in the next chapter.

Creating Points

The **Point** class allows you to automatically create point data without having to define custom objects each time or use arrays. Faking a point using linear arrays requires that you populate and retrieve the array data in the correct order. Here is an example:

```
var arrayPoint:Array = new Array(0, 0);
trace(arrayPoint[0], arrayPoint[1]);
```

Objects, which sometimes take the form of associative arrays, are a bit clearer because you can associate **x** and **y** property names with the values. Here are two examples:

```
var objPoint:Object = {x:0, y:0};
trace(objPoint.x, objPoint.y);

var objPoint2:Object = new Object();
objPoint2.x = 0;
objPoint2.y = 0;
trace(objPoint2.x, objPoint2.y);
```

All these examples correctly trace the values of 0 for x and y to the Output panel; however, in these examples, you still can't benefit from strong data type checking and error reporting. For example, it is possible to store many data types in arrays.

An instance of the **Point** class comes complete with **x** and **y** properties, and creating an instance is as easy as using the **new** operator. Using an empty constructor, as seen in the first line of the following code block, will automatically create a default point of (0, 0). However, you can reference another location by passing **x** and **y** values into the constructor, as seen in the second example that follows. A different way of retrieving the data, as separate coordinate values or as a single point, and the varied results, are shown in the **trace()** methods of each example.

```
var pt:Point = new Point();
trace(pt.x, pt.y);
//0 0
```

```
var pt2:Point = new Point(100, 100);
trace(pt2);
//(x=100, y=100)
```

What really sets the **Point** class apart from faking points with objects is not the ability to use **Point** as a data type. It's the properties and methods that come along with the class, including the subset that follows in the next code block. These methods greatly simplify the mathematical operations you must sometimes perform when using points. Lines 1 and 2 of this example create two points to work with. Line 3 demonstrates the **offset()** method, moving the point 50 pixels in the x and y directions.

Lines 6 and 8 demonstrate adding and subtracting points. These methods work on the point x and y values independently, creating a *new* point that is calculated from the sum or difference of the two original points.

You can also check to see if two points are the same using the **equals()** method (line 10). This is very handy for conditionals because you don't have to test for x and y values independently, or use the **&&** (and) operator to make sure both x and y coordinates match before the conditional evaluates to **true**.

```
1   var pt1:Point = new Point(100, 100);
2   var pt2:Point = new Point(400, 400);
3   pt1.offset(50, 50);
4   trace(pt1);
5   //(x=150, y=150)
6   trace(pt1.add(pt2));
7   //(x=550, y=550)
8   trace(pt2.subtract(pt1));
9   //(x=250, y=250)
10  trace(pt1.equals(pt2));
11  //false
```

Two very convenient **Point** methods are **distance()** and **interpolate()**, which really simplify animation math. Essentially, **distance()** performs the work of the Pythagorean theorem discussed in the previous chapter, so you don't have to do it yourself. The **interpolate()** method will calculate the perfect location for an interim point between two specified points. The method's third parameter determines how close to either point you want the interim location. A value closer to 0 is nearer the proximity of the second point, while a value approaching 1 is closer to the first point.

```
12  trace(Point.distance(pt1, pt2));
13  //353.5533905932738
14  trace(Point.interpolate(pt1, pt2, 0.5));
15  //(x=275, y=275)
```

As you've probably seen throughout this book, and will continue to see here and in the coming chapters, point data is indispensable for positioning objects. However, this is not limited to display objects. You will see when working with bitmaps later in the next chapter that points are used for reference locations in a variety of techniques.

Creating Rectangles

Rectangles are defined in a very similar way using the **Rectangle** class. Like point data, creating and manipulating rectangle areas using ActionScript can be very helpful for establishing boundaries within which something must remain or occur, such as the location of a movie clip or the collision of two objects. You will also find rectangles valuable for defining areas of data, much the way a marquee selection or cropping tool behaves in a drawing tool. Here is an example of creating a rectangle:

```
var rect:Rectangle = new Rectangle(0, 0, 100, 100);
trace(rect.x, rect.y);
//0 0
trace(rect);
//(x=0, y=0, w=100, h=100)
```

You can check a rectangle's location, width, and height in one call simply by querying the rectangle instance itself, as seen in the previous code. However, like the **Point** class, the **Rectangle** class does not limit you to these values. Three sets of properties give you a more granular look at location and dimension values of the rectangle. Line 2 of the following script demonstrates the **left**, **top**, **right**, and **bottom** properties, which allow you to query the four edge locations of the rectangle. Line 4 uses the **topLeft** and **bottomRight** properties to retrieve the eponymously named bounding *points* of the rectangle. Line 6 shows that you can acquire the same data made available directly by the Rectangle instance, but by querying individual properties.

```
1    var rect:Rectangle = new Rectangle(50, 50, 200, 100);
2    trace(rect.left, rect.top, rect.right, rect.bottom);
3    //50 50 250 150
4    trace(rect.topLeft, rect.bottomRight);
5    //(x=50, y=50) (x=250, y=150)
6    trace(rect.x, rect.y, rect.width, rect.height);
7    //50 50 200 100
```

You can move the rectangle with one call to the **offset()** method (line 8), instead of changing both the rectangle's **x** and **y** properties, and you can increase the width and height on all sides surrounding the rectangle's center point using the **inflate()** method. The first parameter of this method is added to both left and right horizontal dimensions, and the second parameter is similarly applied to the top and bottom vertical dimensions.

```
8   rect.offset(10, 10);
9   trace(rect.left, rect.top, rect.right, rect.bottom);
10  //60 60 260 160
11  rect.inflate(20, 20);
12  trace(rect.left, rect.top, rect.right, rect.bottom);
13  //40 40 280 180
```

Finally, you can use a handful of methods to compare rectangles with points and other rectangles. The following code block compares two new rectangles, **rect1** and **rect2**, and a new point, **pnt**. Lines 17, 19, and 21 determine whether a location is inside a rectangle. Line 17 checks to see if x and y locations are both inside the rectangle. Line 19 performs the same test, but allows you to pass in a point instead of discreet x and y values. Line 21 checks to see whether an entire rectangle is within another rectangle.

```
14  var rect1:Rectangle = new Rectangle(0, 0, 100, 50);
15  var rect2:Rectangle = new Rectangle(50, 25, 100, 50);
16  var pnt:Point = new Point(125, 50);
17  trace(rect1.contains(25, 25));
18  //true
19  trace(rect2.containsPoint(pnt));
20  //true
21  trace(rect1.containsRect(rect2));
22  //false
```

Line 23 checks to see if two rectangles overlap, while line 25 returns any area shared by both rectangles. Line 27 returns the union of the two specified rectangles—a new rectangle created from the minimum-bounding area that fully encompasses both original rectangles.

```
23  trace(rect1.intersects(rect2));
24  //true
25  trace(rect1.intersection(rect2));
26  //(x=50, y=25, w=50, h=25)
27  trace(rect1.union(rect2));
28  //(x=0, y=0, w=150, h=75)
```

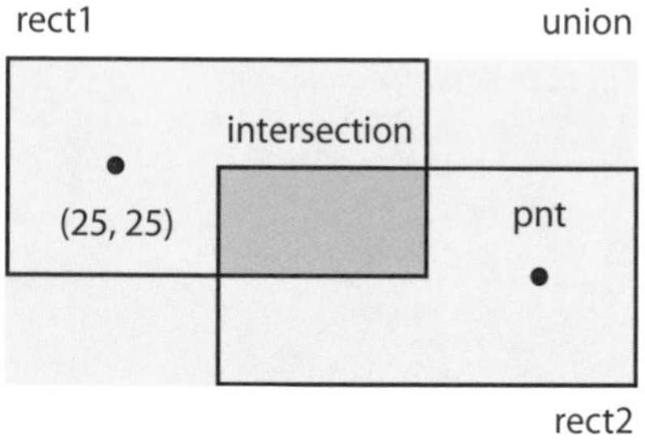

Figure 8-5 shows the position of the rectangles and points discussed, illustrating why the referenced points are contained within the rectangles, but also why the second rectangle is not within the first rectangle. The green and yellow areas depict the new rectangles referenced by the intersection and union, respectively, of the two original rectangles.

Figure 8-5. Rectangle class methods demonstrated

Using Matrices

ActionScript offers predefined properties for affecting a display object's scale, rotation, and x and y locations, all of which are specified individually. However, there are certain types of objects to which these properties do not apply, such as the gradient fill discussed previously and similar bitmap properties we'll introduce in the next chapter.

To affect these changes on objects like gradient fills, you must use a *matrix*. A matrix is a series of related values, called *elements*, that are expressed in a grid, and that can be used independently or together to perform complex transformations. Combinations of elements, such as scale and rotation, can be stored as a matrix for convenient reuse, or even to achieve affects that are otherwise not possible with ActionScript, such as skewing.

You can also use matrices for more advanced operations such as determining the post-transformation coordinates of a point from the original object. In other words, the upper-left corner of a rectangle originally at point (0, 0) will not be at point (0, 0) after a 90-degree rotation. The **Matrix** class can tell you the new location to which that point has moved, or even the change in location between the new and original points, with ease.

The **Matrix** class provides a basic 3 x 3 matrix for use in several transformation processes. Its structure can be seen in Figure 8-6. Built-in **Matrix** properties **a** and **d** affect scaling, properties **b** and **c** affect skewing (also known as shearing), and values **tx** and **ty** affect location. Together, elements **a**, **b**, **c**, and **d**, affect rotation. ActionScript does not support true three-dimensional transformations, so the last three values intended for this purpose, u, v, and w, are not used.

```
[ a,  b,  tx
  c,  d,  ty
  u,  v,  w ]
```

Figure 8-6. Matrix properties

Table 8-1 shows the transformations possible with a matrix. The first column shows the type of transformation, the second column lists related properties and a simplified class method for accomplishing the goal (if one exists), and the third column shows the values that must be adjusted, if you need to do so manually. It is almost always more convenient to use existing methods, or the **a**, **b**, **c**, **d**, **tx** and **ty** properties, but writing out the matrix explicitly is useful when you want to make several changes at once. Finally, the last column depicts a representative change in an object when the transformation is applied.

Table 8-1. Matrix values and how they transform objects

Transformation	Properties Methods	Matrix	Result

Identity
Default matrix, null transformation
	`a, b, c, d, tx, ty`
	`identity()`
		`[ 1,  0,  0`
		`  0,  1,  0`
		`  0,  0,  1 ]`	

Translation
Changes position, x and y, respectively, using pixels
	`tx, ty`
	`translate(tx, ty)`
		`[ 1,  0,  tx`
		`  0,  1,  ty`
		`  0,  0,  1 ]`	

Scale
Scales along the x and y axes, respectively, using percent
	`a, d`
	`scale(a, d)`
		`[ sx,  0,  0`
		`   0,  sy,  0`
		`   0,  0,  1 ]`	

Rotation
Rotates, using radians
	`a, b, c, d`
	`rotate(q)`
		`[ cos(q),  sin(q),  0`
		`  -sin(q),  cos(q),  0`
		`      0,       0,  1 ]`	

Skew (Shear)
Skews along the x and y axes, respectively, using pixels
	`b, c`
	None (see the `MatrixTransformer` discussion in "The Motion Package" section)
		`[      1, tan(zx),  0`
		`  tan(zy),       1,  0`
		`       0,       0,  1 ]`	

Skewing with matrices

To test this information, let's use the **Matrix** class to do something you can't do with a built-in property or method—skew a display object. The following script creates a rectangle with the **Graphics** class and then skews it.

To start with, lines 1 through 6 create a translucent green rectangular sprite with a 1-pixel black border and add it to the display list. The function spanning lines 8 through 10, originally discussed in Chapter 7, converts degrees to radians for use with the **Matrix** skewing element.

```
1   var rect:Sprite = new Sprite();
2   rect.graphics.lineStyle(1, 0x000000);
3   rect.graphics.beginFill(0x00FF00, 0.4);
4   rect.graphics.drawRect(0, 0, 100, 50);
5   rect.graphics.endFill();
6   addChild(rect);
7
8   function deg2rad(deg:Number):Number {
9       return deg * Math.PI / 180;
10  }
11
12  var mtrx:Matrix = rect.transform.matrix;
13  mtrx.c = Math.tan(deg2rad(20));
14  rect.transform.matrix = mtrx;
```

Finally, lines 12 through 14 apply the skewing effect. Line 12 creates a matrix based on the existing object's matrix, to make sure you are starting from the current transformation, whatever that may be. This is accomplished by querying the **matrix** property of the sprite. You can both get and set the matrix using this property of the sprite's **transform** object, which is also how we'll apply the new matrix.

Line 13 sets the **c** property of the matrix, which skews along the x-axis using the angle specified. It requires radians instead of degrees, so a value of 20 degrees is passed to the conversion function to get back the required radian value. Finally, the matrix is applied to the object in line 14. The result is seen in the top illustration in Figure 8-7.

Note that the skew is applied to the bottom edge of the sprite. This is important because if you wanted to give the sprite the appearance that it was slanted right rather than left, you need to compensate with the correct angle. Angles between 90 and 180 degrees and between 270 and 360 degrees will slant an object to the right but it's easier to use negative values. The following change to the existing script uses -20 degrees instead of 20 degrees, and the result appears in the middle illustration of Figure 8-7.

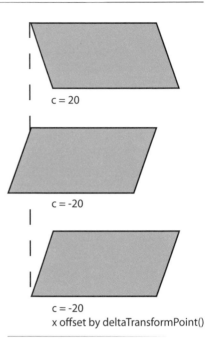

c = 20

c = -20

c = -20
x offset by deltaTransformPoint()

Figure 8-7. A sprite skewed with the Matrix *class*

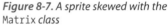

```
12   var mtrx:Matrix = rect.transform.matrix;
13   mtrx.c = Math.tan(deg2rad(-20));
14   rect.transform.matrix = mtrx;
```

Calculating changes in points after transformations

The sprite slants to the right but, because horizontal skewing affects only the bottom edge, the sprite now appears offset to the left. To compensate, we can use the occasionally life-saving methods that calculate the change in point location as a result of a transformation. We'll demonstrate this feature first. Putting aside the correction we're seeking for a moment, let's trace the new position of a sprite point, as it exists after the skew.

```
12   var mtrx:Matrix = rect.transform.matrix;
13   mtrx.c = Math.tan(deg2rad(-20));
14   rect.transform.matrix = mtrx;
15   trace(mtrx.transformPoint(new Point(0, 50)));
```

In line 15, we're passing the lower-left corner of the sprite into the **transformPoint()** method, and the new point will trace as approximately point (18, 50), having moved from point (0, 50). It can require fairly involved trigonometry to calculate this information on your own, so this is very handy.

If we stopped here, we could determine the difference between the two points and change the location of the sprite accordingly. However, there's already a method that eliminates the need to calculate the offset. The **deltaTransformPoint()** method determines the *change* in the before and after locations of a point, rather than the absolute locations. Therefore, all we need to do is correct the location of the sprite using the x value of the deltaTransformPoint() method, as seen here and in the bottom illustration in Figure 8-7.

```
16  rect.x -= mtrx.deltaTransformPoint(new Point(0, 50)).x;
```

Creating better gradient fills

Now that you know a little bit about matrices, you can exert greater control over gradient fills. The first time we introduced gradient fills, we filled a rectangle with a radial gradient but were unable to position the epicenter of the fill. Using matrices, you can control a number of fill attributes, including the width, height, rotation, and translation options described in this section. To simplify this process, the **createGradientBox()** method was added to the **Matrix** class. This method allows you to affect all of these properties with a single method call, and accepts these parameters:

```
createGradientBox(width, height, rotation, tx, ty);
```

Let's see how the optional addition of a matrix to the **beginGradientFill()** method improves our gradient, by starting with the simplest use of the **createGradientBox()**. Continuing to derive from our prior example, we've added a matrix in lines 2 and 3, and then added that matrix to the fill creation in line 9.

```
1   //radial gradient
2   var gradType:String = GradientType.RADIAL;
3   var matrix:Matrix = new Matrix();
4   matrix.createGradientBox(100, 100, 0, 0, 0);
5   var colors:Array = [0xFF0000, 0x000000];
6   var alphas:Array = [1, 1];
7   var ratios:Array = [0, 255];
8   var canvas = new Sprite();
9   canvas.graphics.beginGradientFill(gradType, colors, alphas, ratios,
    matrix);
10  canvas.graphics.drawRect(0, 0, 100, 100);
11  canvas.x = canvas.y = 100;
12  addChild(canvas);
```

The bottom image in Figure 8-8 shows that, by matching the width and height of the gradient box to the size of the rectangle, the radial gradient is now entirely visible. By adding translation values to the method, you can easily reposition the epicenter of the gradient. Using 30 pixels for **tx** and **ty** would place the epicenter of the gradient in the lower-right corner of the rectangle.

Figure 8-8. A radial gradient before (top) and after (bottom) matrix transformations

```
3   var matrix:Matrix = new Matrix();
4   matrix.createGradientBox(100, 100, 0, 30, 30);
```

To demonstrate the rotation of a gradient, we'll change the script in two small ways. First, we'll switch the gradient type from radial to linear so the rotation is more noticeable (line 2). Then we'll send a rotation value into the **createGradientBox()** method (line 4). The degree-to-radian conversion function rounds out the script in lines 14 through 16 of the following script below. Figure 8-9 shows before and after rotating a linear gradient 90 degrees.

```
1   //radial gradient
2   var gradType:String = GradientType.LINEAR;
3   var matrix:Matrix = new Matrix();
4   matrix.createGradientBox(100, 100, deg2rad(90), 0, 0);
5   var colors:Array = [0xFF0000, 0x000000];
6   var alphas:Array = [1, 1];
7   var ratios:Array = [0, 255];
8   var canvas = new Sprite();
9   canvas.graphics.beginGradientFill(gradType, colors, alphas, ratios,
    matrix);
10  canvas.graphics.drawRect(0, 0, 100, 100);
11  canvas.x = canvas.y = 100;
12  addChild(canvas);
13
14  function deg2rad(deg:Number):Number {
15      return deg * (Math.PI / 180);
16  }
```

Figure 8-9. A linear gradient before (top) and after (bottom) rotation with the Matrix class

Finally, just as with Flash's Color Mixer panel, you can control the way a gradient behaves when it fills an area larger than its own dimensions. In the Color Mixer panel this feature is called *overflow*, but in ActionScript it is a parameter of **beginGradientFill()** and is called *spread method*. The default behavior, specified as the **SpreadMethod.PAD** constant, is equivalent to *extend* in the Color Mixer panel. This setting continues the last color in the gradient throughout the remaining visible area to which the gradient is applied. This can be seen in all prior figures depicting gradients, as well as in the first illustration of Figure 8-10.

The other two options, **SpreadMethod.REFLECT** and **SpreadMethod.REPEAT**, share the same names and functionality in both the Color Mixer panel and ActionScript. The former reverses the colors as many times as is needed to occupy the available space filled by the gradient, as if the gradient was held against a mirror. The latter fills the visible area in a similar fashion but starts over at the first color as if tiled.

NOTE

The change in nomenclature for the gradient fill spread method was required because overflow *and* extend *both have important separate meanings in ActionScript.*

To control this feature, we must add another optional parameter to the **beginGradientFill()** call. The entire example is reproduced here for clarity, showing the spread method value for reflecting the gradient. Note line 5, in which the width and height of the gradient has been reduced to half the size of the rectangle to show the feature in action. If both the gradient and rectangle were 100 x 100 pixels, no overflow would occur. Figure 8-10 shows all three effects.

```
1   //using a matrix to control gradiant appearance
2   var gradType:String = GradientType.LINEAR;
3   var spread:String = SpreadMethod.REFLECT;
4   var matrix:Matrix = new Matrix();
5   matrix.createGradientBox(50, 50, deg2rad(90), 0, 0);
6   var colors:Array = [0xFF0000, 0x000000];
7   var alphas:Array = [1, 1];
8   var ratios:Array = [0, 255];
```

```
9    var canvas = new Sprite();
10   canvas.graphics.beginGradientFill(gradType, colors, alphas, ratios,
     matrix, spread);
11   canvas.graphics.drawRect(0, 0, 100, 100);
12   canvas.x = canvas.y = 100;
13   addChild(canvas);
14
15   function deg2rad(deg:Number):Number {
16       return deg * (Math.PI / 180);
17   }
```

Figure 8-10. Gradient fill spread method options pad (top), reflect (middle), and repeat (bottom)

The Motion Package

We couldn't conclude this chapter without mentioning the time- and labor-saving **MatrixTransformer** class added to ActionScript 3.0 as part of the **Motion** package. This class makes matrix transformations even easier than the dedicated methods of the **Matrix** class. For instance, although you can specify individual properties and set translation, scale, and rotation using methods of the **Matrix** class, the **MatrixTransformer** class has dedicated getters and setters for every matrix setting.

What's more, when angles are required, a getter and setter pair is provided for both radians and degrees, eliminating the need to convert your angle values to radians before use. Here is an example of using the **MatrixTransformer** class to skew a display object (instantiated as **dispObj**) 20 degrees, as seen in the previous "Skewing with matrices" section.

```
var mat:Matrix = new Matrix();
MatrixTransformer.setSkewX(mat, 20);
dispObj.transform.matrix = mat;
```

A matrix is still required, and it's still applied to the display object **transform.matrix** property to institute the change. However, using the static **MatrixTransformer** class, you need only call the **setSkewX()** method to accomplish your goal.

The class also has the very cool ability to rotate an object around any point, preventing you from having to calculate your own custom transform points. Using the **rotateAroundExternalPoint()** method, you can pass the matrix, a point, and an angle in degrees to the method and watch the fun.

```
1    import fl.motion.*;
2
3    var down:Boolean = false;
4
5    stage.addEventListener(MouseEvent.MOUSE_UP, onUp, false, 0, true);
6    stage.addEventListener(MouseEvent.MOUSE_DOWN, onDown, false, 0,
     true);
7    addEventListener(Event.ENTER_FRAME, onLoop, false, 0, true);
8
9    function onDown(evt:MouseEvent):void {
10       down = true;
11   }
12
```

```
13   function onUp(evt:MouseEvent):void {
14       down = false;
15   }
16
17   function onLoop(evt:Event):void {
18       if (down) {
19           var mat:Matrix = dispObj.transform.matrix;
20           MatrixTransformer.rotateAroundExternalPoint(mat,
                     mouseX, mouseY, 20);
21           dispObj.transform.matrix = mat;
22       }
23   }
```

original

scaled with distortion

9-slice scaling enabled

scaled without distortion

9-Slice Scaling

Scaling vectors is usually a pleasure because the crispness of the vector art is not lost when it is resized the way bitmaps become pixilated when enlarged significantly. This is because the vectors are recalculated every time an object is scaled. However, one of the downsides of this default behavior is that certain visual characteristics, such as stroke weight and rounded corners, can become distorted during scaling. This phenomenon can be seen in Figure 8-11.

To reduce distortion caused by scaling in many types of display objects, you can use a feature called *9-slice scaling*. This feature virtually slices a display object into nine pieces and controls scaling of these pieces independently. A typical grid of nine slices can be seen in Figure 8-11. The four corners are not scaled. The top and bottom slices between the corners are scaled only horizontally, the left and right slices between the corners are scaled only vertically, and the center slice is scaled in both directions.

To enable this feature using ActionScript, you must set the corresponding **scale9grid** property to a rectangle that, in essence, defines the object's center slice. ActionScript then extrapolates the corners and perimeter slices by extending the sides of the rectangle. The illustration in Figure 8-11 marked "9-slice scaling enabled" shows this by darkening the **scale9grid** and outlining the slices with dashed lines. To demonstrate this feature, the following exercise will create a sprite with rounded corners and then scale it using the mouse.

Lines 1 through 9 follow our familiar routine of creating a sprite, drawing vector assets, and positioning and adding the sprite to the display list. However, there's one new twist to this process. The **lineStyle()** method in line 3 contains two optional parameters we haven't discussed. The third parameter tells the method to give the line an alpha value of 100 percent. This is the default behavior and, because we haven't yet had a need for a semitransparent stroke, has been omitted up to this point.

We now need to include this default value in the method call because we want to set the fourth optional parameter of the method. (It is not possible to vary the order in which parameters are supplied to this method, so the first three must be present to use the fourth.) This last parameter enables *stroke hinting*, which aligns strokes along whole pixels, improving legibility. Specifically, this parameter reduces the apparent loss of stroke thickness due to anti-aliasing and improves the look of rounded corners, which is central to this exercise.

```
1   var sp:Sprite = new Sprite();
2   with (sp.graphics) {
3       lineStyle(1, 0x000000, 1, true);
4       beginFill(0xFFFF00, 0.5);
5       drawRoundRect(0, 0, 100, 50, 15);
6       endFill();
7   }
8   sp.x = sp.y = 50;
9   addChild(sp);
10
11  var slice9rect:Rectangle = new Rectangle(15, 15, 70, 20);
12  sp.scale9Grid = slice9rect;
13
14  addEventListener(Event.ENTER_FRAME, onLoop, false, 0, true);
15
16  function onLoop(evt:Event):void {
17      sp.width = Math.max(mouseX - sp.x, 30);
18      sp.height = Math.max(mouseY - sp.y, 30);
19  }
```

Lines 11 and 12 create a rectangle that is inset from all four sides of the sprite by 15 pixels, and sets the **scale9Grid** property of the sprite to the specified rectangle.

Finally, an event listener calls the **onLoop()** function every enter frame, setting the width and height of the sprite to the mouse coordinates, minus any offset x and y values from the sprite location. One potentially new element, introduced in lines 17 and 18, limits how small the rectangle can become. The **max()** method of the static **Math** class determines which of the two values provided to it are larger and uses that value. Therefore, if you offer a choice between the x coordinate of the mouse and 30, and the mouse is at point (100, 100), 100 will be returned by the method. Conversely, if the mouse is at point (10, 10), 30 will be used. This prevents the rectangle from getting any smaller than 30 x 30 pixels.

If you want to see a live comparison between using and not using 9-slice scaling, add the following code to your script. Every time you click the mouse, the feature will toggle between on and off.

```
16  function onLoop(evt:Event):void {
17      sp.width = Math.max(mouseX - sp.x, 30);
18      sp.height = Math.max(mouseY - sp.y, 30);
19  }
20
21  stage.addEventListener(MouseEvent.CLICK, onClick, false, 0, true);
22
23  function onClick(evt:Event):void {
24      if (sp.scale9Grid) {
25          sp.scale9Grid = null;
26      } else {
27          sp.scale9Grid = slice9rect;
28      }
29  }
```

Applied Examples

Let's use much of what we've covered in this chapter to two applied examples. In the first exercise, we'll create the graphical elements of a basic color picker. Then we'll create a custom button class that can serve as a lightweight, code-only alternative to components.

A Simple Color Picker

Let's start by creating a slightly more complex display object that uses two gradients, alpha values, and a matrix rotation. We'll build the display portion of a simple color picker, a bit like the one seen in Flash's Color Mixer panel. In the next chapter, we'll show you how to retrieve values from the picker using your mouse.

The picker will contain two separate pieces: a color spectrum in vertical blended stripes, and a transparent-to-black gradient overlay, as seen in Figure 8-12. The overlay will allow you to vary how much black is added to a color.

Figure 8-12. A color picker

Creating the two layered gradients for the picker requires the same code with only minor variance in some of the settings. So, it makes sense to define a function to handle the work without a lot of repetition. This way, we can vary the parameters sent to the function and create multiple gradients with the same code. Our custom function accepts parameters for the size of the drawing canvas to be created (the picker will be square, so only one value will be used for width and height), arrays for colors, alphas, and distribution ratios, as previously described, and a rotation setting for the matrix used when drawing the gradient.

Line 2 creates a drawing canvas, line 3 creates an identity matrix, and line 4 specifies a linear gradient fill type. Line 5 defines a gradient box with equal width and height, custom rotation, and no translation. Line 6 creates the fill using a linear gradient fill type as well as the arrays sent in for color, alpha, and ratios, and the newly created matrix. The rectangle is then drawn in line 7 using no change in x or y and the same width and height sent into the function. Finally, the sprite is returned to the function call.

```
1   function drawGradientBox(size:uint, col:Array, alph:Array, rat:
    Array, matRot:Number):Sprite {
2       var sp:Sprite = new Sprite();
3       var mat:Matrix = new Matrix();
4       var fill:String = GradientType.LINEAR;
5       mat.createGradientBox(size, size, matRot, 0, 0);
6       sp.graphics.beginGradientFill(fill, col, alph, rat, mat);
7       sp.graphics.drawRect(0, 0, size, size);
8       return sp;
9   }
```

With our reusable function defined, the script continues by creating a container for the color picker (line 10). This will simplify working with the multipart picker and make it easier to reposition or transform it in the future. The first piece we add to the container is a linear gradient in a spectrum of colors. Lines 12 through 14 set the values used to create the gradient. It contains seven colors (line 12), all at 100-percent alpha (line 13), and evenly distributed (line 14). The **drawGradientBox()** function then creates the **spectrum** sprite using a 100-pixel size, the gradient property arrays, and a 0-degree rotation. The spectrum is then added to the color picker, and we can move on to the next picker layer.

```
10  var colorPicker:Sprite = new Sprite();
11
12  var colors:Array = [0xFF0000, 0xFFFF00, 0x00FF00, 0x00FFFF,
    0x0000FF, 0xFF00FF, 0xFF0000];
13  var alphas:Array = [1, 1, 1, 1, 1, 1, 1];
14  var ratios:Array = [0, 42, 84, 126, 168, 210, 255];
15  var spectrum:Sprite = drawGradientBox(100, colors, alphas,
    ratios, 0);
16  colorPicker.addChild(spectrum);
```

The gradient creation process is repeated with the overlay in lines 17 through 21. Two evenly distributed black color values, one opaque and one transparent, are used. By default, a dynamically created gradient will run horizontally, and we want our overlay to run vertically. Therefore, we must rotate the gradient counterclockwise 90 degrees. Remember that radians are required for the **createGradientBox()** method, so our degree-to-radian conversion function is required and can be found at the end of the script. Once the semitransparent overlay is created, it is added to the picker.

```
17  colors = [0x000000, 0x000000];
18  alphas = [1, 0];
19  ratios = [0, 255];
20  var overlay:Sprite = drawGradientBox(100, colors, alphas, ratios,
    deg2rad(-90));
21  colorPicker.addChild(overlay);
22  colorPicker.x = 100;
23  colorPicker.y = 100;
24  this.addChild(colorPicker);
25
26  function deg2rad(deg:Number):Number {
27      return deg * (Math.PI / 180);
28  }
```

Lastly, the finished picker is positioned to show the convenience of using a parent container, and then added to the display list. Don't forget that this example just demonstrates the dynamic creation of the picker. (No assets— all code!) In the next chapter, we'll show you how to retrieve color values from the picker so you can use it in your own projects.

A Custom Button Class

This applied example is a class that creates functioning buttons entirely with code, and it's based on your work with the **Graphics** class in this chapter. You can use the **CreateRoundRectButton** class to provide a small number of appearance attributes when instantiating the class, and the resulting button will have up, over, down, and hit states, as well as cursor feedback. All that remains is that you attach a listener to the button after instantiation for the button to trigger some aspect of your application.

The class makes use of two new concepts. First is the ability to automatically interpolate a color that falls between two given colors. For example, you can provide red and blue and be given purple in return. This is accomplished through the use of the **Color** class, which will also be discussed in the next chapter. The second new concept is dynamically created text. This will be covered in detail in Chapter 10, but we've introduced just enough here to allow you to create a small text field and use a system font to display text.

The class starts with the standard package syntax through line 15, declaring the package, importing classes and packages, and declaring the class and class properties. Two items worth noting are the import of the **text** and **Color** classes (lines 4 and 5) to support the new functionality, and the use of unsigned integers (positive only) to store color data (lines 13 and 14).

```
1    package {
2
3        import flash.display.*;
4        import flash.text.*;
5        import fl.motion.Color;
6
7        public class CreateRoundRectButton extends Sprite {
8
9            private var _w:Number;
10           private var _h:Number;
11           private var _rad:Number;
12           private var _linW:Number;
13           private var _col:uint;
14           private var _txtCol:uint;
15           private var _txt:String;
```

The constructor begins by populating the class variables with the parameter values passed in when instantiating the class. It follows with the creation of a button and text field (which we'll discuss in just a moment), and adding both to the display list of the class instance. Lastly, the text label is prevented from trapping mouse events because the user will not be editing, or otherwise interacting directly with, this text field. This is important because if this step is not taken, the cursor will change to the I-beam text-editing cursor and the button will not be clickable where covered by the text field.

```
16          public function CreateRoundRectButton(w:Number, h:Number,
            rad:Number, linW:Number, col:uint, txt:String, txtCol:uint){
17              _w = w;
18              _h = h;
19              _rad = rad;
20              _linW = linW;
21              _col = col;
22              _txt = txt;
23              _txtCol = txtCol;
24
25              var btn:SimpleButton = createBtn();
26              addChild(btn);
27              var labl:TextField = createLabel();
28              addChild(labl);
29              labl.mouseEnabled = false;
30          }
```

The **createBtn()** method assembles the button using the new ActionScript 3.0 **SimpleButton** class. This class automatically constructs a button by allowing you to assign display objects to the up, over, down, and hit states. In this case, because we want a code-only solution, we need to build each state using the **createRoundRect()** method. That method, reviewed in just a moment, will likely be familiar to you as it uses the **Graphics** class to draw the button assets. It requires only one parameter, which is the color used for the button.

We determine the colors for the button's over and down states in lines 32 and 33 using the **Color** class; a static class from the **Motion** package. Given two colors, the method calculates a color between the two. A third parameter indicates how close to either color the new value should be. For example, if you provided black and white and a weighting of .1, the new color would be closer to the first, or a charcoal gray. A weighting of .9 would be closer to the second color, or near-white.

To create the over-state color, we calculate a value 30 percent between the main button color (visible in the button's up state) and white. To determine the down-state color, we calculate a value 30 percent between the main button color and black. The final button returned to the constructor then has a lighter over state and darker down state, based on the button's main color.

```
31          private function createBtn():SimpleButton {
32              var ovCol:uint = Color.interpolateColor(_col,
                OxFFFFFF, 0.3);
33              var dnCol:uint = Color.interpolateColor(_col,
                Ox000000, 0.3);
34              var btn:SimpleButton = new SimpleButton();
35              btn.upState = createRoundRect(_col);
36              btn.overState = createRoundRect(ovCol);
37              btn.downState = createRoundRect(dnCol);
38              btn.hitTestState = btn.upState;
39              return btn;
40          }
```

The `createRoundRect()` method (lines 41–48), presents no new material, but reviews an idea discussed in Chapter 4 about display lists. ActionScript 3.0 allows you to create shapes dynamically. The rounded rectangle is being returned to a button state of the **SimpleButton** class, so it doesn't need to be controlled by ActionScript and doesn't need to be a sprite or a movie clip.

```
41          private function createRoundRect(col:uint):Shape {
42              var rRect:Shape = new Shape();
43              rRect.graphics.lineStyle(_linW, _col);
44              rRect.graphics.beginFill(col, 0.5);
45              rRect.graphics.drawRoundRect(0, 0, _w, _h, _rad);
46              rRect.graphics.endFill();
47              return rRect;
48          }
```

Lastly, we create the button's text to give our button a label. We could do this with existing knowledge by using an already created movie clip, but we want to demonstrate a code-only solution, so let's dive in.

Lines 50 through 52 create a new text field with the same width and height as the button. Lines 54 through 59 create an instance of the **TextFormat** class, which is used to format, or style, the text in a field. This formatter uses a 10-point, bold, center-aligned, Verdana font, that is colored with the color specified in the class constructor. Lines 61 through 63 apply the format to the text field, populate the field with the text specified in the class constructor, and prevent the text from being selected by the user. Finally, line 65 returns the newly created text field to the constructor.

```
49          private function createLabel():TextField {
50              var txt:TextField = new TextField();
51              txt.width = _w;
52              txt.height = _h;
53
54              var format:TextFormat = new TextFormat();
55              format.font = "Verdana";
56              format.color = _txtCol;
57              format.size = 10;
58              format.bold = true;
59              format.align = TextFormatAlign.CENTER;
60
61              txt.defaultTextFormat = format;
62              txt.text = _txt;
63              txt.selectable = false;
64
65              return txt;
66          }
67      }
68  }
```

Using this class is one way to present interface buttons to the user without having to pre-create them in the Flash interface. This restricts the ability to use custom artwork for individual buttons but keeps file size to a minimum. This is a simple demonstration, so the class is not particularly robust when it comes to button styling options. However, that fact presents an ideal opportunity for you to practice what you've learned. Try to improve on this class by

Project Package

The project package for this chapter includes the custom button class, **CreateRoundRectButton**. We will make use of this class in future chapters to create small exercise files without building custom assets, and to increase your comfort with using classes. For more information about the companion web site project, see Chapter 6.

drawing specialized button shapes or, perhaps, by offering a choice between circular, rectangular, or rounded button shapes.

What's Next?

For many reasons, mostly subjective, manipulating visual assets in Flash is one of the most fun and most satisfying ways to learn ActionScript. Drawing vectors does more than minimize file size. It also provides literally limitless possibilities for creating generative art. Combining data from other corners of the ActionScript world (user input, sound, mathematical calculations, random numbers, and so on) with vectors opens the door to compelling and instructional experiments. Vectors, however, are only half of the puzzle. Flash also provides an impressive range of classes for manipulating pixel-based assets at runtime.

In the next chapter, we'll look at working with bitmaps, including:

- Drawing bitmaps at runtime
- Applying blend modes such as lighten, screen, and new Flash-specific options
- Using simple filters like drop shadow, bevel, and blur, to enhance assets
- Using complex filter techniques like convolution, color mixing, and displacement maps for special effects
- Encoding custom bitmap data as JPEGs and sending the data to a server

DRAWING WITH PIXELS

While largely known for its focus on vector assets, Flash has been gaining attention in the field of manipulating pixel-based assets, as well. This began in earnest with the introduction of Flash 8, as a large new set of bitmap-related functionality was introduced. Included was a set of blend modes, basic filters (like drop shadow and bevel, akin to Photoshop layer styles), and advanced filter effects (like convolution and displacement mapping, akin to Photoshop filters). Even the ability to temporarily treat vectors like bitmaps, behind the scenes with no loss in vector quality, was introduced for a dramatic performance improvement.

Today, the speed increases afforded by ActionScript 3.0, in Flash Player 9 and later, make bitmap manipulation practical in more processor-intensive scenarios than ever before. In this chapter, we'll discuss several ways to add pixel-pushing to your projects, including:

- **Bitmap Caching.** Moving pixels on screen is a lot more efficient than recalculating the math required to display moving vectors upon every frame rate. Temporarily caching a bitmap representation of a vector-based asset can reduce this strain and increase performance.

- **The BitmapData Class.** Just as the **Graphics** class is used to draw with vectors, the **BitmapData** class can be used to draw with pixels. We'll look at a small subset of its most useful methods.

- **Blend Modes.** Another useful and efficient bitmap compositing tool is the blend mode. Flash offers a standard set of blend modes, including lighten, darken, screen, multiply, and so on, as well as a few Flash-specific blend modes. They can be applied to sprites and movie clips whether they contain vectors or bitmaps.

- **Bitmap Filters.** Advanced filtering techniques such as convolution, color transformation, and displacement map effects can be applied to bitmaps at runtime. Familiar basic filters, such as blur, bevel, and drop shadow, can even be applied to vector symbol instances as well as bitmaps, without first having to rasterize the vectors, and without losing any fidelity or access to vector properties.

- **Color Changes.** ActionScript 3.0 offers a few ways to manipulate color, including the convolution filter, a color transform object, and even a handy new class originally introduced to recreate timeline animations.

- **Image Encoding.** The encoding process involves sending bitmap data to an image encoding class, `ByteArray`, in order to save it in an external graphics format.

Bitmap Caching

A typical first reaction when discussing bitmap manipulation in Flash is resistance or confusion, based on the assumed loss of crisp, clean vectors. However, there are multiple ways to work with bitmap information in Flash, and we'd like to start off with an example that drives home the point that vectors and bitmaps can coexist to great effect.

Vector-based experiences, such as animations, can sometimes lag behind comparable bitmap-based experiences because it is much more processor intensive to animate with vectors. The math needed to recalculate all the vectors every time an update is required is invariably more demanding than moving and compositing bitmaps.

With that in mind, Flash has the capability of caching a version of a vector asset as a bitmap and then working with the bitmap instead of the original until it is no longer optimal to do so. For example, consider a complex vector background over which other vectors are changing. If the background is unchanging, there's no need to redraw the vector background repeatedly. Instead, it is more efficient to work with the changing foreground elements on top of a bitmap. This situation is ideal for bitmap caching, the syntax for which is shown here:

```
displayObject.cacheAsBitmap = true;
```

By setting the `cacheAsBitmap` property to **true**, you can tell Flash Player to create a *surface*, a cosmetically identical bitmap representation, of a symbol to use for display purposes. This visual change is unnoticed by the viewer because the bitmap snapshot of the symbol is always kept current, through any changes, to prevent degradation of image quality. For example, if the symbol is scaled, the original cached bitmap is discarded and a new version is generated.

If you are not significantly altering your vector assets, you can realize noticeable performance gains by using this feature. Some features, including those that use bitmap compositing techniques, require `cacheAsBitmap`. For example, a default mask can contain only hard edges, because vector masks do not support varying degrees of alpha transparency. Any non-transparent pixel, no matter what alpha value it uses, is considered opaque when added to the mask. However, using bitmap caching for both the mask and maskee, the two elements can be composited as bitmaps. This allows alpha masks to composite semitransparent pixels using their actual alpha values to create a soft edge. Here is a look at the syntax, and the effect can be seen in Figure 9-1.

```
masker.cacheAsBitmap = true;
maskee.cacheAsBitmap = true;
maskee.mask = masker;
```

Similarly, you will learn in this chapter that simple bitmap filter effects, like drop shadow, can be applied to vector assets. To simplify support for this feature, Flash Player will automatically enable bitmap caching when needed.

Bitmap caching isn't the perfect solution in every situation, however. It is really optimized for assets that are relatively static. In fact, you can realize even greater gains when applying the feature to assets with solid backgrounds, because the transparency values of the asset no longer need to be calculated. You can even add an opaque background with ActionScript to take advantage of this feature. The following syntax will apply an opaque white background to a movie clip that contains a circle. As a result, the formerly transparent corners of the movie clip will not be a factor.

```
circle.cacheAsBitmap = true;
circle.opaqueBackground = 0xFFFFFF;
```

The byproduct of adding a background behind the circle means this is best suited for a white stage with no other elements between the circle and stage. With this setup, the white background will not be visible. If your stage is not white, the color of the bitmap background can be set to a color that will more closely match the stage. The feature can also be disabled by assigning it a value of null.

Don't enable caching when you are materially altering the appearance of your display object. For example, scaling, rotating, or altering the opacity of a display object will require the object to be redrawn and a new cache created each time a change is made.

Use bitmap caching first and foremost as a performance-enhancing tool. Storing a bitmap surface requires RAM that may be needed elsewhere. Avoid the temptation to cache everything, even when circumstances indicate caching may be helpful. Instead, use caching when you think it's needed, as one of multiple possible techniques to improve upon known performance lags.

In fact, the automatic enabling of this feature when filters are applied is also automatically disabled when the filter is no longer in place. If the filter use ceases, Flash Player returns the **cacheAsBitmap** property to its state prior to the filter use.

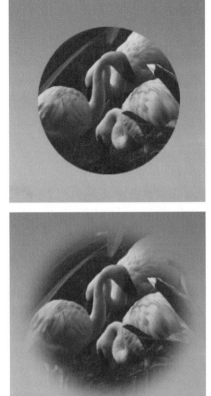

Figure 9-1. The same alpha mask applied without bitmap caching (above) and with bitmap caching (below)

The BitmapData Class

It is also possible to manipulate bitmaps directly through the use of the **BitmapData** class. The target of the manipulation needn't be an actual bitmap. Just as Flash Player can create a bitmap surface of a display object automatically, you can create such a surface explicitly. Think of this process as working with a screenshot. Whether the display object contains a bitmap or a vector shape is immaterial. You can capture the bitmap data of that object in either case. Let's start by looking at creating bitmap data from scratch and highlighting the difference between bitmap data and a bitmap.

Creating Bitmaps

There are two parts to working with a bitmap. One is the bitmap display object, and the other is the bitmap data. Think of the bitmap display object as the picture you see on stage, and the bitmap data as a detailed description of the number of pixels used, their individual colors and alpha values, and so on. You will find out later in this chapter that it is sometimes advantageous to work with bitmap data without ever actually displaying a bitmap.

In the following example, we want to see the fruit of our labors, so we will work with both elements. The first line of the script creates a new instance of the **BitmapData** class, populating it with content. The first two parameters sent to the class are the dimensions of the object, 100 x 100 pixels.

The third parameter tells the class that the object will not be transparent. The last parameter is the color specified, using the 32-bit 0xAARRGGBB hexadecimal format, which adds two digits for alpha data at the beginning of the number. This example specifies FF or 100-percent opaque.

The second and third lines of the script create a bitmap display object and add it to the display list, resulting in a 100 x 100-pixel navy blue square in the upper-left corner of the stage.

```
var bmd:BitmapData = new BitmapData(100, 100, false, 0xFF000099);
var bm:Bitmap = new Bitmap(bmd);
addChild(bm);
```

To create a bitmap data object with transparency requires changing the third parameter of the class constructor to **true** and reducing the opacity of the color. The following, for example, creates a forest green square that is approximately 50-percent transparent.

```
var bmd:BitmapData = new BitmapData(100, 100, true, 0x7F009900);
```

Using a Bitmap from the Library

If you need to work with an actual bitmap image, rather than creating your own **BitmapData** object, you can add an imported bitmap dynamically from the library. You can use the *library_bitmap.fla* file from the accompanying source code for this exercise, or use your own image. You must have an image already imported into the library, and have given it a class name in the Linkage Properties dialog.

When adding a class name to a bitmap's Linkage Properties dialog, you needn't actually create a class file first. Flash will create an internal place-holder for you, which will automatically be replaced by an actual class should you later decide to create one. For more information, see the "Adding Symbol Instances to the Display List" section of Chapter 4.

In our sample source file, an image of penguins has been given the class name **Penguins**. The base class for a library bitmap is **BitmapData** to allow you to easily access the data without creating a **Bitmap** display object. Therefore, the first step in adding a bitmap to the stage must be to create a new **BitmapData** object.

For tutorial purposes, we have clarified this first step of the exercise by typing the newly created instance as **BitmapData**, rather than the subclassed **Penguins**, which might be more typical.

Another important thing to be aware of is that using a bitmap from the library this way is one of the few examples where parameters are required during instantiation of a symbol instance. Fortunately, the exact width and height values are not required. The values are ignored, and the image data is placed into the instance variable without scaling. To remind you that you're not necessarily working with the real width and height, we advise using 0 for both values.

The following three lines create a **Bitmap** instance using the data object, and add the bitmap to the display list.

```
var penguinsBmd:BitmapData = new Penguins(0, 0);
var penguins:Bitmap = new Bitmap(penguinsBmd);
addChild(penguins);
```

Copying Pixels

Another way to populate a **BitmapData** object is to copy pixels from another **BitmapData** object. The exercise that follows uses the **copyPixels()** method to duplicate a penguin image by copying a segment from one image and creating another. The method is called from the new destination object and requires three parameters: the source object, a rectangle defining the pixels to be copied, and the destination point in the new object to which the pixels should be pasted.

This exercise builds on the previous exercise, so you can use the file from the previous section or open *copy_pixels_stage_click.fla* from the accompanying source files. There are no changes to lines 1 through 3, which add a bitmap to the stage from the library. Line 5 adds a listener to the stage to call the **onClick()** function when the mouse is clicked.

NOTE

Loading a bitmap from an external source is discussed in Chapter 13.

Figure 9-2. The source image with the isolated area to be copied marked in red

Line 7 creates a new **BitmapData** object that is the width and height of the pixels to be copied from the original—just enough to enclose a penguin. Line 8 defines the rectangle required to isolate the penguin, including not only its width and height but also its x and y location in the source, as seen in Figure 9-2. Line 9 rounds out the copy process by copying the pixels into the new **BitmapData** object at its origin (defined by creating a new point in the last parameter of the method).

Finally, a new bitmap is created from the duplicated pixels, placed next to the original penguin, and added to the display list. The result is seen in Figure 9-3.

```
1    var penguinsBmd:Penguins = new Penguins(0, 0);
2    var penguins:Bitmap = new Bitmap(penguinsBmd);
3    addChild(penguins);
4    stage.addEventListener(MouseEvent.CLICK, onClick, false, 0, true);
5
6    function onClick(evt:MouseEvent):void {
7        var penguinCopyBmd:BitmapData = new BitmapData(95, 170);
8        var rect:Rectangle = new Rectangle(290, 196, 95, 170);
9        penguinCopyBmd.copyPixels(penguinsBmd, rect, new Point());
10
11       var penguinCopy:Bitmap = new Bitmap(penguinCopyBmd);
12       penguinCopy.x = 385;
13       penguinCopy.y = 196;
14       addChild(penguinCopy);
15   }
```

Figure 9-3. A detail of the image after the pixels have been copied

This exercise is a good example that not all display objects are interactive. The preceding code attached the mouse listener to the stage because we cannot attach a listener to a bitmap. However, if you wanted a bitmap to serve as a button, you would need to place the bitmap into an interactive display object, such as a sprite.

In the code that follows, note that the step to add the bitmap to the stage, and the stage listener, have both been removed. Instead, starting at line 15, the bitmap is placed inside a new sprite and a listener is attached to that sprite, rather than the stage. See the code work in *copy_pixels_sprite_click.fla*.

```
1    var penguinsBmd:Penguins = new Penguins(0, 0);
2    var penguins:Bitmap = new Bitmap(penguinsBmd);
3
4    function onClick(evt:MouseEvent):void {
5        var penguinCopyBmd:BitmapData = new BitmapData(95, 170);
6        var rect:Rectangle = new Rectangle(290, 196, 95, 170);
7        penguinCopyBmd.copyPixels(penguinsBmd, rect, new Point());
8
9        var penguinCopy:Bitmap = new Bitmap(penguinCopyBmd);
10       penguinCopy.x = 385;
11       penguinCopy.y = 196;
12       addChild(penguinCopy);
13   }
14
15   var sp:Sprite = new Sprite();
16   sp.addChild(penguins);
17   addChild(sp);
18   sp.addEventListener(MouseEvent.CLICK, onClick, false, 0, true);
```

Getting and Setting Pixels

In Chapter 8, we created the visual component of a color picker (shown in Figure 9-4) but did not add any functionality to the exercise. In this chapter we will show you how to get and set pixels using methods of the **BitmapData** class.

Get Pixel

We'll start by retrieving pixel values from the picker with the mouse. We'll include the script again here for context. If you have any questions about this material, please review the section "A Simple Color Picker" in Chapter 8.

```
1   function drawGradientBox(size:int, col:Array, alph:Array, rat:Array,
    matRot:Number):Sprite {
2       var sp:Sprite = new Sprite();
3       var mat:Matrix = new Matrix();
4       var fill:String = GradientType.LINEAR;
5       mat.createGradientBox(size, size, matRot, 0, 0);
6       sp.graphics.beginGradientFill(fill, col, alph, rat, mat);
7       sp.graphics.drawRect(0, 0, size, size);
8       return sp;
9   }
10
11  var colorPicker:Sprite = new Sprite();
12
13  var colors:Array = [0xFF0000, 0xFFFF00, 0x00FF00, 0x00FFFF,
    0x0000FF, 0xFF00FF, 0xFF0000];
14  var alphas:Array = [1, 1, 1, 1, 1, 1, 1];
15  var ratios:Array = [0, 42, 84, 126, 168, 210, 255];
16  var spectrum:Sprite = drawGradientBox(100, colors, alphas, ratios,
    0);
17  colorPicker.addChild(spectrum);
18
19  colors = [0x000000, 0x000000];
20  alphas = [1, 0];
21  ratios = [0, 255];
22  var overlay:Sprite = drawGradientBox(100, colors, alphas, ratios,
    deg2rad(-90));
23  colorPicker.addChild(overlay);
24  colorPicker.x = 100;
25  colorPicker.y = 100;
26  this.addChild(colorPicker);
27
28  function deg2rad(deg:Number):Number {
29      return deg * (Math.PI / 180);
30  }
```

After creating the visual aspect of the picker, we need to query color values with the mouse. First, we'll create a variable in line 31 to store the chosen color. Next we need to create a **BitmapData** object of the picker to be able to poll its colors. Line 33 creates an opaque object with the width and height of the picker. Because we want the entire picker, it is again simpler to use the **draw()** method to insert all the bitmap data from the source into the new object, as seen in line 34.

NOTE

To copy all the pixels from one object to another, use the **draw()** *method without having to define a rectangle of pixels to copy. We'll discuss the* **draw()** *method again when literally drawing, with a brush, into a bitmap. A quick example can be found in the* copy_displayObject_bmd.fla *source file, in which a source movie clip instantiated as* **p** *is off-stage right.*

```
var w:Number = p.width;
var h:Number = p.height;
var bmd:BitmapData;
var p2:Bitmap;

bmd = new BitmapData(w, h);
bmd.draw(p);

p2 = new Bitmap(bmd);
addChild(p2);
```

Figure 9-4. The color picker created in Chapter 8

Note that we are not adding the data object to the display list because the color picker is already on the stage. We must, however, add an event listener to the picker, as seen in line 36, so we can click it to retrieve a color value.

```
31  var col:uint;
32
33  var bmd:BitmapData = new BitmapData(colorPicker.width, colorPicker.
    height, false, 0xFFFFFFFF);
34  bmd.draw(colorPicker);
35
36  colorPicker.addEventListener(MouseEvent.MOUSE_DOWN, onClick, false,
    0, true);
```

The main functionality of the listener is seen in line 39. The getPixel() method of the BitmapData class populates the col variable with the color beneath the mouse. Because the method is relative to the BitmapData object derived from the picker, the mouse coordinates must also be relative to the same (0, 0) point. Therefore, they are relative to the spectrum. The coordinates are relative to the spectrum layer, rather than the parent picker, in case the picker changes size due, perhaps, to a border or other interface element.

Two additional things are going on in this function, however. The first is that the pixel value is being retrieved only while the mouse is over the spectrum. Line 38 uses the hitTestPoint() method of the DisplayObject class to determine if a collision occurs between the mouse and the spectrum. This prevents invalid colors from being retrieved.

```
37  function onClick(evt:MouseEvent):void {
38      if (spectrum.hitTestPoint(mouseX, mouseY, true)) {
39          col = bmd.getPixel(spectrum.mouseX, spectrum.mouseY);
40          trace(prependZeros(col));
41      }
42  }
43
44  function prependZeros(hex:uint):String {
45      var hexString = hex.toString(16).toUpperCase();
46      var cnt:int = 6 - hexString.length;
47      var zeros:String = "";
48      for (var i:int = 0; i < cnt; i++) {
49          zeros += "0";
50      }
51      return "#" + zeros + hexString;
52  }
```

Second, the retrieved color value is traced to the Output panel. However, it is first run through a function to make it look like a traditional hexadecimal color value. All the prependZeros() function does is convert the numeric color value to an uppercase string, prepend any necessary zeros to ensure a six-digit format, and prepend a number sign.

This last step is only for display purposes. To make practical use of the color, you need only the value of the col variable from the onClick() listener function, which we'll demonstrate in the next section. This display effort may still be helpful should you decide to show text feedback of the active color in some future project.

Set Pixel

To set a pixel in a `BitmapData` object, you need to furnish a color as well as x and y coordinates. Let's add a small canvas to the color picker exercise, and set pixels based on the color chosen from the picker.

Lines 53 through 56 create a 100 x 100-pixel canvas and position it just beneath the picker, adding it to the display list. Lines 58 through 60 create a black `BitmapData` object of the same size, create a bitmap from the data, and add the object to the `canvas` sprite.

```
53   var canvas:Sprite = new Sprite();
54   canvas.x = 100;
55   canvas.y = 220;
56   addChild(canvas);
57
58   var canvasBmd:BitmapData = new BitmapData(100, 100, false,
     0xFF000000);
59   var canvasBm:Bitmap = new Bitmap(canvasBmd);
60   canvas.addChild(canvasBm);
61
62   addEventListener(Event.ENTER_FRAME, onLoop, false, 0, true);
63
64   function onLoop(evt:Event):void {
65       var rndX:Number = Math.round(Math.random() * 100);
66       var rndY:Number = Math.round(Math.random() * 100);
67       canvasBmd.setPixel(rndX, rndY, col);
68   }
```

Figure 9-5. Setting pixels in a canvas

Setting the pixels is accomplished in the listener function. Line 62 adds an enter frame listener to the main timeline that triggers the **onLoop()** function. Therein, random x and y coordinates within the 100 pixel-square range of the canvas size are chosen, and the **setPixel()** method sets the **canvasBmd** pixel at that coordinate to the color most recently defined by the color picker. Figure 9-5 shows the exercise in action.

Drawing into a Bitmap

We've mentioned once or twice in this chapter that it's possible to draw the contents of one `BitmapData` object into another. Let's demonstrate this by actually painting on a canvas. As seen in *brush_eraser.fla*, we'll create a simple, one-color circular brush and an eraser, and the user will be able to switch between them with the press of a key. Figure 9-6 shows an example of a painted area with a swatch of color erased in the middle.

The no-interface functionality of this basic example calls for a dual role for the mouse—both painting and erasing. So we start the exercise by declaring a pair of Boolean variables that will later be used to track its functionality. We then create an empty canvas to hold our bitmap painting. Lines 7 through 11 prepare the drawing surface by creating an empty white `BitmapData` object the size of the stage, populating a bitmap with that data, and adding it to the canvas sprite.

Figure 9-6. A detail of drawing into a BitmapData object with brush and eraser

NOTE

In this painting example, note that neither brush nor eraser is added to the display list. You may want to create brush and eraser icons to follow the mouse to provide feedback for the user, but the sprite does not need to be added to the display list to access its bitmap data.

Lines 13 through 22 round out the tool setup by creating a brush and an eraser. Both tools are created by the same function, each passing in a different color—blue for the brush and white for the eraser. The **createBrush()** function returns a new sprite with an opaque circle of the color requested, with a 20-pixel radius.

```
1    var mouseIsDown:Boolean;
2    var erasing:Boolean;
3
4    var canvas:Sprite = new Sprite();
5    addChild(canvas);
6
7    var w:Number = stage.stageWidth;
8    var h:Number = stage.stageHeight;
9    var bmd:BitmapData = new BitmapData(w, h, false, 0xFFFFFFFF);
10   var bm:Bitmap = new Bitmap(bmd);
11   canvas.addChild(bm);
12
13   var brush:Sprite = createBrush(0x000099);
14   var eraser:Sprite = createBrush(0xFFFFFF);
15
16   function createBrush(col:uint):Sprite {
17       var sp:Sprite = new Sprite();
18       sp.graphics.beginFill(col, 1);
19       sp.graphics.drawCircle(0, 0, 20);
20       sp.graphics.endFill();
21       return sp;
22   }
```

A trio of listeners controls the brush/eraser functionality. The mouse down listener (lines 27 through 32) first sets the **mouseIsDown** Boolean to **true** so the app will know to alter the canvas. Based on whether or not the **shiftKey** property of the incoming mouse event is **true**, the function knows whether or not the user is holding down the shift key when the mouse is clicked. If so, the **erasing** Boolean is set to **true**. The mouse up listener (lines 34 through 37) resets both Booleans to **false**, as the user is neither painting nor erasing. This combination of listeners toggles the paint/erase functionality with every mouse click.

The enter frame listener (lines 39 through 49) starts with a conditional to determine the appropriate tool mode. If both the **mouseIsDown** and **erasing** variables are **true**, the eraser follows the mouse. If **erasing** is **false**, the brush follows the mouse. In both cases, the bitmap data from the appropriate tool is drawn into the **BitmapData** object used by the canvas.

```
23   canvas.addEventListener(MouseEvent.MOUSE_DOWN, onDown, false, 0,
     true);
24   canvas.addEventListener(MouseEvent.MOUSE_UP, onUp, false, 0, true);
25   this.addEventListener(Event.ENTER_FRAME, onLoop, false, 0, true);
26
27   function onDown(evt:MouseEvent):void {
28       mouseIsDown = true;
29       if (evt.shiftKey) {
30           erasing = true;
31       }
32   }
```

```
33
34  function onUp(evt:MouseEvent):void {
35      mouseIsDown = false;
36      erasing = false;
37  }
38
39  function onLoop(evt:Event):void {
40      if (mouseIsDown && erasing) {
41          eraser.x = mouseX;
42          eraser.y = mouseY;
43          bmd.draw(eraser, eraser.transform.matrix);
44      } else if (mouseIsDown) {
45          brush.x = mouseX;
46          brush.y = mouseY;
47          bmd.draw(brush, brush.transform.matrix);
48      }
49  }
```

By default, no transformations from the source or destination `BitmapData` objects are used by the `draw()` method. The effect is that the bitmap data from the source object at point (0,0) will be drawn into the canvas at point (0,0). That wouldn't make a very interesting painting program. In this case, we are not merely copying the data; we also rely on the location of the brush or eraser relative to the canvas. Therefore, we pass the transform matrix from the source object into the `draw()` method so the appropriate translation values for x and y can be calculated and the new pixels will be drawn into their correct locations.

Blend Modes

Not every bitmap manipulation requires building `BitmapData` objects from the ground up. Sometimes you may only need to apply a quick effect to get the result you need. One of the most basic, yet very useful, effects you can apply is a *blend mode*. ActionScript supports a set of these compositing algorithms behaviors by which one element is blended into another, similar to the blending modes used in Photoshop. Though Flash's set of blend modes is understandably smaller than Photoshop's, many of the most widely used modes (such as Darken, Lighten, Screen, Multiply, Overlay, and Hard Light) are available.

The syntax required to apply a blend mode to a display object or `BitmapData` object is very simple. The `blendMode` property is set to one of the constants of the `BlendMode` class that identifies each mode by name. Here is an example:

```
dispObj.blendMode = BlendMode.DARKEN;
```

Let's take a look at a practical example that makes use of a couple blend modes. One of the modes used is Darken, which preserves the darker of each of the red, green, and blue color components of every overlapping (foreground and background) pixel. This mode is typically used for dropping out a light background of an image without an alpha channel.

The second mode used is Overlay, which adjusts the compositing method of the foreground element dynamically, based on the darkness of the

Figure 9-7. A collage of original assets prior to the use of blend modes

Figure 9-8. The finished composition with gradient fill and blend modes

background. If the background is lighter than 50-percent gray, the elements are screened, resulting in a bleaching effect. If the background is darker than 50-percent gray, the elements are multiplied, resulting in a darkening effect.

The Darken mode will be used to composite a JPEG of text onto an image, removing a white background from the text element. The Overlay mode will be used with a gradient fill to alter the color of an island sky to mimic the color-rich sunsets typical of tropical areas. Figure 9-7 shows a detail of the parts that will be used. Notice the white background in the partially visible text element, and the mixture of light and dark grays and blues in the sky where the overlay will be applied. Figure 9-8 shows the finished effect.

This exercise uses the accompanying source file *blend_modes_darken_overlay.fla*, which contains a bitmap of a beach and a bitmap of text. The former has the class name **Beach**, and the latter uses the class name **Waikiki**.

Lines 1 through 3 of this script review the process of adding library bitmap symbols to the display list. The beach image is the first to be added to the stage. Lines 5 through 15 review the steps required to create a gradient fill, as described in Chapter 8. This fill is linear, evenly distributes an orange from 100-percent opaque to 100-percent transparent, and measures 310 x 110 pixels. This size occupies the width of the beach image, and the height spans from the top of the beach image to its horizon. In line 7, the linear gradient is rotated 90 degrees to transition from top to bottom, rather than the default left to right, so the necessary utility function for converting familiar degrees to required radians is found in lines 23 through 25.

The blend modes are applied in lines 14 and 20. The overlay is assigned the Overlay mode, changing a harsh orange gradient to a simulated sun-saturated skyline, in which the orange is applied based on the density of the gray levels in the clouds and the sky. The text is assigned the Darken mode, so only the word "Waikiki" remains visible after compositing, the white background having dropped out because white is lighter than all red, green, and blue color components of the background.

```
1   var beachBmd:Beach = new Beach(0, 0);
2   var beach:Bitmap = new Bitmap(beachBmd);
3   addChild(beach);
4
5   var gradType:String = GradientType.LINEAR;
6   var matrix:Matrix = new Matrix();
7   matrix.createGradientBox(310, 110, deg2rad(90), 0, 0);
8   var colors:Array = [0xFF6600, 0xFF6600];
9   var alphas:Array = [1, 0];
10  var ratios:Array = [0, 255];
11  var canvas = new Sprite();
12  canvas.graphics.beginGradientFill(gradType, colors, alphas, ratios, matrix);
13  canvas.graphics.drawRect(0, 0, 310, 110);
14  canvas.blendMode = BlendMode.OVERLAY;
15  addChild(canvas);
16
```

```
17  var waikikiBmd:Waikiki = new Waikiki(0, 0);
18  var waikiki:Bitmap = new Bitmap(waikikiBmd);
19  addChild(waikiki);
20  waikiki.blendMode = BlendMode.DARKEN;
21  waikiki.y = 10;
22
23  function deg2rad(deg:Number):Number {
24      return deg * (Math.PI / 180);
25  }
```

Even if you only glance at Figure 9-8, you will probably recognize the effects of these more traditional blend modes. However, we'd like to call your attention to three Flash-specific blend modes that aren't as easy to grasp: Layer, Alpha, and Erase.

Layer is an extremely useful and welcome problem solver. In brief, Layer composites the children of a display object container to which it is applied, allowing any subsequently applied effects to transform the object, or "layer," as a whole, rather than as individual children of the object. This can be made clearer by demonstrating this effect.

Figure 9-9. Before (above) and after (below) the use of the Layer blend mode when setting the alpha value of the enclosing parent to 50 percent

Assume you have a movie clip, and within that clip are two adjacent squares, red and blue. A green square of the same dimensions is centered on top of the underlying red and blue squares. If you were to apply a 50-percent alpha value to the parent movie clip, you might expect the parent movie clip opacity to be reduced by 50 percent, producing a lighter version of exactly what you saw. Unfortunately, Flash goes into the parent clip and applies a 50-percent alpha reduction to each of the children individually.

This produces an unpleasant effect, which can be seen in the top illustration of Figure 9-9. Because each of the squares is partially transparent, their colors blend, creating four bands. Left to right, the first is 50-percent red, the second is 50-percent red and 50-percent green, the third is 50-percent blue and 50-percent green, and the fourth is 50-percent blue.

When applying the Layer blend mode, the children of the clip are composited together as a single item and the alpha value is correctly applied to the container, not each child within. As a result, you see the expected appearance of the original three colors all at 50 percent, as seen in the bottom half of Figure 9-9.

The Layer mode also facilitates the use of two more blend modes, Alpha and Erase. The functionality of each is straightforward. Given a foreground display object with alpha data, such as a movie clip with a semi-transparent PNG inside, the two modes behave this way: Alpha will knock out a background element using the foreground element's alpha channel, and Erase will do the opposite, knocking out the background using the non-transparent pixel data. The effects of each can be seen in Figure 9-10. (The white areas are actually missing from the background element, showing the stage beneath the image.)

The important item to note, however, is that these effects will work only when inside a display object container to which the Layer blend mode is applied. The child elements must be composited together first for the effect to be

Figure 9-10. The Erase (above) and Alpha (below) blend modes

visible. In other words, if you took the same movie clip with semitransparent PNG therein, and placed it on top of a background element on the stage (rather than in a display object container), the background would not drop out even if the Alpha or Erase blend modes were applied. Instead, it would cause the foreground element to disappear altogether.

Bitmap Filters

Filters have been a mainstay of graphics editing programs for years, adding a touch of realism to images and illustrations with a minimum of effort. Along with Flash 8's introduction of powerful bitmap editing capabilities came a set of filters with which most graphics editors will be familiar.

Although there is no official category labeled as such, we've divided our brief look at filters into two sections: basic and advanced. Using Adobe Photoshop for comparison, basic filters are like Layer Styles—quick, easy-to-apply effects with limited functionality—while advanced filters are more robust and are more like the features found in Photoshop's Filters menu.

Basic Filters

A good place to start when learning how to control filter effects with code is a subset of filters found simultaneously in the Flash Property Inspector and in dedicated ActionScript classes. This convenient overlap lets you play around with a GUI interface to see how various properties affect the appearance of the filter. These filters include **DropShadow**, **Blur**, **Glow**, **Bevel**, **GradientGlow**, and **GradientBevel**.

For the most part, the properties of the ActionScript filter classes correlate closely with the properties found in the Flash Property Inspector for the same filter, providing a smooth transition to ActionScript without much effort. Let's use the **DropShadow** filter in the next example, shown in Figure 9-11.

We begin the script by creating the drop shadow filter. Once created, it can be applied to objects at any time. An instance of the aptly named class is created in line 1, using the default values of the filter. Individual properties can be set when the instance is created or adjusted thereafter. In this case, the distance from the display object and the degree of blur in the x and y directions are increased slightly, and the opacity of the shadow is decreased to 60 percent.

Figure 9-11. An interactive element with **DropShadowFilter** *applied (above) and removed (below) to simulate the pressing of a raised button*

Lines 7 through 14 use the **Graphics** class to create a basic, yellow rectangle with rounded corners and add it to the display list. Line 15 is where the shadow is applied. The display object has a property called **filters**, which is an array that allows multiple filters to be applied. This means, for example, that you could use **Bevel** and **DropShadow** at the same time. In this example, only **DropShadow** is in use so the **ds** filter instance is placed into the **filters** array. At this point, the application of the filter is complete. However, this example changes with user input, so let's look at its interactive elements.

```
1   var ds:DropShadowFilter = new DropShadowFilter();
2   ds.distance = 5;
3   ds.blurX = 10;
4   ds.blurY = 10;
5   ds.alpha = 0.6;
6
7   var sp:Sprite = new Sprite();
8   with (sp.graphics) {
9       lineStyle(1, 0x000000, 1, true);
10      beginFill(0xFFFF00, 1);
11      drawRoundRect(0, 0, 100, 50, 15);
12      endFill();
13  }
14  addChild(sp);
15  sp.filters = [ds];
```

Because we went the simple route of using a sprite for our interactive element (rather than building a multistate button with the **SimpleButton** class, as seen in the applied example at the end of Chapter 8), we set the **buttonMode** property of the sprite to **true** in line 16. This won't create the multistate button of a true button, but it will provide cursor feedback.

The listeners in lines 17 through 19 trigger functions based on mouse behavior. The mouse down function clears the **filters** array, removing the drop shadow effect from the sprite. Both the mouse up and mouse out behaviors repopulate the **filters** array with the drop shadow, restoring the elevated "up" appearance to the sprite.

```
16  sp.buttonMode = true;
17  sp.addEventListener(MouseEvent.MOUSE_DOWN, onDown, false, 0, true);
18  sp.addEventListener(MouseEvent.MOUSE_UP, onUp, false, 0, true);
19  sp.addEventListener(MouseEvent.MOUSE_OUT, onUp, false, 0, true);
20
21  function onDown(evt:MouseEvent):void {
22      sp.filters = [];
23  }
24  function onUp(evt:MouseEvent):void {
25      sp.filters = [ds];
26  }
```

Another way to handle this task would be to leave the **ds** filter active, but change some of its properties. For example, if you wanted to simulate casting a shadow from a moving light source, you could vary the distance, angle, and alpha values of the filter.

Filters can be used in creative ways. For example, a basic motion blur can significantly improve the appearance of animated objects or simulate depth of field. If you place the following two lines at the end of your brush/eraser exercise, from the "Drawing into a Bitmap" section of this chapter, it will change your standard brush to an airbrush. This filter will blur the brush 40 pixels in both x and y directions, significantly softening its edges (see Figure 9-12). If you apply the same filter to the eraser, you can soften its edges, too.

Figure 9-12. A Blur filter applied to both brush and eraser in the "Drawing into a Bitmap" exercise

```
var blur:BlurFilter = new BlurFilter(40, 40);
brush.filters = [blur];
```

Advanced Filters

A number of more advanced ActionScript filters exist, allowing scripters to produce some impressive visual effects usually reserved for prerendered assets produced in external applications. We will focus on the **Convolution**, **DisplacementMap** and **PerlinNoise** filters in this section, and then group a trio of color tools together in the following section.

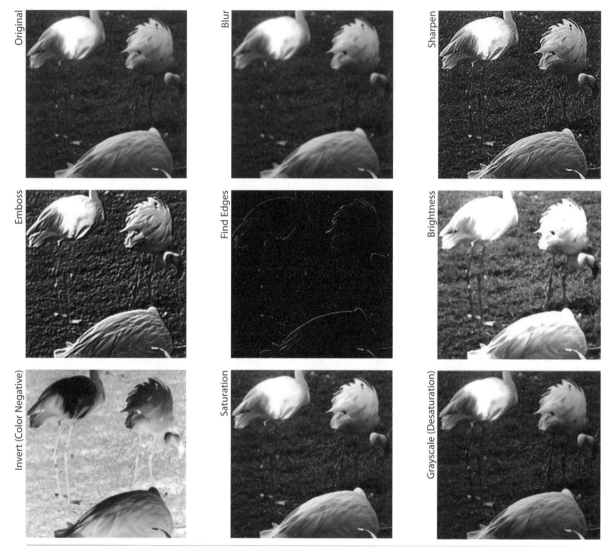

Figure 9-13. Advanced filter effects

ConvolutionFilter

Convolution filtering is typically a part of multiple visual effects in most, if not all, pixel-editing applications. Photoshop offers direct access to a convolution filter (renamed to *Custom...* some years ago, and found in the Filters→Other menu), but usually the filter works quietly behind the scenes.

This is not surprising because using the filter effectively requires at least a working knowledge of matrices. The transformation capabilities made possible by matrices calculate pixel color values by combining values from adjacent pixels to produce a wide variety of image effects. These effects include, but are not limited to, blurring, sharpening, embossing, edge detection, and brightness.

The ConvolutionFilter doesn't use the same matrix format discussed in Chapter 8. You can define any number of rows and columns in a convolution matrix, and the structure of the matrix determines how each pixel is affected. It probably isn't necessary that you acquire a detailed understanding of how a convolution matrix works. In most circumstances, you'll probably use experimentation to determine a satisfactory setting, and then create a class of presets for specific projects. However, if you want a little guidance for your experimentation, read the sidebar, "ConvolutionFilter: A Quick Look Inside."

Here's a handful of representative presets that you can use in your projects. This example code has been written with a reusable function so you can see multiple effects on instances of a single image. Import a small image into Flash and create a movie clip from that image. Drag several copies to the stage, instantiating them as

---

ConvolutionFilter: A Quick Look Inside

A lengthy discussion of the math behind the **ConvolutionFilter** is beyond the scope of this book. However, for a high-level overview, we can focus on three key structural elements of the matrix: the center value in the grid, the symmetry of the surrounding grid elements, and the sum of all of the grid elements. Consider a typical 3 x 3 matrix. The center value in the matrix represents the current pixel (all pixels in an image are analyzed), while the remaining elements are the 8 adjacent pixels. The numbers in each matrix element determine how the color values of that pixel should be used to affect the values of the current pixel.

Therefore, a convolution matrix consisting of all zeros will turn an image black because no color values are used for any pixel. A matrix with all zeros except for the center value of 1 will not change the image because the current pixel uses its own existing color values of 1, while no color values from surrounding pixels are used. For the last example, if the matrix contains all zeros except a center value of 2, the image will be brighter because the color values of the current pixel are being considered at a factor of 2.

Basic syntax for the circumstances discussed follows, with each example, in turn, affecting a display object instantiated as **dispObj**. The **ConvolutionFilter** constructor requires two parameters, the number of rows and the number of columns,

both of which will be 3 in our examples. Another parameter is the matrix used to affect the image. If you do not include this parameter, a default no-change matrix (all zeros but the center element, which is 1) will be created. This can be used to reset any changes made by prior convolution filters.

```
var conv:ConvolutionFilter;

var black:Array = [0, 0, 0,
                   0, 0, 0,
                   0, 0, 0];
conv = new ConvolutionFilter(3, 3, black);
dispObj.filters = [conv];

var noChange:Array = [0, 0, 0,
                      0, 1, 0,
                      0, 0, 0];
conv = new ConvolutionFilter(3, 3, noChange);
dispObj.filters = [conv];

var brighter:Array = [0, 0, 0,
                      0, 2, 0,
                      0, 0, 0];
conv = new ConvolutionFilter(3, 3, brighter);
dispObj.filters = [conv];
```
—Continued—

ConvolutionFilter: A Quick Look Inside (continued)

For the next set of examples, let's focus on the symmetry of the surrounding pixel color values. The **embossUp** example darkens the three pixels to the upper left of the current pixel by 2, and brightens the three pixels to the lower right of the current pixel. The result is a traditional embossing effect where the lighter colors seem to pop out of the image.

By contrast, the **embossDown** example flips the negative polarity on the surrounding pixels, causing the upper-left pixels to be darkened and the lower-right pixels to be brightened, so the image seems to be reverse-embossed, appearing as if the lighter colors are stamped into the image.

```
var embossUp:Array = [-2, -2, 0,
                      -2,  1, 2,
                       0,  2, 2];
conv = new ConvolutionFilter(3, 3, embossUp);
dispObj.filters = [conv];


var embossDown:Array = [2,  2,  0,
                        2,  1, -2,
                        0, -2, -2];
conv = new ConvolutionFilter(3, 3, embossDown);
dispObj.filters = [conv];
```

Finally, let's consider a matrix that, when all elements are added up, does not result in a value of 1. The following example is a matrix that uses the left, top, right, and bottom adjacent pixel color values to affect the current pixel. The result is a blurring effect. However, a dramatic brightening of the image obscures this because the sum of the matrix elements is 5. This means the image's affected state will be five times brighter than its original state.

If increased brightness is not desired, you can compensate by using an optional fourth parameter of the **ConvolutionFilter** class, called a *divisor*. As its name implies, you can divide the sum of the matrix by this number to return to a total value of 1, eliminating any brightening effect. The first **conv** instance below uses only the first three parameters without compensating for brightness. The second **conv** instance adds the divisor in the fourth parameter.

```
var blur:Array = [0, 1, 0,
                  1, 1, 1,
                  0, 1, 0];
conv = new ConvolutionFilter(3, 3, blur);
dispObj.filters = [conv];


conv = new ConvolutionFilter(3, 3, blur, 5);
dispObj.filters = [conv];
```

dispObj0, **dispObj1**, and so on. You can also see the accompanying source file, *convolution_filter.fla*.

```
1   var conv:ConvolutionFilter;
2
3   function convFilter(dispObj:DisplayObject, matrix:Array,
    divisor:int):void {
4       var conv:ConvolutionFilter =
        new ConvolutionFilter(3, 3, matrix, divisor);
5       dispObj.filters = [conv];
6   }
7
8   var blur:Array = [0, 1, 0,
9                     1, 1, 1,
10                    0, 1, 0];
11  convFilter(dispObj0, blur, 5);
12
13  var sharpen:Array = [ 0, -1,  0,
14                       -1,  5, -1,
15                        0, -1,  0];
16  convFilter(dispObj1, sharpen, 1);
17
18  var emboss:Array = [-1, -1, 0,
19                      -1,  1, 1,
20                       0,  1, 1];
```

```
21  convFilter(dispObj2, emboss, 1);
22
23  var edges:Array = [0, -1,  0,
24                    -1,  4, -1,
25                     0, -1,  0];
26  convFilter(dispObj3, edges, 1);
27
28  var brightness:Array = [0, 0, 0,
29                          0, 2, 0,
30                          0, 0, 0];
31  convFilter(dispObj4, brightness, 1);
```

Other Flash effects

Two other very useful and entertaining effects supported by Flash are the **PerlinNoise** generator and the **DisplacmentMap** filter. Perlin noise is widely used for generating naturalistic animated effects like fog, clouds, smoke, water, and fire, as well as textures like wood, stone, and terrain. Displacement maps are used to translate (or displace) pixels to add extra dimension to surfaces. They are commonly used to add realism to textures (such as a pitted or grooved surface) as well as distort images as if seen through a refracting material like glass or water.

Figure 9-14. Displacement map filter using Perlin noise to simulate waves and distort foreground elements during animation

This exercise will create an animated Perlin noise texture that will then be used as the source for a displacement map. The combined effect will be applied to a foreground image that will appear to undulate as if experiencing the effect of water currents. The source material we'll use is a picture of a reef aquarium, as seen in Figure 9-14. The soft corals that move with water current in real life have been pulled into the foreground image, and will be affected by the filters, while the rock remains in the background so it, too, doesn't appear to move with the virtual current.

Perlin noise

The first step in the process is to create a **BitmapData** object to contain the Perlin noise. Our image will cover the stage, so we pass the stage width and height into the object to size it appropriately. Lines 2 and 3 (on the next page create) a bitmap using the bitmap data, and then add that bitmap to the display list. However, the lines are commented out because we do not want to see the Perlin noise. We want to have access only to the data created by the algorithm for the displacement map we will create. However, it is often very helpful to see the Perlin noise as you work so you can experiment with various settings, as seen in Figure 9-15. If you wish to do so after creating the noise generator, simply comment in lines 2 and 3 until you are satisfied with the effect, and then comment out these lines again when moving on to displacement.

NOTE

Ken Perlin developed the Perlin noise algorithm while creating the special effects for the 1982 film, Tron. At the time, the extensive use of effects in that film may have been cost-prohibitive using traditional multiexposure film compositing techniques. Perlin noise was used to manipulate the near-constant computer-generated glows and shadings, among other effects. Mr. Perlin won an Academy Award for Technical Achievement in 1997 for his contributions to the industry.

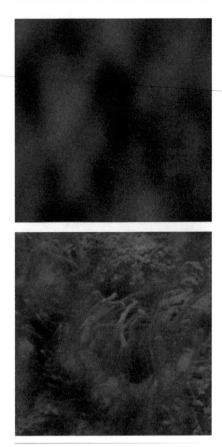

Figure 9-15. Perlin noise detail without alpha data (top) and with (bottom)

NOTE

Perlin noise layers are called octaves because, like musical octaves, each one doubles the frequency of the previous octave, increasing detail within the texture. It's also important to note that the processor power required to generate noise patterns increases with the number of octaves used.

The Perlin noise generator has a number of settings that will produce dramatically different results when adjusted. As we discuss these settings, we will reference natural phenomena, like water and smoke, as what will hopefully be common experiences to which you can relate. We will first discuss the settings of the filter and then simply pass these settings into the constructor later on in line 28.

```
1   var bmpData:BitmapData = new BitmapData(stage.stageWidth,
    stage.stageHeight);
2   //var bmp:Bitmap = new Bitmap(bmpData);
3   //addChild(bmp);
4
5   var baseX:Number = 50;
6   var baseY:Number = 75;
7   var numOctaves:Number = 2;
8   var randomSeed:Number = Math.random();
9   var stitch:Boolean = true;
10  var fractalNoise:Boolean = true;
11  var channelOptions:Number = BitmapDataChannel.BLUE;
12  var grayScale:Boolean= false;
13  var offsets:Array = new Array(new Point(), new Point());
```

Lines 5 and 6 set the scale of the texture in the x and y directions. Think of this as influencing the number of waves you can see at one time in water. A very large scale might result in the look of a swelling sea, and a small scale might look like a babbling brook.

Line 7 determines the number of *octaves*, which are discreet layers of noise that function independently of each other. A single-octave noise will not be as complex as a multioctave noise and, during animation, you can move a single-octave noise in only one direction at a time. You can create interesting animations with single octaves, like the look of running water, but a multioctave noise can animate each layer in a different direction. The combined effect can appear like colliding waves moving in multiple directions.

A random seed, or randomly chosen starting point (much like a seed is the start of a plant), for the texture is set in line 8. To appear more natural—one of the most important concepts behind Perlin noise—you don't want the same texture every time. This seed allows you to vary the origin of the calculation to create seemingly random outcomes with each value you use.

Line 9 determines whether the edges of the area defined when creating the noise pattern are stitched together in an attempt to create a seamless tile. When creating small textures, this "stitching" is not usually needed, but it is recommended when animating the effect.

Using fractal noise or turbulence techniques when generating the effect is dictated in line 10. Fractal noise generates a smoother effect while turbulence produces more distinct transitions between levels of detail, useful for sharper changes from one part of the texture to the next. For example, fractal noise might be used to create a terrain map of rolling hills or an oceanscape, while turbulence might be better suited to a terrain of mountains or water surfaces over a reef.

Line 11 chooses which channels of bitmap data are used: red, green, blue, and/ or alpha. These can be indicated by constants from the `BitmapDataChannel` class, or with integers. You can also use the bitwise OR operator (|) to combine channels to create multicolor effects or combine color with alpha. For example, combining alpha with grayscale noise (discussed next) can create fog or smoke with transparent areas through which a background can be seen.

In this example, because we are generating only the pattern to provide data for a displacement map, we need only one channel. Blue was chosen arbitrarily because this will ultimately be used for a water effect, and it might be a little easier to visualize when experimenting with settings and a visible bitmap. You can improve the visualization a bit by adding an alpha channel to the mix, so you can see the underlying image through the pattern. Figure 9-15 shows the visible BitmapData object with and without the alpha channel. You only have to *change* line 11 (this is not an additional line of script) to this:

```
11  var channelOptions:Number = BitmapDataChannel.BLUE |
    BitmapDataChannel.ALPHA;
```

The grayscale parameter set in line 12 desaturates the pattern so it generates only grays. This setting conveniently converts the red, green, and blue colors to grayscale within the function so you don't have to apply additional color transformation techniques (which we'll discuss later in the chapter).

Lastly, line 13 creates an array of offset points, one for each octave, that control the location of the noise pattern generated. During animation, you will alter the position of these points to move the pattern.

Having set all the values required to create a Perlin noise pattern, we will supply the values to the `perlinNoise()` method during the animation process discussed in just a moment. First, we need to set up the displacement map settings.

DisplacementMap

The `DisplacementMap` filter is significantly simpler. It also requires an x and y scale, as seen in lines 15 and 16. Think of this as the size of the waves when looking through water, or the degree of refraction when looking through glass, in each direction.

Next, lines 17 and 18 determine which color channel will affect the distortion in each direction. We will be using the Perlin noise pattern as source data for the displacement, and we used the blue channel for the noise, so we use the same channel here.

Line 19 sets the displacement mode to *clamp*, which clamps the displacement to the edge of the source data. Another option, as a comparison, is *wrap*, which wraps the distortion from edge to edge. For example, if a displacement pushed the image beyond its left edge, the distortion would reappear on the right edge of the image. This is fine for tiled patterns but not useful for affecting a realistic image of a recognizable object. You don't want to see the top of

NOTE

You can reuse the same random seed value in a Perlin noise calculation to achieve the same result at another time. The random seed is not a Boolean that says randomize or don't randomize. Instead, it is the starting point from which the calculation arrives at its outcome.

a person's head appearing beneath their feet as a displacement wraps from top to bottom edge.

Finally, we create the **DisplacementMapFilter** in line 20. This will use the same **BitmapData** object that is being affected by the Perlin noise pattern, so the degree of displacement will be determined by that image data. When we apply the filter to an image, the image will be distorted accordingly.

```
14   var dMap:DisplacementMapFilter;
15   var xScale:Number = 15;
16   var yScale:Number = 10;
17   var componentX:uint = BitmapDataChannel.BLUE;
18   var componentY:uint = BitmapDataChannel.BLUE;
19   var dMode:String = DisplacementMapFilterMode.CLAMP;
20   dMap = new DisplacementMapFilter(bmpData, new Point(), componentX,
       componentY, xScale, yScale, dMode);
```

To animate this effect, we start with a listener that triggers the **onLoop()** function every enter frame. The first thing the function does is update the offset points for each octave of the Perlin noise pattern, seen in lines 24 and 25. This example moves the first octave down by adding 2 pixels to its y offset, and moves the second octave to the left by subtracting 1 pixel from its x offset, every enter frame.

With each change to the offset points, the **perlinNoise()** method is called (line 26), applying all the previously set parameters along with the offset updates. Finally, with each change to the Perlin noise, the **DisplacementMap** filter source data is updated, so the new values of the **DisplacementMap** filter must be reapplied to the display object in line 28.

```
21   addEventListener(Event.ENTER_FRAME, onLoop, false, 0, true);
22
23   function onLoop(evt:Event):void {
24       offsets[0].y += 2;
25       offsets[1].x -= 1;
26       bmpData.perlinNoise(baseX, baseY, numOctaves, randomSeed,
           stitch, fractalNoise, channelOptions, grayScale, offsets);
27
28       tank_mc.filters = [dMap];
29   }
```

Color Effects

There are multiple ways to apply color effects using ActionScript, and we will focus on three. The first is a relatively straightforward way of altering the emphasis of individual color channels in an image using the **ColorTransform** class. The second is a more powerful technique that uses the **ColorMatrixFilter** to apply a detailed matrix to simultaneously affect change to all color channels and alpha, which we will use to desaturate an image. The last method discussed is the simplest, using the static **Color** class to apply a tint to a display object.

ColorTransform

The `ColorTransform` class can be used to easily adjust individual color and alpha channels of a display object or `BitmapData` object. We will focus exclusively on color in the examples that follow, and use the class to invert an image (create a color negative), and apply a simple saturation effect.

The class offers two ways to change color. First, you can multiply a color channel by a fraction to increase or decrease its effect. For example, you can double the weight of the color by using a value of 2, and you can reduce the weight of the color in half by using 0.5 as a multiplier. Second, you can offset a color channel from -255 to 255 after the multiplier is applied. For example, assuming a default multiplier of 1, an offset value of 255 would maximize the red channel, 0 would apply no change, and -255 would remove all red from the image.

The following exercise manipulates three hypothetical movie clips instantiated as `mc0`, `mc1`, and `mc2`. Line 1 instantiates the `ColorTransform` class, and the last line of each of the following three code blocks applies the transformation to the `colorTransform` property of the movie clip's `transform` object.

Lines 3 through 12 represent a default color transform. By using a multiplier of 1 and an offset of 0, you can effectively reset any prior color transformation. Although we're focusing on color in this example, alpha multiplier and offset values have been included to show the complete syntax of a reset.

The next code block inverts all color in the image. The multiplier for all color channels is set to -1, which effectively turns the image black, and then the offset values are set to full to revert back to color. This effect can be seen in the "Invert (Color Negative)" example from Figure 9-13.

Finally, the last block demonstrates a simple change in saturation. The original offset values of all colors remain unchanged, but the color multipliers are increased by 0.5 for each channel. This effect can be seen in the "Saturation" example from Figure 9-13. You could also partially desaturate an image using the same technique but applying a multiplier value of less than 1 to each color channel.

```
1    var ct:ColorTransform = new ColorTransform();
2
3    //no change
4    ct.redMultiplier = 1;
5    ct.greenMultiplier = 1;
6    ct.blueMultiplier = 1;
7    ct.alphaMultiplier = 1;
8    ct.redOffset = 0;
9    ct.greenOffset = 0;
10   ct.blueOffset = 0;
11   ct.alphaOffset = 0;
12   mc0.transform.colorTransform = ct;
13
14   //invert
15   ct.redMultiplier = -1;
```

```
16  ct.greenMultiplier = -1;
17  ct.blueMultiplier = -1;
18  ct.redOffset = 255;
19  ct.greenOffset = 255;
20  ct.blueOffset = 255;
21  mc1.transform.colorTransform = ct;
22
23  //basic saturation
24  ct.redMultiplier = 1.5;
25  ct.greenMultiplier = 1.5;
26  ct.blueMultiplier = 1.5;
27  ct.redOffset = 0;
28  ct.greenOffset = 0;
29  ct.blueOffset = 0;
30  mc2.transform.colorTransform = ct;
```

ColorMatrixFilter

The next color effect uses the **ColorMatrixFilter** class. This class uses a 4 x 5 matrix to transform red, green, blue, and alpha values of the image, and can be used to create advanced hue, saturation, and contrast changes, among other effects. The following example shows using luminance constants to desaturate an image to create a color grayscale.

The identity matrix for the **ColorMatrixFilter** class is as follows:

```
        Rs, Gs, Bs, As, Os
Rnew =  1,  0,  0,  0,  0,
Gnew =  0,  1,  0,  0,  0,
Bnew =  0,  0,  1,  0,  0,
Anew =  0,  0,  0,  1,  0
```

The rows represent the sum of changes in red, green, blue, and alpha values for each pixel, while the columns represent the source R, G, B, and A values. The first four columns are the multipliers for red, green, blue, and alpha values of the source, and the fifth column is the offset value for each row. The identity matrix shows a default multiplier of 1 and offset of 0 for each color channel, and no change to the other source color multiplier or offset values for that channel—that is, new red equals old red, the new green equals old green, and so on.

By introducing changes to the other color values, the appearance of each pixel will change. For example, you can affect subtle contrast or saturation changes by adding a little green and blue into the new red channel, or a little red and blue into the new green channel, and so on.

A good way to make this clear is to demonstrate the creation of a color grayscale image. When creating the new red value for a pixel, instead of using a multiplier of 1 for red and 0 for green and blue, you can use a *partial* value of 1 for all colors (with no change in alpha or offset). There will be no change in brightness because the sum of each row will still be 1. The alpha row receives no change to R, G, or B values, and the standard alpha multiplier of 1 is used with no offset.

The only question is, what partial values should be used for each color? Knowing that hexadecimal values of gray are created with equal values of each color (0x666666, for example), it is common to see a value of .33 used for each R, G, and B component of every pixel. However, it turns out that an unequal value of red, green, and blue combine to create better grayscale. We can take advantage of research completed before us to try to achieve color grayscales that are more pleasing to the eye, using what are known as *luminance constants*.

By applying these constants to the source R, G, and B values, the new red, green, and blue values for each pixel will be optimized for grayscale display. The newly created matrix is passed to the filter constructor (line 8), and the result is applied to the filters array of the display object (line 13).

NOTE

Luminance is the amount of light that is reflected or emitted by a color. In lay terms, luminance is brightness (which is more of a human perception than a measured quantity). NTSC broadcast luminance constants (TV grayscale) published in 1954 were replaced by values better tuned to CRT monitors and computer displays.

For many years, Paul Haeberli's luminance vectors of .3086 for red, .6094 for green, and .0820 for blue, published in 1993, were used for color grayscale. Recently, these values have been adjusted for HDTV standards and are now slightly different. Red has reduced slightly, and green and blue have increased slightly, over previous values. The current standard is .2127 for red, .7152 for green, and .0722 for blue. Experiment to see which combination you prefer.

```
1    //ITU-R BT.709-5 Parameter Values for the HDTV
2    //  Standards for Production, 2002
3    var lumRd:Number = .2127;
4    var lumGr:Number = .7152;
5    var lumBl:Number = .0722;
6
7    //grayscale
8    var grayscale:ColorMatrixFilter =
         new ColorMatrixFilter([lumRd, lumGr, lumBl, 0, 0,
9                                lumRd, lumGr, lumBl, 0, 0,
10                               lumRd, lumGr, lumBl, 0, 0,
11                                   0,     0,     0, 1, 0]);
12
13   dispObj.filters = [grayscale];
```

Color

The last color manipulation is the simplest. It uses the **Color** class to set the tint of a display object. The tint is set the same way line and fill styles are set using the graphics class. Two parameters, color and alpha, are used to define the tint. Once the tint is created, it is applied to the **colorTransform** property of the display object's transform object, as in previous examples.

```
import fl.motion.Color;
var blueTint:Color = new Color();
blueTint.setTint(0x0000FF, 1);
mc.transform.colorTransform = blueTint;
```

Finally, we want to reemphasize a really cool feature of the **Color** class that we made use of in our custom button class in Chapter 8. Given two colors, and a weighting between them, the **interpolateColor()** method can determine a new color. This example passes in red and blue and gets purple in return.

```
import fl.motion.Color;
var newColor:uint = Color.interpolateColor(0xFF0000, 0x0000FF,.5);
trace(newColor.toString(16));
//7f007f
```

The final color is equivalent to 127 red, 0 green, and 127 blue, or half-red/half-blue, which is purple.

Image Encoding and Saving

The last thing we want to cover is encoding a **BitmapData** object and then transmitting that data to a server for saving or downloading. The encoding process involves sending your bitmap data to an image encoding class. Fortunately, JPEG and PNG encoders have been created and provided by Adobe. Adobe's distribution license prohibits us from including the classes with our companion source files, but you can download them from their code archive in Google Code.

They are both part of Adobe's AS3 Core Library. Information can be found at *http://labs.adobe.com/wiki/index.php/ActionScript_3:resources:apis:libraries*, and a direct link to the library at *http://code.google.com/p/as3corelib/* will allow you to download individual classes and an archive of the library, or use an SVN client to read the most current branch or trunk. Because you will be downloading the classes to make use of this exercise, you must follow the class paths used in the library, or edit your file and the classes if you wish to move them.

The saving portion of the exercise is accomplished using PHP. You must have a server that supports PHP to try this, or substitute your own server-side technology to accomplish the same functionality.

ActionScript

The heavy lifting of this exercise is done during the encoding process by Adobe's **JPGEncoder** class. The class itself is a bit outside the scope of this book, so we'll cover its use but not its inner workings. The actual saving process is not very demanding. After importing the **JPGEncoder** class in line 1, line 3 adds a mouse click listener to a button that will serve to trigger the save.

Lines 6 and 7 (on the next page) create a **BitmapData** object and use the **draw()** method to quickly place the entire contents of a hypothetical painting canvas, instantiated as **canvas**, into that object. This is the same name as the canvas used in the "Drawing into a Bitmap" section of this chapter, so you can add this feature to that exercise, if you wish.

Line 9 instantiates the **JPGEncoder** class, passing the image quality setting of 100 into the constructor when doing so. Line 10 creates a **ByteArray** that stores all the binary data that results when the **JPGEncoder** encodes the image.

Line 12 creates a **URLRequestHeader**, identifying the data as a binary file (as opposed to text, for example). Line 14 creates a **URLRequest** instance, specifying the location of the PHP script as well as adding a name/value pair, containing a variable called **img** with the string "mydrawing.jpg" as its data. This will serve as the file name of the saved file. Lines 15 through 17 add the headers, method, and image data to the **URLRequest**.

Finally, the **URLRequest** is sent via the **naviagateToURL()** method, specifying a new window as the return destination. The PHP script, which we'll discuss next, handles the portion of the process that forces the browser to download the file.

```
1    import com.adobe.images.JPGEncoder;
2
3    saveJPG_btn.addEventListener(MouseEvent.CLICK, onSaveJPG, false, 0,
     true);
4
5    function onSaveJPG(evt:Event):void {
6        var paintGrab:BitmapData = new BitmapData (550, 450);
7        paintGrab.draw(canvas);
8
9        var myEncoder:JPGEncoder = new JPGEncoder(100);
10       var byteArray:ByteArray = myEncoder.encode(paintGrab);
11
12       var header:URLRequestHeader = new URLRequestHeader
         ("Content-type", "application/octet-stream");
13
14       var saveJPG:URLRequest =
         new URLRequest ("savejpg.php?img=mydrawing.jpg");
15       saveJPG.requestHeaders.push(header);
16       saveJPG.method = URLRequestMethod.POST;
17       saveJPG.data = byteArray;
18
19       navigateToURL(saveJPG, "_blank");
20   }
```

PHP

Discussing the PHP server-side language in detail is also beyond the scope of this book. However, this is a basic description of how this script works. Lines 1 and 11 identify the script as PHP. Lines 2 and 3 check to see if any data has been sent via the POST HTTP method to the script and, if so, populates the **$jpg** variable with that data. Knowing the data is there, line 4 retrieves the image data from the **img** form variable and populates the **$img** PHP variable with that data. Lines 5 and 6 add HTTP headers identifying the content as an image and as an attachment to force your browser to download the image rather than display it inline. Finally, line 7 sends the combined data back to your browser:

```
1    <?php
2    if (isset($GLOBALS["HTTP_RAW_POST_DATA"])) {
3        $jpg = $GLOBALS["HTTP_RAW_POST_DATA"];
4        $img = $_GET["img"];
5        header("Content-Type: image/jpeg");
6        header("Content-Disposition: attachment; filename=".$img);
7        echo $jpg;
8    } else {
9        echo "Encoded JPEG information not received.";
10   }
11   ?>
```

To work with the syntax used in the ActionScript portion of this exercise, this file should be saved as *savejpg.php* and reside in the same directory as your SWF host HTML file. You may face server security issues, such as when working with a hosting company that restricts executable scripts to specific direc-

NOTE

If you're already familiar with PHP, or a comparable server scripting language that you prefer to use, the **ByteArray** *class even supports ZLib compression via the* **compress()** *method. You could add server-side decompression (using the* **gzuncompress()** *method in PHP, for example), or save zip archives instead of images, to support transmission of compressed data. This would cut down on server traffic, but might affect performance due to the compression and decompression time required.*

Project Package

The project package for this chapter includes **ColorPicker**, a class for creating a functioning color picker similar to the utility of the same name in the Flash Color Mixer Panel. It also includes **FadeRollOver**, a custom class that extends **Sprite** and fades items using the Zeno's paradox technique discussed in Chapter 7. For more information about the companion web site project, see Chapter 6.

tories, but you can easily revise the path to the PHP file in the ActionScript code as long as it's in the same domain.

The result can vary depending on which browser you are using and the way your browser is set up but, essentially, the "Content-disposition: attachment" HTTP header should force a browser to download the image. You may be prompted to open or save the file, or you may set up a default action to automatically save the file to your download directory.

Another option is to save the file to the server, and then, perhaps, build a file browser or image-sharing system so that users can share their drawings with others. Other file formats are also available. The aforementioned Adobe encoding library includes a PNG encoder you could use if that format is more appropriate for your needs. One of the benefits of the PNG format over JPEG, for example, is that PNG supports transparency.

What's Next?

One of the most surprising things to come to light after each major Flash upgrade is how small the engineering team manages to keep Flash Player. The bitmap manipulation and compositing features discussed in this chapter are by no means a complete list of related capabilities available. Theoretically, if you spent some time and effort on the project, you could make a fairly respectable graphics-editing application using only Flash (and, perhaps, a server technology like PHP for file management). Yet Flash Player still remains small and easy to install and update. Bravo, past and present Flash and Flash Player engineers.

Now it's time to change direction and focus on the oft-overlooked workhorse of the Flash family: text. Text can be as fruitful a subject for experimentation and eye-candy as vectors and bitmaps, but it also serves a very important utilitarian purpose. Creating, styling, and parsing text are fundamental needs that you will frequently encounter.

In the next chapter, we'll look at a variety of ways to work with text, including:

- Creating text fields on the fly

- Initializing basic text field appearance and behavioral attributes

- Formatting text, including default formats for text fields, as well as changing formats across entire fields or partial text selections

- Using HTML and Cascading Style Sheets, for limited HTML rendering and global styling

- Embedding ActionScript triggers in HTML anchor tags

- Parsing paragraph, line, and character data from text fields using points and indices

TEXT

Part III focuses exclusively on text, and covers a variety of text uses. Chapter 10 begins with the dynamic creation of text fields and the styling of text elements using `TextFormat` objects. Using this approach, text styles can be precreated and applied to individual text fields at any time. For global styling, you can use a combination of HTML and Cascading Style Sheets (CSS). Both the HTML content and the CSS styles can be created internally or loaded from external sources. By using HTML and CSS, you can establish styles that apply to an entire project, if desired. Further, CSS styles can be edited easily in one central location, and all text to which the styles are applied will be automatically updated.

IN THIS PART

CHAPTER 10

TEXT

Working with text can be a basic affair, such as drawing a text box in the Flash interface and populating it with text at authoring time, or as complex as your needs require, perhaps including the dynamic creation of individual text fields for every character in a string to create an animated text effect. Learning how to move from authoring-only manual manipulations to runtime ActionScript control, however, can dramatically improve your text-handling capabilities and open a lot of creative doors.

In this chapter we'll focus mostly on how to display, populate, and format existing text data. We'll cover:

- **Creating Text Fields.** Text fields can be created with ActionScript like any display object, freeing you from the Flash Property Inspector and allowing you to create fields on the fly.

- **Setting Text Field Characteristics.** How you set up your text field will determine how the field will appear and function.

- **Selecting Text.** You can select segments of text fields using ActionScript by specifying the start and end of a selection block.

- **Formatting Text.** Text can be formatted easily by creating a formatting object that can be applied to one or more text fields at any time, including partial content of these fields.

- **Formatting with HTML and Cascading Style Sheets.** It is also possible to use a limited subset of supported HTML and Cascading Style Sheets (CSS) features to format and style your text globally or on a field-by-field basis. Both HTML and style sheets can be created internally or loaded from external sources.

- **Triggering ActionScript from HTML.** In addition to standard links in HTML text that may, for example, open a web site, you can also use links to trigger ActionScript. This makes it easy for external HTML files to control your project and provides another way of dynamically generating triggers. For example, rather than having to create buttons, a text field could contain many links to serve this purpose.

- **Parsing Text Fields**. New to ActionScript 3.0 is a variety of methods that allow you to walk through a text field by character, or line, or paragraph.

Creating Text Fields

Creating text fields dynamically is as simple as creating any other display object, and we will be using this method in most of the examples in this chapter. This example creates a text field and adds it to the display list. It uses the **text** property to populate the field, as seen in *text1.fla*.

```
var txtFld:TextField = new TextField();
addChild(txtFld);
txtFld.text = "Hello Skinny";
```

This minimum-required code will create the field using default values and automatically place it at point (0, 0) of the parent display object, in this case, the stage. The field defaults are fairly straightforward, such as black text, no field styling (for example, background or border), and a single-line format without wrapping. In other words, no assumptions are made by Flash about the way you want to display the text.

By default, a text field created with ActionScript will be a **dynamic** field type, to allow programmatic control. Later on we will show you how to switch to an **input** field to allow user input. Another notable item about the default state of a text field is that it starts at a size of 100 pixels wide by 100 pixels tall. This is worth noting because, until you set the display characteristics of the field, it will crop your content to that size.

Setting Text Field Characteristics

It is unlikely that you will be satisfied with the text field display defaults, so you will quickly need to learn how to affect field appearance and functionality. We will run through a common set of properties to demonstrate the typical use of a field with this first example, as seen in *text2.fla*.

Dynamic Text Fields

Lines 1 and 18 will already be familiar to you from the prior discussion about creating text fields. Everything else is new, including how to populate the field. Line 2 merely sets the location of the field, and is consistent with all display objects. Line 3, however, sets the width of the field. This is a direct change to the field width itself, which prevents distortion of the text inside the field. By contrast, if you were to set the width of a parent movie clip, for example, the text would appear to stretch or condense accordingly.

```
1    var txtFld:TextField = new TextField();
2    txtFld.x = txtFld.y = 20;
3    txtFld.width = 200;
4    txtFld.border = true;
5    txtFld.borderColor = 0x000033;
```

```
6    txtFld.background = true;
7    txtFld.backgroundColor = 0xEEEEFF;
8    txtFld.textColor = 0x000099;
9    txtFld.selectable = false;
10   txtFld.multiline = true;
11   txtFld.wordWrap = true;
12   txtFld.autoSize = TextFieldAutoSize.LEFT;
13
14   for (var i:Number = 0; i < 25; i++) {
15       txtFld.appendText("word" + i + " ");
16   }
17
18   addChild(txtFld);
```

Lines 4 through 8 set the color of the background, border, and text of the field. In this case, the border is enabled and set to a dark blue, and the background is enabled and set to a light blue. This is very handy because, although many of these properties can also be set in Flash's Property Inspector, the border and background can only be turned on or off, and will always be black and white, respectively. Line 8 sets the color of the text inside the field.

Line 9 prevents the text from being selectable. This is very important to understand for dynamic text fields because you may not want the user to be able to copy the contents of the field, and you may not want the visual and functional feedback that comes with selectable text. For example, the cursor will change over a selectable field and selected text will be highlighted.

Lines 10 through 12 set the ability for long passages of text to display properly. The **multiline** property allows the field to display more than one line. If this is not enabled, even carriage returns won't display more than one line. The **wordWrap** property wraps the line to the width of the text field. On its own, it will wrap to the width of the field you set and become cropped by the height setting, including the default value of 100 pixels.

Line 12, however, allows the field to resize to accommodate varying amounts of text. Depending on how you allow it to automatically resize, the field will expand to the right, to the left, on both sides, or not at all. In any case other than no resizing, the field will also expand down to contain your text. In this example, we've set the feature to auto-size from the left, using the accompanying constant, **TextFieldAutoSize.LEFT**. This means the left side will be anchored and the field will grow to the right and down; you are not specifying the direction in which the field will expand but rather its starting point—much like you would specify a text field's justification.

To demonstrate this feature, lines 14 through 16 populate the field using a **for** loop. This loop puts multiple instances of the text "word" into the field, adding the instance number to the word as it goes. The result will be "word0 word1 word2" and so on. This approach uses the **appendText()** method, which adds the text to the end of the field.

NOTE

The **appendText()** *method executes faster than using the* **+=** *compound operator (txtFld.text += "new value") and is recommended for this purpose.*

Input Text Fields

The only step required for allowing user input in a text field is to set its **type** property to that of an input field. This is accomplished by using the **TextFieldType.INPUT** constant. However, additional features may be useful.

Consider, for example, a password field. When entering passwords, you usually want to obscure the password itself by replacing its characters with symbols. You may also want to limit input in a field to a specific number of characters or range of allowable input. To demonstrate, consider the following script, seen in *text3.fla*:

```
1    var txtFld:TextField = new TextField();
2    txtFld.x = txtFld.y = 20;
3    txtFld.width = 100;
4    txtFld.height = 20;
5    txtFld.border = txtFld.background = true;
6    txtFld.type = TextFieldType.INPUT;
7    txtFld.maxChars = 10;
8    txtFld.restrict = "0-9";
9    txtFld.displayAsPassword = true;
10   addChild(txtFld);
11   stage.focus = txtFld;
```

Lines 1 through 5, as well as line 10, are consistent with the prior example. We've simplified this a bit by removing the color styling. Input text fields should obviously be selectable, but we wanted to keep the background and border visible to show the user where to enter his or her password.

Line 6 sets the field to an input field, and lines 7 through 9 define the password-related behavior. The **maxChars** property limits the number of characters that can be entered. The **restrict** property limits the characters that can be entered to a specified group of valid characters. These characters can be expressed individually or in logical ranges, such as the 0 through 9 number range used in this example. Line 9 performs the task of automatically switching the typed character for an asterisk to hide the password. Finally, line 11 gives the field focus so the user can begin typing without first selecting the field with the mouse.

NOTE

If you have trouble using the Backspace/ Delete key when testing your movie, it is not because the **restrict** *property prohibits its operation. This is a function of keyboard behavior in Flash's built-in player. You can either test in a browser, or disable keyboard shortcuts via the Control menu while in the player. This will remove the functional limitation on the Backspace/Delete key. Just remember to reenable keyboard shortcuts when returning to Flash.*

Selecting Text

Your control over text and text fields is not limited to styling or input. You can also track user selections or even select portions of a field programmatically, replacing that content if desired.

The following example, seen in *text4.fla*, creates two buttons, using the button creation class discussed in Chapter 8, that allow you to select and replace a word of text. The first 10 lines are consistent with prior examples with one exception. The first line imports the external class to allow us to use it for data typing. The new functionality begins with the two functions starting at line 11.

```
1    import CreateRoundRectButton;
2
3    var txtFld:TextField = new TextField();
4    txtFld.x = txtFld.y = 20;
5    txtFld.width = 200;
6    txtFld.multiline = txtFld.wordWrap = true;
7    txtFld.autoSize = TextFieldAutoSize.LEFT;
8    txtFld.type = TextFieldType.INPUT;
9    txtFld.text = "Lorem ipsum dolor sit amet, consectetur adipisicing
     elit, sed do eiusmod tempor incididunt ut labore et dolore magna
     aliqua. Ut enim ad minim veniam, quis nostrud exercitation ullamco
     laboris nisi ut aliquip ex ea commodo consequat.";
10   addChild(txtFld);
```

The new functions define the selection and replacement behaviors. Line 12 programmatically selects characters bound by indices 6 and 11. In this example, that's the second word, "ipsum." Line 13 is a new feature that allows the selected area to be visible even when the field no longer has focus. This is very handy and a welcome addition to ActionScript. In prior versions, selections would disappear when the user clicked or tabbed away from the field.

```
11   function onSelectWord(evt:MouseEvent):void {
12       txtFld.setSelection(6, 11);
13       txtFld.alwaysShowSelection = true;
14   }
```

Having made the selection, the **onReplaceWord()** function replaces the word with another. The first line ensures that a selection has been made by checking that the start and end of the current section are not equal. If these values are equal, that means there is no selection and only the insert carat (the vertical "I-beam" cursor position for selecting text) exists. That is, if you selected characters 1 through 4, the beginning of the selection would be index 0, and the end would be 4. (The last value is 4 not 3 because the selection range spans from the first character affected through the last character and stops at the next unaffected character.) However, if you click prior to the first word, with no selection, the insert caret places both beginning and end values at 0.

```
15   function onReplaceWord(evt:MouseEvent):void {
16       if (txtFld.selectionBeginIndex != txtFld.selectionEndIndex) {
17           txtFld.replaceSelectedText("LOREM");
18           var len:Number = txtFld.length;
19           txtFld.setSelection(len, len);
20           stage.focus = txtFld;
21           trace(txtFld.caretIndex);
22       }
23   }
```

Line 17 replaces the selected text with the new word, and then, to further demonstrate the selection and caret property, we introduce a new property, **length**. This is the total number of characters in the field and is placed into a variable in line 18. Line 19 then sets a new selection with both beginning and ending indices at the end of the file, line 20 sets the focus to show the blinking caret, and line 21 traces its position to the output window using the **caretIndex** property.

Lastly, the **CreateRoundRectButton** custom class is used to create a button to trigger each function. For more information about this class and its arguments, see Chapter 8.

```
24   var selBtn:CreateRoundRectButton = new CreateRoundRectButton(110,
     20, 10, 2, 0x000033, "Select Word 2", 0xFFFFFF);
25   selBtn.x = 300;
26   selBtn.y = 20;
27   selBtn.addEventListener(MouseEvent.CLICK, onSelectWord, false, 0,
     true);
28   addChild(selBtn);
29
30   var repBtn:CreateRoundRectButton = new CreateRoundRectButton(110,
     20, 10, 2, 0x330000, "Replace Word 2", 0xFFFFFF);
31   repBtn.x = 300;
32   repBtn.y = 60;
33   repBtn.addEventListener(MouseEvent.CLICK, onReplaceWord, false, 0,
     true);
34   addChild(repBtn);
```

Formatting Text

Now that you can create, style, and populate text fields, and select their contents, it's time to learn how to format the text therein. This is accomplished with another class called **TextFormat**. The process is to set up a **TextFormat** instance that controls all the desired formatting, and then apply that object to all or part of a field.

You can apply the object in two ways: by establishing it as the default format for the field, affecting all future input, or by applying it on a case-by-case basis, affecting only a specific formatting step. Let's start with an example of using the object as the default format, as seen in *text_fmt1.fla*.

Creating the format happens up front, in lines 1 through 7. A new instance of the format is created in line 1, and a variety of properties are set, including changes to the font, color, size, leading, left and right margins, and indent. The **font** property is the name of the font you wish to use. You can use system fonts or embedded fonts, which we'll talk about in a moment. The **color** property is a hexadecimal color value in the 0xRRGGBB format. The **size**, **leftMargin**, and **rightMargin** properties are measured in pixels.

The **leading** property is also measured in pixels but it is based on the space between lines, rather than including the line height as in typical typography usage. For example, if you wanted 10-point type on 12-point leading, **size** would be set to 10 and **leading** would be set to 2. Finally, **indent** indents the first line of every paragraph by a measure of pixels (in contrast to **blockIndent,** which will indent the entire passage).

```
1   var txtFmt:TextFormat = new TextFormat();
2   txtFmt.font = "Verdana";
3   txtFmt.color = 0x000099;
4   txtFmt.size = 10;
5   txtFmt.leading = 4;
```

NOTE

Using the recommended appendText() *method to add text to a field will maintain the formatting of the last character. Using the compound assignment operator will reset the field to use its default format.*

```
6    txtFmt.leftMargin = txtFmt.rightMargin = 6;
7    txtFmt.indent = 20;
```

The next portion of the script is familiar territory, with the exception of line 14. This is where, and how, the format is applied. In this case, the **default-TextFormat()** method is used to ensure that all future text insertions will be formatted using these settings. This format instance uses a 10-point Verdana font, colors it blue, gives it a leading of 4 pixels between lines, gives it a left and right margin of 6 pixels, and indents the paragraph 20 pixels.

```
8    var txtFld:TextField = new TextField();
9    txtFld.x = txtFld.y = 20;
10   txtFld.width = 200;
11   txtFld.border = txtFld.background = true;
12   txtFld.multiline = txtFld.wordWrap = true;
13   txtFld.autoSize = TextFieldAutoSize.LEFT;
14   txtFld.defaultTextFormat = txtFmt;
15
16   for (var i:Number = 0; i < 25; i++) {
17       txtFld.appendText("word" + i + " ");
18   }
19   addChild(txtFld);
```

The remainder of the script shows how to apply a format that is not the field default formatting instance. The principle is exactly the same except the way it is applied. To apply any format to text—controlling the appearance of the text for that change rather than all future changes—use the **setTextFormat()** method. The following new five lines of code, added to the prior example, demonstrate an additional optional step, which is to format only a segment of the text. This additional code can be found in source file *text_fmt2.fla*.

```
20   var txtFmt2:TextFormat = new TextFormat();
21   txtFmt2.color = 0xFF0000;
22   txtFmt2.bold = true;
23   txtFmt2.underline = true;
24   txtFld.setTextFormat(txtFmt2, 0, 5);
```

The optional second and third parameters seen in line 24 indicate that the format should be applied only to character indices 0 through 5 (the first word, in this case). The effect would be to make the first word bold, underline, and red.

Tab Stops

Another handy feature made possible by the **TextFormat** class is tab stops. It can be very difficult to format text in columns using the Flash interface, but it's simple using ActionScript. The next example uses the **TextFormat** class to set two tab stops so that text including tab characters will line up at these stops, forming columns. See file *text_fmt3.fla* to try this yourself.

Let's get to the code. The first 13 lines of this script include only previously discussed material—creating and configuring **TextFormat** and **TextField** objects.

However, we've delayed adding the tab stops to show how to change a **TextFormat** object after it has been created. We'll look at that process in just a moment.

```
1   var txtFmt:TextFormat = new TextFormat();
2   txtFmt.font = "Verdana";
3   txtFmt.size = 10;
4   txtFmt.leading = 4;
5   txtFmt.leftMargin = txtFmt.rightMargin = 6;
6
7   var txtFld:TextField = new TextField();
8   txtFld.x = txtFld.y = 20;
9   txtFld.width = 300;
10  txtFld.border = txtFld.background = true;
11  txtFld.multiline = txtFld.wordWrap = true;
12  txtFld.autoSize = TextFieldAutoSize.LEFT;
13  txtFld.defaultTextFormat = txtFmt;
```

Lines 14 through 16 populate the field, **txtFld**, that you just set up in lines 7 through 13. There are two new items. The first is the inclusion of the **\t** escape character. The backslash prevents this character from being understood as the letter "t," so this is instead interpreted as a tab instruction. The second new item is simply a random number generator that has nothing to do with text formatting. It merely creates a random number in the indicated range to simulate a product's price and quantity for this demo.

Since the text has tab characters, we need tab stops to ensure the columns line up nicely. These are applied in line 19, using an array of pixel values to indicate the location of each tab stop. We applied this property later, in line 19, for demonstration purposes. You may go back and edit a **TextFormat** instance at any time. In this case, all we did was add tab stops to the existing formatting, so no new **TextFormat** instance was required. Having made this change, the format must be *reapplied* to the text field, as seen in line 20, to show any change. In other words, edits to a **TextFormat** instance don't automatically cascade down to objects using that instance. After the same format is reapplied in line 20, the tab stops take effect.

```
14  for (var i:Number = 0; i < 10; i++) {
15      txtFld.appendText("product" + i + "\t$" + getRandom(1000) +
        "\t" + getRandom(100) + "\n");
16  }
17  addChild(txtFld);
18
19  txtFmt.tabStops = [120, 200];
20  txtFld.setTextFormat(txtFmt);
21
22  function getRandom(range:Number):Number {
23      return Math.round(Math.random() * range);
24  }
```

Embedded Fonts and Custom Anti-Aliasing

When a custom font is required, you must embed that font to ensure that it displays properly on all machines. The first step to do so in Flash is to create a new font symbol from the Library panel's menu, seen in Figure 10-1. In the resulting Font Symbols Properties dialog, seen in Figure 10-2, choose the font and font style you wish to embed. Each font symbol can contain only one font style: plain, bold, italic, or a combination thereof. So, for example, to include plain and bold font styles, you would need a symbol for plain and a symbol for bold. When referencing the font in ActionScript, the original font name will be used, so name these font symbols descriptively—"Verdana Plain" and Verdana Bold," for example.

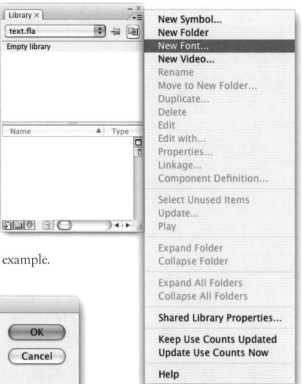

Figure 10-1. Library menu

Figure 10-2. Choosing which font and font style to embed

The second step is to make this font available to ActionScript through the Linkage option in the Library panel menu. As you did in Chapter 4, make this symbol available by clicking Export for ActionScript, as seen in Figure 10-3. The default class name used is probably fine, as long as it is unique. Again, ActionScript will use the original name of the font used when creating the font symbol.

All that remains is to tell the field to use embedded fonts. You specify which font to use in the `TextFormat` instance, as usual, but each applicable text field must be told to use embedded fonts, rather than system fonts. Don't worry: Like other symbol types, file size is affected only by the insertion of the font symbol, not by its repeated use.

Figure 10-3. The Linkage Properties dialog used for making the font available to ActionScript

The new bold lines below, added to the previous example to form file *text_fmt4.fla*, use embedded fonts (line 25) and a new feature: custom anti-aliasing. By changing the **antiAliasType** property to advanced with the **AntiAliasType.ADVANCED** constant, you control the thickness (-200 to 200) and sharpness (-400 to 400) to improve the legibility of small type sizes.

```
25  txtFld.embedFonts = true;
26  txtFld.antiAliasType = AntiAliasType.ADVANCED;
27  txtFld.thickness = 100;
28  txtFld.sharpness = -100;
```

Formatting with HTML and CSS

The **TextFormat** class is great for simple formats of dynamically generated text. But managing a large Flash project this way might become unwieldy if several formats are required. An alternative to this approach is to use HTML and CSS to style the project globally.

HTML

Flash supports a limited subset of HTML tags, as seen in Table 10-1.

Table 10-1. The HTML tags supported by Flash Player

HTML Tag	Notes
`<font>`	Supported attributes include: **color, face, size**
`<b>`	Bold version of font must exist to work
`<i>`	Italic version of font must exist to work
`<u>`	Underlines text
`<span>`	Supported attributes include: **class**
`<p>`	**multiline** must be enabled to work. Supported attributes include: **align, class**
` `	**multiline** must be enabled to work
`<li>`	All lists are bulleted; ordered and unordered qualifiers are ignored
`<img>`	Supported attributes include: **src, width, height, align, hspace, vspace, id**; can embed external images (JPG, GIF, PNG) and SWF files with automatic text flow around the images
`<a>`	Supported attributes include: **href, event, target**
`<textformat>`	Used to apply a limited subset of **TextFormat** properties to text; supported attributes include: **blockindent, indent, leading, leftmargin, rightmargin, tabstops**

To use HTML in a text field, you need only switch from using the **text** property to using the **htmlText** property. For example, the following code will put the word "Flash" in bold in a text field:

```
txtFld.htmlText = "<b>Flash</b>";
```

You should look at the accompanying tables for anything that might vary from traditional usage, or have an added Flash issue, especially if you are seeing unexpected results. For example, it should make sense that line breaks (`<p>` and `<br>` tags) require a `multiline` field just like carriage returns without HTML require this setting. However, it may not be obvious that `<ol>` and `<ul>` have no effect on list items, and they are all bulleted.

NOTE

The more efficient `appendText()` method does not work with HTML, so you must use traditional compound addition (+=) to append HTML text to a field.

CSS

Flash supports a limited subset of CSS properties, as seen in Table 10-2. Style sheets require a bit more setup. We'll begin by demonstrating how to create style sheets on the fly, and then the final chapter exercise will describe loading both the HTML and CSS data from external files.

Table 10-2. The CSS properties supported by Flash Player

CSS Property	Notes
`color`	Font color in 0xRRGGBB format
`display`	Controls display of an item. Values include: `none block inline`
`font-family`	Font name
`font-size`	Font size in pixels
`font-style`	Font style. Values include: `italic normal`
`font-weight`	Font style. Values include: `bold normal`
`kerning`	Turns kerning on or off. Values include: `true false`
`leading`	Font leading in pixels. Not officially supported. Similar to: `text-height`. Works well in internal style object, but may not be reliable in loaded CSS
`letter-spacing`	Specified in pixels
`margin-left`	Specified in pixels
`margin-right`	Specified in pixels
`text-align`	Aligns text. Values include: `left right center justify`
`text-decoration`	Underlines text. Values include: `underline none`
`text-indent`	First-line paragraph indent specified in pixels

The process of building a style sheet involves creating an instance of the **StyleSheet** class, and then adding styled objects for each tag or class to the instance. For each tag or class, a custom object is created to which the relevant CSS properties are added. Once complete, each object is associated with the tag or class and added to your style sheet using the **setStyle()** method.

In the following example, seen in *text_css_gen.fla*, line 1 creates the style sheet, lines 3 through 5, 7 through 13, and 15 through 19 each create a style for the **body** tag, **heading** CSS class, and **byline** CSS class, respectively—all using the subset of supported CSS properties described in Table 10-2. Finally, lines 21 through 23 add each style to the **css** instance of the **StyleSheet** class.

```
1   var css:StyleSheet = new StyleSheet();
2
3   var body:Object = new Object();
4   body.fontFamily = "Verdana";
5   body.textIndent = 20;
6
7   var heading:Object = new Object();
8   heading.fontSize = 18;
9   heading.textIndent = -20;
10  heading.leading = 10;
11  heading.letterSpacing = 1;
12  heading.fontWeight = "bold";
13  heading.color = "#FF6633";
14
15  var byline:Object = new Object();
16  byline.fontSize = 14;
17  byline.leading = 20;
18  byline.fontStyle = "italic";
19  byline.textAlign = "right";
20
21  css.setStyle(".heading", heading);
22  css.setStyle(".byline", byline);
23  css.setStyle("body", body);
```

The remainder of the script is consistent with prior examples with two important qualifications. First, the previously discussed change in populating the text field demonstrates the use of the **htmlText** property and compound addition. More importantly, however, we must stress that the style sheet must be applied before the HTML is added to the field. If this rule is not followed, the style sheet will not be applied. Note that, in this example, the style sheet is applied in line 30, before the HTML is added to the field beginning at line 31.

```
24  var txtFld:TextField = new TextField();
25  txtFld.x = txtFld.y = 20;
26  txtFld.width = 500;
27  txtFld.multiline = true;
28  txtFld.wordWrap = true;
29  txtFld.autoSize = TextFieldAutoSize.LEFT;
30  txtFld.styleSheet = css;
31  txtFld.htmlText = "<body>";
32  txtFld.htmlText += "<span class='heading'>ActionScript 10.0 Adds
    Time Travel to Flash</span><br>";
33  txtFld.htmlText += "<span class='byline'>by Walter Westinghouse</
    span><br><br>";
34  txtFld.htmlText += "<p>Lorem ipsum dolor sit amet, consectetur
    adipisicing elit, sed do eiusmod tempor incididunt ut labore
    et dolore magna aliqua. Ut enim ad minim veniam, quis nostrud
    exercitation ullamco laboris nisi ut aliquip ex ea commodo
    consequat.</p>";
35  txtFld.htmlText += "<p>Duis aute irure dolor in reprehenderit
    in voluptate velit esse cillum dolore eu fugiat nulla pariatur.
    Excepteur sint occaecat cupidatat non proident, sunt in culpa qui
    officia deserunt mollit anim id est laborum.</p>";
36  txtFld.htmlText += "</body>";
37  addChild(txtFld);
```

Triggering ActionScript from HTML Links

In addition to supporting standard HTML links, ActionScript can also trigger functions from anchor tags. This is accomplished by replacing the Internet protocol **http://** with **event:**. This change instructs ActionScript to fire a **TextEvent.LINK** event that can be trapped and processed. (If you are familiar with prior versions of ActionScript, this replaces the equivalent **asfunction:** protocol.)

The following example, seen in *text_event.fla*, shows both a conventional **http://** link and ActionScript **event:** link in action. The traditional link is in line 10. The ActionScript **event:** link can be seen in line 9. The link is still constructed using the anchor tag and href attribute but, instead of pointing to a URL, a string is specified—in this case, "showMsg." To respond to a user, click this custom link, and an event listener is added to the field in line 11, listening for the **TextEvent.LINK** event.

When the user clicks the conventional link, the normal behavior ensues automatically. Flash launches or switches to the default browser and navigates to the site. However, when the user clicks the "Show Message" link, the listener traps the event and calls the **linkHandler()** function, passing the link information into the argument. A conditional queries the text from the event and, if it matches the specified string, traces a message to the Output panel.

```
1   var txtFmt:TextFormat = new TextFormat();
2   txtFmt.size = 18;
3   txtFmt.bullet = true;
4
5   var txtFld:TextField = new TextField();
6   txtFld.autoSize = TextFieldAutoSize.LEFT;
7   txtFld.multiline = true;
8   txtFld.defaultTextFormat = txtFmt;
9   txtFld.htmlText = "<a href='event:showMsg'>Show Message</a><br />";
10  txtFld.htmlText += "<a href='http://www.google.com'>Google</a>";
11  txtFld.addEventListener(TextEvent.LINK, linkHandler);
12  addChild(txtFld);
13
14  function linkHandler(evt:TextEvent):void {
15      if (evt.text == "showMsg") {
16          trace("Dynamic links are useful");
17      }
18  }
```

Parsing Text Fields

For certain kinds of text-heavy work, especially word games, educational exercises, and similar activities, ActionScript has been lacking in the ability to quickly access partial content from text fields. It has always been possible to accomplish some text parsing tasks by working with the text data within the field, using string manipulation. However, it was not previously possible, or in some cases not very easy, to get information about a specific line or paragraph or, in particular, mouse-text interaction.

ActionScript 3.0 comes closer to what some of us are looking for with the addition of a handful of methods for looking directly into fields. To demonstrate these features, we've divided them up into two groups of methods. The first focuses on characters and fields, the second on lines. In both cases, data originates from mouse interaction. In each of the two source files we'll discuss, the user drags a virtual loupe, or magnifying glass, around the screen that reveals information from a text field below the mouse.

These examples are presented in a diagnostic fashion, but the methods they demonstrate have many practical uses. Being able to pull text from a single line of a text field, and knowing where the lines break in a field, are two good examples. This information can be great for truncating lines that may be too long for an interface, or for determining when to insert a page break.

Retrieving Line Data

The first exercise we'll discuss is in the *text_line_data.fla* file from the accompanying source code and focuses on lines. It shows an enlarged view of the target line in its loupe, and places additional information in a secondary field at the bottom of the screen, as seen in Figure 10-4.

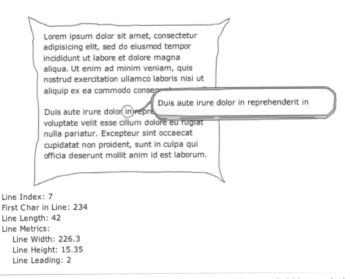

Figure 10-4. Mouse interaction reveals line data about the text field beneath the mouse

The first instruction of this script is to hide the mouse, so the experience of dragging the loupe around will be more immersive. Line 3 adds an enter frame event listener to the timeline to trigger the **onLoop()** function every time the playhead enters the frame. Lines 5 and 6 make the loupe metaphor possible by placing the loupe at the mouse location. The instance name of the loupe is **detail**, and its **x** and **y** properties are set to the **mouseX** and **mouseY** properties, respectively.

```
1    Mouse.hide();
2
3    addEventListener(Event.ENTER_FRAME, onLoop, false, 0, true);
4
5    function onLoop(evt:Event):void {
6        detail.x = mouseX;
7        detail.y = mouseY;
```

Line 8 provides the first piece of information from the field, which will be used in additional queries later in the script. The instruction uses the mouse location to determine the number of the line in the field that happens to be under the mouse at any given time. (Specifically, it will return the line index of any line at any point, but we're sending the **mouseX** and **mouseY** properties into the method, so the point at which the mouse is located is the point used.) When the mouse is not over a line of text, the value returned is -1, which we use as the basis for a conditional beginning at line 10. If the value of the index variable is anything other than -1, the mouse (loupe) is over a line of text and the script can continue.

In that case, the script uses the **getLineText()** method to put the line of text under the mouse into the text field inside the loupe (**detail.info**). It also sets the alpha of the loupe to 1, or full opacity, to draw attention to the line being displayed. (You will see in just a moment that, when the loupe is not over a line, the alpha of the loupe will be set to 10 percent for a muted appearance.)

```
8        var index:int = body.getLineIndexAtPoint(body.mouseX,
         body.mouseY);

9
10       if (index != -1) {
11           detail.info.text = body.getLineText(index);
12           detail.alpha = 1;
```

The next nine lines populate the **info** field at the bottom of the stage. We're appending multiple lines of text so we start by emptying the field in line 13. The next line shows the index determined in line 11, which will be used as the value for the next three method arguments. The **getLineOffset()** method in line 15 returns the index of the first character in a line, relevant to the field. For example, if a field had many lines of 10 characters each, the first index in each of the first few lines would be 0, 10, 20, and so on. The last line in this block, line 16, returns the total number of characters in a line.

```
13           info.text = "";
14           info.appendText("Line Index: " + index + "\n");
15           info.appendText("First Char in Line: " + body.
             getLineOffset(index) + "\n");
16           info.appendText("Line Length: " + body.getLineLength(index)
             + "\n");
```

Line 18 returns an object that includes information about the text metrics, or typographical measurements of a line. This text metrics object includes information like measurements of character ascent (for example, how far the top of an f, d, or t character is above the other characters), and descent (for example, how far the bottom of a y, g, or q falls below the baseline). In lines 19 through 21, we're displaying a subset of that data—the leading and actual width and height of the *text* (as opposed to the width and height of the text *field*), which we'll use in the next exercise as an error-checking device. Finally, if the loupe is not over a line of text, lines 24 through 27 clear both fields and set the alpha of the loupe to 10 percent.

```
17          info.appendText("Line Metrics:\n");
18          var txtMtr:TextLineMetrics = body.getLineMetrics(index);
19          info.appendText("    Line Width: " + txtMtr.width + "\n");
20          info.appendText("    Line Height: " + txtMtr.height +
            "\n");
21          info.appendText("    Line Leading: " + txtMtr.leading +
            "\n");
22      } else {
23          detail.info.text = "";
24          detail.alpha = 0.1;
25
26          info.text = "";
27      }
28  }
```

Retrieving Character and Paragraph Data

This next script comes from *text_char_data.fla* and looks at characters and paragraphs. The structure of this example is the same as the prior example, but with a smaller loupe that isolates one character at a time, as seen in Figure 10-5.

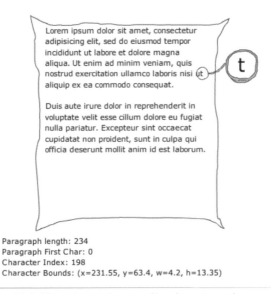

Paragraph length: 234
Paragraph First Char: 0
Character Index: 198
Character Bounds: (x=231.55, y=63.4, w=4.2, h=13.35)

Figure 10-5. Mouse interaction revealing character and paragraph data about the text field beneath the mouse

The catalyst for the data in this file is **getCharIndexAtPoint()** (line 9), which returns the index of a single character (again, under the mouse, in this case), rather than a line. Because of the similarity in scripts, we'll focus only on new material in this discussion.

```
1    Mouse.hide();
2
3    addEventListener(Event.ENTER_FRAME, onLoop, false, 0, true);
4
5    function onLoop(evt:Event):void {
6        detail.x = mouseX;
7        detail.y = mouseY;
8
9        var index:int = body.getCharIndexAtPoint(body.mouseX,
         body.mouseY);
```

Line 11 uses the string method **charAt()** to determine the text field character at that index. Line 15 returns the length of a paragraph, rather than the length of the line, and then line 16 determines the first character in the paragraph, rather than the first character in the line, as in the previous example. Finally, line 18 uses the **getCharBoundaries()** method to determine the minimum-bounding rectangle surrounding the character under the mouse. This can be used for simulating unsupported CSS features like and borders and collision detection.

```
10       if (index != -1) {
11           detail.info.text = body.text.charAt(index);
12           detail.alpha = 1;
13
14           info.text = "";
15           info.appendText("Paragraph length: " +
             body.getParagraphLength(index) + "\n");
16           info.appendText("Paragraph First Char: " +
             body.getFirstCharInParagraph(index) + "\n");
17           info.appendText("Character Index: " + index + "\n");
18           info.appendText("Character Bounds: " +
             body.getCharBoundaries(index) + "\n");
19       } else {
20           detail.info.text = "";
21           detail.alpha = 0.1;
22
23           info.text = "";
24       }
25   }
```

The last thing we'd like to discuss is how we can improve upon this example by using the **textHeight** property. Remember that this property returns the height of the text, not the height of the text field. If you've downloaded the source file we created for this exercise, you may notice that we intentionally increased the height of the field beyond the height needed to accommodate the text. This increase was made so you could see that dragging over the bottom of the field, after the last line of text has ended, still produces the same effect as dragging over actual lines. (If you choose not to download the accompanying source files, just create a large dynamic text field so there is plenty of extra space in the field after including all your text. This will leave extra room between the last line of text and the bottom edge of the field.)

Described another way, imagine three lines of text placed inside a field large enough to accommodate 10 lines of text. If you dragged your mouse over the first three lines, you would see the previously described feedback for the first, second, and third line, respectively. However, if you dragged your mouse anywhere over the remainder of the field, at the bottom where nonexistent lines 4 through 10 might appear, Flash will still display the data from line 3.

Using the `textHeight` property, we can further limit the conditional in this script to work only when dragging over actual text, not for the gap at the end of the field. Edit line 10 to reflect this change.

```
10        if (index != -1 && mouseY < (body.y + body.textHeight)) {
```

This way, the line index still must be non-negative, but the mouse also has to be higher than the bottom of the last line of text (the location of the field plus the height of the text, rather than the height of the field). This will prevent the phantom recognition of characters when the text doesn't fill the bottom of the field and can be used in all such cases.

Loading HTML and CSS

The last exercise of the chapter focuses again on HTML and CSS, but this time by loading both from external sources. None of the text field code is new, and the HTML and CSS are quite straightforward, but it's useful to understand how to load the files and apply the results. We'll discuss loading again in Chapter 13, in many contexts, but here we'll just focus on loading text files.

The assets you'll need for this exercise are included with the source code from the companion web site, but here are the setup files if you wish to recreate them on your own. The following files should go in the same directory as your host *.fla* file.

HTML: (*demo.html*)

```
<body>
<span class='heading'>ActionScript 10.0 Adds Time Travel to Flash</
    span><br>
<span class='byline'>by Walter Westinghouse</span><br><br>
<p>Lorem ipsum dolor sit amet, <a href="event:ActionScript control
    from URLs">consectetur</a> adipisicing elit, sed do eiusmod tempor
    incididunt ut labore et dolore magna aliqua. Ut enim ad minim
    veniam, quis nostrud exercitation ullamco laboris nisi ut aliquip
    ex ea commodo consequat.</p>
<p>Duis aute irure dolor in <a href="http://www.google.com" target="_
    blank">Google</a> in voluptate velit esse cillum dolore eu fugiat
    nulla pariatur. Excepteur sint occaecat cupidatat non proident,
    sunt in culpa qui officia deserunt mollit anim id est laborum.</p>
</body>
```

CSS: (*demo.css*)

```
body {
    font-family: Verdana;
    text-indent: 20px;
}

.heading {
    font-size: 18px;
    font-weight: bold;
    text-indent: -20px;
    letter-spacing: 1px;
    color: #FF6633;
}

.byline {
    font-size: 14px;
    font-style: italic;
    text-align: right;
}

a:link {
    color: #990099;
    text-decoration: underline;
}

a:hover {
    color: #FF00FF;
}
```

ActionScript: (*load_html_css.fla*)

Loading the HTML and CSS from external files requires use of the **URLLoader** and **URLRequest** classes. The process discussed, loading a text file, is the same for both HTML and CSS, so we'll focus on one and discuss the other briefly. You'll use two events: **Event.COMPLETE** to move on after the loading is complete, and **IOErrorEvent.IO_ERROR** to listen for any I/O errors.

Lines 1 through 14 set up the standard package, class, and constructor format, including importing the necessary classes and declaring the necessary variables. The script uses a text field for display, **URLLoader** instances to load both documents, a **StyleSheet** instance to hold the style sheet, and a string variable to hold the HTML data.

```
1   package {
2
3       import flash.display.Sprite;
4       import flash.text.*;
5       import flash.net.*;
6       import flash.events.*;
7
8       public class LoadHTMLCSS extends Sprite {
9
10          private var _txtFld:TextField;
11          private var _html:String;
12          private var _htmlFile:URLLoader;
13          private var _css:StyleSheet;
14          private var _cssFile:URLLoader;
```

The constructor sets up the CSS load, so we'll focus on that in detail. Line 16 creates an instance of the **URLLoader** class that you can monitor. Line 17 adds a listener to that instance, and calls the **onLoadCSS()** function when the load is complete. Line 18 adds a listener for I/O errors and calls the **ioErrorHandler()** in such an event. (One example of such an error is if the file can't be found.) Finally, line 19 loads the CSS file. To do so, a **URLRequest** instance is required. This is used for all loads from URLs and it allows for consistent handling of URLs throughout ActionScript 3.0.

```
15          public function LoadHTMLCSS() {
16              _cssFile = new URLLoader();
17              _cssFile.addEventListener(Event.COMPLETE, onLoadCSS,
                false, 0, true);
18              _cssFile.addEventListener(IOErrorEvent.IO_ERROR,
                ioErrorHandler, false, 0, true);
19              _cssFile.load(new URLRequest("demo.css"));
20          }
```

When the CSS document loads in the next code block, line 22 creates a new **StyleSheet** instance, and line 23 parses the CSS data sent to the listener function. The style sheet is now ready to be applied, but neither the HTML nor the text field exist yet. Next on the to-do list is the exact same procedure for the HTML file.

```
21          private function onLoadCSS(evt:Event):void {
22              _css = new StyleSheet();
23              _css.parseCSS(evt.target.data);
24              _htmlFile = new URLLoader();
25              _htmlFile.addEventListener(Event.COMPLETE, onLoadHTML,
                false, 0, true);
26              _htmlFile.addEventListener(IOErrorEvent.IO_ERROR,
                ioErrorHandler, false, 0, true);
27
28              _htmlFile.load(new URLRequest("demo.html"));
29          }
```

Once the HTML is fully loaded, it is put into the **_html** variable (line 31), and the text field is created. The **initTextField()** function does nothing new, but please note three things. First, the CSS is applied before the HTML is added to the field (lines 43 and 44). Second, a listener is added to trap any link-based ActionScript triggered by an **event: href**. Finally, as a best practice, the loading and I/O error listeners are removed once the process is complete.

```
30          private function onLoadHTML(evt:Event):void {
31              _html = evt.target.data;
32              initTextField();
33          }
34
35          private function initTextField():void {
36              _txtFld = new TextField();
37              _txtFld.x = _txtFld.y = 20;
38              _txtFld.width = 500;
39              _txtFld.multiline = true;
40              _txtFld.wordWrap = true;
41              _txtFld.autoSize = TextFieldAutoSize.LEFT;
42              _txtFld.selectable = false;
```

```
43          _txtFld.styleSheet = _css;
44          _txtFld.htmlText = _html;
45          _txtFld.addEventListener(TextEvent.LINK, onTextEvent,
            false, 0, true);
46          addChild(_txtFld);
47
48          _cssFile.removeEventListener(Event.COMPLETE,
            onLoadCSS);
49          _cssFile.removeEventListener(IOErrorEvent.IO_ERROR,
            ioErrorHandler);
50          _htmlFile.removeEventListener(Event.COMPLETE,
            onLoadHTML);
51          _htmlFile.removeEventListener(IOErrorEvent.IO_ERROR,
            ioErrorHandler);
52      }
53
54      private function onTextEvent(evt:TextEvent):void {
55          trace(evt.text);
56      }
57
58      private function ioErrorHandler(evt:IOErrorEvent):void {
59          trace("The following file could not be loaded: " +
            evt.text);
60      }
61  }
62 }
```

The last two functions react to events. The **onTextEvent()** function traces any **event:** link text to the Output panel, and the **ioErrorHandler()** function traces an I/O error warning to the Output panel.

With this exercise as a basis for future work, you can control the text formatting for very large projects by applying the project-wide CSS document to every applicable text field. This also makes your development process much easier because you can edit the external CSS file and its styles will be updated everywhere the file is used. The document in Figure 10-6 was created using external HTML data and formatted using a CSS document.

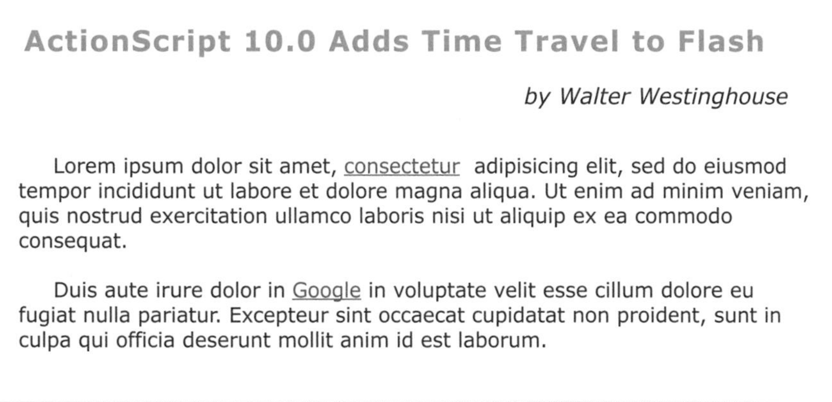

ActionScript 10.0 Adds Time Travel to Flash

by Walter Westinghouse

Lorem ipsum dolor sit amet, consectetur adipisicing elit, sed do eiusmod tempor incididunt ut labore et dolore magna aliqua. Ut enim ad minim veniam, quis nostrud exercitation ullamco laboris nisi ut aliquip ex ea commodo consequat.

Duis aute irure dolor in Google in voluptate velit esse cillum dolore eu fugiat nulla pariatur. Excepteur sint occaecat cupidatat non proident, sunt in culpa qui officia deserunt mollit anim id est laborum.

Figure 10-6. Text loaded and styled from external HTML and CSS data.

What's Next?

Text is fundamental to most Flash products, and this chapter should give you the starting knowledge you need to explore further text usage. Once you've become more comfortable with text as a general category (including tasks like displaying and formatting), start to delve deeper into the raw data that makes up text. Look into strings directly, and learn how to build and parse the paragraphs, words, and characters you see every day. Try to think of imaginative ways of generating, deconstructing, and otherwise manipulating text, such as combining string methods and properties with arrays and other ActionScript elements.

In the next chapter, we'll look at many ways of using sound in ActionScript, including:

- Understanding the new granular components of sound management, including individual sound channels and a global sound mixer

- Playing, stopping, and pausing internal and external sounds

- Controlling the volume and pan of sounds

- Working with microphone input

- Parsing data from sounds, including ID3 tags from MP3 files

- Visualizing frequency amplitudes

SOUND AND VIDEO

PART **IV**

Part IV covers sound and video, the media types that arguably contributed most significantly to the ubiquitous use of Flash on the web. Chapter 11 covers the use of internal and external sound, and features examples of controlling sound playback, as well as manipulating volume and stereo panning. The chapter also includes a brief overview of parsing ID3 metadata from MP3 sounds, for display during audio playback. The chapter concludes with a sound visualization exercise that uses the `Graphics` class from Chapter 8 to draw a waveform in real time.

Chapter 12 contains information about encoding video using the free Flash Video Encoder that ships with Flash. This coverage includes instruction on how to create cue points. The chapter also discusses two approaches to authoring video playback. By using components, you're able to focus more on the balance of your design and application as most of the ActionScript is taken care of for you. However, this chapter also includes the information necessary to code your own video player, so you can keep file size down if you choose not to rely on the video components. Finally, Chapter 12 provides true full-screen video examples, and covers accessibility and multilanguage projects through the use of video captioning.

CHAPTER 11

SOUND

ActionScript 3.0 introduces a new way to work with sound. In addition to adding new classes that afford more granular control over sound management, you can now also access raw sound data including amplitude and frequency spectrum analysis while a sound is playing.

In this chapter, we'll look at the following topics:

- **ActionScript Sound Architecture.** Beyond the `Sound` class, new classes including `SoundChannel` and `SoundMixer` have been added to easily manage multiple channels of sound. Additional classes consolidate volume and pan (moving between stereo channels) manipulation, parsing metadata from MP3 sounds, and more.

- **Internal and External Sounds.** We'll show you how to work with internal sounds found in your library, as well as load external MP3 sounds on the fly.

- **Playing, Stopping, and Pausing Sounds.** In addition to playing and stopping sounds, you'll learn how to pause and resume playback, as well as stop sound playback in all active channels at once.

- **Buffering Streaming Sounds.** To optimize playback across slower connections, sounds can be buffered, or preloaded. This ensures that sounds play longer without interruption while data continues to download.

- **Changing Sound Volume and Pan.** The `SoundTransform` class gathers volume and panning features, allowing you to increase or decrease volume, and move sounds between the left and right speakers, respectively.

- **Reading ID3 Metadata from MP3 Sounds.** During the encoding process, metadata including artist name, track title, and more can be injected into an MP3 file. The `ID3Info` class allows you to parse this information from MP3 files for use in your application.

- **Visualizing Sound Data.** Perhaps the most dramatic change to the ActionScript 3.0 sound architecture is the possibility to dynamically poll the amplitude and frequency spectrum data of a sound live, during playback. You can use the information gathered to display visualizations of the sound, such as waveforms, peak meters, and artistic interpretations while the sound plays.

- **Working with Microphone Data.** You can also access the microphone and check the activity level periodically to visualize the amplitude of a live sound source.

ActionScript Sound Architecture

The ActionScript 3.0 sound scripting architecture is composed of several new classes that contribute to a finer degree of control over sound data and sound manipulation than previously available. Along with this control, however, comes an increased verbosity in sound-related scripts. Before moving on to specific examples, it will help to understand the primary purposes of the main sound classes we'll be discussing.

Sound

The **Sound** class is the first stop in working with sound. It is used to load a sound, play a sound, and manage basic sound properties.

SoundChannel

The **SoundChannel** class is used to create a separate channel for each new sound played. The use of the word channel, in this case, does not refer to the left and right channel of a stereo sound. Sounds in channels can be either mono or stereo. Instead, a channel created by the **SoundChannel** class is analogous to multitrack recording techniques. By placing each sound in its own channel, you can work with multiple sounds but control each sound separately.

SoundMixer

As the name implies, the **SoundMixer** class creates a central mixer object through which all sound channels are mixed. Changes to the mixer will affect all playing sounds. For example, this class can be used to conveniently stop all sounds that are playing.

SoundLoaderContext

Used in conjunction with the **load()** method of the **Sound** class, you can use the **SoundLoaderContext** class to specify how many seconds of a sound file to buffer.

SoundTransform

This class is used to control the volume and panning between left and right stereo channels of a source. It can be used to affect a single sound channel, a mixer object to globally affect all playing sounds, the microphone, and even the sound of a video.

ID3Info

The **ID3Info** class is used to retrieve metadata written into ID3 tags found in an MP3 file. ID3 tags are used to store information about the MP3, including artist name, song name, track number, and genre.

Microphone

Using the **Microphone** class, you can control the gain, sampling rate, and other properties of the user's microphone, if present. You can also check the activity level of the microphone, and create simple visualizations of microphone amplitude values.

We will demonstrate many of the capabilities of these classes, without exhaustively illustrating all possible features. Experimenting with sound is one of the most rewarding ways to learn more about what ActionScript has to offer, so be sure to carry on your learning after working through this chapter.

Internal and External Sounds

Typically, the use of sound in your projects will entail loading sounds from external sources. Keeping your sounds external to your primary SWF has many benefits. It can keep the file size of your SWF from becoming too large, and it's easy to change the audio file without having to recompile your SWF, just to cite two examples.

Most of the examples we'll cover in this chapter use external sound files, but it is possible to use internal sounds without having to rely on the timeline. To prepare for the remaining examples, we'll show you how to store a reference to both an internal and an external sound. These references can then be used to play the sound, create a sound channel, and otherwise manage and manipulate the sound in examples that will soon follow.

Working with Sounds in Your Library

Creating an instance of a sound from your library is consistent with creating an instance of a display symbol, as described in Chapter 4 during our discussion of the display list. After importing a sound, open the Symbol Properties or Linkage dialog, and click the Export for ActionScript check box. This will create a linkage identifier, in the form of a class name, by which you can refer to the sound. If you need to review any part of this process, see Chapter 4.

By default, the class name will be assigned automatically based on the name of the imported sound. This is important because the name of the sound may have a three-character extension, such as *.mp3*, or similar extensions for WAVE or AIFF files. You may also notice that, if your file name has spaces in it, the Flash interface will automatically remove the spaces. Neither spaces nor periods are allowed in class names, so you may need to adjust the identifier used. Following best practices, you may also wish to make sure the class name starts with a capitalized alpha character (rather than a numeral).

In this example, consider the file name *song to play.mp3*. The linkage identifier class name automatically created when exporting this sound for ActionScript will be "`songtoplay.mp3`" because the spaces will be automatically removed. The period must be removed and, with best practices in mind, a capital first letter of each word should be used, ultimately giving us "SongToPlay" as the class name, shown in Figure 11-1. Appropriately, the Base class that is automatically assigned is the **Sound** class, giving you access to all properties, methods, and events of this class when you instantiate your sound.

Figure 11-1. Choosing a custom class name for ActionScript instantiation

With that process completed, you can create an instance of that sound the same way you instantiated a custom movie clip in Chapter 4. The consistency with which you can create new instances (considering sound objects and display objects, in this discussion) is one of the hallmarks of ActionScript 3.0, and will be reinforced in upcoming examples. To create an instance of the library-bound sound, use this code:

```
var snd:Sound = new SongToPlay();
```

Thereafter, you can manage the instance of this sound by referring to the variable **snd**. Before we demonstrate playing the sound by using the variable, look at what is required to load an external sound, in the next section.

Loading External Sounds

Simply loading a sound requires a little more than invoking the **load()** method on any sound instance. There are two more small steps that we haven't yet covered. The first is to create a new sound instance. It probably won't be surprising when you realize that this process follows the same techniques we've used before, as shown in line 1 of the following code:

```
1    var snd:Sound = new Sound();
2    snd.load(new URLRequest("song.mp3"));
```

The loading process shown in line 2, however, requires the use of a new class called **URLRequest**. We'll discuss this in greater detail in Chapter 13, when we look at loading a variety of external assets. For now, however, it is important only to know that this class standardizes the use of external URLs by passing on any information you may need to provide to Flash Player. In more complex scenarios, for example, you may need to submit data to a URL, or dictate whether the GET or POST method is used when submitting your request. In these cases, we need to specify only a path to the sound we wish to load.

Once we've completed this process, we are again theoretically ready to start working with the sound stored in the **snd** variable. When working with external sounds, however, there are additional factors to consider that warrant a little extra safety code. For simplicity, we'll cover these concepts here in our discussion about loading external audio files, but we won't always include these additional measures in every example. None of these steps are required, but know that they are recommended.

The first additional consideration is to trap any possible errors encountered when trying to load the sound. You can present these errors to the end user as part of your interface, or just look for them during the authoring process by tracing to the Output panel, as is the case in this example.

To trap the errors, you need to add an event listener to the sound instance; it listens for an I/O (input/output) error event. The code that follows uses the listener structure discussed in Chapter 3 and used throughout the book. Its function traces the error text to the output window to aid in your debugging efforts.

```
3    snd.addEventListener(IOErrorEvent.IO_ERROR, onIOError, false, 0,
     true);
4    function onIOError(evt:IOErrorEvent):void {
5        trace("An error occurred when loading the sound:", evt.text);
6    }
```

The next consideration—and this is the least necessary of these recommended optional steps—is to provide feedback to the user during the loading process. Again, adding a listener to the sound instance, this time looking for a progress event, the listener function increases the width of a progress bar. The progress bar, in this case, is simply a movie clip in the shape of a horizontal bar, with its registration point aligned to its left edge, and an instance name of **progBar**. As the width increases, the movie clip grows to the right to indicate progress.

```
7    snd.addEventListener(ProgressEvent.PROGRESS, onLoadProgress, false,
     0, true);
8    function onLoadProgress(evt:ProgressEvent):void {
9        progBar.width = 100 * (evt.bytesLoaded / evt.bytesTotal);
10   }
```

The event **ProgressEvent.PROGRESS** carries with it information, including the number of bytes in the target object (in this scenario a sound that is being loaded), as well as the number of bytes loaded at the moment the event was fired. By dividing the latter by the former, you end up with a fraction. For example, if 500 bytes of a total 1,000 bytes have loaded, the progress is 500/1,000 or .5, indicating that the object is 50-percent loaded. By multiplying that times a desired width of the progress bar, the bar will start at a zero-pixel width and grow to the final desired size (100 pixels, in this example) when the file is 100-percent loaded.

The last option we'll introduce here is responding to the completion of the sound loading process. The structure is similar to the prior two examples, this time using the **Event.COMPLETE** event to trigger the listener function.

```
11   snd.addEventListener(Event.COMPLETE, onLoadComplete, false, 0,
     true);
12   function onLoadComplete(evt:Event):void {
13       trace("The sound is completely loaded.");
14   }
```

In this example, the function merely traces a notice of the completed load to the Output panel, but you'll see in a moment why this is a highly recommended step. In the next section, we'll use this event to play the sound, ensuring that no attempt is made to play the sound before loading is complete. Before we can do that, we need to demonstrate how to play the sound.

Playing, Stopping, and Pausing Sounds

As with loading, playing a sound can be accomplished merely by invoking the **play()** method of the sound instance. However, also true with loading, there is an additional step that you should take to make future work easier. That additional step is creating a channel in which this sound can reside.

When you think of your average recording device, you probably have only one channel, or track, in which to record. You may be able to record multiple sources simultaneously, but you must do so live, to one channel. Once recorded, you can no longer isolate one of your original sources for manipulation. Instead, you can work only with the combined final recording. Multitrack recorders, however, allow you to record separate channels, which can be manipulated later as discrete sources. This functionality is analogous to ActionScript 3.0's new **SoundChannel** class.

Playing Sounds

You can easily preserve each sound as a discrete entity by creating a channel when issuing a play command:

```
var channel:SoundChannel;
channel = snd.play();
```

Now that you know how to play the sound and create a new channel, reconsider the previous loading discussion. If you load an external sound file and then immediately attempt to play it, it will very likely fail because the sound will likely still be loading. However, if you capitalize on the load-complete example discussed previously, you can play the file only after the sound has loaded.

Repeating the last section of code from the loading discussion, you can simply replace the trace instruction with a play command. Line 11 creates the channel variable. Line 14 identifies the target of the event (the file having just completed loading) and casts it as a sound, because many types of files can be loaded. (For more information about casting, see "Casting a Display Object" in Chapter 4.) Finally, line 15 populates the created channel by playing the sound.

```
11  var channel:SoundChannel;
12  snd.addEventListener(Event.COMPLETE, onLoadComplete, false, 0,
        true);
13  function onLoadComplete(evt:Event):void {
14      var localSnd:Sound = evt.target as Sound;
15      channel = localSnd.play();
16  }
```

Stopping Sounds

Stopping a single sound in a channel requires only the **stop()** method. Unlike playing the sound, however, this method is invoked from the channel, not from the sound itself. Continuing with the use of **channel** as the sound channel instance:

```
channel.stop();
```

> **NOTE**
>
> *Hereafter, we will standardize all examples to load an external sound and create a sound channel. If not specifically noted to the contrary, please assume any sound example in this chapter begins with the following first steps:*
>
> ```
> var snd:Sound = new Sound();
> snd.load(new URLRequest
>     ("song.mp3"));
>
> var channel:SoundChannel = new
>     SoundChannel();
> channel = snd.play();
> ```

It is also possible to stop all sounds using the **SoundMixer** class. As in real-world scenarios, multichannel playback funnels through a sound mixer. You can manipulate all the sounds going through the mixer, allowing you to stop all sounds.

Unlike the previous classes discussed, the **SoundMixer** is a static class, which means it does not need to be instantiated using the **new()** method. Therefore, to stop playing the sounds in all channels, you need only write:

```
SoundMixer.stopAll();
```

Pausing Sounds and Resuming Playback

Pausing a sound is a bit different. Currently, there is no sound pause command. Instead, you must rely on an optional parameter of the **play()** method that allows you to play the sound starting from a particular number of seconds offset from the beginning of the sound.

To use this feature, the first step is to store the current position of the sound in the desired channel (using the aptly named **position** property), stop the sound in that channel, and then, later, play the sound from the stored position. Assuming the sound and channel instances are referenced by the same variables we've been using in this chapter (**snd** and **channel**, respectively), here is an example of pausing and resuming playback of the sound:

```
var pausePos:Number = channel.position;
channel.stop();
```

At some later point, you can resume playback from where you left off:

```
channel = snd.play(pausePos);
```

Buffering Streaming Sounds

Previously, we discussed waiting to play a sound until it was fully loaded, to prevent errors or stutters that might occur when attempting to play a sound during the load process. An alternative approach is to preload only a portion of the sound prior to playback, and then play the sound while it continues to stream to Flash Player in the background. The principle behind this approach is to preload a buffer that can stay ahead of playback during the time required to download the remainder of the sound.

How much of the sound you should preload depends on your connection speed. Theoretically, if you have no load time, you usually need no buffer time, because the sound loads instantly. This is usually true of local files, when you are not loading the sound from the Internet. Following that concept, if you have a fast connection, you need a shorter buffer time, but a slow connection requires a longer buffer time. In this way, your connection speed can dictate how much sound needs to be preloaded to prevent the sound playback from catching up with the download state and stalling your sound.

To specify the buffer time, you must use the **SoundLoaderContext** class at the time of sound loading. Instantiating the class requires one parameter, which is the number of milliseconds of the sound you wish to buffer. After instantiating the class, you then pass the resulting instance into the sound **load()** method, as a second parameter following the **URLRequest**. The following example, as a variant on our standard sound loading sequence, buffers 10 seconds of the loaded sound before the **play()** method will have any effect:

```
var snd:Sound = new Sound();
var context:SoundLoaderContext = new SoundLoaderContext(10000);
snd.load(new URLRequest("song.mp3"), context);
var channel:SoundChannel = new SoundChannel();
channel = snd.play();
```

NOTE

For simplicity, we will omit loading listeners and buffering from the sample code snippets. You will probably not need them when loading local files, but consider their use for online work.

Changing Sound Volume and Pan

During playback, it is possible to manipulate the volume and pan of individual channels, as well as the global mixer containing all sounds. Doing so requires the **SoundTransform** class.

The process involves storing a reference to the transform object of the channel or mixer, setting the volume and/or pan setting, and then repopulating the original transform object with the newly altered reference transform. For example, this script will set the volume of the single channel in our ongoing discussion to 50 percent.

```
var trans:SoundTransform = new SoundTransform();
trans.volume = 0.5;
channel.soundTransform = trans;
```

Most ActionScript 3.0 settings that use percentage values use a unit range of 0 to 1. For example, volume is expressed as a range of 0 (muted) to 1 (full volume) with any interim value expressed as a percentage of full volume. To determine a value that describes a pan setting between left and right stereo channels, a percentage left and percentage right is required. Therefore, the units are expressed as a range of -1 (full left) through 0 (centered) to 1 (full right). Negative interim values reflect some degree of pan left, and positive interim values reflect some degree of pan right. The following script sets the channel in the prior example to a pan setting of full left:

```
var trans:SoundTransform = new SoundTransform();
trans.pan = -1;
channel.soundTransform = trans;
```

To transform all playing sounds at once, simply substitute the specified channel with the global mixer. For example, the following script mutes all sounds:

```
var trans:SoundTransform = new SoundTransform();
trans.volume = 0;
SoundMixer.soundTransform = trans;
```

To tie this together, let's examine *soundTransform.fla* (Figure 11-2) from the accompanying source code. This sample file uses coordinates of the mouse to control volume and pan. Moving the mouse left and right pans the sound left and right. Moving the mouse up and down fades the volume up and down.

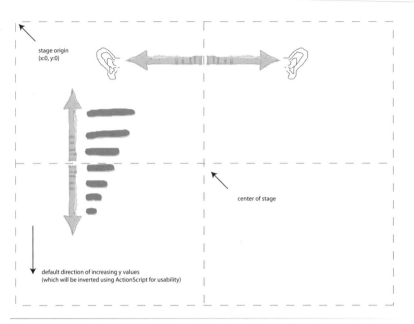

Figure 11-2. Using the mouse with soundTransform.fla *to adjust the sound volume and panning*

The first several lines of the source code are pretty basic. Line 1 instantiates the **Sound** class, and line 2 loads the sound. Line 4 creates a sound channel, and line 5 populates that channel by playing the sound.

```
1    var snd:Sound = new Sound();
2    snd.load(new URLRequest("song.mp3"));
3
4    var channel:SoundChannel = new SoundChannel();
5    channel = snd.play();
```

The next line creates a **SoundTransform** instance so we can change the volume and pan values.

```
6    var trans:SoundTransform = new SoundTransform();
```

The final set of lines creates a listener that updates the transform every time an **ENTER_FRAME** event occurs.

```
7    this.addEventListener(Event.ENTER_FRAME, onLoop, false, 0, true);
8    function onLoop(evt:Event):void {
9        trans.volume = 1 - mouseY / stage.stageHeight;
10       trans.pan = mouseX / (stage.stageWidth / 2) - 1;
11       channel.soundTransform = trans;
12   }
```

Line 9 affects the volume. In basic terms, dividing the y position of the mouse by the height of the stage will give you a fraction that fits nicely into the volume unit range of 0 to 1. However, in a Cartesian coordinate system like that used for the Flash stage, the upper-left corner of the stage is (0, 0), and the y values increase as you go *down*. This means the volume would increase toward the bottom of the stage, not the top, which is counter-intuitive when you think of a volume slider.

So, to invert the value, we subtract it from 1. When the mouse is near the bottom of the stage, the `mouseY`/`stageHeight` fraction might ordinarily equate to 0.9 for a loud sound, but 1 minus 0.9 is 0.1, giving you a soft sound. Similarly, at the top of the stage, when an unaltered fraction might yield 0.1, 1 minus 0.1 is 0.9 resulting in a louder sound. This more closely mimics our expectations of volume sliders.

Line 10 affects the pan. This calculation is similar to the volume calculation, but we need -1 for full left, 0 at the center of the stage, and 1 for full right. Therefore, we need to divide the mouse x location by half the stage, and then subtract 1. If the mouse is in the center of a 400-pixel wide stage, the calculation is this: half the stage width is 200, 200 divided by 200 is 1, minus 1, resulting in a value of 0 for a centered pan. At the far left of the stage, you end up with 0 divided by 200 is 0, minus 1, giving you a value of -1 for a full-left pan. Finally, at the far right of the stage, 400 divided by 200 is 2, minus 1 is 1 for a full-right pan.

After calculating the volume and pan values based on the mouse position, and altering the volume and pan properties of the **trans** transform object you created, all that remains is updating the **transform** property of the desired channel by replacing it with the new data. This occurs in line 11.

Again, if you want to transform every sound playing at a given moment, the same technique can be used, simply by substituting **SoundMixer** for the specific channel in line 11.

Reading ID3 Metadata from MP3 Sounds

During the encoding process, MP3 encoders can inject metadata into the MP3 sounds, storing this data in tags established by the ID3 specification. How much metadata that is included is decided during the encoding process, but version 2 of the ID3 specification, supported by Flash, can contain quite a bit of information.

Accessing this read-only information is accomplished via the **ID3Info** class. The simplest way to query the primary supported ID3 tags is through the use of logically named properties of the **id3** property of the **Sound** class.

For example, you can query the artist and song names of an MP3 file, loaded by our **snd** sound instance, this way:

```
snd.id3.artist;
snd.id3.songName;
```

There are seven main tags supported in this direct fashion, as seen in Table 11-1. The remainder of the supported tags can be accessed through the same **id3** property of the **Sound** class, but using the tag's four-character name.

Table 11-1. The most common ID3 tags and their corresponding ActionScript property names

ID3 2.0 tag	ActionScript property
COMM	Sound.id3.comment
TALB	Sound.id3.album
TCON	Sound.id3.genre
TIT2	Sound.id3.songName
TPE1	Sound.id3.artist
TRCK	Sound.id3.track
TYER	Sound.id3.year

Table 11-2 shows supported tags that do not also have accompanying property names all their own. Accessing the beats-per-minute data, for example, would require the following syntax:

```
snd.id3.TBPM;
```

If you prefer a consistent approach, it is also possible to access all ID3 tag information using the four-character tag names, including the seven tags that have their own dedicated property names. However, for quick access to the most commonly used properties, you will likely find the descriptive names to be more useful.

Table 11-2. Supported ID3 tags without dedicated ActionScript property names

ID3 2.0 tag	Description
TBPM	Beats per minute
TCOM	Composer
TFLT	File type
TIME	Time
TIT1	Content group description
TIT3	Subtitle/description refinement
TKEY	Initial key
TLAN	Languages
TLEN	Length

Table 11-2. Supported ID3 tags without dedicated ActionScript property names (contd.)

ID3 2.0 tag	Description
TMED	Media type
TOAL	Original album/movie/show title
TOFN	Original filename
TOLY	Original lyricists/text writers
TOPE	Original artists/performers
TORY	Original release year
TOWN	File owner/licensee
TPE2	Album artist/band/orchestra/accompaniment
TPE3	Conductor/performer refinement
TPE4	Interpreted, remixed, or otherwise modified by
TPOS	Disc/position in set
TPUB	Publisher
TRDA	Recording dates
TRSN	Internet radio station name
TRSO	Internet radio station owner
TSIZ	Size
TSRC	ISRC (international standard recording code)
TSSE	Software/hardware and settings used for encoding
WXXX	URL link frame

Finally, using a **for..in** loop, it is possible to access ID3 2.0 tags. You can add a listener to the sound instance (which continues to be **snd** in these examples) that listens for the **Event.ID3** event.

```
1    snd.addEventListener(Event.ID3, onID3Info, false, 0, true);
2    function onID3Info (evt:Event):void {
3        var id3Props:ID3Info = evt.target.id3;
4        for (var propName:String in id3Props) {
5            trace("ID3 Tag", propName, "=", id3Props [propName]);
6        }
7    }
```

When ID3 information is detected and the listener function is triggered, an **ID3Info** object is created to store the incoming data. The **for..in** loop walks through all the properties stored and, in this case, traces them to the Output panel. The data could also be displayed in a custom MP3 player interface, placed into an ongoing database to rank most often played songs, and so on.

NOTE

*In all cases, if a tag has not been encoded into the MP3, querying the tag will return **undefined** as a value.*

Visualizing Sound Data

One of the most inviting new pieces of eye candy in ActionScript 3.0 is sound visualization. It is now possible to analyze a sound during playback and pull raw data from the sound in real time to create a visual representation of that sound.

You can visualize three basic sets of values: the amplitude at any given moment of the left and/or right stereo channels; the amplitude of the sound over time (like when represented by a traditional waveform); and an analysis of the frequency spectrum using a Fourier transform, to depict the values of low-, mid-, and high-range frequency bands.

We'll start off with the first option, as it is the easiest to approach. At any point during playback, you can query the amplitude of a specific sound channel's left or right stereo channel. All you need to do is read the **leftPeak** and **rightPeak** properties of the desired sound channel, like so:

```
channel.leftPeak;
channel.rightPeak;
```

These properties will return a value between 0 and 1 to represent the amplitude at the moment the sample occurred. Therefore, to create a basic amplitude meter, you need do little more than manipulate the height of a movie clip. You could multiply the desired full-height of the amplitude meter (instantiated as **lftMeter** and **rghtMeter** in this example) by the fraction returned by the properties. The following code demonstrates a basic meter that is 100 pixels high at full amplitude. Therefore, a **leftPeak** or **rightPeak** value of .5 will cause the meter to rise to half-height, or 50 pixels.

```
lftMeter.height = 100 * channel.leftPeak;
rghtMeter.height = 100 * channel.rightPeak;
```

If you wanted something slightly less conventional, you might scale a graphic with the amplitude values. For example, you could create pictures of left and right speakers that increase in size based on the amplitude values. Scale is also measured in units from 0 to 1; so, to prevent the speakers from disappearing during silent sections, you should add the amplitude to an original scale of 1 (100 percent). Therefore, the speakers will remain unchanged during silence and potentially grow to twice their size at 100 percent amplitude.

```
lftSpeaker.scaleX = lftSpeaker.scaleY = 1 + channel.leftPeak;
rghtSpeaker.scaleX = rghtSpeaker.scaleY = 1 + channel.rightPeak;
```

We're going to show you a slightly more realistic meter, based on a peak meter that you might see on a home stereo. If you've never seen a peak meter before, it is usually a series of 6 to 10 consecutive lights, which glow in sequence depending on the amplitude of the sound. Typically, the lights begin in green or cool colors for acceptable amplitudes, then switch to yellow or warm colors when the amplitude approaches possible distortion levels, and finally switch to red or hot colors when the amplitude exceeds acceptable levels. A representation of this type of meter is shown in illustration A of Figure 11-3.

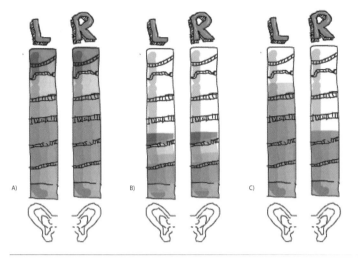

Figure 11-3. The visual layout of the sample file

Because of the color changes, we can't simply scale the color bars. The effect would not look like a standard peak meter because all the colors would be visible, including the hot colors, even at partial amplitude. This can be seen in illustration B of Figure 11-3. What we need, instead, is to see only those colors representative of the amplitude, be they cool or hot, as seen in illustration C of Figure 11-3.

This can be accomplished by creating a mask for the color bars, and scaling only the mask. The entire peak meter is a movie clip, within which another movie clip exists, instantiated as **barMask**. Because the mask dictates what is seen in the masked layer, scaling the mask will reveal only the desired portion of the color bars, as seen in Figure 11-4. Also, the registration point of the mask can be placed at the bottom of the clip to simplify the scaling process. Any scaling will be relative to the bottom edge.

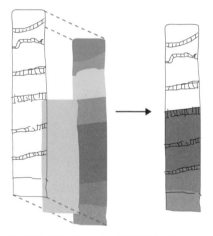

Figure 11-4. A peak meter controlled by scaling a mask

This is the code included in *channelPeaks.fla*. The first five lines are the standard opening we've been using throughout the chapter, and the remaining lines are a standard event listener, responding to enter frame events.

```
1   var snd:Sound = new Sound();
2   snd.load(new URLRequest("song.mp3"));
3
4   var channel:SoundChannel = new SoundChannel();
5   channel = snd.play();
6
7   this.addEventListener(Event.ENTER_FRAME, onLoop, false, 0, true);
8
9   function onLoop(evt:Event):void {
10      lPeak.barMask.scaleY = channel.leftPeak;
11      rPeak.barMask.scaleY = channel.rightPeak;
12  }
```

All the function needs to do is set the **scaleY** property of the mask (**barMask**) inside the left and right peak meters (**lPeak** and **rPeak**), to the value of the respective amplitude values that are returned by the **leftPeak** and **rightPeak** properties. Because these are audio peak meters, we want the bar to disappear during silent passages, so we don't want to scale up from 100 percent, as discussed previously. Instead, we want 0 percent, 100 percent, and all the values in between.

The result is a pair of peak meters, tuned to the left and right stereo channels of a sound, that bounce with amplitude as the sound plays. We'll look at a more complex example at the end of the chapter, at which time we'll visualize the sound's waveform.

Working with Microphone Sound

It is also possible to access some information about microphone input, although it is not possible to record without the use of a remote server like the Flash Media Server, nor is it currently possible to use **computeSpectrum()** to analyze the waveform, as demonstrated with MP3 source material. Instead, we can reflect something akin to the amplitude of the sound, which, in the parlance of the ActionScript 3.0 **Microphone** class, is called **activityLevel**.

Much of the code in this example will be familiar to you by now, so we'll jump right in to explain the *microphone.fla* source file. The first six lines of this script are important in that they initialize the microphone for use.

Line 1 creates an instance of the microphone using the **getMicrophone()** method of the static class **Microphone**. In order to work with the data of the microphone, you'll need to loop it back into Flash, in line 2. When doing so, it is best to use echo suppression, shown in line 3, to minimize feedback from your speakers during recording. Finally, lines 4 through 6 initialize the gain (amplitude of the recording), sample rate (11.050 kHz for basic voice input), and silence level. The latter is a convenient filter, if you will, to tell Flash what level of input, sustained for how many milliseconds, should be ignored as inactivity. This helps reduce the input of background noise.

```
1    var mic:Microphone = Microphone.getMicrophone();
2    mic.setLoopBack(true);
3    mic.setUseEchoSuppression(true);
4    mic.gain = 80;
5    mic.rate = 11;
6    mic.setSilenceLevel(5, 1000);
```

Despite echo suppression, if your microphone is close to your speakers (particularly when using a laptop with a built-in microphone), feedback can still occur. Therefore, if you're not recording the mic input using a remote server, you may wish to set the volume of the mic to zero. This is not the same as muting, or deactivating, the microphone; it merely sets the volume of the *active* mic to an inaudible level.

```
7    var trans:SoundTransform = mic.soundTransform;
8    trans.volume = 0;
9    mic.soundTransform = trans;
```

The next 20 lines are optional and provide feedback about the mic. If you are not getting any results from your code, it is helpful to know whether your microphone is disabled. The **onMicStatus** listener responds to any microphone status updates, such as when the mic is muted or unmuted. If the user has allowed access to the mic, the **showMicInfo()** function is then called.

```
10   mic.addEventListener(StatusEvent.STATUS, onMicStatus);
11   function onMicStatus(evt:StatusEvent):void {
12       if (evt.code == "Microphone.Unmuted") {
13           showMicInfo();
14       } else if (evt.code == "Microphone.Muted") {
15           trace("Microphone access was denied.");
16       }
17   }
```

Another reason that you may not get the results you expect from microphone input is if the wrong input (or possible multiple inputs) has been selected. The first structure of the **showMicInfo()** function, in lines 19 through 24, loops through all possible microphone names and traces them to the Output panel, followed by the name of the currently selected microphone. This allows you to verify that the desired mic is active.

The last of the optional diagnostic measures takes place in lines 26 through 31, tracing the primary microphone settings to the Output panel.

```
18   function showMicInfo():void {
19       var sndInputs:Array = Microphone.names;
20       trace("Available sound input devices:");
21       for (var i:int = 0; i < sndInputs.length; i++) {
22           trace("    " + sndInputs [i]);
23       }
24       trace("Sound input device name:", mic.name);
25
26       trace("Muted:", mic.muted);
27       trace("Echo suppression:", mic.useEchoSuppression);
28       trace("Gain:", mic.gain);
29       trace("Rate:", mic.rate, "kHz");
30       trace("Silence level:", mic.silenceLevel);
31       trace("Silence timeout:", mic.silenceTimeout);
32   }
```

Next, we begin to get into the visualization section of the file. This example will plot a graph of microphone activity levels over time. To do this, we need to use the **Graphics** class and draw lines from point to point, as discussed in Chapter 8.

We start with a real-world canvas to draw onto so it can be repositioned later, if desired. Also, because we don't need a timeline, we can save a bit on file size by using a sprite instead of a movie clip. Lines 33 and 34 create the sprite and add it to the display list, and line 35 stores a concise reference to the sprite's **Graphics** object, specified by the canvas's **graphics** property.

```
33  var canvas:Sprite = new Sprite();
34  addChild(canvas);
35  var g:Graphics = canvas.graphics;
```

The last bit of prep work before we can begin drawing is to initialize the canvas. The canvas is cleared, a line style is specified, and the first drawing point is then moved to the starting position of the graph. This plot will arbitrarily begin at the left edge of the stage, 300 pixels from the top, and remap once the drawing reaches 550, or the right side of the stage when using the default Flash movie size. (All these settings can be stored into variables for a more flexible solution, which we'll demonstrate at the end of the chapter in a summary exercise.)

```
36  initCanvas();
37  function initCanvas():void {
38      g.clear();
39      g.lineStyle(0, 0x6600CC);
40      g.moveTo(0, 300);
41  }
```

Next, we script the plotting of the graph. One way to graph the microphone's activity level is to draw the next point in the graph when the microphone is stimulated by a change in activity (determined both by input and your silence level settings). This can be accomplished using the **ActivityEvent.ACTIVITY** event. However, we want this graph to be a continuous display of activity, so we will use a frequently occurring event.

For greater accuracy, we've used a timer object that triggers an event every 50 milliseconds. The timer object can be adjusted with a finer granularity than the movie tempo, and won't affect other animations that use enter frame events. (For more information on the **Timer** event, see Chapter 3.) We also initialize a counter that we will increment to draw the graph.

```
42  var myTimer:Timer = new Timer(50);
43  myTimer.addEventListener("timer", timerHandler);
44  myTimer.start();
45
46  var xInc:int = 0;
```

The listener function then simply draws lines from point to point. The x coordinate of each point is retrieved from the **xInc** variable, which starts at zero and increments by 2 pixels with each plot. The y coordinate is always the arbitrary baseline (300, in this case) minus the activity recorded by the mic. So, if the value is 50, the y coordinate will be 300 minus 50, or 250. Because y values increase down to the bottom of the stage, a *lower* y value will appear as an increase in amplitude. Finally, when the x coordinate exceeds the width of this stage, it is reset to 0, and the canvas is reinitialized so the plot can continue.

```
47    function timerHandler(ev:TimerEvent):void {
48        g.lineTo(xInc, 300 - mic.activityLevel);
49        if (xInc > 550) {
50            xInc = 0;
51            initCanvas();
52        } else {
53            xInc += 2;
54        }
55    }
```

Figure 11-5 shows an example of the script's output. The first segment of the plot was created with staccato whistling, similar to the call of a robin or other songbird. The sharp rise and fall of activity is characteristic of this type of sound. The second segment was created by a human voice steadily increasing the amplitude of a single tone to crescendo and then diminishing again to silence. The fact that the rise and fall of the tone are not represented by straight lines is attributed to the natural wavering of the average human voice when attempting this exercise.

Figure 11-5. A visualization of a microphone's activity level

Waveform Visualization

Having visualized raw sound data during playback as a representation of a simple set of left and right peak meters, and then moved on to draw a graph of amplitudes of microphone input, let's combine those ideas and draw waveforms of a sound playing in real time. Figure 11-6 shows a screenshot of *soundVis.fla* in action, using the code we're about to explain. It depicts the left stereo channel in green and the right stereo channel in orange, with load and playback progress bars in the lower-left corner, and play, pause, and stop buttons in the lower-right corner.

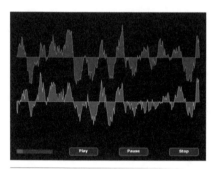

Figure 11-6. A visualization of left and right channel waveforms

This exercise is composed of three classes: a main document class that is responsible for playback, another class responsible for the buttons, and a third class responsible for the visualization.

The SoundPlayBasic Class

The first part of this system is a class that controls the playback of the sound. Lines 1 through 25 are the standard opening lines for packages, beginning with Line 1, which defines the package itself. Lines 3 through 12 import the needed classes, including two custom classes in lines 11 and 12: the class responsible for the visualization of the sound data, and a class defined in Chapter 8 for drawing code-only buttons.

```
1    package {
2
3        import flash.display.Sprite;
4        import flash.display.Graphics;
5        import flash.geom.Point;
6        import flash.net.URLRequest;
7        import flash.media.*;
8        import flash.utils.ByteArray;
9        import flash.utils.Timer;
```

```
10        import flash.events.*;
11        import Visualization;
12        import CreateRoundRectButton;
13
14        public class SoundPlayBasic extends Sprite {
15
16            private var _snd:Sound = new Sound();
17            private var _channel:SoundChannel = new SoundChannel();
18            private var _pausePosition:int = 0;
19            private var _loadBar:Sprite;
20            private var _playBar:Sprite;
21            private var _playBtn:Sprite;
22            private var _pauseBtn:Sprite;
23            private var _stopBtn:Sprite;
24            private var _isPlaying:Boolean;
25            private var _vis:Visualization;
```

Line 14 defines the class, which extends **Sprite**. We need a display object with some movie clip attributes, but we don't need a timeline, so a sprite will serve us well. Lastly, lines 16 through 25 declare the variables that will be private to this class. In this class, we will be focusing on sound playback only, so we won't need any visualization variables other than the instance of the **Visualization** class itself, **_vis**.

In the next block of code, lines 26 through 38 encompass the class constructor. The constructor is brief, consisting of a series of listeners, the sound loading instruction, and function calls that create two display objects. Line 27 adds a listener that will listen for errors that may occur while loading the sound. Line 28 will monitor loading progress, and line 29 will react when the sound loading is complete. We'll discuss all the listener functions in just a moment.

```
26        public function SoundPlayBasic() {
27            _snd.addEventListener(IOErrorEvent.IO_ERROR, onIOError,
              false, 0, true);
28            _snd.addEventListener(ProgressEvent.PROGRESS,
              onLoadProgress, false, 0, true);
29            _snd.addEventListener(Event.COMPLETE, onLoadComplete,
              false, 0, true);
30
31            var context:SoundLoaderContext = new
              SoundLoaderContext(5000, false);
32            _snd.load(new URLRequest("song.mp3"), context);
33
34            _loadBar = drawBar(0x003388);
35            addChild(_loadBar);
36            _playBar = drawBar(0x0066CC);
37            addChild(_playBar);
38        }
```

Line 32 loads the sound using the standard **URLRequest()** method for interacting with all URLs. This example also includes a buffer, through the **SoundLoaderContext** class, of five seconds (5000 milliseconds) to compensate a bit for slower connections.

The last four lines of this script segment are responsible for creating load and playback progress bars. Lines 34 and 35 draw the loader bar and then add it to the display list, respectively, and lines 36 and 37 accomplish the same tasks for the playback bar.

The **drawBar()** function itself can be seen in the next code block, in lines 39 through 48. When called, it will create and return a sprite with a horizontal rectangle drawn within. The function defines a hairline stroke and 100-percent alpha fill, in lines 41 and 42 respectively, using the color sent into the **col** argument. It then draws a rectangle starting at point (0, 0), and spans 1-pixel wide and 10-pixels high. Finally, it positions the bar at point (20, 370) (the bottom of the stage in this example) and returns the finished sprite to the constructor so it can be added to the display list.

```
39          private function drawBar(col:uint):Sprite {
40              var bar:Sprite = new Sprite();
41              bar.graphics.lineStyle(0, col);
42              bar.graphics.beginFill(col, 1);
43              bar.graphics.drawRect(0, 0, 1, 10);
44              bar.graphics.endFill();
45              bar.x = 20;
46              bar.y = 370;
47              return bar;
48          }
```

The next two functions are callback functions. The first traces any error that occurs during loading, and the second sets the width of the bar used to indicate loading progress. The width of the progress bar is determined by multiplying the final width of the bar by the fraction of bytes loaded over bytes total. Therefore, 100 pixels times 50-percent loaded equals 50 pixels.

```
49          private function onIOError(evt:IOErrorEvent):void {
50              trace("An error occurred when loading the sound:",
                    evt.text);
51          }
52
53          private function onLoadProgress(evt:ProgressEvent):void {
54              _loadBar.width = Math.round(100 * (evt.bytesLoaded /
                    evt.bytesTotal));
55          }
```

The next segment of ActionScript, in lines 56 through 75, contains the listener function, triggered when the sound loading is complete. This is important for a few reasons. It creates the control buttons and visualization and also removes three unneeded listeners.

```
56        private function onLoadComplete(evt:Event):void {
57            createControlButtons();
58
59            removeEventListener(IOErrorEvent.IO_ERROR, onIOError);
60            removeEventListener(ProgressEvent.PROGRESS,
                  onLoadProgress);
61            removeEventListener(Event.COMPLETE, onLoadComplete);
62
63            //add sound visualization
64            var visObj:Object = new Object();
65            visObj.waveHeight = 100;
66            visObj.leftBase = 60;
67            visObj.rightBase = 120;
68            visObj.visLoc = new Point(20,0);
69            visObj.visScale = 2;
70            visObj.fft = false;
71
72            _vis = new Visualization(visObj);
73            addChild(_vis);
74            _vis.stage.frameRate = 20;
75        }
```

Creating the visualization is a two-part process. Lines 64 through 70 set up the parameters that will be passed into the **Visualization** class, and lines 72 and 73 instantiate it and add it to the display list.

To be as flexible as possible, the class was designed to accommodate a number of optional parameters. One way to support a variable number of values is to pass them in as properties of a custom object. That way, only one parameter is required, but an unlimited number of properties can be added to the object. In the **Visualization** class, you can then check to see which parameters were actually sent in, and apply any default values required in the event of any absences.

The properties added here include the size and y coordinate of the waveform for both left and right channels, the location and scale of the final visualization, and a Boolean that determines whether to display a regular waveform or a frequency spectrum analysis that maps the amplitude of low, mid, and high frequencies. We'll discuss these options in greater detail when we look at the **Visualization** class.

Lastly, line 74 increases the frame rate to make the visualization graphics appear smoother. The frame rate chosen will be revisited later, when discussing the visualization.

The next code block, lines 76 through 83, is responsible for monitoring playback as well as improving performance. The **onPlayProgress()** function controls the width of a playback progress bar in a similar manner as the aforementioned load progress bar. This time the final bar width is multiplied by the fraction of current sound position over sound length. The length is also adjusted by the percentage of the sound that has loaded, to make the available length of the sound more accurate during loading.

```
76          private function onPlayProgress(evt:Event):void {
77              var sndLength:int = Math.ceil(_snd.length /
                    (_snd.bytesLoaded / _snd.bytesTotal));
78              _playBar.width = 100 * (_channel.position /
                    sndLength);
79          }
80
81          private function onPlaybackComplete(evt:Event):void {
82              soundStopped();
83          }
```

The **onPlaybackComplete()** method is triggered when the sound finishes playing and, in turn, calls **soundStopped()**. This allows **soundStopped()** to be called from other methods and reduces code duplication.

The next four methods control playback. The **onPlaySnd()** method creates listeners for progress and visualization, plays the sound, and sets a playing flag to **true**. Checking for this flag before continuing limits playback to one sound. The **onStopSnd()** method again calls **soundStopped()**, which stops playback, resets the progress bar and visualization timer, and removes the applicable listeners.

```
84          private function onPlaySnd(evt:MouseEvent):void {
85              if (!_isPlaying) {
86                  this.addEventListener(Event.ENTER_FRAME,
                        onPlayProgress, false, 0, true);
87                  _vis.addVisTimer();
88                  _channel = _snd.play(_pausePosition);
89                  _channel.addEventListener (Event.SOUND_COMPLETE,
                        onPlaybackComplete, false, 0, true);
90                  _isPlaying = true;
91              }
92          }
93
94          private function onPauseSnd(evt:MouseEvent):void {
95              _pausePosition = _channel.position;
96              _channel.stop();
97              _isPlaying = false;
98          }
99          private function onStopSnd(evt:MouseEvent):void {
100             soundStopped();
101         }
102
103         private function soundStopped():void {
104             _pausePosition = 0;
105             _channel.stop();
106             _channel.removeEventListener(Event.SOUND_COMPLETE,
107                 onPlaybackComplete);
108             this.removeEventListener(Event.ENTER_FRAME,
                    onPlayProgress);
109             _playBar.width = 0;
110             _vis.removeVisTimer();
111             _isPlaying = false;
112         }
```

The **_pausePosition** variable is used throughout these methods. There is no ActionScript pause method, so pausing is accomplished by resuming playback from the last known sound position. The **onPauseSnd()** method records this position before the sound is stopped. By contrast, the **onStopSnd()** method sets the variable to 0 to ensure that replaying the sound starts at its beginning. It also removes the listener controlling the playback bar, resets the bar's width to 0, and removes the listener controlling the visualization.

In the very last block of code, spanning lines 113 through 130 the aforementioned **createControlButtons()** method creates play, pause, and stop buttons. The **CreateRoundRectButton** class introduced in Chapter 8 accepts a width, height, corner radius, stroke weight, color, text, and text color, and returns a sprite with a simple button therein. Each button is then positioned and assigned an event listener that triggers the methods described in the previous code block. If you need to review this class, see Chapter 8.

```
113        private function createControlButtons():void {
114            _playBtn = new CreateRoundRectButton(80, 20, 10, 2,
               0x0066CC, "Play", 0xFFFFFF);
115            _playBtn.x = 170;
116            _playBtn.y = 365;
117            _playBtn.addEventListener(MouseEvent.MOUSE_UP,
               onPlaySnd, false, 0, true);
118            addChild(_playBtn);
119            _pauseBtn = new CreateRoundRectButton(80, 20, 10, 2,
               0x0066CC, "Pause", 0xFFFFFF);
120            _pauseBtn.x = 310;
121            _pauseBtn.y = 365;
122            _pauseBtn.addEventListener(MouseEvent.MOUSE_UP,
               onPauseSnd, false, 0, true);
123            addChild(_pauseBtn);
124            _stopBtn = new CreateRoundRectButton(80, 20, 10, 2,
               0x0066CC, "Stop", 0xFFFFFF);
125            _stopBtn.x = 450;
126            _stopBtn.y = 365;
127            _stopBtn.addEventListener(MouseEvent.MOUSE_UP,
               onStopSnd, false, 0, true);
128            addChild(_stopBtn);
129        }
130    }
131 }
```

The Visualization Class

As the **SoundPlayBasic** class was responsible for playing the sound in this example, the **Visualization** class is specifically responsible for drawing with sound data during playback. The opening salvo of the class imports the necessary classes and declares the variables it will be using.

This is relatively standard fare, but you may notice the absence of the **Sound** and **SoundChannel** classes. While the sound is played in the **SoundPlayBasic** class, the more important point is that analyzing the sound data going through the global **SoundMixer** is what drives the visualization.

```
1    package {
2
3        import flash.display.Sprite;
4        import flash.display.Graphics;
5        import flash.geom.Point;
6        import flash.media.SoundMixer;
7        import flash.utils.ByteArray;
8        import flash.utils.Timer;
9        import flash.events.*;
10
11       public class Visualization extends Sprite {
12
13           private var _bytes:ByteArray = new ByteArray();
14           private var _visLoc:Point;
15           private var _visScale:Number;
16           private var _waveHeight:Number;
17           private var _leftBase:Number;
18           private var _rightBase:Number;
19           private var _fft:Boolean;
20           private var _g:Graphics;
21           private var _timer:Timer;
```

The first task of the class constructor is to parse the properties of the argument object and store them in the variables declared previously. Immediately thereafter, the **initVars()** function is called to ensure that any important values are present. The class parameter values are designed to be optional, but that is not necessarily because they are unneeded. They have been made optional to allow the default values of the class to be used instead.

The **initVars()** function in lines 41 through 47 first checks to see whether a property has been omitted and, if so, substitutes a default value. It is important to note that ActionScript 3.0 changes the way programmers check for default values. For example, you can no longer sweepingly look to see whether a variable is undefined. Instead, different data types require different tests. A **Number** has a default value of **NaN** (not a number), integers (both signed and unsigned) default to 0, and Booleans default to **false**, just to name a few data types.

```
22           public function Visualization(obj:Object) {
23               _waveHeight = obj.waveHeight;
24               _leftBase = obj.leftBase;
25               _rightBase = obj.rightBase;
26               _visLoc = obj.visLoc;
27               _visScale = obj.visScale;
28               _fft = obj.fft;
29               initVars();
30
31               var canvas:Sprite = new Sprite();
32               addChild(canvas);
33               canvas.x = _visLoc.x;
34               canvas.y = _visLoc.y;
35               canvas.scaleX = canvas.scaleY = _visScale;
36               _g = canvas.graphics;
37
38               addVisTimer();
39           }
40
```

```
41          private function initVars():void {
42              if (isNaN(_waveHeight)) { _waveHeight = 150; }
43              if (isNaN(_leftBase)) { _leftBase = 125; }
44              if (isNaN(_rightBase)) { _rightBase = 235; }
45              if (!(_visLoc is Point)) { _visLoc = new Point(); }
46              if (isNaN(_visScale)) { _visScale = 1; }
47          }
```

Lines 31 through 36 of the constructor set up a canvas onto which we can draw the sound waves. A new sprite is created, positioned, and scaled by the incoming parameters, and then a shorthand citation is created to make subsequent references simpler.

The last line of the constructor (line 38) establishes an event listener to control the visualization. This can be seen in the **addVisTimer()** function. If the timer does not yet exist, a new timer is created to fire every 50 milliseconds. An event listener is added to the timer, to call the **onVisualize()** function, and the timer is then started.

Previously, in the **SoundPlayBasic** class, the frame rate of the Flash SWF was set to 20 frames per second after the **Visualization** class was instantiated. Increasing the frame rate improves the quality of the drawing, just like increasing the frame rate of video improves the look of the video. More frames per second equate to smoother, more fluid playback. However, the choice of 20 frames per second was not coincidental.

Firing a timer event every 50 milliseconds coincides with 20 frames per second (1000 divided by 50 equals 20). If we did not change the SWF default frame rate of 12 frames per second, the sampling of the wave data would occur 20 times per second, but the frame updates would occur only 12 times per second. In effect, the SWF would be working nearly twice as hard as it needed to. By synchronizing the frame update and sample rate, the display will be much improved without an ineffectual impact on CPU cycles.

```
48          public function addVisTimer():void {
49              if (_timer == null) {
50                  _timer = new Timer(50);
51                  _timer.addEventListener("timer", onVisualize);
52                  _timer.start();
53              }
54          }
55
56          public function removeVisTimer():void {
57              removeEventListener("timer", onVisualize);
58              _timer = null;
59          }
```

Also included in the previous code block is the **removeVisTimer()** function. Called from the **SoundPlayBasic** class, this function removes the timer listener and removes the **_timer** object from memory when the sound playback is complete. When the **SoundPlayBasic** play button is clicked again, the **addVisTimer()** function is called again, recreating the timer for subsequent display of the visualization. This optimizes performance because events aren't firing needlessly.

All that remains is the visualization itself, found at the end of the class in lines 60 through 78. The first step in the process is to extract the raw data from the sound. This is achieved using the **computeSpectrum()** method in line 61. This method pulls out 512 samples of amplitude data from the sound at the point at which the method is called—256 samples for the left stereo channel and 256 for the right stereo channel. The result is 512 samples 20 times per second, or 10,240 samples per second.

Storing and retrieving the data quickly is a challenge that is handled by the **ByteArray** class. A byte array is an optimized array that can be used to store any kind of bytes, including external file data, image data for export and, in this case, sound amplitudes. The first argument of the **computeSpectrum()** method is a byte array into which the spectrum data is stored. The second parameter is a Boolean that determines whether the data will be formatted as the positive and negative amplitudes of a normal waveform (between -1 and 1) or positive-only amplitudes (between 0 and 1) divided into frequency bands of low, mid, and high frequencies. We'll illustrate the impact of this parameter in a bit. The final parameter determines the resolution of the sound samples. The default value of 0 samples at 44.1 kHz, 1 samples at 22.050 kHz, 2 samples at 11.025 kHz, and so on.

```
60          private function onVisualize(evt:TimerEvent):void {
61              SoundMixer.computeSpectrum(_bytes, _fft, 0);
62              _g.clear();
63              plotWaveform(0x00CC00, _leftBase);
64              plotWaveform(0xFFCC00, _rightBase);
65          }
66
67          private function plotWaveform(col:uint,
            chanBaseline:Number):void {
68              _g.lineStyle(0, col);
69              _g.beginFill(col, 0.5);
70              _g.moveTo(0, chanBaseline);
71              for (var i:Number = 0; i < 256; i++) {
72                  _g.lineTo(i, chanBaseline - (_bytes.readFloat() *
                    _waveHeight));
73              }
74              _g.lineTo(i, chanBaseline);
75              _g.endFill();
76          }
77      }
78  }
```

Once the data has been stored in the byte array, the drawing canvas is cleared, and a new waveform is drawn for the left and right channels. The function call sends the color of the waveform and the y coordinate, or baseline, of the waveform into the function. The **plotWaveform()** function creates a hairline stroke and 50-percent transparent fill of the desired color, and then begins drawing a line that connects the amplitude values of all 256 samples per channel, creating a waveform.

Line 70 moves the starting point of the waveform to the left of the canvas and y coordinate of the specified baseline. A **for** loop pulls out each value of the byte array, drawing a line to an x coordinate of the next iteration of the loop (0, 1, 2, and so on, until it reaches 256 pixels across), and a y coordinate based on the amplitude of the sound times the wave height (a value of 1 or -1 is full wave height, 0.5 or -0.5 is half wave height)—all offset from the specified baseline.

The last steps are to return the drawing point of the wave to the baseline, and then end the fill in the illustrated wave.

Notice, in line 72, that the loop counter (**i**) is being used as the x coordinate of the drawing point, but not to pull a value from the byte array. The **read-Float()** method does this much faster, and automatically advances to the next item in the array. This means that at the end of the first **plotWaveform()** call, the byte array remains at position 256, or the end of the left channel, and the second **plotWaveform()** call picks up at position 257, or the start of the right channel. In other words, just because the **for** loop iterates from 0 to 256 does not mean it is reading the indices 0 to 256 each time. Because the **readFloat()** method auto-advances the array, it is correctly reading first 0 to 256 and then 257 to 512.

The Impact of Select Parameters

Varying the values of the object properties that get passed into the **Visualization** class will have differing effects on the visualization. Figure 11-6, represents the result of the values in this example, set in lines 79 through 85: a wave height of 100, separate left and right baselines of 60 and 120, a location of (20, 0), and a scale of 200 percent. A nice effect can also be achieved by setting the left and right baselines to the same value. Because each channel appears in a different color, you can see both channels working together on the same baseline.

```
79          var visObj:Object = new Object();
80          visObj.waveHeight = 100;
81          visObj.leftBase = 60;
82          visObj.rightBase = 120;
83          visObj.visLoc = new Point(20, 0);
84          visObj.visScale = 2;
85          visObj.fft = false;
```

Figure 11-7 illustrates two changes in the exercise values: The left and right baselines are the same, and the scale is set to 100 percent.

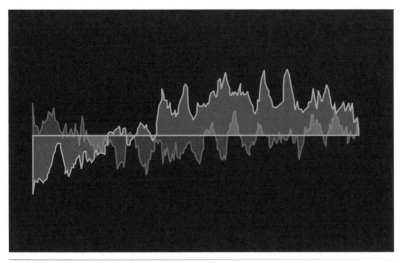

Figure 11-7. The visualizer when the left and right baselines are the same

Setting the **_fft** parameter to **true** plots the amplitude of individual frequency bands, with values of 0 to 1. An FFT plot distributes positive amplitudes of different frequencies across the baseline, much like an equalizer. Low frequencies of each channel appear on the left, and high frequencies appear on the right, as seen in Figure 11-8.

NOTE

FFT refers to "Fast Fourier Transform," a method for efficiently computing the component frequencies that make up a signal like a sound or light wave.

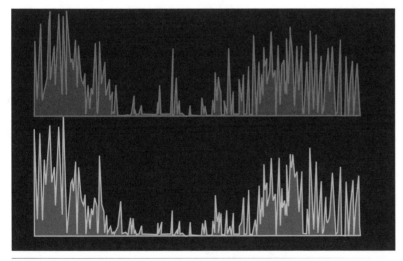

Figure 11-8. Visualizing frequency values with an FFT display

This is just one example visualization, with a simple display. The kind of art you can create is limited only by what you can manipulate with numbers in real time and your imagination. Think of numerical values and you'll realize you can easily include color, opacity, location, size, rotation, and more.

Project Package

The project package for this chapter is based on the document class of the final visualization exercise. Using this package, you can pass an external sound file path to an initialization class, and the class will automatically prepare the necessary elements for playback and error reporting. Then, you can manipulate playback with your preferred controls. For more information about the companion web site project, see Chapter 6.

What's Next?

This chapter covered quite a bit of ground regarding ActionScript control of sound, but there is much left to explore and many fun experiments left to try. The companion web site for this book can serve as a starting point for this ongoing study. The web site includes a more elaborate object-oriented example akin to a desktop sound mixer, in which you can mix three samples and visualize the resulting mix in multiple ways. The site will also continue to add sound examples as time goes on.

Next, we make the logical jump to another media type: video. We'll not only demonstrate how to deliver Flash video in a number of ways—including both with components and ActionScript-only solutions—but we'll also briefly discuss how to encode videos into a Flash-compatible format.

In the next chapter, we'll discuss:

- Encoding Flash video, or FLV, files; mentioning a couple of commercial options but focus primarily on the Flash Video Encoder application that ships with Flash CS3

- Using components for video playback requiring little to no ActionScript

- Writing your own simple ActionScript-only video player to reduce file size

- Displaying video in a browser in true full-screen resolution

- Adding captions to video playback

CHAPTER 12

VIDEO

Video playback is largely responsible for dramatic increases in Flash use over the past few years, and it's not hard to understand why. Flash not only offers an easy entry into video delivery with components (precreated collections of user interface assets and ActionScript), but it also provides extensive control over nearly every aspect of video playback. This simultaneous ease of use and control, added to the video quality and pervasiveness of Flash Player, has made Flash video (FLV) one of the most attractive video delivery formats available.

While we won't be able to cover every aspect of FLV development, we will concentrate on a variety of ways to present video, as well as cover some key new features introduced in Flash CS3. In this chapter, we'll discuss:

- **Encoding.** The scope and size of this book doesn't allow us to delve extensively into Flash video encoding, but a little background will be enough to get you started and will be useful when discussing captioning with cue points—video time markers that can contain additional information and that can be inserted during encoding.

- **Components**. It's very easy to get going with Flash video by using the FLVPlayback component. We'll explore components further when discussing full-screen video and captions.

- **Full-screen Video**. The Flash engineers have made full-screen video a very simple effect to achieve. We'll discuss the steps required to present your video in a true full-screen environment, where your video fills the screen entirely—rather than just filling a browser window.

- **Captions.** Flash CS3's new FLVPlayback companion component, aptly named FLVPlaybackCaptioning, simplifies accessibility and multilanguage subtitling efforts. We'll also discuss some limitations and workarounds with the cue point implementation of captions.

- **ActionScript Code.** While components are valuable tools, we also want to show you how to create the same functionality strictly with code. Eliminating the use of components means you can make use of video content without any internal assets and reduce your SWF file size in the process.

Let's start with a look at what it takes to create the assets we'll be using throughout this chapter. This text assumes you have video files, possibly QuickTime, AVI, or even a newly digitized DV file from your own video camera. Before moving on, you may want to gather one or two short clips to serve as your raw material. For optimal results in the full-screen section, start with clips from high-quality sources and digitize from the largest size available.

Encoding

There are several FLV encoders available today, and more hitting the marketplace as time goes on. The three leading applications in this arena are Adobe's Flash Video Encoder, On2's Flix Pro, and Sorenson's Squeeze. In this text, we will focus on Adobe's Flash Video Encoder, as it is installed free with the purchase of Flash CS3. However, the book's companion web site will contain additional information about the other products, as well as streaming and live encoding options from Adobe, On2, and others.

Let's start with the basics of the Flash Video Encoder. The application's interface is quite simple, and the first step in using the encoder is to add your source material to the encoding queue. This can be done either through drag and drop or by browsing for your file using the Add button.

The next step is to choose your video and audio encoding settings, by clicking the Settings button, which reveals the main interface elements you'll be using. For brevity, we'll rely on the optimized default settings that ship with the application, shown in Figure 12-1. Because we'll be exploring full-screen video later on, we'll use the "Flash 8 – High Quality (700kbps)" setting, as seen in the visible menu. This setting uses the On2 VP6 video codec at 700kbps and the MP3 audio format at 128kbps, stereo.

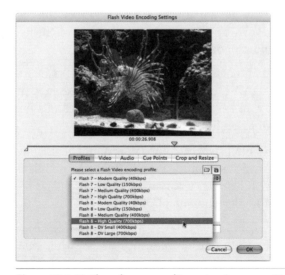

Figure 12-1. Until you have a need to customize your settings for a specific project, start with one of the Flash 8 presets; these settings use the On2 VP6 codec

Clicking the OK button registers your settings choice, closes the dialog, and returns you to the queue window. Without need for further customization, you're ready to encode. Just click the Start Queue button.

Figure 12-2 shows the Flash Video Encoder with information displayed for the settings and the status of the encoding process.

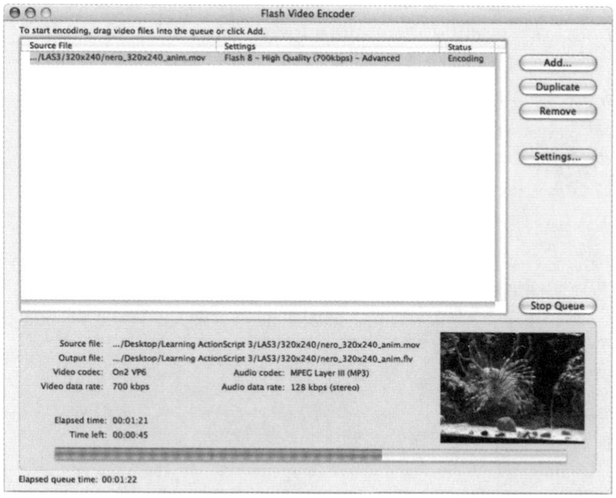

Figure 12-2. During encoding, the Flash Video Encoder displays a progress bar with estimated times and a small preview of the video

If you're using the default preference settings, your new FLV will be placed in the same directory as the source file when the encoding is finished. Currently, if you're using Adobe's Flash Video Encoder, there is no easy way to view FLV files immediately after encoding. This is changing rapidly, however. A number of third-party FLV viewers/players are available, as well as Adobe's Media Player. If you are using Flash CS3 as a part of a larger Creative Suite install, Bridge CS3 can now display FLV files, too.

In any case, you should now have a new Flash video file with the .flv extension. If you chose to use the On2 VP6 codec, through one of the Flash 8 presets, you will need Flash Player 8 or later. For our purposes, we are using Flash CS3 so you shouldn't have any problems.

Support for Additional Video Formats

Adobe has announced plans for the next version of Flash Player—tentatively titled Flash Player 9 Update 3 (Beta 1 at the time of this writing). In this announcement, Adobe detailed limited support for: H.264-encoded (video) and AAC-encoded (audio) MPEG-4, 3GP, and QuickTime movie formats; 3GPP timed text (a standardized subtitle format for 3GP files); sample rates from 8Khz to 96Khz (meaning you are no longer restricted to 11.025Khz, 22.050Khz, or 44.1Khz to avoid nasty resampling); (unencrypted) audio chapter markers; and the 'ilst' atom, which is the ID3-like expanded metadata created by iTunes.

If even a subset of these features—already functional in the beta release of Flash Player—make it to the final release of Flash Player, this update will have a dramatic effect on web video distribution. This update is expected to expand the available production workflows that create web video by eliminating the need to encode the final file into FLV format and, therefore, eliminate the need to convert assets that already exist in any of the newly supported formats.

Further, while official comments are conservative at the time of this writing, it is likely that expanded features sets made available by these formats, such as multi-track audio or video files, and multi-channel AAC files (the cited beta release mixes down to two channels and resamples to 44.1Khz), will also be supported in the future.

Bravo to the Flash Player engineering team. This is a huge step forward for web video delivery using the world's most ubiquitous playback engine.

Components

The fastest way to add video to your Flash application is through the use of the FLVPlayback component. Shown in Figure 12-3, this component will take care of most of your needs without having to write much, or any, code yourself.

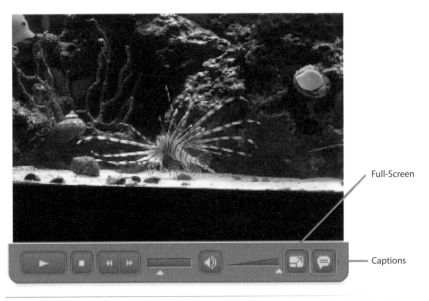

Full-Screen

Captions

Figure 12-3. The FLVPlayback component simplifies adding video to most Flash projects

If you have a fair amount of experience working with Flash (or the Flash community), you'll know that there is a love-hate relationship between Flash developers and components. Certainly, using components has its pros and cons. The obvious benefit is that you don't have to reinvent the wheel each time you need to code a task that a component can handle. This makes components popular for users new to ActionScript. On the down side, you may not like the appearance or out-of-the box functionality of the component. It's also not uncommon for a component to have one or more bugs. Perhaps the biggest issue, however, is that there is an inherent file-size increase, as well as a possible performance hit (either with the component or your entire file), as a result of using components.

If you prefer to avoid components, we will show you how to play video entirely with ActionScript. However, if you are open to the use of components, consider this: The FLVPlayback component, specifically, has a few additional related benefits that address some of the negative issues.

First, you can pick from several preconfigured controllers, or skins, and it is relatively easy to create your own controller. This allows you to create the appearance and functionality that you need. Second, you can use the component without any skin at all. This allows you to take advantage of the prewritten ActionScript to handle your video display needs, but still control the video playback with your own code. Finally, the FLVPlayback component has a few additional features that make working with video in specific situations a bit easier.

For example, the component will automatically determine whether or not you wish to stream a video from a streaming server, just by parsing the URL of the video source. If so, it will handle the necessary initial communication with the streaming server for you so you don't have to script those connections yourself.

These and other factors will influence your decision whether or not to use components. Ultimately, it is a good idea to know how they work and to be familiar with what they do well and where they are lacking. This will prepare you to work with clients and colleagues who may prefer components, and it will also help you decide which approach to video playback is best in any given situation.

Working with the FLVPlayback Component

For many component users, one of the major attractions is that you don't need to know a lot of ActionScript to use them. You can rely nearly exclusively on the Flash interface and its Parameters or Components Inspector panels to configure the required component values. However, we want to focus on ActionScript here, so we're going to instantiate and configure them dynamically with code.

To do so, the components must be in your file's library (or, for experienced users, a Shared Library that your file has access to without security or cross-domain restrictions). We will be working with a single file, so all you need to do is create a new *.fla* and drag the FLVPlayback component to the library. Alternatively, you can drag it to the stage and then delete it from the stage. In either case, the components will then be placed into your library and you'll be ready to begin.

We'll be looking at captioning later in the chapter so, from a tutorial standpoint, you may wish to do the same with the FLVPlaybackCaptioning component. However, in production scenarios, it's a good idea not to bloat your file size with unused assets. So, if you don't intend to caption your *.flv* files, then you don't need to take this step.

Let's begin with timeline-based code for tutorial simplicity, adding the following lines to the first frame of your file:

```
1   import fl.video.*;
2
3   var vid:FLVPlayback;
4
5   vid = new FLVPlayback();
6   vid.source = "nero_320x240_cp.flv";
7   addChild(vid);
```

The first line is the familiar **import** statement that we've seen throughout the past several chapters. This will provide access to the **FLVPlayback** class. Line 3 types the instance variable, and line 5 creates an instance of the FLVPlayback component. Using that instance variable, line 6 populates the **source** property for the component (telling it which video to play). Finally, line 7 adds the component instance to the DisplayList, which shows it on the stage.

This code is simpler than it might be in a typical case because we are relying on default parameters such as **autoplay**, an implied (x, y) location of (0, 0), and no skin, among others. However, you will be able to see the video automatically play only once and then remain onscreen without the ability to control it in any way.

To add an existing skin, we need to pick from the available options. In short, there are two main categories of shipping skins—those that sit on top of, or "over," the video (close to the bottom edge of the picture), and those that sit outside, or "under," the video, immediately below the picture. Each of these main skin groups contains a wide variety of configurations that allow you to pick which functions are included. You can opt for many combinations of play, pause, stop, seek, mute, volume, full-screen, and captioning.

You can see a list of these skins by looking at the **skin** parameter in the Component Inspector shown in Figure 12-4. To preview skins that ship with Flash, click the **skin** parameter in the Component Inspector.

Clicking the skin option in the Component Inspector will open a dialog that allows you to preview each skin, and you can see the skin names here for quick reference. Figure 12-5 shows how you can quickly view the names of all skins that ship with Flash and can be specified with ActionScript.

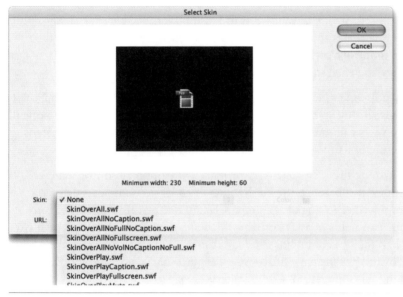

Figure 12-4. The Flash Component Inspector

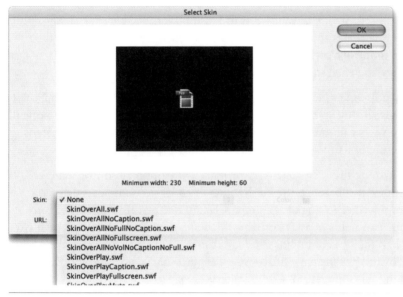

Figure 12-5. Skins that ship with Flash

Once you choose a skin, you can pick a color and opacity for that skin. These settings can help blend the controller into the video when using "over" skins, or the blend into the application background (if any) when using "under" skins.

All that remains is to add the following three lines to your existing script. Line 7 specifies your skin choice, line 8 specifies the color, and line 9 specifies the alpha.

```
1   import fl.video.*;
2
3   var vid:FLVPlayback;
4
5   vid = new FLVPlayback();
6   vid.source = "nero_320x240_cp.flv";
7   vid.skin = "SkinUnderPlayStopSeekMuteVol.swf";
8   vid.skinBackgroundColor = 0xAEBEFB;
9   vid.skinBackgroundAlpha = 0.5;
10  addChild(vid);
```

NOTE

Remember that in ActionScript 3.0 percentage values (such as alpha) are specified as a value between 0 and 1, rather than 0 and 100.

By incorporating these script lines, you will add a controller to your video and then be able to control its playback interactively. An example of this script, with the sample video depicted in the figures in this chapter, can be seen in *full_screen_tt_01.fla*.

Full-Screen Video

One of the most visually arresting new features in the Flash video arena is true full-screen video, available as of Flash Player 9. The term *true full-screen video* indicates that the image occupies the entire screen (much like the full-screen mode of a software DVD player), rather than inside a browser or player window stretched to cover most of the available screen area.

Flash CS3 offers accessor methods for full-screen video via ActionScript, which we'll look at in just a bit, but also through the FLVPlaybackComponent. Before we get to implementation, we need to cover two preliminary steps to make sure our full-screen video works well.

The first of these two steps is to start with optimal source material. To encourage this practice, the Flash Video Encoder now supports deinterlacing for improved encoding of DV sources. Deinterlacing is the process of converting the two fields of a DV source (which are like video frames but each contain half the horizontal lines and are displayed twice as fast) into the frames used by the FLV format. One common artifact that is more pronounced when working with interlaced source material is jagged lines visible along sharp edges in your videos. Deinterlacing the source during encoding significantly reduces this effect.

If you select one of the new DV presets that ship with the Flash CS3 Video Encoder, this option will automatically be enabled and the encoded video will also be resized to a standard 640 x 480 pixels. If you prefer, you can maintain the size and aspect ratio of the original source material, for a "wider screen" look, by manually disabling the resize option. Alternatively, you can manually enable the deinterlacing option in the Video settings, as shown in Figure 12-6.

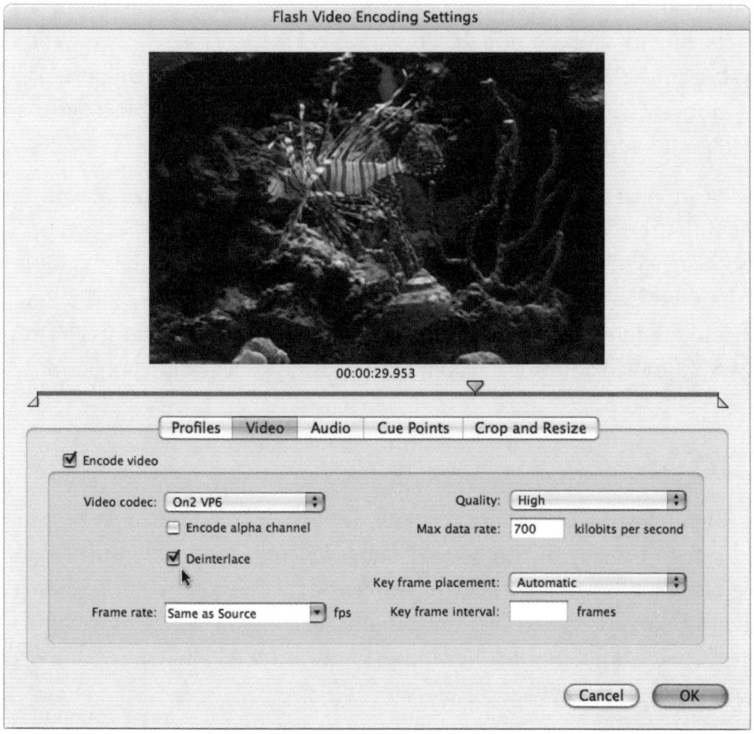

Figure 12-6. Deinterlacing is available in the version of the Flash Video Encoder that ships with Flash CS3

The second step you must take is to instruct Flash Player to allow the conversion to full-screen display. If you think about it for a moment, you certainly don't want the decision to switch to full-screen mode left in the hands of content developers. If that were the case, every Flash advertisement would take over your screen, leaving you no control. Instead, the developer must enable the feature, and the user must switch back and forth between normal and full-screen modes.

To enable the feature, you must add the new **allowFullScreen** parameter, with a value of **true**, to the file's host HTML file. One way to do this is to add this parameter manually to the object and embed tags, as seen in the following example.

```
1   <object>
2       ...
3       <param name="allowFullScreen" value="true" />
4       <embed ... allowfullscreen="true" />
5   </object>
```

Another quick and easy solution, handy during testing, is to choose the "Flash Only – Allow Full Screen" publishing template in the HTML section of the Publish Settings dialog.

Once you've taken these steps, you can test your file by using the Publish Preview command (File→Publish Preview→HTML). This is usually the default value in the Publish Preview menu, but you can select any available HTML option. If HTML is not available at all, go to the File→Publish Settings menu dialog and add HTML as a publishable format.

After adding support for full-screen video in your HTML host file, you're ready to enable the full-screen option. To automatically do so in the FLVPlayback component, choose any skin that supports full screen or has "all" in its name. Examples include SkinOverPlayFullscreen.swf and SkinUnderAll.swf. These, and similar skins will add the Full Screen button shown in Figure 12-3. Later in this chapter, we'll show you how to add full-screen playback using your own ActionScript.

Captions

Captions, also referred to in some contexts as subtitles, consist of text that is displayed synchronously during video playback. Captions are very useful for providing alternate language tracks to bring your video to a wider audience. Captions are also appreciated by the deaf and hearing impaired, as they provide a much needed accessible alternative for audio tracks when it comes to dialog and descriptive audio services.

The United States government passed a law, commonly known as Section 508 (because it is Section 508 of the Rehabilitation Act of 1973), which introduced certain accessibility mandates for content developed for government use. Many private entities, particularly those serving the educational markets, also require accessible content. As the demand for this requirement increases, captions will play an increasingly more important role in digital video.

Flash supports captioning via the FLVPlaybackCaptioning component, when used in conjunction with the FLVPlayback component. Adding the FLVPlaybackCaptioning component to the stage at authoring time, or dynamically at runtime with ActionScript, opens the door for caption use.

NOTE

If you are using the FLVPlayback component for caption display, and you are using a stock skin, be sure to choose a skin that has the word "Caption" in it. This will enable a button that will toggle the captions on and off at the user's request. This button can be seen at the far right in Figure 12-7. It is labeled in Figure 12-3.

The simplest way to display captions is to use the FLVPlayback component itself. In fact, with only one FLVPlayback instance on stage at a time, the default behavior of the captioning component is to automatically detect the playback component, and target its internal text element as the destination for the captions. You can also manually specify any FLVPlayback component as the captioned content (in case you require more than one at any given time), as well as your own target for the captions (in the event that you want to use another text element—perhaps integrated into your interface, rather than the video). The result will look like Figure 12-7.

Figure 12-7. Captions can be displayed within the FLVPlayback component

Creating Captions with Timed Text

Before we take the steps to display the captions, we need to create the caption data. There are two ways to easily create captions. The preferred way to create an XML file using the W3C Timed Text format—also referred to by its formal name, Distribution Format Exchange Profile (DFXP), or familiarly as TT.

We'll cover a subset of Timed Text here, but you can learn more about the format by visiting the W3C page at *http://www.w3.org/AudioVideo/TT/*. More importantly, you can learn about the subset of features supported by Flash CS3 by searching the built-in help system for "Timed Text Tags." MAGpie, the captioning tool developed by accessibility leaders, the National Center for Accessible Media (NCAM), already supports the DFXP format, and the Manitu Group has announced plans to support DFXP in their product, Captionate, by the time this book is in print.

You can easily write your own Timed Text files. The example XML that follows this paragraph is a slightly edited excerpt of the file provided with our sample video, *nero_720x480_cp.flv*. For brevity, this printed version includes only two captions, and the style of the second caption has been changed to show all the features represented in the longer file. We will discuss this abbreviated form because it includes most of the features you are likely to use for an average captioning project. Please remember, however, that this is not a complete resource on this topic.

WARNING

The Flash help system entry "Timed Text Tags" specifies that all attributes of the **<tt>** *tag are ignored. However, if you delete the* **xmlns:tts** *attribute, Flash CS3 will throw errors in the* **TimedTextManager**, **EventDispatcher**, *and* **URLLoader** *classes. If you omit only the* **xmlns** *attribute, you will not receive any errors, but the captions will not be styled. You should consider both of these attributes as required.*

NOTE

Be sure to consult the "Timed Text Tags" Flash help citation for a complete list of supported and unsupported properties. Here are a few noteworthy mentions:

- **fontFamily** *supports device fonts, as seen in our example.*

- **fontSize** *supports only the first vertical size found, if more than one exists. It supports absolute and relative sizes but not percentages.*

- **lineHeight**, **padding**, *and* **overflow**, *although potentially useful for captions, are among several options that are not supported.*

```
1   <?xml version="1.0" encoding="UTF-8"?>
2   <tt xmlns="http://www.w3.org/2006/04/ttaf1"
3     xmlns:tts="http://www.w3.org/2006/04/ttaf1#styling">
4     <head>
5       <styling>
6         <style id="1"
7           tts:textAlign="center"
8           tts:fontFamily="_sans"
9           tts:fontSize="18"
10          tts:fontWeight="bold"
11          tts:color="#FFFF00FF" />
12        <style id="2" tts:backgroundColor="#00000000" />
13        <style id="3" tts:backgroundColor="#000000FF" />
14        <style id="trans" style="1 2" />
15        <style id="opaq" style="1 3" />
16      </styling>
17    </head>
18    <body>
19      <div>
20        <p begin="00:00:05.00" dur="00:00:04.00" style="opaq">Nero is
          a Lionfish<br />
21        (<span tts:fontStyle="italic">Pterois volitans</span>),</p>
22        <p begin="00:00:09.00" dur="00:00:02.00" style="trans">at home
          in his reef aquarium.</p>
23      </div>
24    </body>
25  </tt>
```

Lines 1 through 3 include two default tags used to validate the file. The first is the xml declaration tag, and we recommend specifying an encoding of UTF-8 (both in this tag and when writing the file) to support special characters. This is especially important when captioning using world languages. The second tag is the document's root tag. Be sure to see the accompanying note describing the use of attributes in this tag.

A single balanced **<head>** tag (lines 4 and 17) is optional, but we recommend its use because it makes styling your captions much easier. A single balanced **<styling>** tag (lines 5 and 16) is also optional but required if you intend to create *styles*. Styles are itemized in lines 6 through 15 and are Cascading Style Sheet (CSS) entities for the Timed Text document. You can have as many styles as you like, but each must have a unique **id** attribute. The style attributes that are actually responsible for the formatting are very similar to CSS properties, but are preceded by the **tts:** prefix.

It is possible to assign styles directly by their id, but it is also possible to manage formatting efficiently by creating new styles consisting of multiple existing styles. Take a look at the styles in our example. We wanted to achieve two looks for our captions: one with a black background, for use over light areas of video, and one with a transparent background, to allow more of the video to show through the text.

Style *1* consists of all styling attributes common to both looks, which means background alpha is not included. Styles *2* and *3* itemize only the background color and specify transparent and opaque, respectively. The Timed Text format uses #RRGGBBAA color notation, where AA is alpha, but the Flash components support only opaque and transparent settings. All zeros will be seen as transparent, but *any* value other than zero will be opaque. We've used the opposite of zero for alpha, FF, to remind us that this is opaque. The resulting value of #000000FF is, therefore, an opaque black background.

It is possible to assign multiple styles at the caption level (such as *id="1 2"*), but it is also possible to create a new style the same way. This allows you to give it an easily recognizable name. We've done this in lines 14 and 15, specifying that "trans" is transparent because it uses ids *1* and *2*, and "opaq" is opaque because it uses ids *1* and *3*.

One balanced `<body>` tag (lines 18 and 24) is required and can be used to apply styles throughout all captions. One balanced `<div>` tag (lines 19 and 23) is required. The documentation discussing this requirement was a bit ambiguous. When we removed the `<div>` tag, we got an error saying that paragraph tags were not supported in the body tag. So, we reiterate that the div tag is required. We found the same situation to be true with `<p>` tags (lines 20 through 22). The "Timed Text Tags" Flash help system entry says zero or more paragraph tags are supported, but we didn't find a logical way of applying time and style attributes to individual captions without them. For example, `<span>` tags (line 21) are supported, but not in the `<body>` tag. Therefore, we suggest you consider `<p>` tags required for each caption.

For each caption (in our case, in each `<p>` tag), a `begin` attribute is required to set the time of the caption. The attributes `dur` (duration) and `end` (the time at which the caption should end) are optional. If omitted, the caption will remain onscreen until the next caption appears. Time can be specified in full clock format (HH:MM:SS.m, where m is milliseconds), partial clock format (MM:SS.m or SS.m), or offset time (with units, such as "1s" for one second). Ticks or frames are not supported.

NOTE:

For more information about using alpha in hex color values, see Chapter 9. Note that the TimedText format places its alpha value at the end of the string.

NOTE

In our main Timed Text example, we used full clock format for clarity and consistency, even when the duration matched the time at which the next caption appeared. However, you can simplify this by using partial clock format, and omitting any duration or end attributes when the caption is to remain onscreen until replaced. As an illustration, we have formatted our Spanish-language example this way, which we'll discuss shortly.

Using the Timed Text File

Using the default implementation of Timed Text captions, which is displaying them within the FLVPlayback component, requires only that we add the component to the stage and assign its attribute. The new code, augmenting our FLVPlayback example, is represented in bold, in the following code.

```
1   import fl.video.*;
2
3   var vid:FLVPlayback;
4   var cap:FLVPlaybackCaptioning;
5
6   vid = new FLVPlayback();
7   vid.source = "nero_720x480_tt.flv";
8   vid.skin = "SkinUnderAll.swf";
9   vid.skinBackgroundColor = 0xAEBEFB;
10  vid.skinBackgroundAlpha = 0.5;
11  addChild(vid);
12
13  cap = new FLVPlaybackCaptioning();
14  cap.source = "nero_timed_text.xml";
15  addChild(cap);
```

NOTE

It is best practice, when using the caption button, to turn the **showCaptions** *property to* **false** *to begin with, so the user can elect whether or not to view the captions. However, for these examples, we've omitted that step for faster testing.*

Line 4 types the instance variable, line 13 creates the component instance, line 14 assigns its source, and line 15 adds it to the DisplayList. Note, too, the change of the skin used, in line 8, to make sure we have access to the caption on/off toggle button (and, in this case, the full screen button as well). With these changes in place, you will now be able to show and hide the video captions at will.

Creating Captions with Cue Points

Another way to add captions is by embedding the information in time markers called *cue points* when encoding the video. This has the advantage of the caption information always being present, but is also permanent. Changing the embedded cue points requires reencoding the video.

Inserting a cue point is simple. When assigning the encoding settings, as discussed earlier, go to the Cue Points section and drag the slider beneath the video preview to the time you want to caption. Then, in the interface below the video, click the plus (+) button and fill in the appropriate values. This process is partially illustrated in Figure 12-8.

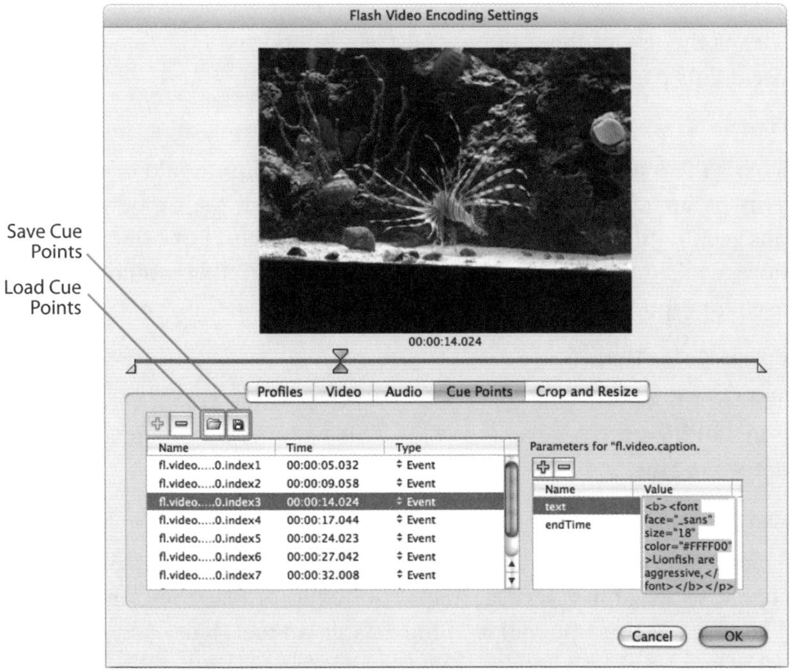

Figure 12-8. Captions embedded into FLV files using cue points

The values required for captioning follow specific guidelines created for the FLVPlaybackCaptioning component. You can learn more about them by searching the Flash CS3 Help system for "cue point standards." In brief, the cue point attributes are

Time

This is populated by the slider position in the Flash Video Encoder.

Name

This must begin with "fl.video.caption.2.0." and be followed by a string with a positive, incrementing integer (for example, "fl.video. caption.2.0.index1," "fl.video.caption.2.0.index2").

Type

This must be **Event**.

The actual captions are then added as cue point parameters. Adding parameters to a cue point is similar to adding a cue point to a video. With the cue point selected, click the plus (+) button, and a name-value pair will be added. The parameter options include:

text

> This is the text of the caption, and Flash-supported HTML tags may be used. This parameter is required.

endTime

> This is the number of seconds for which the caption should be displayed. This parameter is optional, but if it is not used, the caption will stay onscreen until the end of the video. This has the effect of combining captions, which we do not find useful. In our opinions, this should always be used for captioning.

backgroundColorAlpha

WARNING

See the sidebar "Issues with Cue Point Captioning" for important notes regarding this process.

> This is a Boolean value that specifies transparency. **true** means the caption will have no background color. This parameter is optional, and the default is **true**.

wrapOption

> This is also a Boolean value, and specifies whether or not the caption should wrap, adding vertical lines required to display the complete text. This parameter is optional, and the default is **true**.

Inserting cue points manually can be a laborious process, particularly due to the size and editing limitations imposed by the interface. Fortunately, a great new feature in Flash CS3 makes this process easier. It is now possible to import and export cue point lists in XML format. This means you can add your cue points manually, using the video preview for accurate timings, but without worrying about all the available parameters. You can then export that information to an external file, and use a standard text editor to fill in the remaining details. The Load and Save buttons are the open folder and floppy disk icons, respectively, shown in Figure 12-8.

We've provided a cue point XML file for the video used in this chapter, so you can test the process and encode a video of your own using this data. An excerpt of the file can be seen in the XML that follows this paragraph. It is a straightforward XML document, including the use of the CDATA tag when HTML is used in the caption text. However, a few particulars bear notice. See the sidebar "Issues with Cue Point Captioning" for important notes regarding creating similar files.

```
1   <?xml version="1.0" encoding="UTF-8" standalone="no"?>
2   <FLVCoreCuePoints>
3       <CuePoint>
4           <Time>5032</Time>
5           <Type>event</Type>
6           <Name>fl.video.caption.2.0.index1</Name>
7           <Parameters>
8               <Parameter>
9                   <Name>text</Name>
10                  <Value><![CDATA[<p align="center"><b><font
                    face="_sans" size="18" color="#FFFF00">Nero is a
                    lionfish<br>(<i>Pterois volitans</i>),
                    </font></b></p>]]></Value>
11              </Parameter>
12              <Parameter>
13                  <Name>endTime</Name>
14                  <Value>9.000</Value>
15              </Parameter>
16              <Parameter>
17                  <Name>backgroundColorAlpha</Name>
18                  <Value>true</Value>
19              </Parameter>
20          </Parameters>
21      </CuePoint>
22  </FLVCoreCuePoints>
```

Using the FLV Cue Point Captions

Displaying cue point captions is similar to displaying Timed Text captions. However, because the captions are embedded into the video, there is one less line of ActionScript required. The **source** property of the FLVPlaybackCaptioning component is not needed because the captions are automatically parsed from the FLV file. The changes to our ongoing example appear here in bold. Line 7 changes our source to an embedded cue point source, and line 8 eliminates the full-screen option from the skin. Lines 13 and 14 are bolded not because they are new, but because they surround the omitted caption source assignment.

```
1   import fl.video.*;
2
3   var vid:FLVPlayback;
4   var cap:FLVPlaybackCaptioning;
5
6   vid = new FLVPlayback();
7   vid.source = "nero_320x240_cp.flv";
8   vid.skin = "SkinUnderAllNoFullscreen.swf";
9   vid.skinBackgroundColor = 0xAEBEFB;
10  vid.skinBackgroundAlpha = 0.5;
11  addChild(vid);
12
13  cap = new FLVPlaybackCaptioning();
14  addChild(cap);
```

Regardless of how you choose to pursue adding captions to your project, it is possible to make the captions appear, and function similarly.

Issues with Cue Point Captioning

Using the resources initially available in the shipping version of Flash CS3 to create FLV captions via embedded cue points will result in a misstep or two. Not to worry, however, because we have workarounds and a replacement component that will help rectify the situation.

Problems exist in two categories: minor bugs with the FLVPlaybackCaptioning component, and formatting issues when creating encoding cue points by importing an external XML file. We'll discuss the bugs first, because they are the most important and easily fixed.

The first bug is in the assignment of the **backgroundColorAlpha** property value. This property tells the FLVPlaybackComponent to remove the background color from its internal caption field. The documentation says this property requires a Boolean value, but, unfortunately, the value is actually interpreted as a string. Consequently, you can start off with an opaque background by default, but any cue point assignment of this property will be interpreted as **true**. This means you can switch to a transparent background once but can't ever go back to an opaque background.

The second bug is in the assignment of the **track** property value. This property will be explained in the upcoming section, "Providing Captions in Multiple Languages," but, in short, it's designed to allow you to switch caption sets. For example, you can switch among multiple language captions, or between subtitles and descriptive text. However, the track value is not actually assigned in the shipping component, so no captions other than the default values in the **text** property are ever used.

The companion web site for this book explains how to change the code if you are so inclined. It also makes available a replacement component that you can simply drop into your installation directory (instructions provided) to correct this functionality. (Thanks to Jeff Kamerer for helping to confirm the *backgroundColorAlpha* issue.)

With the known bugs out of the way, we want to save you some time by pointing out a few formatting issues when writing your own caption XML file for the Flash Video Encoder. The Encoder uses its own file structure for this asset, so don't attempt to make the XML valid prior to importing it. For example, if you unify the tag case, the import will fail. Just follow the example provided, and you should be fine.

Next, it's helpful to notice that the required attribute **Time** is in milliseconds, while the optional parameter **endTime** is in seconds. For example, our first caption starts at 5032 milliseconds and ends at 9.000 seconds. These units are not interchangeable.

Finally, unlike the Timed Text format, omitting the optional **endTime** parameter will not cause the caption to be replaced when the next caption is reached. Instead, the newer caption will be added to the text field. This allows you to build a two- or three-line caption field one piece at a time, but is not the typical behavior for caption updates. For this reason, we suggest that you consider the **endTime** parameter as required, rather than optional.

Providing Captions in Multiple Languages

Feature-rich DVD titles frequently have multiple caption programs available, each in a different language. This broadens the reach of the title across cultures and supports a wider audience with accessibility needs. It is possible to achieve the same thing using Flash CS3's FLVPlaybackCaptioning component. In this chapter, we've discussed two ways to use the component: using an external Timed Text (DXFP) XML file, and using embedded cue points. Both support multiple languages but in very different ways.

Timed Text

In the case of the Timed Text approach, all you need to do is prepare multiple DXFP files, one for each language, and switch among them when needed. Off the shelf, however, the FLVPlaybackCaptioning component does a couple of things that make this an odd experience.

First, in between caption changes, it is designed to overwrite the caption field only when the original content consists exclusively of white space. If that is not the case (such as when switching captions from one language to another), it adds the new text to the existing caption until the next cue point overwrites it. As a result, you end up with English and Spanish, for example. Second, the method it uses to determine whether or not the DXFP file has already been loaded results in no immediate change. Therefore, you must wait for the next caption to come along to see a language update.

The companion web site has more information about this, but, fortunately, there's an easy workaround. All you have to do is turn off caption display before making the DXFP source switch, and then turn the display back on again. The example file, *full_screen_tt.fla*, demonstrates this using the Button component to toggle the caption source files. You must have this component, found in the User Interface category of the Components panel, in your library.

NOTE

If needed, review the section "Working with the FLVPlayback Component" for more information about adding components to your file.

```
1   import fl.video.*;
2   import fl.controls.Button;
3
4   var vid:FLVPlayback;
5   var cap:FLVPlaybackCaptioning;
6   var capsLangBtn:Button;
7   var vidSize:Rectangle;
8
9   vid = new FLVPlayback();
10  vid.source = "nero_720x480_tt.flv";
11  vid.skin = "SkinUnderAll.swf";
12  vid.skinBackgroundColor = 0x0066CC;
13  vid.skinBackgroundAlpha = 0.5;
14  addChild(vid);
15
16  cap = new FLVPlaybackCaptioning();
17  cap.source = "nero_timed_text.xml";
18  addChild(cap);
19
20  capsLangBtn = new Button();
21  capsLangBtn.label = "English/Spanish";
22  vidSize = vid.getBounds(this);
23  capsLangBtn.x = vidSize.right + 20;
24  capsLangBtn.y = vidSize.bottom;
25  addChild(capsLangBtn);
26  capsLangBtn.addEventListener(MouseEvent.CLICK, onSwitchTTCaps,
    false, 0, true);
27
28  function onSwitchTTCaps(evt:MouseEvent):void {
29      cap.showCaptions = false;
30      switch(cap.source) {
31          case "nero_timed_text.xml":
32              cap.source = "nero_timed_text_sp.xml";
33              break;
34          case "nero_timed_text_sp.xml":
35              cap.source = "nero_timed_text.xml";
36              break;
37      }
38
39      cap.showCaptions = true;
40  }
```

Line 2 of the previous code imports the **Button** class so we can instantiate and manipulate the Button component. Lines 6 and 7 type the instance variables. A rectangle will be used to position the button in the lower-right corner of the FLVPlayback component. Lines 20 through 24 create and set the properties of the button, including its text label and location on stage. The **getBounds()** method in line 22 uses the coordinate system of the main timeline (referenced by the **this** keyword) to get the **x, y, width**, and **height** values of the FLVPlayback component. Line 25 adds the button to the DisplayList, and line 26 adds an event listener to call the **switchTTCaps()** function upon a **click** mouse event. Finally, the **switchTTCaps()** function (lines 28 through 40) turns off caption display, checks to see which caption source is in use, switches to the other file, and then turns caption display back on again.

You might need to improve this approach if more than two languages need to be supported. Our implementation is by no means complete. Instead, it is a proof of concept that requires minimal code and custom assets. If you want to pursue this technique, we suggest adding features such as showing the caption language switcher only when the **showCaptions** property is **true**, indicating which language is currently active, and adding an off state to the cycle. Try using the *subtitles* feature on your DVD player for another example implementation.

Cue points

Multilanguage captions require that you embed the additional language during the encoding process also. Any number of languages can be added, and they are separated by a positive integer used by the FLVPlaybackCaptioning component's **track** property. By default, the **track** property is not used, and the **text** parameter is the source of the caption. However, setting the **track** property to a non-zero positive integer, such as *n*, will cause the component to use captions found in the parameter **text***n*. For example, a track value of **1** would use captions identified by **text1**. A value of **2** would use captions found in the **text2** parameter, and so on.

Here is an example of the previous XML file, with a second language:

```
1    <?xml version="1.0" encoding="UTF-8" standalone="no"?>
2    <FLVCoreCuePoints>
3        <CuePoint>
4            <Time>5032</Time>
5            <Type>event</Type>
6            <Name>fl.video.caption.2.0.index1</Name>
7            <Parameters>
8                <Parameter>
9                    <Name>text</Name>
10                   <Value><![CDATA[<p align="center"><b><font face="
                     sans" size="18" color="#FFFF00">Nero is a
                     lionfish<br>(<i>Pterois volitans</i>),</font><
                     b></p>]]></Value>
11               </Parameter>
12               <Parameter>
13                   <Name>text1</Name>
```

```
14                          <Value><![CDATA[<p align="center"><b><font face="_
                            sans" size="18" color="#FFFF00">Nero es un
                            lionfish<br>(<i>Pterois
                            volitans</i>),</font></b></p>]]></Value>
15                      </Parameter>
16                      <Parameter>
17                          <Name>endTime</Name>
18                          <Value>9.000</Value>
19                      </Parameter>
20                      <Parameter>
21                          <Name>backgroundColorAlpha</Name>
22                          <Value>true</Value>
23                      </Parameter>
24                  </Parameters>
25          </CuePoint>
26  </FLVCoreCuePoints>
```

To switch languages, you need to set the **track** property. Note that a **track** value of 1 is used to display the Spanish **text1** cue point parameters in this example, while a track value of 0 returns the component to the English **text** parameter for each cue point. Switching languages does not show any side effects such as combined captions, so you don't have to turn the captions off and on again. In the following code, only the lines that are different from the Timed Text approach are shown in bold.

```
1   import fl.video.*;
2   import fl.controls.Button;
3
4   var vid:FLVPlayback;
5   var cap:FLVPlaybackCaptioning;
6   var capsLangBtn:Button;
7   var vidSize:Rectangle;
8
9   vid = new FLVPlayback();
10  vid.source = "nero_320x240_cp.flv";
11  vid.skin = "SkinUnderAllNoFullscreen.swf";
12  vid.skinBackgroundColor = 0x0066CC;
13  vid.skinBackgroundAlpha = 0.5;
14  addChild(vid);
15
16  cap = new FLVPlaybackCaptioning();
17  addChild(cap);
18
19  capsLangBtn = new Button();
20  capsLangBtn.label = "English/Spanish";
21  vidSize = vid.getBounds(this);
22  capsLangBtn.x = vidSize.right + 20;
23  capsLangBtn.y = vidSize.bottom;
24  addChild(capsLangBtn);
25  capsLangBtn.addEventListener(MouseEvent.CLICK, onSwitchFLVCaps,
    false, 0, true);
26
27  function onSwitchFLVCaps(evt:MouseEvent):void {
28      if (cap.track == 0) {
29          cap.track = 1;
30      } else {
31          cap.track = 0;
32      }
33  }
```

Coding Your Own Video Playback

Up to this point, we've relied exclusively on components for FLV playback. However, it's important to reiterate that creating your own code can reduce file size, allow you to customize your own functionality, and free you from relying on the FLVPlayback component for user interface controls. Code-only solutions are advantageous for these reasons. However, they do have design limitations because code-only files can't use your own custom art. Therefore, using code-only approaches should be the result of a balanced analysis of their pros and cons, rather than the ultimate goal in every situation.

This last section of this chapter provides a complete class called **BasicVideo** to create a very simple video player entirely from code. Even the buttons are drawn dynamically, using techniques discussed in Chapter 8. As a result, the generated SWF file is only 4 K. As usual, this class can be created in any text editor and should be saved in a text file called *BasicVideo.as*.

```
1    package {
2
3        import flash.display.*;
4        import flash.net.*;
5        import flash.media.Video;
6        import flash.events.*;
7        import CreateRoundRectButton;
8
9        public class BasicVideo extends Sprite {
10
11           private var _vidConnection:NetConnection;
12           private var _vidStream:NetStream;
13           private var _vid:Video;
14           private var _vidURL:String;
15           private var _vidPlaying:Boolean;
16           private var _infoClient:Object;
17           private var _playBtn:Sprite;
18           private var _pauseBtn:Sprite;
19           private var _stopBtn:Sprite;
```

The first 19 lines cover the basic package structure. This includes the package declaration (1), external class import directives (3 through 7), class declaration (9), and variable declarations (11 through 19). Note that we are using a **Sprite** display object for both the simple controller buttons and the class itself. (Also, don't forget the balancing braces for the class declaration and package at lines 99 and 100.)

```
20           public function BasicVideo () {
21
22               _vidConnection = new NetConnection();
23               _vidConnection.connect(null);
24               _vidStream = new NetStream(_vidConnection);
```

The class constructor, starting at line 20, begins with the **NetConnection** class. This is the first step in creating a video player because it allows you to establish a connection with a remote streaming server, such as the Flash Media Server or one of the increasing number of alternative services. To use progressive download FLV files, either locally or from the web, you simply inform the class that no streaming will occur by passing a **null** value, instead of a URL to the streaming application, to the class instance through the **connect()** method, as seen in line 23.

Next, you must instantiate the **NetStream** class and reference the **NetConnection** instance you just created, as seen in line 24. This is the stream through which the video will be controlled, even in the case of progressive download files.

```
25          _infoClient = new Object();
26          _infoClient.onMetaData = onMetaData;
27          _infoClient.onCuePoint = onCuePoint;
28          _vidStream.client = _infoClient;
29          _vidConnection.addEventListener(NetStatusEvent.
            NET_STATUS, onNetStatus, false, 0, true);
30          _vidConnection.addEventListener(AsyncErrorEvent.
            ASYNC_ERROR, onAsyncError, false, 0, true);
31          _vidStream.addEventListener(NetStatusEvent.NET_STATUS,
            onNetStatus, false, 0, true);
32          _vidStream.addEventListener(AsyncErrorEvent.ASYNC_ERROR,
            onAsyncError, false, 0, true);
```

Lines 25 through 32 create a basic network of event, status, and error handling. This can be accomplished in a variety of ways, but this example includes the most basic way. Programmatic feedback is captured in two ways: by predefined callback handlers, such as *onMetaData* and *onCuePoint*, and by creating event listeners and trapping event-related information yourself.

Lines 25 through 28 create a custom object that will be used to process information received from the **NetStream** instance. By assigning the object to the stream's **client** property, any metadata or cue point information will be sent to that object. If **onMetaData()** and **onCuePoint()** methods are created (assigned in lines 26 and 27, and defined a bit later on), you can use that information as it becomes available.

Lines 29 through 32 accomplish a similar task using event listeners. Through their use, this class will trap events related to status reports and asynchronous errors both when connecting to, and handling, the video stream. You can use this technique to take advantage of incoming data or just to prevent errors from being displayed.

```
33          _vid = new Video();
34          _vid.attachNetStream(_vidStream);
35          _vidURL = "nero_320x240_cp.flv";
36          _vidStream.play(_vidURL);
37          addChild(_vid);
38
39          createControlButtons();
40      }
```

Lines 33 through 37 are primarily responsible for the actual display of the video. The first step is to dynamically create a video display object. The previously created **NetStream** instance is then attached to that display object to allow control, a video is specified and played, and the video object is added to the DisplayList so it appears on stage.

The last line of the constructor (line 39) calls a function that creates three buttons for playing, pausing, and stopping the video. This function's at the very end of the script, lines 80 through 96, which we'll highlight for you.

```
41    private function onMetaData(info:Object):void {
42        trace(info.duration);
43    }
44
45    private function onCuePoint(info:Object):void {
46        trace(info.parameters.text);
47    }
48
49    private function onAsyncError(evt:AsyncErrorEvent):void {
50        trace(evt.text);
51    }
52
53    private function onNetStatus (evt:NetStatusEvent):void {
54        trace(evt.info.level + ": " + evt.info.code);
55        if (evt.info.code == "NetStream.Play.Start") {
56            _vidPlaying = true;
57        } else if (evt.info.code == "NetStream.Play.Stop") {
58            _vidPlaying = false;
59        }
60    }
```

Next we find the functions invoked by the _vidConnection callbacks and event listeners. As a metadata example, the *onMetaData()* function (line 42) traces the FLV's duration. Similarly, the *onCuePoint()* function (line 46) traces the text of each cue point. Any asynchronous errors that may occur are traced by the *onAsyncError()* function (line 50), and status messages are traced by *onNetStatus()* (line 54). We've also taken advantage of the *onNetStatus()* function to create a basic way of telling us when an FLV is playing. The *NetStatus.Play.Play* event code is issued upon play, and the *NetStatus.Play.Stop* event code is issued when the video is stopped.

```
61    private function onPlayVid(evt:MouseEvent):void {
62        if (_vidPlaying) {
63            _vidStream.resume();
64        } else {
65            _vidStream.play(_vidURL);
66        }
67
68        _vidPlaying = true;
69    }
70
71    private function onPauseVid(evt:MouseEvent):void {
72        _vidStream.togglePause();
73    }
74
75    private function onStopVid(evt:MouseEvent):void {
76        _vidPlaying = false;
77        _vidStream.close();
78        _vid.clear();
79    }
```

Next are the button functions. When issuing a stream *play()* method, playback will begin at the start of the file. Therefore, the *onPlayVid* function (line 61) needs to know when the movie is paused and stopped so it doesn't just start the video over with every click of the play button. We can use the *_vidPlaying* Boolean populated in the *onNetStatus()* function in a simple conditional to make that decision. The *onPauseVid()* function at line 71 uses the *togglePause()* method to alternately pause and resume the video stream.

The *onStopVid()* (line 75) uses the **close()** method to fully stop playback rather than just pause it. This function also demonstrates the video object **clear()** method so the frame visible when the video was stopped doesn't linger onscreen. Depending on the frame, this can give the incorrect appearance of having paused the video.

```
80        private function createControlButtons():void {
81            _playBtn = new CreateRoundRectButton(80, 20, 10, 2,
               0x0066CC, "Play");
82            _playBtn.x = 20;
83            _playBtn.y = 260;
84            _playBtn.addEventListener(MouseEvent.MOUSE_UP,
               onPlayVid, false, 0, true);
85            addChild(_playBtn);
86            _pauseBtn = new CreateRoundRectButton(80, 20, 10, 2,
               0x0066CC, "Pause");
87            _pauseBtn.x = 120;
88            _pauseBtn.y = 260;
89            _pauseBtn.addEventListener(MouseEvent.MOUSE_UP,
               onPauseVid, false, 0, true);
90            addChild(_pauseBtn);
91            _stopBtn = new CreateRoundRectButton(80, 20, 10, 2,
               0x0066CC, "Stop");
92            _stopBtn.x = 220;
93            _stopBtn.y = 260;
94            _stopBtn.addEventListener(MouseEvent.MOUSE_UP,
               onStopVid, false, 0, true);
95            addChild(_stopBtn);
96        }
97    }
98 }
```

Finally, you'll find the **createControlButtons()** function called in the last line of the class constructor. It instantiates an external class used to create each button and position it below the video. You can see the custom class import statement at line 7. You can look at the source to inspect the **CreateRoundRectButton** class, but it is a simple implementation of material covered in Chapters 8 and 10, so we won't go over it again here. All you need to focus on is that it adds an event listener to each button, which is triggered by a mouse up event and calls an appropriately named function for controlling the video.

While this is not a fully comprehensive class, it demonstrates how to play video with ActionScript. For a more feature-rich class, we might add seek functionality, audio control, and even caption display for cue point captions, if present. However, this is a project you can grow into after understanding

Project Package

The project package for this chapter is based on the last exercise in this chapter, "Coding Your Own Video Playback." Using this package, you can pass an external video file path to an initialization class and that class will automatically prepare the necessary elements for playback and error reporting. Then, you can manipulate playback with your preferred controls. For more information about the companion web site project, see Chapter 6.

the basics. On the companion web site, we discuss some of these issues further, as well as provide an example of a more robust NetStream client, and an alternate coding approach using the `VideoPlayer` class. After working with the examples in these pages, you may want to investigate the additional exercises and topics on the web site.

What's Next?

This chapter provided a couple of video playback methods to choose from. We've explained simple uses of prebuilt components, including both the FLVPlayback component for video display and the FLVPlaybackCaptioning component for accessibility and multilanguage captions. We also demonstrated how to create a rudimentary player by writing your own ActionScript. Don't forget to check the companion web site, which has several additional exercises that will take these examples to the next level.

In the next chapter, we'll begin Part V of book, covering input and output. Chapter 13 covers the basics of loading external assets, including:

- Using the universal URLRequest class
- Loading visual assets, including graphics and other SWF files
- Loading external MP3s
- Loading text and variables

INPUT/OUTPUT

Part V homes in on two of the possible input and output methods used for transferring data and assets in the Flash world. Chapter 13 covers several ways to load external assets. It also includes a discussion of text, with an in-depth look at loading variables. Similar to the text-loading example, the chapter takes a close look at best practices for loading external SWF and image formats. The chapter wraps up with a look at communication between ActionScript 3.0 SWFs and SWFs compiled using prior versions of the language, and how security sandboxes affect the process of loading assets.

Chapter 14 provides a detailed look at what may be the most common format for structured data exchange: XML. In addition to the creation of XML documents in their own right, the chapter discusses reading, writing, and editing XML on the fly. Finally, the chapter covers XML communication between client and server.

CHAPTER 13

LOADING ASSETS

Not every project requires assets to be loaded at runtime, but the ability to load files from external sources is extremely important and cannot be overemphasized. Loading assets on the fly reduces initial file size and, therefore, load times, and also increases the degree to which a Flash experience can change. Such change includes not only the all-important dynamic nature of updateable content, but also a streamlined editing process that allows external assets to be altered without having to republish the *.fla* file every time an update occurs.

The main purpose of this chapter is to cover loading external SWFs and images, to augment prior discussions regarding sound, video, and plain text. However, we also want to briefly address two issues very closely related to loading from remote sources: communication among SWF files of differing ActionScript versions, and security concerns. In this chapter, we'll look at:

- **Loading Sound and Video.** Necessity required that we cover loading sound and video in Chapters 11 and 12, respectively, including fairly robust, dedicated classes that separate the loading of the assets from their use. However, we'll briefly cover the basics here again to consolidate discussions of loading each major asset type into one chapter.

- **Loading Text.** We also discussed loading text in Chapter 10 but limited our coverage to loading of plain text to support HTML and CSS exercises. In this chapter, we'll also look at loading URL-encoded variables, and introduce a multipurpose class for all text loading.

- **Loading Display Objects.** We'll cover loading images and other SWFs into your main SWF file at runtime. As with text, we'll introduce a multipurpose class for loading SWFs and a variety of image formats.

- **Communicating Across ActionScript Virtual Machines.** As discussed in Chapter 1, the origination of ActionScript 3.0 as a wholly separate code base left a compatibility rift between ActionScript 3.0 assets and those of previous versions. While the new version of ActionScript cannot coexist with prior versions in the same file, it is possible to communicate between ActionScript 3.0 and ActionScript 1.0- or 2.0 SWFs loaded at runtime.

- **A Brief Look at Security**. Finally, we'll discuss some of the security issues that ActionScript developers face when loading assets from remote sources.

Loading Sound and Video

In Chapter 11, within the "Waveform Visualization" exercise, we covered the loading of sound. In that simple OOP example, the loading process was included in the **SoundPlayBasic** class, separated from the waveform visualization code. This compartmentalizing of functionality is a hallmark of object-oriented programming and a practice you'll see again, here in our video discussion, as well as throughout the remainder of this section.

For a more complete loading example, including error checking and progress feedback, review the **SoundPlayBasic** class. The following example, however, includes the minimum code required to load and play external sounds, and is included here as coverage of loading a variety of external asset types.

Line 1 creates an instance of the **Sound** class to load and play the sound, while line 2 instantiates a **SoundChannel** object to separate the sound from other audio for possible ActionScript control. Line 4 loads the local sound using a **URLRequest** object, and a listener is created to trigger a function upon completion of the load process. When that event occurs, the sound is played in line 9.

```
1    var snd:Sound = new Sound();
2    var channel:SoundChannel = new SoundChannel();
3
4    snd.load(new URLRequest("song.mp3"));
5
6    snd.addEventListener(Event.COMPLETE, onComplete, false, 0, true);
7
8    function onComplete(evt:Event):void {
9        channel = snd.play();
10   }
```

Loading video is more direct, and a common code set for use with streaming servers and progressive download video files already exists. As such, there is no need to create a dedicated loading step in the process of playing video. A more complete code structure, including error and status events, is covered in the "Coding Your Own Video Playback" section of Chapter 12 in the **BasicVideo** class. Here, again, is a streamlined set of instructions for playing external video files.

Line 1 creates an instance of the **NetConnection** class, responsible for connecting to a streaming server or progressive download file. Using null as the parameter for the class's connect method (line 2) prepares the class instance for loading a progressive download video, rather than working with a server asset. Line 4 instantiates a **NetStream** object that will be used to play the video, and references the connection previously created. Lines 6 through 8 create a video object for display, add it to the display list, and attach the NetStream object to the video display, respectively. As a result, anything streamed or downloaded across the established connection will appear on stage. Finally, line 10 plays the specified video.

```
1    var vidConnection:NetConnection = new NetConnection();
2    vidConnection.connect(null);
3
4    var vidStream:NetStream = new NetStream(vidConnection);
5
6    var vid:Video = new Video();
7    addChild(vid);
8    vid.attachNetStream(vidStream);
9
10   vidStream.play("video_name.flv");
```

NOTE

See Chapter 12 for information regarding handling errors related to meta data, cue points, and asynchronous operations.

Loading Text

Loading text makes available a greater number of variants than working with sound or video. Specifically, you can load plain text (such as text, HTML, CSS and so on, which will return a string), URL-encoded variables (such as HTML form and server responses, which will return an instance of the **URLVariables** class that contains a collection of name-value pairs), and even binary data (such as a compressed archive of data, which returns a **ByteArray**).

We covered loading plain text in the "Loading HTML and CSS" section of Chapter 10, so we'll focus on loading variables in our first example, and then discuss a universal class you can use for loading most kinds of text.

NOTE

Loading XML assets will be discussed in Chapter 14, "XML and E4X."

Loading Variables

The key difference between previous examples and the following exercise is the optional **dataFormat** property. Like our prior examples of loading text, we start with a **URLLoader** instance (line 1), add an **onComplete()** event listener (line 3) to react when the text is loaded, and then load the text (line 5).

However, line 2 sets the **dataFormat** property to **URLLoaderDataFormat.VARIABLES** constant, changing the default value from plain text to URL-encoded variables. This automatically changes the text returned from the loading process to a **URLVariables** object with properties named for the variable names in the result, and values corresponding to the values from the result. Lines 8 through 11 trace each property name and value to the Output panel.

```
1    var vars:URLLoader = new URLLoader();
2    vars.dataFormat = URLLoaderDataFormat.VARIABLES;
3    vars.addEventListener(Event.COMPLETE, onComplete, false, 0, true);
4
5    vars.load(new URLRequest("vars.txt"));
6
7    function onComplete(evt:Event):void {
8        var urlVars:URLVariables = evt.target.data;
9        for (var prop in urlVars) {
10           trace("urlVars." + prop + " = " + urlVars[prop]);
11       }
12   }
```

Therefore, starting with a typical URL-encoded string of "name=Sally&age=1" that might be returned from a server or a text file, the result is this:

```
//urlVars.name = Sally
//urlVars.age = 1
```

Using a Multiuse Text Loader

The following class can be used to load any of the three main kinds of text data discussed to date: plain text, URL-encoded variables, and binary data.

LoadText.as

The class starts with a typical structure of compiler directives (line 3 and line 4) and private properties (lines 8 through 13), but does contain one minor difference when compared to our prior examples. Because we are not creating a display object, the class extends **EventDispatcher** rather than **Sprite** or **MovieClip** (line 6). This is a style choice and was picked because the class dispatches events upon load completion to let your application know its work is done.

The constructor begins on line 15 and populates the **_verbose** property with the associated parameter received from instantiation, as well as sets the **data-Format** property discussed in the prior example. A half-dozen event listeners follow in lines 19 through 24, identifying functions to call when the relevant events occur. Included are opening the loading process, progress during the load, completion of the process, input/output errors, and security errors when trying to load content from other domains. The last step in the constructor attempts to load the text with any errors caught and a friendlier error message traced only during authoring.

```
1    package {
2
3        import flash.events.*;
4        import flash.net.*;
5
6        public class LoadText extends EventDispatcher {
7
8            private var _loader:URLLoader = new URLLoader();
9            private var _loaderData:*;
10           private var _verbose:Boolean = false;
11           private var _loadProgress:String = "";
12           private var _bytesLoaded:Number = 0;
13           private var _bytesTotal:Number = 0;
14
15           public function LoadText(path:String, verbose:
                 Boolean=false, format:String="text") {
16               _verbose = verbose;
17               _loader.dataFormat = format;
18
19               _loader.addEventListener(Event.OPEN, onOpen, false, 0,
                     true);
20               _loader.addEventListener(ProgressEvent.PROGRESS,
                     onProgress, false, 0, true);
```

```
21          _loader.addEventListener(HTTPStatusEvent.HTTP_STATUS,
            onHTTPStatusEvent, false, 0, true);
22          _loader.addEventListener(Event.COMPLETE, onComplete, false,
            0, true);
23          _loader.addEventListener(IOErrorEvent.IO_ERROR, onIOError,
            false, 0, true);
24          _loader.addEventListener(SecurityErrorEvent.SECURITY_ERROR,
            onSecurityError, false, 0, true);
25
26          try {
27              _loader.load(new URLRequest(path));
28          } catch (err:Error) {
29              trace("Unable to load document:\n" + err.message);
30          }
31      }
```

The next function uses the **bytesLoaded** and **bytesTotal** properties to create a string describing how much of the asset has loaded. If the **_verbose** property is **true**, it will trace this information to the Output panel during authoring. For a runtime equivalent, sample getters have been created to return the same string at runtime (lines 40 through 42), or a two-item array containing only the numerical bytes properties (lines 44 through 46). The latter would be more useful if you wanted to update a progress bar, for example.

```
32          private function onProgress(evt:ProgressEvent):void {
33              var loadPercent:int = Math.round((evt.bytesLoaded /
                evt.bytesTotal) * 100);
34              _bytesLoaded = evt.bytesLoaded;
35              _bytesTotal = evt.bytesTotal;
36              _loadProgress = ("The document is " + loadPercent
                + " % loaded: " + _bytesLoaded + " bytes of " +
                _bytesTotal + " total bytes");
37              if (_verbose) { trace(_loadProgress); }
38          }
39
40          public function get progressString():String {
41              return _loadProgress;
42          }
43
44          public function get progressNumberArray():Array {;
45              return [_bytesLoaded, _bytesTotal];
46          }
```

The **onComplete()** method first removes the listeners that were only applicable prior to the complete loading of the data, then populates the private property **_loaderData** with the text loaded (line 55), and finally dispatches an event to the instance of the class so the rest of your project knows the data is available (line 56). This asynchronous approach means you don't have to wait around for the data to be loaded. Once you receive notification of completion, you can query the **urlData()** getter in lines 59 through 61 for the data.

```
47          private function onComplete(evt:Event):void {
48              _loader.removeEventListener(Event.OPEN, onOpen);
49              _loader.removeEventListener(ProgressEvent.PROGRESS,
                onProgress);
50              _loader.removeEventListener(HTTPStatusEvent.HTTP_STATUS,
                onHTTPStatusEvent);
```

```
51                          _loader.removeEventListener(Event.COMPLETE,
                               onComplete);
52                          _loader.removeEventListener(IOErrorEvent.IO_ERROR,
                               onIOError);
53                          _loader.removeEventListener(SecurityErrorEvent.
                               SECURITY_ERROR, onSecurityError);
54
55                          _loaderData = evt.target.data;
56                          dispatchEvent(new Event("dataLoaded", true));
57                      }
58
59                      public function get urlData():* {
60                          return _loaderData;
61                      }
```

Finally, the series of event listener methods targeted in lines 62 through 76
will trace their results if requested by the **_verbose** property when the class
was instantiated.

```
62                      private function onOpen(evt:Event):void {
63                          if (_verbose) { trace("Loading has begun."); }
64                      }
65
66                      private function onHTTPStatusEvent(evt:HTTPStatusEvent):
                           void {
67                          if (_verbose) { trace("HTTP status code: " + evt.
                               status); }
68                      }
69
70                      private function onSecurityError(evt:SecurityErrorEvent):
                           void {
71                          if (_verbose) { trace("A security error occured:\n",
                               evt.text); }
72                      }
73
74                      private function onIOError(evt:IOErrorEvent):void {
75                          if (_verbose) { trace("A loading error occurred:\n",
                               evt.text); }
76                      }
77                  }
78          }
```

To use this class, all you need to do is specify the path to the data and the
type of data you need to load, including the optional verbose instruction if
desired. In the following example, we trace the variables by name, rather than
using a **for..in** loop, to demonstrate this standard syntax:

```
1    import LoadText;
2
3    var loader:LoadText = new LoadText("vars.txt", true,
     URLLoaderDataFormat.VARIABLES);
4    loader.addEventListener("dataLoaded", onComplete, false, 0, true);
5
6    function onComplete(evt:Event):void {
7        var urlVars:URLVariables = loader.urlData;
8        trace(urlVars.name);
9        trace(urlVars.age);
10   }
```

Loading Display Objects

Loading display objects follows a similar pattern, but uses the **Loader** class, rather than the **URLLoader** class. Another important distinction is, to react to the load instruction in line 2, the event listener is attached to the **content-LoaderInfo** property of the loader, rather than the loader itself, as seen in line 3. This is a built-in instance of the related **LoaderInfo** class, which traffics all information about the loaded content. Finally, in this example, the content is added to the display list once it has finished loading.

```
1    var ldr:Loader = new Loader();
2    ldr.load(new URLRequest("toLoad.swf"));
3    ldr.contentLoaderInfo.addEventListener(Event.COMPLETE, loaded,
     false, 0, true);
4
5    function loaded(evt:Event):void {
6        addChild(evt.target.content);
7    }
```

This process applies not only to SWF files, but also to JPG, PNG, and GIF files. Like the class included in the text loading example, the following class can be used to load these display objects. The benefit of writing the much more elaborate and verbose class is that it bundles all the error checking and event processing (such as progress monitoring) into one reusable class. Once the class is written, you don't have to add that material to your projects over and over again.

You will notice that this class is very close in structure to the text loading class, and that it functions in a very similar manner. The only principal differences in use is that there is no optional **dataFormat** property (because SWF and image formats are loaded the same way), and because this class extends Sprite, you can add an instance of the class to the display list for easy manipulation.

The class setup and constructor follow the same pattern established in the **LoadText** class, with three small differences. First, in line 7, this class extends Sprite, as previously mentioned. Second, the **contentLoaderInfo** property is again used as the target for the event listeners, which is consistent with the simplified example we just covered. The last difference is that the event listeners are changed very slightly, dropping the security event and adding events for initializing (line 26) and unloading (line 27) the content. We'll discuss the merits of each of these new events when we discuss their methods.

LoadDisplayObject.as

```
1    package {
2
3        import flash.display.*;
4        import flash.events.*;
5        import flash.net.URLRequest;
6
7        public class LoadDisplayObject extends Sprite {
8
```

```
9        private var _loader:Loader = new Loader();
10       private var _loaderInfo:LoaderInfo;
11       private var _verbose:Boolean = false;
12       private var _loadProgressString:String = "";
13       private var _bytesLoaded:Number = 0;
14       private var _bytesTotal:Number = 0;
15
16       public function LoadDisplayObject(path:String, verbose:
         Boolean) {
17           _verbose = verbose;
18           _loader.addEventListener(MouseEvent.CLICK, onClick,
             false, 0, true);
19
20           _loaderInfo = _loader.contentLoaderInfo;
21           _loaderInfo.addEventListener(Event.OPEN, onOpen, false,
             0, true);
22           _loaderInfo.addEventListener(ProgressEvent.PROGRESS,
             onProgress, false, 0, true);
23           _loaderInfo.addEventListener(HTTPStatusEvent.HTTP_STATUS,
             onHTTPStatusEvent, false, 0, true);
24           _loaderInfo.addEventListener(Event.COMPLETE, onComplete,
             false, 0, true);
25           _loaderInfo.addEventListener(IOErrorEvent.IO_ERROR,
             onIOError, false, 0, true);
26           _loaderInfo.addEventListener(Event.INIT, onInit, false,
             0, true);
27           _loaderInfo.addEventListener(Event.UNLOAD,
             onUnloadContent, false, 0, true);
28
29           try {
30               _loader.load(new URLRequest(path));
31           } catch (err:Error) {
32               trace("Unable to load content:\n" + err.message);
33           }
34
35       }
```

Progress monitoring is the same as the material explained in the **LoadText** class, and the **onComplete()** method is also the same but with one exception. The loaded content is added to the instance of this class automatically. A custom event is still dispatched that allows you to monitor the completion of the loading but, because the SWF or image has been added as a child to this class instance, you don't have to use a getter to fetch its content.

```
36       private function onProgress(evt:ProgressEvent):void {
37           var loadPercent:int = Math.round((evt.bytesLoaded /
             evt.bytesTotal) * 100);
38           _bytesLoaded = evt.bytesLoaded;
39           _bytesTotal = evt.bytesTotal;
40           _loadProgressString = (loadPercent + " % loaded: " +
             _bytesLoaded + " bytes of " + _bytesTotal +
             " total bytes");
41           if (_verbose) { trace(_loadProgressString); }
42       }
43
44       public function get progressString():String {
45           return _loadProgressString;
46       }
47
```

```
48          public function get progressNumberArray():Array {
49              return [_bytesLoaded, _bytesTotal];
50          }
51
52          private function onComplete(evt:Event):void {
53              _loaderInfo.removeEventListener(Event.OPEN, onOpen);
54              _loaderInfo.removeEventListener(ProgressEvent.PROGRESS,
                onProgress);
55              _loaderInfo.removeEventListener(
                HTTPStatusEvent.HTTP_STATUS, onHTTPStatusEvent);
56              _loaderInfo.removeEventListener(Event.COMPLETE,
                onComplete);
57              _loaderInfo.removeEventListener(IOErrorEvent.IO_ERROR,
                onIOError);
58
59              addChild(_loader);
60              dispatchEvent(new Event("displayObjectLoaded", true));
61          }
```

The event listener methods common to the **LoadText** class function the same way. However, there are three new event listener methods. The **onInit()** method is triggered when the content of the loaded asset is available to ActionScript. This makes the method a reliable place to query or manipulate properties or methods of the content, but the **Event.INIT** event occurs before **Event.COMPLETE** and can be used for more immediate results or even in conjunction with **Event.COMPLETE**, executing instructions in tandem.

In this example, several properties of the **LoaderInfo** class are displayed. The URL and a Boolean, indicating whether or not the loaded content is in the same domain as the loading file, appear regardless of the loaded content (lines 79 and 80). However, only if the **contentType** is consistent with a SWF (line 81) are the **swfVersion**, **actionScriptVersion**, and **frameRate** reported by lines (82 through 84).

```
62          private function onOpen(evt:Event):void {
63              if (_verbose) { trace("Loading has begun."); }
64          }
65
66          private function onHTTPStatusEvent(evt:HTTPStatusEvent):
            void {
67              if (_verbose) { trace("HTTP status code: " + evt.
                status); }
68          }
69
70          private function onIOError(evt:IOErrorEvent):void {
71              if (_verbose) { trace("A loading error occurred:\n",
                evt.text); }
72          }
73
74          private function onInit(evt:Event):void {
75              _loaderInfo.removeEventListener(Event.INIT, onInit);
76              //properties of loaded asset now accessable
77              if (_verbose) {
78                  trace("Content initialized. Properties:");
79                  trace("    url:", evt.target.url);
80                  trace("    Same Domain:", evt.target.sameDomain);
```

```
81                          if (evt.target.contentType == "application/x-
                            shockwave-flash") {
82                              trace("    SWF Version:",
                                evt.target.swfVersion);
83                              trace("    AS Version:",
                                evt.target.actionScriptVersion);
84                              trace("    Frame Rate:",
                                evt.target.frameRate);
85                          }
86                      }
87              }
```

The content is unloaded only when it is clicked (lines 88 through 90), triggering the **onUnloadContent()** method (lines 92 through 95). In this example, an event report is traced to the output window. However, it is highly advisable that you determine the best way to stop any streaming content in the loaded file before ultimately unloading the asset. In some cases content can continue to stream to your file, preventing proper cleanup and eating bandwidth, and, in an even worse user experience, sounds can continue to play.

```
88              private function onClick(evt:MouseEvent):void {
89                  _loader.unload();
90              }
91
92              private function onUnloadContent(evt:Event):void {
93                  _loaderInfo.removeEventListener(Event.UNLOAD,
                    onUnloadContent);
94                  if (_verbose) { trace("unLoadHandler:\n", evt); }
95              }
96          }
97      }
```

Using this class is nearly identical to using the **LoadText** class. This example shows the loading of a SWF that is ultimately scaled. Line 1 imports the custom class for use in data typing, and line 3 instantiates the class with a path-name and verbose reporting. Line 4 adds an event listener that listens for the custom event dispatched by the class, **displayObjectLoaded**, and line 5 adds the loaded asset to the display list. Lines 7 through 10 are a simple example of reacting to the completion of a load. The method scales the loader to 75 percent, but also includes a trace to demonstrate that this event occurs after the aforementioned initialization of the loaded asset.

```
1   import LoadDisplayObject;
2
3   var loader:LoadDisplayObject = new LoadDisplayObject("toLoad.swf",
    true);
4   loader.addEventListener("displayObjectLoaded", onComplete, false, 0,
    true);
5   addChild(loader);
6
7   function onComplete(evt:Event):void {
8       trace("loaded complete received");
9       loader.scaleX = loader.scaleY = 0.75;
10  }
```

Communicating Across ActionScript Virtual Machines

One of the most difficult things to deal with when migrating from prior versions of ActionScript to version 3.0 is that prior versions of the language cannot commingle with version 3.0. As discussed in Chapter 1, this is because ActionScript 3.0 resides in its own ActionScript virtual machine (AVM2) in Flash Player 9, while ActionScript 1.0 and 2.0 exist in another, wholly separate virtual machine (AVM1). SWFs created with ActionScript 1.0 or 2.0 can be loaded into an ActionScript 3.0 file, but the host file cannot access any of the scripted content *or assets* of the loaded SWF. As a result, it is difficult to mix legacy projects and new work.

Figure 13-1 shows an example of this phenomenon. The head is an animation in a SWF that was published using ActionScript 2.0. That SWF has been loaded into an ActionScript 3.0 shell where the controls exist. By default, you cannot issue commands in the shell to stop or play the loaded animation.

The workaround is to use a *local connection*, which is a conduit between two instances of Flash Player on the same machine. Two SWFs in a browser can talk to each other (even in separate windows), two Flash desktop projectors can communicate with each other, and a Flash projector can even communicate with a browser-bound SWF. This technique can be extended to allow communication across virtual machines.

Figure 13-1. AVM communication between AS3 (control panel at bottom) and AS1/AS2 (character at top)

The process for using a local connection is to create an instance of the `LocalConnection` class in one file, sending any messages to external SWFs using a specific string as a type of access code, if you will. By default, any external SWFs within the same domain that know the unique identifying string can subscribe to that connection.

Let's look at the AVM1 file first. As the project designer, you know you will be sending messages to this file using "avm2" as the unique connection identifier. Therefore, you must create a `LocalConnection` object (line 1) and use the `connect()` method (line 2) to subscribe to the connection of the same name.

Thereafter, you can create methods of that object to accomplish goals within this file. For example, the `playClip()` and `stopClip()` methods of the `avm2LC` object play and stop the animated head movie clip, respectively.

NOTE

You must be able to add the described code to legacy SWF files to support the `LocalConnection` *process. This means that if you don't have the source files for an older SWF, you can load it but not interact with it via ActionScript 3.0.*

```
1    var avm2LC:LocalConnection = new LocalConnection();
2    avm2LC.connect("avm2");
3
4    avm2LC.playClip = function():Void {
5        head.play();
6    };
7
8    avm2LC.stopClip = function():Void {
9        head.stop();
10   };
```

Now in the ActionScript 3.0 host file, you need to send messages using the "avm2" unique identifier string. First, let's dispense with the simplest possible loading code so we can concentrate on the local connection. Lines 1 through 3 load the older SWF and add it to the display list. Next, line 5 creates a **LocalConnection** object that will be used to send messages and monitor for errors.

Lines 7 through 16 create two event listeners that, when activated by the mouse clicks on the control buttons, send messages using the **LocalConnection** instance, specifying "avm2" as the connection specific to this task. The Play button sends "playClip" to execute the same-named method in the loaded legacy SWF, and the Stop button does likewise with the "stopClip" message.

```
1    var loader:Loader = new Loader();
2    loader.load(new URLRequest("avm1.swf"));
3    addChild(loader);
4
5    var avm2LC:LocalConnection = new LocalConnection();
6
7    playBtn.addEventListener(MouseEvent.CLICK, onPlayBtn, false, 0,
     true);
8    stopBtn.addEventListener(MouseEvent.CLICK, onStopBtn, false, 0,
     true);
9
10   function onPlayBtn(evt:MouseEvent):void {
11       avm2LC.send("avm2", "playClip");
12   }
13
14   function onStopBtn(evt:MouseEvent):void {
15       avm2LC.send("avm2", "stopClip");
16   }
17
18   avm2LC.addEventListener(StatusEvent.STATUS, onLCStatus, false, 0,
     true);
19
20   function onLCStatus(evt:StatusEvent):void {
21       if (evt.level == "error") {
22           trace("AVM2 LocalConnection could not send message.");
23       }
24   }
```

NOTE

Grant Skinner has created an open-source class called **SWFBridge** *designed to simplify this process, if you are already comfortable with the use of classes. It can be found at http://www. gskinner.com/blog/archives/2007/07/swf-bridge_easie.html. Another resource is the solution created by Robert Taylor called FlashInterface, which makes use of* **ExternalInterface** *and includes additional discussion on the topic, as well as examples. http://www.flashextensions. com/products/flashinterface.php.*

For those not yet ready to embrace classes, an unsupported free component called ActionScript Bridge (JumpEye Components) also existed at the time of this writing: http://www.jumpeyecompo-nents.com/Flash-Components/Various/ActionScript-Bridge-91/.

This is a simple example to illustrate the technique behind communicating across ActionScript virtual machines. The companion web site has two additional extensions of this example (retrieving a variable and triggering a function in the loaded file) as well as discussions about additional techniques for communicating with legacy assets, such as using the **ExternalInterface** class to communicate through JavaScript while in a browser. Additional information and techniques may also be available on the companion web site.

Taking a Brief Look at Security

Throughout the book, we've periodically discussed loading external data and content, but have avoided discussing security issues in every instance to avoid inevitable repetition. Here, consolidated in one location focusing on loading assets, we would like to present a brief overview of Flash security issues.

We must stress the fact that this is a quick rundown because security can be a serious matter and you should take the time to learn everything you can about its ramifications. You should be concerned not only about the obvious issues of possible security breaches, but also about the limitations imposed by the Flash security model on your projects. You don't want to start developing an important project only to discover in the eleventh hour that you need a workaround due to a security problem.

The best source for information about Flash security is the Adobe white paper, *Flash Player 9 Security*: *http://www.adobe.com/devnet/flashplayer/articles/flash_player_9_security.pdf*. This PDF is a comprehensive detailing of Flash security features and should, along with other Adobe resources, be considered one of the ultimate sources for information on the matter. The points we cover here are meant to introduce you to the topic but not to serve as an authoritative resource.

Security Sandboxes

The first Flash security concept to understand is the *security sandbox*. A sandbox is a limited, protected realm within which you may function with impunity. Crossing from one sandbox to another, however, is either not permitted or requires that you take significant measures to overcome the barriers. By segmenting the runtime and authoring experiences into multiple sandboxes, the use of the Flash platform is more secure. However, it can be very invasive. In fact, when some of the measures were introduced with Flash Player 8, it was one of the first, and very pervasive, disruptions that actually broke huge numbers of existing files.

Local versus network

The first two sandboxes we'd like to discuss are the local and network realms. By default, it is possible to work entirely in a local realm (loading assets from your local file system) or entirely within a network (loading assets from network URLs), but it is not permitted to do both. As an example, consider an e-learning situation. It is not possible to load an XML file of quiz questions from your local drive and submit an email of results to your instructor. Loading the local XML file puts your project firmly in the local realm, but accessing the network to send an email carries you into the network realm. Alas, never the twain shall meet. There are workarounds to this issue, which we'll discuss in the "Inter-Sandbox Access Solutions" section at the end of the chapter. For now, however, let's go over domain-based sandboxes.

Same versus cross-domain

The next sandbox we'll cover is the idea of a dedicated domain. By default, you can load data from the domain within which your main file resides. However, loading data from another domain is prohibited. For example, a hypothetical host file may reside at the location, *http://www.yourdomain.com/flash/host.swf*. From there, you can load assets at *http://www.yourdomain.com/flash/loaded/loadme.swf*. However, you cannot load the exact same file from another domain such as *http://www.mydomain.com/flash/loaded/loadme.swf*.

It's useful to note, however, that this restriction applies to data, not content. Content is defined as media Flash Player can display, or audio, video, or a SWF file that is used for display purposes (rather than for accessing data or scripting). You can load content using classes such as **Loader** (display objects), **Sound** (sound), and **NetStream** (video).

Data is information available only to ActionScript and which may even be derived from content, including content that has already been successfully loaded. Data can be loaded from an external source (like an XML file, which we'll discuss in the next chapter) using classes like **URLStream**, **URLLoader**, or extracted from media content. The latter is often overlooked and includes examples such as creating bitmaps or using the **BitmapData.draw()** method, discussed in Chapter 9, or extracting data from sounds by means of the **Sound.id3** property, or the **SoundMixer.computeSpectrum()** method, discussed in Chapter 11.

For instance, look at the following two examples, lines 2 through 4 demonstrate a legal loading of a display object, loading the Google logo with the **Loader** class. The **onComplete()** listener function, however, details an illegal operation, attempting to access the bitmap data from the Google logo with the **draw()** method.

NOTE

When testing the cross-domain example code, remember two things. First, the path to the example graphic may have changed, and any JPG, PNG, or GIF from a remote domain will suffice. Second, you must test this code within a browser, rather than the Flash authoring environment. The version of Flash Player integrated into Flash is automatically deemed a trusted realm and, therefore, will not behave as the browser-based Player will. For more information, see the "Inter-Sandbox Access Solutions" section of this chapter.

```
1   //allowed: loading content from another domain
2   var loader:Loader = new Loader();
3   loader.load(new URLRequest("http://www.google.com/intl/en_ALL/
    images/logo.gif"));
4   addChild(loader);
5
6   loader.contentLoaderInfo.addEventListener(Event.COMPLETE,
    onComplete, false, 0, true);
7
8   //disallowed: loading data from another domain
9   function onComplete(evt:Event):void {
10      var bmd:BitmapData = new BitmapData(276, 110);
11      bmd.draw(loader);
12      var bm:Bitmap = new Bitmap(bmd);
13      bm.x = bm.y = 100;
14      addChild(bm);
15  }
```

Inter-Sandbox Access Solutions

There are several ways to work around many of the security limitations we've discussed. They differ in approach, however, and are broken out into categories.

Administrator and user controls for local and network realms

To grant access to local files within SWF files that are earmarked for network access only, you must install what is called a *trust file*. This requires an installer that the user must download and run, which is an invasive procedure. However, it is the only way to grant this access *for* the user, rather than rely on the user doing this correctly. Further, if you are dealing with closed systems, such as intranets, this procedure is more tolerable.

To create a trust file, you must use a text editor capable of saving in Unicode format. You then add the paths to the directories you wish to trust—either on a project-by-project basis (such as a browser-based CD-ROM, or for a centralized location to which you plan to save your files. We've provided one sample path for the Mac OS X environment and one for the Windows environment, merely for examples. You would not likely have paths to more than one platform in any single trust file because these files are installed on a per-computer basis. The lines preceded by the number (or pound) sign (#) are comments and are optional.

```
#Mac
/FlashContent
#Windows
C:\FlashContent
```

This file must then be installed (using an installer application, or similar, that has access to system directories) in the appropriate location on the user's hard drive. The four paths that follow represent example locations. The first two are for end-user access, and the second two are for system-level access that administrators can grant for all users of a computer:

```
Windows user – c:\Documents and Settings\<user>\Application Data\
    Macromedia\Flash Player\#Security\FlashPlayerTrust
Mac user – /Users/<user>/Library/Preferences/Macromedia/Flash Player/
    #Security/FlashPlayerTrust
Windows Admin – c:\WINNT\system32\Macromed\Flash\FlashPlayerTrust
Mac Admin – /Library/Application Support/Macromedia/FlashPlayerTrust
```

NOTE

This discussion is about how you, as a Flash developer, can work with security issues, not how an end user can grant access on a SWF-by-SWF basis. As such, we will discuss only distributable solutions. For information about user settings, see the white paper referenced at the start of the section, "Taking a Brief Look at Security."

Web site controls (cross-domain policy files)

At the server level, you can install a cross-domain policy file, provided you have access to the server that will be hosting the loaded file. A cross-domain policy file is nothing but a simple XML file that grants access to identified sources to the directory in which it is placed, as well as all nested directories. For example, if you place a policy file in the root directory of a site, any identified source will have access to the entire site. If you place the same file in a single directory, with no child directories, the identified sources will have access only to that one directory.

To create a cross-domain policy file, you need to use the following syntax. You can identify legal sources by IP or domain and use the asterisk (*) as a wild card.

```
<?xml version="1.0"?>
<cross-domain-policy>
    <allow-access-from domain="192.168.1.100" />
    <allow-access-from domain="www.yourdomain.com" />
    <allow-access-from domain="*.yourdomain.com" />
    <allow-access-from domain="*" />
</cross-domain-policy>
```

To grant access to an XML Socket (discussed in the next chapter), you must also include the ports to which access is granted. For example:

```
<?xml version="1.0"?>
<cross-domain-policy>
    <allow-access-from domain="192.168.1.100" to-ports="507" />
    <allow-access-from domain="www.yourdomain.com" to-ports="507,516" />
    <allow-access-from domain="*. yourdomain.com" to-ports="507,516-523"
    />
    <allow-access-from domain="*" to-ports="*" />
</cross-domain-policy>
```

Author (developer) controls

When working with SWFs, you, as a developer, can also allow access on a per-asset basis. In the loaded asset (not the main file that will be doing the loading, but the remote SWF you intend to load into your main file), you can grant permission for a host to load the file. You can grant this permission for all loading attempts via the **Security** class, using the **allowDomain()** method and/or the **allowInsecureDomain()** method (when crossing *https* and *http* realms). With ActionScript 3.0 assets (for which Flash Player 9 is required) you can specify domains using text and IP address, and also use the asterisk (*) wildcard. For example:

```
Security.allowDomain("www.yourdomain.com");
```

You can also sometimes grant permission on a class-by-class basis. For example, you can use the same approach to grant access only to local connections. This example grants access to all subdomains of this domain, as well, through the use of the wildcard.

```
<localconnectioninstance>.allowDomain("*.yourdomain.com");
```

Caveat emptor

Please remember that we have only scratched the surface in this Flash discussion on security issues. Additional security is available, including all the way down to such intimate levels as traversing the display list. Also, additional methods of granting access exist, including on a user-by-user basis that you may choose to explain in a site-wide help system. Please explore the resources listed here, as well as discovered through your own research, before committing to a security solution.

NOTE

For more information about Flash Player 9 security issues, see Chapter 19 of Colin Moock's **Essential ActionScript 3.0.**

What's Next?

Throughout this book, we've demonstrated a few examples of loading external assets. Previously, we discussed loading sound (Chapter 11) and video (Chapter 12). In this chapter, we focused on loading text and variables, as well as SWF and image assets. We also covered one technique for communicating between ActionScript 3.0 and ActionScript 2.0 SWF assets, and briefly discussed some of the security issues facing access of external data in a number of forms. With this information as a head start, you should be able to begin working with just about any basic external asset, and begin explorations into intermediate to advanced loading issues. Multisandbox security setups, binary data, interrupting loading operations, and more should be within your reach with a little effort.

Next we're going to cover XML, which is among the most important standard formats used for data exchange, and E4X, the dramatically simplified approach to working with XML in ActionScript. XML is very widely used and enables a significant leg up over name-value pairs when it comes to structured data and large data sizes.

In the next chapter, we'll cover:

- The basics of the XML format

- Reading, writing, and editing XML data

- Loading XML assets using the `LoadingText` class from this chapter

- XML communication with servers and other peers

Project Package

The project package for this chapter includes **LoadText** and **LoadDisplayObject**, robust classes for loading external text data, SWFs, and images. **LoadText** supports the ability to load plain text, URL-encoded variables, and binary data. **LoadDisplayObject** supports loading SWFs, regular JPG, PNG, and static GIF formats. Both classes support relatively comprehensive error reporting and partially implemented getters. For more information about the companion web site project, see Chapter 6.

XML AND E4X

XML, which stands for Extensible Markup Language, is a structured, text-based medium for exchanging data. XML is tag-based, like HTML, but is designed for organizing information rather than controlling visual display. Instead of a relatively large library of tags used to lay out pages and build interfaces, XML is wide open with only a handful of preexisting tags that are strictly for administrative purposes. This freedom allows you to structure data in a way that is most efficient for your needs.

E4X (ECMA for XML) is the current World Wide Web Consortium (WC3) standard for reading and writing XML documents, and greatly reduces the amount of code and hoop-jumping required to communicate with XML. It allows you to treat XML objects like any other object with familiar dot syntax, and provides additional shortcuts for traversing XML trees.

In this chapter you'll learn the essentials of E4X. We'll cover:

- **Understanding XML Structure.** XML's flexibility means you can set up files in a manner that best serves your project's requirements. Unlike other tag-based languages, there's no library of tags to memorize—just a few simple rules to follow.

- **Reading XML.** Reading and parsing XML files is significantly easier using E4X than when using prior versions of ActionScript. You can find specific single pieces of information, as well as sweep through the entire document, using simple properties and methods that are consistent with other ActionScript objects.

- **Writing XML.** You can also put the same power, clarity, and ease of use to work when creating XML. You can create XML for internal use or build data structures for use with servers or other clients.

- **Deleting XML.** Whether eliminating unwanted items during reading to simplify the final XML object or removing errant elements when writing, it is sometimes necessary to delete elements.

- **Loading External XML Documents**. Because you determine its structure, XML is highly efficient and often the format of choice for portable data. As a result, external XML documents are very useful for loading data at runtime.

- **Communicating with XML Servers**. Knowing how to write, as well as read, XML, you can use it to improve your communication between servers and other clients. You can send XML to outside URLs and load a response, or open a real-time connection to communicate in real time.

Understanding XML Structure

XML is a vast improvement over the name-value pairs that are used in simple web communications such as HTML forms. An XML document can contain much more data, but can also convey an information architecture, detailing relationships among the data. For example, a list of users—with names, emails, passwords, and similar information—can be organized much the way a traditional database is organized. Records might be represented with tags that define a single user, and nested, or child, tags might serve as the equivalent of database fields, associating data for that user. Once a structure is established, a tag set can be duplicated any time a new record (or user, in this case) is added, and the consistent structure can be reliably navigated when retrieving the data.

Here is an example XML document:

```
<users>
    <user>
        <username>johnuser</username>
        <email>email1@domain.com</email>
        <password>123456</password>
    </user>
    <user>
        <username>janeuser</username>
        <email>email2@domain.com</email>
        <password>abcdef</password>
    </user>
</users>
```

Because you make up the tags as you go along, this document would be just as valid if you replaced the string "user" with "student" throughout. Neither the data nor the data structure would change. The document simply might be more meaningful if you were describing students instead of users.

The easiest way to understand this open format is to remember that XML, itself, doesn't do anything. While HTML defines the layout of a web page and gives instructions for displaying that page to a browser, XML does nothing more than organize data. It's up to the client or server to correctly parse the data. Think of XML as you would any other structuring effort. For example, you might export text from a database or a spreadsheet using XML as a replacement for comma-delimited or tab-delimited formats (records separated by carriage returns, fields separated by commas or tabs, respectively).

There are only a few simple rules to remember when creating an XML document:

- Every XML document must have a root node.

- XML is case-sensitive. It doesn't matter whether you use lowercase or uppercase, but it must be consistent. There are two schools of thought when it comes to choosing a case. The first school advocates uppercase as a means of making it easier to separate tag from content when you glance at the document. A bit more nebulous, the other school pursues lowercase as a de facto standard form used in programming, URLs, and other places.

- All tags must be closed. Relaxed HTML parsers will allow unclosed tags, such as <p>Paragraph text versus <p>Paragraph</p>. However, XML is stricter and requires all tags to be closed. In cases where a tag doesn't have a balancing closing tag (such as <br> from HTML), you can use a self-closing tag. This tag precedes the closing greater-than symbol with a slash. The HTML line break tag would look like this: <br/>.

- All tags must be properly nested. Relaxed HTML parsers may still correctly interpret improperly balanced tags, such as <b><i>term</b></i> versus the correct <b><i>term</i></b>. This is not allowed in XML.

- All attributes must be quoted. The last of the strict changes over lax HTML parsers is quoted attributes. While <span class=headline>News</span> may be allowed elsewhere, XML requires <span class="headline">News</span>.

- A few other items warrant a bit more discussion:

NOTE

As a personal preference, we opt for lowercase. You'll find, later in this chapter, that you can address XML elements using dot syntax the same way you would create custom properties of objects, as described in Chapter 2 in the section "Custom Objects." However, case sensitivity must be preserved. Therefore, a tag called username in lowercase would be represented as .username, while uppercase requires .USERNAME. We prefer to reserve uppercase in ActionScript for the preexisting task of representing constants.

White Space

White space includes all returns, tabs, and spaces between tags, as indicated in the example below:

```
<users>
    <user>
        <username>johnuser</username>
        <email>email1@domain.com</email>
        <password>123456</password>
    </user>
</users>
```

By contrast, the following example has no white space:

```
<users><user><username>richshupe</username><email>email1@domain.com
</email><password>123456</password></user></users>
```

Both are representations of the same document. Version two is a tiny bit smaller due to the reduced number of characters; however, in all but very large documents, this is usually negligible. Version one is much easier for a human to read, so it is usually the preferred formatting approach.

White space is important to understand because this information could be interpreted as text. Return, tab, and space are all legal text entities, so the XML parser must be told to ignore them or they will be counted as such when reading the document. This is because both tags and text are individual objects when parsed. The tags are called *element nodes* and the text entries within the tags are called *text nodes*. Because the white space can be considered text nodes, the previous example would contain a different number of nodes with and without white space.

Human readability usually prevails when formatting XML documents and, fortunately, ignoring white space is the default behavior of ActionScript's E4X implementation.

Declarations

You will likely see additional tags at the start of XML documents that you should be aware of. The first is the XML declaration tag, and it usually looks something like this:

```
<?xml version="1.0" encoding="ISO-8859-1"?>
```

This may differ, depending on the source document, but the purpose of such a tag is usually the same. It tells parsers the version of XML and the type of encoding used when the file was written. Another example of a declaration tag is the document type declaration (DTD), which is used to identify a set of rules against which the parser will compare the XML when validating. An example can be seen here:

```
<!DOCTYPE note SYSTEM \"note.dtd\">
```

Flash ignores these declaration tags. You may work with specific encoding types when creating text documents—such as UTF-8, for example, which is a Unicode format used to encode special characters—but the tag is not required by Flash. Similarly, a server that your Flash client communicates with may validate incoming XML data, so you may need to include this information in the XML you write for sending to a server. However, Flash does not validate or otherwise act on these tags.

Comments and Processing Instructions

XML comments are the same as HTML comments and take the form: <!--comment-->. In Flash, they are ignored by default but can be parsed using E4X and converted to strings if you wish to use them.

Processing instructions are strings typically used when working with style sheets to display XML, and they're not supported by Flash. They take the form: <? instruction ?>. They are ignored by default but can also be parsed using E4X and converted to strings if you wish to use them.

Entities and the CDATA Tag

When writing your XML documents, you must be aware that it is possible to confuse a parser, or even break your document, by including illegal characters. For example, the following document would cause a problem:

```
<example>The symbol < denotes "less than"</example>
```

In this case, the XML parser sees the less than symbol in the text as an opening XML tag. One way around this is to encode the entity for use, as seen here:

```
<example>The symbol &lt; denotes "less than"</example>
```

There are only five entities included in the XML specification, as seen in Table 14-1. Only less than and ampersand are strictly illegal in XML, but you are encouraged to use the correct form for all five entities.

Table 14-1. The five entities included in the XML specification

Entity	Correct Form	Notes
<	<	less than
>	>	greater than
&	&	ampersand
'	'	apostrophe
"	"	quotation mark

To include other special characters, or preserve special formatting, you can use a CDATA tag. This tag wraps around the special content and tells the XML parser to consider everything therein as plain text. This is particularly useful when you want to include HTML or formatted text inside your XML document, because you don't want the HTML tags to be interpreted as nested XML tags. The following example might be used to display a sample ActionScript function. The less than symbol will not cause a problem, and the formatting will be preserved.

```
<stuff>
    <![CDATA[
    function styleBold(txt:String):String {
        return "<b>" + txt + "</b>";
    }
    ]]>
</stuff>
```

Creating an XML Object

The ActionScript 3.0 implementation of E4X uses the **XML** class to replace a trio of legacy classes, simplifying things considerably. There are two ways of creating an XML object from internal sources. (We'll cover loading external XML separately.) The first approach is to write the content when the object is created, as seen here and in *createXML.fla*:

```
1    var authors:XML;
2
3    function fromNodes():void {
4        authors =    <authors>
5                            <author>
6                                <firstname>Rich</firstname>
7                                <lastname>Shupe</lastname>
8                            </author>
9                            <author>
10                               <firstname>Zevan</firstname>
11                               <lastname>Rosser</lastname>
12                           </author>
13                       </authors>;
14       trace(authors);
15   }
16
17   fromNodes();
```

The Flash engineers have considered a few wonderful subtleties of this approach. The XML is treated like XML, rather than like plain text. As a result, an instance of the XML class is automatically created, and you don't need to enclose the XML in quotes or worry about line breaks until the next ActionScript instruction is encountered. Note the absence of quotes in lines 4 and 13 above.

It's even possible to use variables by enclosing the variables in braces, as seen inside the tags in lines 7 and 8 in the following example.

```
1    var authors:XML;
2    var author1First:String = "Rich";
3    var author1Last:String = "Shupe";
4
5    function nodesWithVariables():void {
6        authors =    <authors>
7                            <author>
8                                <firstname>{author1First}</firstname>
9                                <lastname>{author1Last}</lastname>
10                           </author>
11                       </authors>;
12       trace(authors);
13   }
14
15   nodesWithVariables();
```

The second approach is to create the XML object from a string. This is handy for creating the XML object on the fly from user input. The text of a text field could be used as the source. In this case, you must use the XML class constructor explicitly, as seen in line 6.

```
1    var book:XML;
2    var bookStr:String;
3
4    function fromString():void {
5        bookStr = "<book><publisher>O'Reilly</publisher></book>";
6        book = new XML(bookStr);
7        trace(book);
8    }
9
10   fromString();
```

Here, standard variable syntax is used in line 4, joining the strings with the variable.

```
1    var book:XML;
2    var bookStr:String;
3    var publisher:String = "O'Reilly";
4
5    function stringWithVariables():void {
6        bookStr = "<book><publisher>" + publisher + "</publisher>
         </book>";
7        book = new XML(bookStr);
8        trace(book);
9    }
10
11   stringWithVariables();
```

Reading XML

E4X makes reading XML easier than ever before. You can now use syntax consistent with use of other ActionScript objects, including not only properties and methods, but also individual nodes and attributes within an XML instance. For the examples in this section, we will be referring to the following XML object, **book**, and can be seen in *readXML.fla*.

```
var book:XML;

function createBasicStructure():void {
    book =   <book>
                <publisher name="O'Reilly"/>
                <title>Learning ActionScript 3.0</title>
                <subject>ActionScript</subject>
                <authors>
                    <author>
                        <firstname>Rich</firstname>
                        <lastname>Shupe</lastname>
                    </author>
                    <author>
                        <firstname>Zevan</firstname>
                        <lastname>Rosser</lastname>
                    </author>
                </authors>
            </book>;
    trace(book);
}

createBasicStructure();
```

A familial relationship is used to describe nodes. Nested element nodes are children of their parent element nodes, and text nodes and comments are children of their parent element nodes. Nodes at the same level are known as *siblings*.

Element Nodes

Retrieving a single element node from an XML object is as easy as drilling down from biggest to smallest, just like you would access a nested movie clip from the main timeline. For example, to access the **title** tag, you need only use the following script. Metaphorically, the XML instance is the main timeline and **title** is the movie clip. The Output panel results are displayed in comments.

```
trace(book.title);
//Learning ActionScript 3.0
```

Going down another level or two, you can access information about the authors. At first glance, the result may seem odd, but order and method prevail.

```
trace(book.authors.author);
/*
<author>
    <firstname>Rich</firstname>
    <lastname>Shupe</lastname>
</author>
<author>
    <firstname>Zevan</firstname>
    <lastname>Rosser</lastname>
</author>
*/
```

Why did the result include both authors? The syntax requested **author** within **authors**, within **book**. Because that result could return more than one item, the result is an instance of the **XMLList** class and contains a list of all elements that apply. This is a very powerful feature of E4X that allows you to easily pull all values of the same tag from the same hierarchical level.

What's more, the **XMLList** functions like an array so you don't need to create an array variable first to contain the results. All you need to do is use array syntax with the object itself to retrieve the value you want. For example, the following syntax goes one level deeper to pull the first name of an author. Instead of stopping at **firstname**, which would return all elements of that name, an array index of 0 is added to the object address, seeking the first element of the array.

```
trace(book.authors.author.firstname[0]);
//Rich
```

Another powerful feature is the double-dot operator, which allows you to retrieve an **XMLList** across any hierarchy without a direct path to an element. This is useful for creating lists of children within multiple separate parents because you don't have to traverse each parent in the object to get to its children. This example gets all **firstname** text elements, even though they are in different **author** parents.

```
trace(book..firstname);
//<firstname>Rich</firstname>
//<firstname>Zevan</firstname>
```

Finally, you can use an asterisk (*) as a wildcard to include every element in a desired hierarchy. For instance, if you wanted both the first and last names of the authors, you could query the contents of the parent **author** element, without a wildcard, which would retrieve the following:

```
trace(book..author);
/*
<author>
    <firstname>Rich</firstname>
    <lastname>Shupe</lastname>
</author>
<author>
    <firstname>Zevan</firstname>
    <lastname>Rosser</lastname>
</author>
*/
```

However, this requires additional parsing of the author element. Instead, you could add a wildcard to represent all elements beneath **author**, and retrieve all first and last names.

```
trace(book..author.*);
/*
<firstname>Rich</firstname>
<lastname>Shupe</lastname>
<firstname>Zevan</firstname>
<lastname>Rosser</lastname>
*/
```

Using Text Nodes

It is common to think that the text information within an element node's tags is the value of the element node. However, this is not the case. In fact, the text is a node unto itself. This is not always obvious, especially when using E4X, because working with XML has been so simplified. To begin with, when querying an element node the contents of the element node are returned, as seen here:

```
trace(book.title);
//Learning ActionScript 3.0
```

Secondly, when using this value in the context of a string, Flash Player automatically casts the content into the string data type. The following code populates a string variable with no error and then traces a query of the new variable, using the **is** operator to check whether it's a string, and the result comes back positive.

```
var titleAuto:String = book.title;
trace(titleAuto is String);
//true
```

This is the most common use of a text node, so this is a meaningful shortcut. However, both of these steps are niceties provided by Flash Player. Checking the kind of node that **book.title** contains, using the **nodeKind()** method, reveals that it is still an element node.

```
trace(book.title.nodeKind());

//element
```

You can use the **text()** method to specifically retrieve the text node, and verify its node type to see a result of **text**. However, a text node is still XML. In fact, because an element node can contain many things, including other elements, text, comments, and more, its contents are returned as an **XMLList**. Examples of both circumstances are shown here:

```
trace(book.title.text().nodeKind());
//text

trace(book.title.text() is XMLList);
//true
```

Although Flash automatically casts text content to strings, it's a good idea to cast the data type explicitly using the **toString()** method. This remains in line with data typing best practices and prevents unexpected results.

```
trace(book.title.toString() is String);
//true
```

In addition to being a best practice, this step is useful when a specific data type is needed. For example, you can convert to other data types as seen in the following example, found in *typeCastingXMLData.fla*. All XML originates as text and, when text is not the preferred data type, it is helpful to cast to the correct type to take advantage of compiler and runtime error checking.

```
var dataTypes:XML = <root>
                        <value>.5</value>
                        <value>-2</value>
                        <value>1</value>
                        <value>true</value>
                    </root>;
var val0:Number = Number(dataTypes.value[0]);
var val1:int = int(dataTypes.value[1]);
var val2:uint = uint(dataTypes.value[2]);
var val3:Boolean = Boolean(dataTypes.value[3]);
```

Using Attributes

XML element nodes can include attributes the same way HTML nodes can contain attributes. For example, an HTML image tag might contain a width attribute, and the **publisher** node of our **book** XML object contains an attribute called **name** with "O'Reilly" as its content. To access the attribute by name, you first treat it like a child of the node in which it resides but precede its name with an at symbol (@).

```
trace(book.publisher.@name);
//O'Reilly
```

Because an element node can contain multiple attributes, you can also access all attributes as an **XMLList**. You can create the list using the **attributes()** method or a wildcard. The following code serves the same purpose as the prior example.

```
trace(book.publisher.attributes()[0]);
//O'Reilly

trace(book.publisher.@*[0]);
//O'Reilly
```

Finding Elements by Content

Another convenient feature of E4X is the ability to use conditionals within the address of a desired node. For example, instead of looping through the contents of an **XMLList** with a loop and a formal **if** structure, you can simply start with the conditional directly inside the dot-syntax address. Consider the following information, which can be seen in *find_by_content.fla*:

```
var phones:XML =  <phones>
                        <model stock="no">
                            <name>T2</name>
                            <price>89.00</price>
                        </model>
                        <model stock="no">
                            <name>T1000</name>
                            <price>99.00</price>
                        </model>
                        <model stock="yes">
                            <name>T3</name>
                            <price>199.00</price>
                        </model>
                  </phones>;
```

The next two statements check to see if any phone model has a price that is below $100. This check is performed in the first two lines in two ways, in accordance with the prior discussion of casting best practices. The first line is probably the most commonly used because Flash Player automatically casts the value of price to a number during the comparison. The second line explicitly casts the value. The results of both statements are the same, and listed only once following the second line of script. Only the first two models are listed because they are the only models with a price less than 100.

```
trace(phones.model.(price < 100));
trace(phones.model.(Number(price) < 100));
/*
<model stock="no">
  <name>T2</name>
  <price>89.00</price>
</model>
<model stock="no">
  <name>T1000</name>
  <price>99.00</price>
</model>
*/
```

Similarly, the next two lines look for any element one level down that has an attribute named stock with a value of "yes." Both implicit and explicit casting are also represented here, with the same results of both instructions listed only once.

```
trace(phones.*.(@stock == "yes"));
trace(phones.*.(@stock.toString() == "yes"));
/*
<model stock="yes">
  <name>T3</name>
  <price>199.00</price>
</model>
*/
```

Finding Elements by Relationship

In addition to finding elements by name, it is also possible to walk through XML data using position or familial relationship. In this chapter, you've seen several examples of using position in an XMLList instance by using the array bracket syntax and index of an item.

However, you can also create an XMLList instance of an object's children using the children() method. This list includes all possible children: element nodes, text nodes, comments, and processing instructions. The method elements() is usually preferred for this in Flash because it excludes the seldom-used comments and processing instructions from the resulting XMLList. You can also identify an object's parent node, or all descendants (not just children but grandchildren, and so on), using the eponymous parent() and descendants() methods, respectively.

Most of the time, you will exploit the power and simplicity of E4X to parse XML instances using the name of the element or attribute in which you are interested. However, familial relationships can be useful when analyzing all contents of an XML object.

The following script walks through an XML instance recursively, just as you saw in Chapter 4 when looking through the display list. This code can be seen in the source file, *find_by_relationship.fla*. Lines 1 through 20 declare and type two variables and also populate **book** as in previous examples.

```
1    var book:XML;
2    var indentLevel:int = 0;
3
4    function createBasicStructure():void {
5        book =   <book>
6                        <publisher name="O'Reilly"/>
7                        <title>Learning ActionScript 3.0</title>
8                        <subject>ActionScript</subject>
9                        <authors>
10                           <author>
11                                <firstname>Rich</firstname>
12                                <lastname>Shupe</lastname>
13                           </author>
14                           <author>
15                                <firstname>Zevan</firstname>
16                                <lastname>Rosser</lastname>
17                           </author>
18                        </authors>
19                   </book>;
20   }
```

The **displayXML()** function (lines 21 through 32) looks at every node in the XML instance. For each node, it uses the **hasSimpleContent()** method to see if the node contains only a text node, an attribute, an element node with no additional child element nodes, or no children at all. If any of these basic content scenarios exist, the function traces the name and content (if any) of the element, indenting four spaces for each child, and then attempts to trace any attributes. We'll talk about the **padIndent()** and **displayAttributes()** functions in just a moment.

If the content is more complex, meaning additional nested elements exist, it traces the element name, again looks for any attributes, but then calls the **displayXML()** function again to analyze deeper into the detected children each time.

```
21   function displayXML(node:XML, indentLevel:int):void {
22       for each (var element:XML in node.elements()) {
23           if (element.hasSimpleContent()) {
24               trace(padIndent(indentLevel) + element.name() + ": " +
                     element);
25               displayAttributes(element, indentLevel + 1);
26           } else {
27               trace(padIndent(indentLevel) + element.name());
28               displayAttributes(element, indentLevel + 1);
29               displayXML(element, indentLevel + 1);
30           }
31       }
32   }
```

The **displayAttributes()** function (lines 33 through 39) loops through any attributes of each node passed into it. It traces the number of spaces required for the indent level passed into the function, adds an arbitrary at symbol (@) to differentiate the attribute listing from other children, and, finally, adds the attribute name and value.

```
33  function displayAttributes(node:XML, indentLevel:int):void {
34      if (node.attributes().length() > 0) {
35          for each (var attrib:XML in node.attributes()) {
36              trace(padIndent(indentLevel) + "@" + attrib.name() +
                    ": " + attrib);
37          }
38      }
39  }
```

The **padIndent()** function (lines 40 through 46) returns four spaces for every indent level required for attributes or children. Line 48 creates the XML instance you wish to display, and line 49 starts the display process with an indent level of 0.

```
40  function padIndent(indents:int):String {
41      var indent:String = "";
42      for (var i:uint = 0; i < indents; i++) {
43          indent += "    ";
44      }
45      return indent;
46  }
47
48  createBasicStructure();
49  displayXML(book, 0);
```

The result of the display process appears here:

```
/*
publisher:
    @name: O'Reilly
title: Learning ActionScript 3.0
subject: ActionScript
authors:
    author:
        firstname: Rich
        lastname: Shupe
    author:
        firstname: Zevan
        lastname: Rosser
*/
```

Writing XML

You've already seen how to create XML when writing the entire instance at once, but you may also have the need to write the XML over time. For example, you may need to continue to add to an XML object based on user input, or changes in your file. The majority of techniques for adding content to XML mirror the process of reading the data, except this time you're assigning information to a node rather than retrieving it.

In this section, you'll re-create the data used in the "Reading XML" section of this chapter. For expediency, we'll combine discussion of creating element nodes, text nodes, and attributes into this one section, and present these actions in one possible order that you might follow when building the object. If you knew this goal initially, you could simply write out the XML when creating the instance of the **XML** class. For the sake of discussion, assume you are adding to the instance over time. Here is the ultimate object you will build, and it can be seen in the file, *writeXML.fla*:

```
<book>
    <publisher name="O'Reilly"/>
    <title>Learning ActionScript 3.0</title>
    <subject>ActionScript</subject>
    <authors>
        <author>
            <firstname>Rich</firstname>
            <lastname>Shupe</lastname>
        </author>
        <author>
            <firstname>Zevan</firstname>
            <lastname>Rosser</lastname>
        </author>
    </authors>
</book>
```

An XML instance must exist before it can be augmented, and every instance must have a root node, so begin by creating both:

```
1   var book:XML = <book />;
```

Next, it's possible to add an element node by name, just as you would read it by name. We're not including the attribute of this node on purpose, so we can demonstrate adding it after the node is created. However, it's certainly possible to include the attribute when creating the node.

```
2   book.publisher = <publisher />;
```

To add the attribute, use the attribute operator as you did earlier:

```
3   book.publisher.@name = "O'Reilly";
```

To easily create a text node, you assign a string to an element node, just as you retrieve the content of any node using its name. For example, to create the **title** element node, and its child text node at once, use the following:

```
4   book.title = "Learning ActionScript 3.0";
```

Tracing your progress so far should yield this:

```
/*
<book>
    <publisher name="O'Reilly"/>
    <title>Learning ActionScript 3.0</title>
</book>
*/
```

Remember that, while it's not always as attractive from a simplicity standpoint, it's sometimes necessary to add elements using position or familial relationship. In the following block of code, a new element node, **subject**, is added to the end of the instance using the **appendChild()** method.

```
5    book.appendChild(<subject />);
6    book.subject.prependChild("ActionScript");
7    book.insertChildAfter(book.subject, <authors />);
```

You can create text nodes the same way. Although there are no preexisting text children of **subject** (having just created the node), we demonstrate this process using the variant **prependChild()** method, which adds an element to the beginning of an object. Finally, you can insert a child after a specified element, using the **insertChildAfter()** method. We'll look at its sister method, **insertChildBefore()**, in a few moments.

It's also possible to create multiple nodes at once. In the next two lines, both the children **firstname** and **lastname**, and their parent node **author** are created. In the first line, Flash Player checks to see if the **author** node exists and, finding that it does not, creates it. In the next line, the **author** node does exist, so the child is added. (We purposely added the second author of the goal XML first to demonstrate inserting a child before something that already exists.)

```
8    book.authors.author.firstname = "Zevan";
9    book.authors.author.lastname = "Rosser";
```

Your XML object should now look like this:

```
/*
<book>
    <publisher name="O'Reilly"/>
    <title>Learning ActionScript 3.0</title>
    <subject>ActionScript</subject>
    <authors>
        <author>
            <firstname>Zevan</firstname>
            <lastname>Rosser</lastname>
        </author>
    </authors>
</book>
*/
```

A convenient XML writing tool, especially when dealing with large groups of nested tags, is the **copy()** method. It creates an exact copy of the target node and all its descendants. In the following block, we copy the existing author node and place it into a variable. Because the node being copied could have many children, the **copy()** method creates an instance of the **XMLList** class.

It is then a simple matter to change the desired content of the copy. Because the interim variable is a list, you must specify which item you wish to edit. Even though this list contains only one item, the copy of the **author** element node, you must still indicate that you want to work with the first index in the list to change the **firstname** and **lastname** elements to create the other **author** node.

Finally, you can add the new item before the existing **author** node to put it in the location originally indicated.

```
10  var tempList:XMLList = book.authors.author.copy();
11  tempList[0].firstname = "Rich";
12  tempList[0].lastname = "Shupe";
13  book.authors.insertChildBefore(book.authors.author, tempList);
```

At last, your XML object should match your goal:

```
/*
<book>
    <publisher name="O'Reilly"/>
    <title>Learning ActionScript 3.0</title>
    <subject>ActionScript</subject>
    <authors>
        <author>
            <firstname>Rich</firstname>
            <lastname>Shupe</lastname>
        </author>
        <author>
            <firstname>Zevan</firstname>
            <lastname>Rosser</lastname>
        </author>
    </authors>
</book>
*/
```

Deleting XML Elements

We've broken out deleting XML elements into a separate section because you may delete elements when reading or writing XML. When reading XML, you are more likely to just ignore unwanted content, but you may choose to simplify the object by deleting element nodes, text nodes, or attributes you know you won't be using. When writing XML, however, you may find the need to delete an element added in error or that is no longer needed.

To delete an element, simply use the **delete** command on the desired element. Here are a few examples showing how to delete items that exist in the prior **book** example. This code can be seen in the file *deleteXML.fla*.

```
//delete an attribute
delete book.publisher.@name;

//delete an element node and all descendents
delete book.subject;

//delete only a text node, not its parent
delete book.title.text()[0];
```

The resulting object looks like this:

```
/*
<book>
    <publisher/>
    <title/>
    <authors>
        <author>
            <firstname>Rich</firstname>
            <lastname>Shupe</lastname>
        </author>
        <author>
            <firstname>Zevan</firstname>
            <lastname>Rosser</lastname>
        </author>
    </authors>
</book>
*/
```

Loading External XML Documents

One of the most common XML data sources for local assets is an external document that is loaded at runtime. The E4X parsing of the resulting data has been discussed extensively, but it's still important to review the loading process used to get the data into Flash. Additional information about loading external assets has been covered in Chapter 13, so this brief segment is included simply for completeness. It can be seen in *loadXML.fla*.

First, an XML variable is declared to contain the ultimate XML object. Next, lines 3 through 6 create a **URLLoader** instance, with two accompanying event listeners, triggered when the load is complete, or when an I/O error occurs. Finally, the XMLdocument is loaded with a basic **URLRequest**, as no URL properties must be specified to load data.

```
1    var navData:XML;
2
3    var loader:URLLoader = new URLLoader();
4    loader.addEventListener(Event.COMPLETE, onComplete, false, 0, true);
5    loader.addEventListener(IOErrorEvent.IO_ERROR, onIOError, false, 0,
     true);
6    loader.load(new URLRequest("nav.xml"));
7
8    function onComplete(evt:Event):void   {
9        try {
10           navData = new XML(evt.target.data);
11           trace(navData);
12           loader.removeEventListener(Event.COMPLETE, onComplete);
13           loader.removeEventListener(IOErrorEvent.IO_ERROR,
             onIOError);
14       } catch (err:Error) {
15           trace("Could not parse loaded content as XML:\n" + err.
             message);
16       }
17   }
18
```

```
19   function onIOError(evt:IOErrorEvent):void {
20       trace("An error occurred when attempting to load the XML.\n" +
         evt.text);
21   }
```

The onComplete() function (lines 8 through 17) is triggered when the XML file is loaded. The function then tries to convert the loaded text data into XML, and trace the result to the Output panel. If successful, the listeners are removed and the process is complete. If one or more errors prevent the text data from being cast as XML, an error message is traced, often allowing you to locate something that may cause the XML to be malformed.

Communicating with XML Servers

Another frequent use of XML data is for transmission to and from a server. XML is usually the data format used by subscribable information feeds (RSS, ATOM), Web services, and database output. While some of these uses require only loading information, other tasks, including application logins, game high score submission, and so on, also require sending data. We'll cover two methods of communicating with a server, including the most common send-and-load technique as well as a brief overview of XML sockets.

Send and Load

The send-and-load approach is similar to traditional server communications, be they a browser retrieving an HTML file, or a user submitting data via a form. Essentially, the client sends data to the server and waits for a response. The server processes the incoming information, formulates a reply, and sends information back to the client source.

There are many scenarios in which this technique is used but, for simplicity, we'll send a three-node XML object, and then write that to a text file on the server. The server will reply with a simple object for Flash. Writing a text file on the server may not be the most common use of XML submissions, but it is basic enough to illustrate, as seen in *sendLoadXML.fla*.

Lines 1 and 2 create the XML object to send, and line 3 declares a variable to use when receiving a response from the server. Lines 5 through 8 create a URLRequest instance, assigning the XML object to the **data** property, specifying "text/xml" as the **contentType**, and specifying POST as the **method**. Lines 10 through 13 create a URLLoader instance, complete with completion and error event listeners, and then load the URL specified in the URLRequest instance.

```
1   var xmlString:String = "<?xml version='1.0' encoding='utf-
    8'?><root><value>1</value></root>";
2   var book:XML = new XML(xmlString);
3   var xmlResponse:XML;
4
5   var xmlURLReq:URLRequest = new URLRequest("savexml.php");
6   xmlURLReq.data = book;
7   xmlURLReq.contentType = "text/xml";
8   xmlURLReq.method = URLRequestMethod.POST;
9
10  var xmlSendLoad:URLLoader = new URLLoader();
11  xmlSendLoad.addEventListener(Event.COMPLETE, onComplete, false, 0,
    true);
12  xmlSendLoad.addEventListener(IOErrorEvent.IO_ERROR, onIOError,
    false, 0, true);
13  xmlSendLoad.load(xmlURLReq);
```

The **onComplete()** function (lines 14 through 24) attempts to convert the incoming data to an XML object, and populates a stage-bound text field (instantiated as **respTxt**) with the result. The response from the server is shown in comment form in line 17, and we'll discuss that in just a moment. In the meantime, the status node is placed in the text field if successful, showing "File saved." If the response is received, the two listeners are removed, freeing up memory. If the process is unsuccessful, the thrown error is caught and displayed. Finally, if the specified URL cannot be loaded, the **IOErrorEvent** occurs and that error is displayed.

```
14  function onComplete(evt:Event):void {
15      try {
16          xmlResponse = new XML(evt.target.data);
17          //<root><status>File saved.</status></root>
18          respTxt.text = xmlResponse.status;
19          removeEventListener(Event.COMPLETE, onComplete);
20          removeEventListener(IOErrorEvent.IO_ERROR, onIOError);
21      } catch (err:TypeError) {
22          respTxt.text = "A server communication error occured:\n" +
            err.message;
23      }
24  }
25
26  function onIOError(evt:IOErrorEvent):void {
27      respTxt.text = "An XML load error occurred:\n" + evt.text;
28  }
```

The next code block is the server-side PHP script. This is the server destination of your simple XML object and, as specified in line 5 of the ActionScript code, should be called *savexml.php*. The script first checks to be sure POST data has been received (line 3), and then populates the **$data** variable with that data (line 4). In lines 6 through 8, it creates, and opens for writing, a file called *data.txt*, writes the data to the file, and then closes the open file instance. Lastly, it checks to make sure the file was written successfully and sends a simple XML object back to Flash for digestion, as previously described.

savexml.php

```
1    <?php
2
3    if (isset($GLOBALS["HTTP_RAW_POST_DATA"])){
4        $data = $GLOBALS["HTTP_RAW_POST_DATA"];
5
6        $file = fopen("data.txt", "w");
7        fwrite($file, $data);
8        fclose($file);
9
10       if (!$file) {
11           echo("<root><status>PHP write error. Check permissions.</
             status></root>");
12       } else {
13           echo("<root><status>File saved.</status></root>");
14       }
15   }
16
17   ?>
```

Sockets

As a topic for future exploration, an alternative to standard send-and-load server communication is the use of sockets. You can use sockets to establish an ongoing connection between client and server, allowing real-time data transmission. Think of send-and-load connections as akin to letter writing. With each new missive, you must establish a new connection (a new letter) to send the data.

Sockets, on the other hand, are more like telephone calls. Once you establish the connection, the connection remains open while data is transferred to and from, until the client or server closes the connection. This makes sockets ideal for experiences like chat, multiplayer games, and similar real-time environments.

Socket communication requires a running socket server with which the client may interface. These servers are typically created in Java, Perl, or Python, and are, therefore, a bit outside the scope of this book. A number of servers are available, from free products (some of which are open source) like red5 (Java), Pallabre (Python), and Chatter (Perl), to commercial products like Electro Server, SmartFox, and Unity (all Java). The companion web site for this book includes additional information on each of these products.

We'd like to give you a brief overview of the ActionScript client experience to get you going. Lines 1 through 4 declare the relevant variables, including a hypothetical host name identifying the local server, and a hypothetical port of 8080. Your needs may vary. Lines 6 through 9 create listeners for the inevitable asynchronous stages of communication. These include when the socket connection is established, when incoming data is received in response from the server, when the socket connection is closed, and when any possible I/O errors occur.

```
1   var xmlSocket:XMLSocket = new XMLSocket();
2   var hostName:String = "localhost";
3   var port:uint = 8080;
4   var connectionOpen:Boolean = false;
5
6   xmlSocket.addEventListener(Event.CONNECT, onSocketConnection, false,
        0, true);
7   xmlSocket.addEventListener(DataEvent.DATA, onSocketResponse, false,
        0, true);
8   xmlSocket.addEventListener(Event.CLOSE, onSocketClose, false, 0,
        true);
9   xmlSocket.addEventListener(IOErrorEvent.IO_ERROR, onIOError, false,
        0, true);
```

The listener functions respond to the events described previously. When a connection is established (lines 10 through 13), the stage-bound text field instantiated as **conversation** is populated with a message to that effect. Further, a Boolean variable is set to **true** to indicate that the connection is open.

When incoming data is received in lines 15 through 20, an XML object is created for easier parsing, and the text field is updated with the response. A hypothetical response format, indicated in line 17 by an element node with a user attribute and a child text node, is displayed in comment form. The information added to the field begins with the user name from the attribute, and is followed by a colon and the text node. The result is also shown in common form, in line 19.

Finally, in the event of an I/O error, the error is placed in the text field.

```
10  function onSocketConnection(evt:Event):void {
11      conversation.appendText("Server connected.");
12      connectionOpen = true;
13  }
14
15  function onSocketResponse(evt:DataEvent):void {
16      var xmlResponse:XML = new XML(evt.data);
17      //<msg user="IMChatting">Hey, NYC...</msg>
18      conversation.appendText(xmlResponse.@user + ": " +
            xmlResponse.toString());
19      //IMChatting: Hey, NYC...
20  }
21
22  function onIOError(evt:IOErrorEvent):void {
23      conversation.appendText("An error occured: " + evt.text);
24  }
```

All that remains is a hypothetical interface, including buttons to connect, transmit chat text, and close the connection. The listeners in lines 25 through 27 follow the usual form and trigger the functions that follow. The **onSocketConnect()** function establishes the socket connection, and the **onSocketClose()** function closes the connection and sets the **connectionOpen** Boolean back to **false**.

The **onSocketSend()** function in lines 33 through 39 send your chats to the server. Line 34 starts by checking whether a connection is open. Line 35 creates an XML object using your hypothetical user name (itemized here as "chatterNYC") and the contents of another stage-bound text field instantiated as **sendTxt**. Finally, the **XMLSocket** class' **send()** method is used to transmit the information to the server.

```
25   connect_btn.addEventListener(MouseEvent.CLICK, onSocketConnect,
     false, 0, true);
26   send_btn.addEventListener(MouseEvent.CLICK, onSocketSend, false, 0,
     true);
27   close_btn.addEventListener(MouseEvent.CLICK, onSocketClose, false,
     0, true);
28
29   function onSocketConnect(evt:MouseEvent):void {
30       xmlSocket.connect(hostName, port);
31   }
32
33   function onSocketSend(evt:MouseEvent):void {
34       if (connectionOpen) {
35           var xmlSend:XML = <msg user="chatterNYC">{sendTxt.text}</
             msg>;
36           //<msg user="chatterNYC">Anyone there?</msg>
37           xmlSocket.send(xmlSend);
38       }
39   }
40
41   function onSocketClose(evt:Event):void {
42       xmlSocket.close();
43       connectionOpen = false;
44   }
```

An XML-Based Navigation System

If you haven't done so already, you may want to read the last exercise in Chapter 6, before continuing with this exercise. Chapter 6 discusses object-oriented programming and uses a simplified version of this exercise without XML. Instead of creating the menus with XML, it simulates the process using an array. By comparing this exercise with the more basic version in Chapter 6, you can see how incorporating XML changes the system. The result of this exercise will be a five-button navigation bar with submenus, the labels and partial functionality of which are populated through XML.

Before looking at the ActionScript for this exercise, we need to explain a couple of quick things about the directory structure and main *.fla* source file, *LAS3Lab.fla*. This allows you to create your own source files if you don't wish to download the files from the companion web site.

This exercise improves upon the files used in the ongoing book project, that includes material from this text and the companion web site. As such, it uses the directory structure you started in Chapter 6. The main project directory includes the primary *.fla* file and the document class, *LAS3Main.as*. It also contains two directories for classes, *com* (for general packages that you may use in multiple projects), and *app* (for classes specific to this project that you are less likely to reuse). For each class included in this section, the code is preceded by a comment that describes where, in the described directory structure, the class belongs. The qualifying path of the package itself can also demonstrate this, as discussed in Chapter 6.

Finally, the xml file that populates the menus is called *nav.xml* and is found inside a directory called *data*, which also resides in the same folder as your main *.fla* file. The main *.fla* file requires three symbols in the library:

MenuButtonMain

In our example file, this is a library movie clip that looks like a tab. Each main menu button appears above a horizontal line to collectively form a navigation bar. Inside the tab movie clip is a text field, instantiated as `_label`, which contains the label of the button. The symbol's linkage information identifies as its class a class of the same name, but in its appropriate directory, making the class path `app.gui.MenuButtonMain`.

MenuButtonSub

In our example file, this is a rectangular library movie clip the width of the tab used for `MenuButtonMain`. Each main menu button causes a submenu to appear beneath it, and these buttons stack inside that submenu. Inside the rectangular movie clip is a text field, instantiated as `_label`, which contains the label of the submenu button. The symbol's linkage information identifies as its class a class of the same name, but in its appropriate directory, making the class path `app.gui.MenuButtonSub`.

HLineThick

In our example file, this is a library movie clip containing a thick line. This serves as the horizontal plane on which the main menu buttons reside to form the navigation bar. There is no external class for this line, as it has no functionality, but to create it dynamically, it has been given a linkage class of `app.gui.HLineThick`. The nice thing about presupposing a class name in this manner is that, if you ever want to add functionality to this asset, you can create a class in this location and perhaps avoid additional edits to the main *.fla* file.

The first ActionScript file we'll discuss is the project document class, *LAS3Main.as*. Lines 4 through 7 import required classes, including two custom classes, `NavigationBar` and `LoadXML`. The remainder of the script is the class, which extends `Sprite`. It contains two private properties (lines 11 and 12) that will hold instances of the two aforementioned custom classes.

The class constructor occupies lines 14 through 17 and creates an instance of the `LoadXML` file to load the external data. An event listener is also added, waiting for the `xmlLoaded` custom event dispatched by the `LoadXML` class. Because the XML loading process is not the primary focus of this exercise, and because the steps in the process have been discussed at length in the Text and Loading chapters (10 and 13, respectively), we'll discuss `LoadXML` as the last class of the chapter.

NOTE

Although not required, you may also want to draw, or import, a texture or image for the background of your menu file, as the menu system makes use of a nice alpha-based rollover effect that will be easier to see if there is something more than a solid color underneath the submenus.

Once the XML is loaded, the **onLoadXML()** function is called, which creates an instance of the **NavigationBar** class and adds it to the display list. We'll look at that class next, so note that the instantiation call passes the main timeline and the **buttons XMLList** into the **NavigationBar** constructor.

Document class:

```
1    //LAS3Main.as (document class)
2    package {
3
4        import flash.display.Sprite;
5        import flash.events.*;
6        import app.gui.NavigationBar;
7        import com.las3.xml.LoadXML;
8
9        public class LAS3Main extends Sprite {
10
11           private var _navBar:NavigationBar;
12           private var _appData:LoadXML;
13
14           public function LAS3Main() {
15               _appData = new LoadXML("data/nav.xml");
16               _appData.addEventListener("xmlLoaded", onLoadXML,
                     false, 0, true);
17           }
18
19           private function onLoadXML(evt:Event):void {
20               _navBar = new NavigationBar(this, _appData.xml.
                     buttons);
21               addChild(_navBar);
22           }
23       }
24   }
```

You can look at the XML any time at the end of the chapter, but the buttons list contains all buttons (with an attribute for spacing apart the main navigation bar menu buttons), a child node for each main navigation bar menu button (with an attribute for its label), and a child node for each submenu button. The submenu button includes not only a label attribute, but also a path that can be used to load a demo SWF, and a text node that describes the project while it's loaded. Here is a sample subset of the document:

```
<nav>
    <buttons spacing="2">
        <button label="MOTION">
            <project label="flocking" path="motion/glow_worm.swf">
                Flocking with Zeno's paradox
            </project>
        </button>
    </buttons>
</nav>
```

NavigationBar

The **NavigationBar** class instantiates the main and submenu buttons. Lines 1 through 12 are familiar territory, but two things are worth highlighting. First, recall the form of a package path, as seen in line 2, and a reminder that the **HLineThick** class is a symbol linkage class from the Flash file's library.

Lines 14 through 19 encompass the class constructor, receiving the aforementioned main timeline and **buttons XMLList** from the file's document class during instantiation. The constructor populates three private properties, and calls the **build()** function. Before looking at that function, note that the **spacing** attribute of the first child of the **buttons** list is retrieved for use in horizontal spacing of the main menu buttons.

```
1    // app > gui > NavigationBar.as
2    package app.gui {
3
4        import flash.display.Sprite;
5        import flash.filters.DropShadowFilter;
6
7        public class NavigationBar extends Sprite {
8
9            private var _app:Sprite;
10           private var _buttonSpacing:int;
11           private var _hline:HLineThick;
12           private var _navData:XMLList;
13
14           public function NavigationBar(app:Sprite, navData:XMLList) {
15               _app = app;
16               _navData = navData;
17               _buttonSpacing = _navData.@spacing;
18               build();
19           }
```

The **build()** function instantiates the main and submenu buttons. The process begins with a **for** loop that walks through the number of menus. The loop creates an instance of the **MenuButtonMain** class, passing the list label attribute of each button the loop encounters into the constructor. It then positions the button horizontally (accounting for the width and spacing times the number of current buttons, plus a 20-pixel offset from the left edge), at a fixed **y** location for all buttons.

It then retrieves the number of submenu buttons for the next loop, which instantiates a **MenuButtonSub** class for every menu button—this time passing the timeline reference and project node into the new constructor. Because the menu is stacked vertically, the positioning is all in the **y** direction, offset by the height of each button to build the menu.

Next, line 30 is very important because it shows that every submenu button is added to a child of the main menu button called **subMenu**. Note the destination when adding submenu buttons to the display list: **menuBtn.submenu**. You will soon see that this submenu sprite is a container for all the submenu buttons, and it was created in the **MenuButtonMain** class in line 22.

The entire menu, including the main button, submenu, and all submenu buttons, is added to the navigation bar in line 33.

```
20          private function build():void {
21              for (var i:int; i < _navData.button.length(); i++) {
22                  var menuBtn:MenuButtonMain = new MenuButtonMain(
                    _navData.button[i].@label);
23                  menuBtn.x = 20 + (menuBtn.width + _buttonSpacing)
                    * i;
24                  menuBtn.y = 75;
25
26                  var subMenuButtonNum:uint =
                    _navData.button[i].project.length();
27                  for (var j:uint = 0; j < subMenuButtonNum; j++) {
28                      var subMenuButton:MenuButtonSub = new
                        MenuButtonSub(_app,
                        _navData.button[i].project[j]);
29                      subMenuButton.y = ((subMenuButton.height - 2)
                        * j);
30                      menuBtn.subMenu.addChild(subMenuButton);
31                  }
32
33                  addChild(menuBtn);
34              }
```

Finally, the horizontal line from the Flash library is added to the bottom of the menu buttons, mouse functionality is disabled so the line itself doesn't trap mouse events, and a drop shadow is added to the entire navigation bar, allowing all children to inherit its effect.

```
35                  _hline = new HLineThick();
36                  _hline.y = 100;
37                  _hline.mouseEnabled = false;
38                  addChild(_hline);
39
40                  var ds:DropShadowFilter = new DropShadowFilter();
41                  ds.angle = 45;
42                  ds.distance = 5;
43                  ds.alpha = 0.5;
44                  filters = [ds];
45              }
46          }
47      }
```

FadeRollOver

Now we'd like to take a tiny break from the linear progression of menu elements (navigation bar, main menu button, submenu, submenu button) to talk about the **FadeRollOver** class. Up to this point, and including this class, our classes have extended the **Sprite** class to easily adopt the appropriate display object functionality.

Yet, when we discuss the submenu, you'll see that it extends the **FadeRollOver** class. Because this class extended **Sprite**, however, sprite characteristics are still passed down to the subclasses.

NOTE

For more information about inheritance, see the Inheritance section in Chapter 6.

FadeRollOver is very simple. It uses Zeno's paradox to fade an element to a new alpha value. In addition to the standard file setup, the constructor starts with an initial **alpha** value of 65 percent, and a listener for mouse rollover and rollout. Upon rollover, the **alpha** is set to 100 percent and the enter frame listener is created, making the change in the prescribed four steps. On rollout, the same thing happens in reverse until the **alpha** reaches a 1-percent tolerance of the desired 65-percent **alpha** we started with. At that point, the listener is removed for efficiency, and the process doesn't begin anew until another rollover event is received.

```
1    // com > las3 > graphics > FadeRollOver.as
2    package com.las3.graphics {
3
4        import flash.display.Sprite;
5        import flash.events.*;
6
7        public class FadeRollOver extends Sprite {
8
9            private var _alphaDest:Number;
10
11           public function FadeRollOver() {
12               _alphaDest = 0.65
13               alpha = _alphaDest;
14               addEventListener(MouseEvent.ROLL_OVER, onOver, false,
                 0, true);
15               addEventListener(MouseEvent.ROLL_OUT, onOut, false, 0,
                 true);
16           }
17
18           private function onOver(evt:MouseEvent):void {
19               _alphaDest = 1;
20               addEventListener(Event.ENTER_FRAME, onLoop, false, 0,
                 true);
21           }
22
23           private function onOut(evt:MouseEvent):void {
24               _alphaDest = 0.65;
25           }
26
27           private function onLoop(evt:Event):void {
28               if (Math.abs(alpha - _alphaDest) > 0.01) {
29                   alpha += (_alphaDest - alpha) / 4;
30               } else {
31                   removeEventListener(Event.ENTER_FRAME, onLoop);
32               }
33           }
34       }
35   }
```

MenuButtonMain

MenuButtonMain not only creates the main menu button, but it also creates the submenu that will later contain the submenu buttons. In addition, it handles all the showing and hiding of the submenu. The only thing noteworthy among the first 11 lines is the fact that **_label** is a public property. This is because it references the text field inside the button that resides in the library of your main Flash file.

```
1   // app > gui > MenuButtonMain.as
2   package app.gui {
3
4       import flash.display.Sprite;
5       import flash.events.*;
6       import flash.text.TextField;
7
8       public class MenuButtonMain extends Sprite {
9
10          public var _label:TextField;
11          private var _subMenu:Sprite;
```

The constructor receives the string for the button label and puts it into the text field, as seen in line 13. It then disables mouse activity in the text field, so the mouse can respond to the underlying button and update the cursor to a hand when rolling over the button. To enable the hand cursor, the movie clip is set to behave as a button by setting both the **buttonMode** and **useHandCursor** properties to **true**.

In lines 18 and 19, the class creates a sprite container for all the submenu buttons and positions it 5 pixels above the bottom of the main menu button (as determined by the height of the main menu button, minus 5 pixels). This is the same submenu container discussed earlier, when we added the buttons to the display list in the **NavigationBar** class. Finally, an event listener is added and responds to the event triggered when the main menu button is added to the stage. This is important because, remember, the main menu button is not being added to the display list in this class. Instead, it's added to the display list in the previously discussed **NavigationBar** class at the time of instantiation. So, this class waits until the button is added to the stage, and then creates the mouse listener in line 25. (It also removes the other listener because the element has already been added to the stage.)

```
12          public function MenuButtonMain(labl:String) {
13              _label.text = labl;
14              _label.mouseEnabled = false;
15              buttonMode = true;
16              useHandCursor = true;
17
18              _subMenu = new Sprite();
19              _subMenu.y = height - 5;
20
21              addEventListener(Event.ADDED_TO_STAGE, onAdded, false,
                    0, true);
22          }
23
24          private function onAdded(evt:Event):void {
25              addEventListener(MouseEvent.CLICK, onShow, false, 0,
                    true);
26              removeEventListener(Event.ADDED_TO_STAGE, onAdded);
27          }
```

The last portion of this class covers the showing and hiding of the submenus. Click the main menu button and the submenu is displayed and remains visible until you click elsewhere. The **onHide()** and **onShow()** methods remove and add the submenu child each time you mouse up on the stage. The getter returns a reference to the **subMenu** sprite and, though not used, the setter is provided for completion.

```
28          private function onHide(evt:MouseEvent):void {
29              stage.removeEventListener(MouseEvent.MOUSE_UP, onHide);
30              removeChild(_subMenu);
31          }
32
33          private function onShow(evt:MouseEvent):void {
34              stage.addEventListener(MouseEvent.MOUSE_UP, onHide,
                    false, 0, true);
35              addChild(_subMenu);
36          }
37
38          public function get subMenu():Sprite {
39              return _subMenu;
40          }
41
42          public function set subMenu(s:Sprite):void {
43              _subMenu = s;
44          }
45      }
46  }
```

MenuButtonSub

The MenuButtonSub class has only three tasks. First, it pulls the **label** attribute from the **project** node of the XML for the button's label. (Note here, too, that the **_label** property is public, to access the text field inside the library symbol.) Second, it disables the text label's mouse functionality so the underlying button can update the cursor, as with the main menu button. Finally, it adds a mouse click listener that, when triggered, traces the label and path, pulled from the **path** attribute of the project node. This is the example button functionality for this exercise. In the final project that can be found in the accompanying source files on the companion web site, the path is used to load some of the demo files you've been creating throughout the book.

```
1   // app > gui > MenuButtonSub.as
2   package app.gui {
3
4       import flash.display.Sprite;
5       import flash.events.MouseEvent;
6       import flash.text.TextField;
7       import com.las3.graphics.FadeRollOver;
8
9       public class MenuButtonSub extends FadeRollOver {
10
11          public var _label:TextField;
12          private var _app:Sprite;
13          private var _projectNode:XML;
14
15          public function MenuButtonSub(app:Sprite, projectNode:XML) {
```

```
16              _app = app;
17              _projectNode = projectNode;
18
19              _label.text = _projectNode.@label;
20              _label.mouseEnabled = false;
21
22              addEventListener(MouseEvent.CLICK, onClick, false, 0,
                true);
23          }
24
25          private function onClick(evt:MouseEvent):void {
26              trace(_label.text + ":  path = " + _projectNode.@
                path);
27          }
28      }
29  }
```

LoadXML

The LoadXML class is a clean front end for the LoadText class we discussed at length in Chapter 13. It passes the path of the XML document to load, as well as an optional Boolean value to enable verbose tracing of progress to the Output panel. Once the loading has been completed, the LoadText class dispatches a dataLoaded event to the LoadXML class, which triggers the onComplete() method.

The most important step in the onComplete() method is the creation of an XML object from the text string that was loaded. If that is successful, the LoadXML class dispatches an xmlLoaded event to the class that instantiated it. The arrival of that message allows the other class to request the XML at will, using the getter function.

```
1   // com > las3 > xml > LoadXML.as
2   package com.las3.xml {
3
4       import flash.events.*;
5       import flash.net.*;
6       import com.las3.loading.LoadText;
7
8       public class LoadXML extends EventDispatcher {
9
10          private var _xml:XML;
11          private var textXML:String;
12          private var _loader:LoadText;
13
14          function LoadXML(path:String, verbose:Boolean=false) {
15              _loader = new LoadText(path, verbose);
16              _loader.addEventListener("dataLoaded", onComplete,
                false, 0, true);
17          }
18
19          private function onComplete(evt:Event):void {
20              try {
21                  _xml = new XML(_loader.urlData);
22                  dispatchEvent(new Event("xmlLoaded", true));
23              } catch (err:Error) {
24                  trace("Could not parse loaded content as XML\n" +
```

NOTE

This class is actually a subset of the project package for this chapter. It can be reused, in combination with the **LoadText** *class from Chapter 13, to load XML any time you need it.*

```
                                    err.message);
25                          }
26                  }
27
28          public function get xml():XML {
29                  return _xml;
30          }
31      }
32  }
```

XML data file

Finally, here is the XML file, *nav.xml*, found in the *data* folder in the same directory as the main *.fla* file.

```
1   <nav>
2       <buttons spacing="2">
3           <button label="MOTION">
4               <project label="particle system"
                path="motion/particles/particles.swf">
5                   Change the values applied to each particle
6               </project>
7               <project label="flocking" path="motion/glow_worm.swf">
8                   Flocking with Zeno's paradox
9               </project>
10          </button>
11          <button label="DRAWING">
12              <project label="drawing app"
                path="drawing/drawing.swf">
13                  A simple drawing app.
14              </project>
15          </button>
16          <button label="TEXT">
17              <project label="text formatting"
                path="text/formatting.swf">
18                  Format text on the fly
19              </project>
20              <project label="text metrics 1"
                path="text/line_data.swf">
21                  Retrieve line data
22              </project>
23          </button>
24          <button label="SOUND">
25              <project label="volume and pan"
                path="sound/volume_pan.swf">
26                  Control sound volume and pan with the mouse
27              </project>
28              <project label="compute spectrum"
                path="sound/visualizer.swf">
29                  Create visuals based on a sound's frequency
                    spectrum data
30              </project>
31          </button>
32          <button label="VIDEO">
33              <project label="full-screen video"
                path="video/fullscreen.swf">
34                  Show full-screen video
35              </project>
36              <project label="captioned video"
```

```
                   path="video/caption.swf">
37                 Display video captions
38             </project>
39         </button>
40     </buttons>
41 </nav>
```

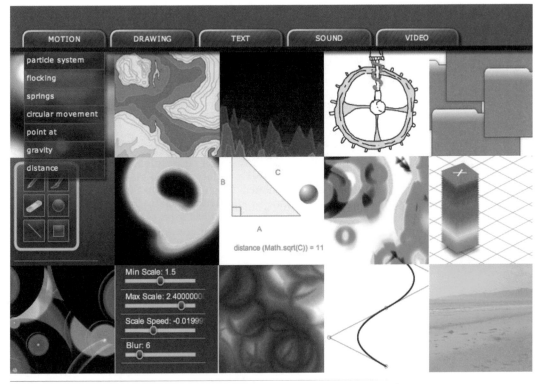

Figure 14-1. A simple navigation system that loads button labels and destinations from XML, seen over a static image background to demonstrate translucency of menus

This simple navigation system, shown in Figure 14.1, brings a lot of power to a project because it allows you to quickly and easily change the main and submenu button names, alter the layout a small degree, modify project descriptions, and change what is loaded when the button is activated, all by configuring an external XML file. In other words, you don't have to edit and republish the Flash file every time you want to make a change.

If you've already read the preceding chapters, you now have enough skills to finalize the ongoing project that highlights most of what you've learned. You've created content in the motion, drawing, text, sound, and video categories, learned how to load the content, and now how to navigate through it using XML. All that is left is to wire it all together, which you can finalize on the companion web site, with access to all source files.

Project Package

As working with E4X is so simple, there's little need for a library of custom methods that are generic enough to work across many projects. The project package for this chapter is designed to minimize the amount of effort needed to load XML documents. For more information about the companion web site project, see Chapter 6.

What's Next?

This chapter has covered many of the capabilities of the `XML` and `XMLList` classes, but the coverage is not exhaustive. For example, it is possible to parse XML comments and processing instructions by setting the `ignoreComments` and `ignoreProcessingInstructions` properties to `false`. From there, you can create `XMLLists` using the `comments()` and `processingInstructions()` methods and convert them to strings. You also have control over XML namespaces used to prevent duplicate element and attribute names—useful when merging XML from multiple sources. For additional information, consult Chapter 18 of Colin Moock's *Essential ActionScript 3.0*.

In the next chapter, we'll take a brief look at planning your code. We'll discuss:

- Basic strategies for mapping out your projects to make coding more efficient

- An example of object-oriented design patterns in the form of the Singleton pattern, used when only a single instance of a class should be created

- A short list of additional resources for continued learning

PROGRAMMING DESIGN AND RESOURCES

This book concludes with Part VI: a high-level overview of coding design and technique. Chapter 15 includes discussions about general programming design principles, as well as an example of using design patterns in object-oriented programming. The chapter wraps up with a short list of resources you can use to enhance your learning.

PROGRAMMING DESIGN AND RESOURCES

Having covered the big bones of ActionScript 3.0, we're now faced with the challenge of building a skeleton. Where do you start? Should you start with the spine of a project and build outward, or perhaps begin with a toe and build up from there? Just how do you add the connecting tissue that holds the whole thing together?

The best answer to these questions is that it depends a lot on each project, and one school of coding may not work in all situations. A lot of factors affect how you approach a programming task including the size of the project, how many programmers are contributing to the code, to what degree the user is involved in the final work, and, of course, your personal style.

We'd like to wrap up this book with a big-picture overview of several programming theories that you can explore further when choosing your first bone.

- **Programming Design Methodologies.** Learning syntax is one thing, but knowing how to pull it all together is another. As you gain experience and develop your own working processes, following a recommended development model can sometimes help get things rolling. We give you a glimpse of a handful of methodologies that have been developed over the years, to see if any suit your needs.

- **Object-oriented Design Patterns.** Good planning is helpful to any programming effort, but object-oriented programming, in particular, can sometimes benefit from established patterns of coding. We'll outline a few widely used design patterns and show you an example of one in practice.

Programming Design Methodologies

Learning any type of programming language is always improved by trial and error—"learn by doing," as the adage goes. Trial and error is embodied by experimentation, or *spiking*, as it is sometimes called in programming. Spiking is trying something experimental, but being willing to throw away the code while retaining what you've learned from the effort. The more

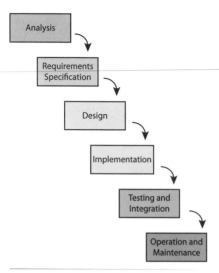

Figure 15-1. A simple Waterfall software development model

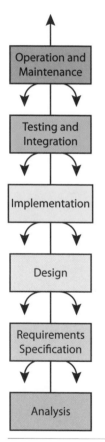

Figure 15-2. The Fountain software development model, a variant on Waterfall

spiking you do, the better you understand the topic you're experimenting with. Focusing on the syntax first—learning how a class, method, or property works and understanding how change affects their outcome—is the first step in becoming fluent in a language.

This idea has driven the design of this book. Taking into consideration an audience that is new to ActionScript 3.0, some of which may even be new to ActionScript in general, we did not want to immediately immerse you in classes. Companion examples in class form are available for every exercise in this book, but the tutorial thread throughout this book has focused on teaching the syntax and functionality of each topic discussed. As the book progressed, we added more discussion about how to write a script, how classes can work as pieces of a larger goal, and how object-oriented practices can be used in some circumstances.

How, though, do you plan an entire project? First, understanding syntax, then how to write a script, and then how scripts work together, how do you progress to designing an application? Unfortunately, there's not one silver bullet that is perfect for all software development. However, there are several schools of thought that may help guide you in planning your project.

Some of the ideas put forward in methodologies may appear to be common sense, while others may seem at odds with your goals. This potential conflict is common and, in fact, has given rise to additional methodologies from one or more existing theories. The important idea is to gain some insight into how a particular application may be planned based on the pros or cons of some of these popular design approaches.

What follows is a subset of development processes that you may wish to learn more about when adopting a style of your own. This is meant as a brief introduction to these theories, and we encourage you to learn more about each one, ideally trying them out when you can, before putting them into practice. A quick place to start your exploration is the Software Development Process entry at Wikipedia (*http://en.wikipedia.org/wiki/Software_development_process/*).

Waterfall

Waterfall is a linear development model that compartmentalizes phases of development into consecutive stages, each of which must be completed prior to moving on to the next. Analysis results in project requirements, the project is then designed, and code implementation begins. Testing follows, and the project is delivered and maintained thereafter. Development flows down through each phase, as seen in Figure 15-1, like water spilling down a waterfall.

In theory, this model is easy to understand and adhere to, and sometimes works well on very big projects when responsiveness to customer needs and market changes are not as crucial. Critics of this model, however, point out that it is not always possible to completely contain each phase. In other words, a project design may change when issues surface during the coding phase, or testing may reveal weaknesses that result in a change in project requirements.

Several theories have been introduced in an attempt to adhere to the basics of the Waterfall method but improve it with new features. The *Fountain* method, for example, represents a small change by inverting the model, as seen in Figure 15-2, allowing later phases to cascade back into previous phases like water dribbling down the tiers of a fountain. More extreme adaptations, such as *Spiral*, which we'll discuss in a moment, combine elements of Waterfall with other models.

Iterative

The *Iterative* model, seen in Figure 15-3, stresses incremental software development, reworking the product throughout its life cycle. Analysis, testing, and revision occur regularly, resulting in ongoing change during development. The key to this model is that revisions are built into the development process and occur not just from user feedback, but also during the testing and coding phases.

The Iterative model was created in answer to the failings of the Waterfall model in smaller projects where timeliness, customer satisfaction, and market awareness are more critical. Typically, project development begins by focusing on small pieces of functionality. At each iteration, known issues are corrected in the planning, design, and coding stages, and additional features are added for the next round of work—that is, rather than just adding functionality in increments, each iteration goes through the entire development phase and attempts to produce a theoretically releasable product.

Prototyping

Prototyping is one example of an iterative process. This method begins with establishing a preliminary set of project specifications, then developing a prototype, or rudimentary functioning version of the project, and then immediately submitting it for user evaluation. After evaluation, changes are made to the specifications; a new prototype is designed and coded, and then it is submitted again for user evaluation. Essentially, this process continues until a satisfactory user response is received, and then the project is finished, tested, and delivered.

Agile

Agile is more a collection of methods than a single approach, but the shared principles of Agile development can be included in this discussion in a general form. Agile is an outgrowth of the Iterative model. However, Agile differs from the Iterative model in several ways, a few of which are highlighted here.

NOTE

Interestingly, software engineer Winston Royce is said to have proposed the Waterfall model, but Royce actually used the then-unnamed theory as an example of an approach needing improvement—proposing the Iterative model instead.

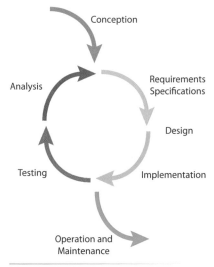

Figure 15-3. The Iterative software development model

First, it favors rapid development, timing iterations in weeks rather than months. Second, it places a significantly greater emphasis on client collaboration and face-to-face communication. Finally, it focuses less on traditional planning practices, starting with fewer project requirements and producing little documentation.

Extreme Programming (XP)

Extreme Programming is an example of an Agile method, designed for small teams working on projects that may be in flux, or when customer or market requirements are changing rapidly. Frequent testing and code integration, as well as a higher number of iterations than other models, are straightforward hallmarks of Extreme Programming, also referred to as XP. More controversial aspects of XP include having the client onsite at all times and use pair programming. Pair programming requires programmers to work in pairs on the same workstation—one coding, while the other tests, for example. Programmers are encouraged to switch roles often during a workday, and switch partners as often as is practical.

Critics point to haste, chaotic work environments, and self-fulfilling testing methods as faults of the approach. Another criticism is insufficient project requirements and documentation in favor of "user stories," which are brief descriptions of user requirements written on note cards. Advocates insist that the approach brings projects to market faster, while simultaneously reducing risk. They claim the near-constant testing cuts down on bugs, and having a client onsite means customer satisfaction and market readiness is at its highest.

V-Model

The *V-Model* is an adaptation of Waterfall, slightly enhanced by processes in the Iterative method. Favored by those who find benefit in Waterfall but recognize the need for improvement, the V-Model basically bends the waterfall diagram back upward at the implementation stage, as seen in Figure 15-4. More than just a different way to present the same model, this new arrangement demonstrates the relationship between planning and testing phases. This encourages, at minimum, validation that the project planning appears successful and, beyond that, promotes redesign if flaws are discovered during the testing phase. However, this model still suffers from reduced responsiveness to the client and user and is not very successful for smaller projects.

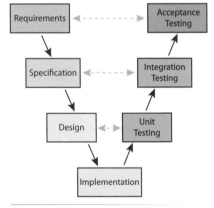

Figure 15-4. A simplified V-Model theory of software development

Spiral

The *Spiral* method is a tighter combination of the Waterfall and Iterative methods, the latter contribution focusing primarily on prototyping. It is still a plan-heavy, predictive method, but passes through multiple iterations from conception to delivery. Essentially, the path of development spirals outward through multiple stages: planning, review, analysis/prototyping, and coding, as seen in Figure 15-5. Each complete spiral represents an iteration typically culminating in a deliverable. In simple terms, the project goes through repeated passes through the waterfall, evolving by means of a prototype at each iteration.

Originally, the Spiral model was conceived for very large projects, with each iteration lasting one to two years. However, increasing numbers of smaller development efforts are adopting a simplified version of the model because it embodies the clarity of the Waterfall model and degrees of responsiveness attributed to Iterative methods.

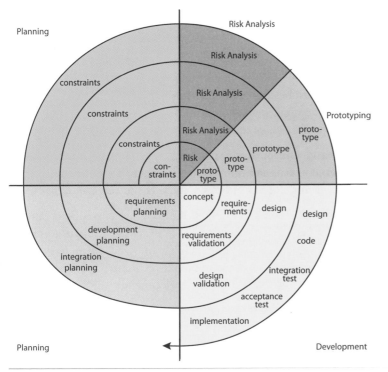

Figure 15-5. The Spiral software development model

No Perfect Solution

The evolution of this variety of methodologies—a small selection of such schools of thought in use today—reinforces the idea that no single solution will work in every situation. In many cases, particularly if you are a single programmer or part of a small development team, trying different theories may yield the best results. You may find that one approach is ideal for one project while an entirely different development method may be better suited for another project.

In general, smaller development teams, and projects that are time-sensitive, tend to adopt some form of an Iterative model—either the original theory, one of the Agile methods, or a custom adaptation. This is primarily because these methods can go to market more quickly and are more responsive to client and user needs. As a rule of thumb, larger projects tend to adopt a Spiral or V-Method approach to development. Both represent improvements over the Waterfall method, perhaps a merging of Waterfall and Iterative methods, because their coding and testing phases inform design and planning in later passes through the system.

We believe there are a number of basic principles that, while not necessarily compatible with every methodology discussed, contribute to a better coding experience:

- Start with clearly defined project requirements. An accurate design document will save unnecessary expense and keep client-vendor relationships (even if that is a metaphor for interdepartmental work within a single company) working smoothly.

- Favor spiking. Don't be afraid to experiment when developing functionality, and, perhaps more importantly, don't be afraid to discard your code if it's not up to snuff.

- Regularly review your progress to make sure you are continuing to achieve the project goals. Periodic client review and focus testing can also help provide varying degrees of objectivity to the reviews.

- Learn from project reviews and adjust the requirements, design, and/or coding phases when needed—*while keeping the design document in mind*. Some change in project specification is likely to be beneficial to the project, but try to avoid "feature creep," the tendency for new features to creep into the project unconstrained during development.

- Test early, test often, and test on many end-user environments. Avoid surprises by testing on a range of processor speeds, RAM quantities, browsers, and platforms.

- Comment and document your code as much as is practical. This is usually mandatory when coding for a client or public distribution, but it should not be overlooked even when coding your own projects. You may revisit your code months later and not be able to determine how everything works.

- Version your code. Don't ruin something that was working because you tried something else without saving your progress. Use versioning systems like our preferred Subversion (SVN) (*http://subversion.tigris.org/*) or Concurrent Version System (CVS) (*http://www.nongnu.org/cvs/*). If you'd rather not use one of these systems, save incremental versions of your code with descriptive names, dates, and possibly even a read me.

Object-Oriented Design Patterns

While many programming methodologies are relatively general, they can also be quite specialized. This is true of object-oriented *design patterns*. One of the greatest benefits of good object-oriented programming is efficient reuse. Design patterns take the idea of reuse and apply it to code *planning* rather than the code itself. Ideally, established patterns can be used when planning many different OOP projects, smoothing the development process to varying degrees.

A design pattern isn't a template into which you can just copy and paste your code, but rather an *approach* to coding that reinforces OOP principles and helps guide code creation. Patterns focus on structure and interaction between classes and objects, rather than the classes and objects themselves, laying down a blueprint from which one or more programmers can build an application. While patterns can be useful for small projects, they really shine when used on larger projects, particularly when multiple programmers are involved. Programmers who are familiar with the pattern or patterns used will more easily understand the project and be able to contribute to the code base in a logical, productive manner that results in fewer conflicts among coding styles.

Design patterns are quite the rage these days, but they are not a requirement of object-oriented programming. If you had to organize several programmers, and all agreed that known patterns would increase efficiency, you would have an ideal scenario for their use. If you don't feel comfortable with patterns, however, you shouldn't feel compelled to use them. Design patterns often introduce multiple levels of abstraction to programming design to increase flexibility. This varying degree of abstraction can sometimes make them difficult to grasp. One of the ways to determine whether a design pattern may be appropriate for a specific project is to look over the benefits and drawbacks of several patterns to see if any fit your needs.

NOTE

For more information on design-pattern use in ActionScript, see ActionScript 3.0 Design Patterns by William Sanders and Chandima Cumaranatunge (O'Reilly).

Select Pattern Descriptions

The following short list of descriptions includes a subset of design patterns gaining popularity in contemporary coding practices.

Creational patterns

This category of patterns focuses primarily on the creation of objects. These patterns have to do with class and object instantiation. Creational patterns often use inheritance and delegation to manage the creation of objects.

Factory

The Factory method adds a flexible interim step between an object and the class used to create that object. Essentially, it allows objects to be created without specifying the exact class used to create the object. It does this by defining a generic method used for instantiation that subclasses can then override to identify the class to be instantiated. This process helps relax the tight coupling of an object with its creator. As an example, think of a real factory from which this pattern takes its name. The factory stands between the client and the product. The factory adds a layer of abstraction to the creation of an object so the client can do its job without concern for how the object was created. As a result, if the product implementation changes, the factory can adapt and the client remains unaffected.

Singleton

Singletons restrict the instantiation of a class to only one object. Singletons are used much in the way a global variable is used, but they offer tighter control. A singleton can alert a developer, for example, when you attempt to create another instance of the class. Global variables have no such alert mechanism. We will provide a sample usage of the Singleton pattern later in this chapter.

Structural patterns

Structural patterns focus on relationships between classes and objects, and scaffold a project to create something larger than the sum of its parts.

Adapter

This pattern is used to give wider use to an existing class. The pattern accomplishes this without changing the existing class by adapting its interface to a form that is more suitable for a particular use.

Composite

As the name implies, this pattern advocates composition, in which case every object has the same interface. This pattern is used to create complex systems of smaller components. Some objects in that system are container objects themselves, and contain smaller components, therefore functioning as composite objects in their own right. The ActionScript 3.0 display list is a composite system that might be well-maintained by the Composite pattern.

Decorator

This pattern helps a system remain lean by providing additional functionality to objects at runtime. Essentially, it wraps objects with new methods and properties without changing entire classes. The Decorator pattern is used as an alternative to extensive inheritance, when adding desired changes through inheritance would result in an inefficiently large quantity of subclasses.

Behavioral patterns

This group of patterns focuses on object behavior and communication, as well as the allocation of responsibility for project tasks.

Observer

Using the Observer pattern, objects are instructed to observe other objects watching for the occurrence of a particular event. On a small scale, we have been using this type of pattern throughout this book, in the form of ActionScript 3.0's event listeners. Similar to the use of the Observer pattern, the target of an event listener is trained to listen for a mouse-up event, for example, and react accordingly.

State

The State pattern provides an efficient way to manage multiple states of an object or application. States can be simple, such as minimized and maximized, or more complex such as the many states of a video-editing application (for example, preferences, media, editing, preview, and export). Managing states, switching between them, and remembering their status throughout can get complicated, and the State pattern can help.

Strategy

This pattern is used to allow you to easily change the functionality of an object at runtime. Consider the arcade game Pac-Man, for example. The initial behavior of the game's antagonists is to pursue Pac-Man with a meal in mind. However, upon consuming the appropriate power-up, Pac-Man can exact his revenge, as the ghosts suddenly become the prey not the predators. This on-the-fly switching of object behavior is handled well by the Strategy pattern.

Again, this list represents a subset of known OOP design patterns. Ideally, this overview gives you an idea of the overall purpose of design patterns, and a possible topic of exploration when furthering your OOP education. To help drive this point home, let's take a closer look at one simple pattern.

The Singleton Pattern

The singleton pattern is used to restrict instantiation of a class to one object. This is useful when one instance of a particular object is needed for an application. Consider a single-player game, for example. There can be only one player score. If you inadvertently create more than one score-tracking object, you'll end up with a fragmented system that will not result in a final cumulative score.

The Singleton pattern is relatively simple to construct. It should contain a class with a method that creates a new instance of the class, or new singleton, if one does not exist. If an instance does already exist, it should return a reference to that object so a new instance is not created.

To make sure that a singleton cannot be instantiated any other way, the constructor is typically made private rather than public, as has been the case with all the classes we've discussed so far. However, ActionScript 3.0 does not allow private constructors so that it may remain compliant with the ECMA standard on which it is based. Therefore, you must adapt the traditional pattern a bit to get around this limitation.

There are many such adaptations, ranging from the use of simple static methods and properties (requiring no instantiation) with no warning errors at all, to robust systems that make use of private classes that supplement the public class constructor. The argument for no runtime warning errors is that they are of marginal use if no compile-time error is presented. The more robust Singleton patterns trigger compile-time errors but are more complex. We offer a compromise in the form of a solution that uses a static method and properties, but also offers a runtime warning—the logic being that a runtime error is better than no error at all.

An example singleton

The following code examples show the structure and use of a singleton. First, let's look at the **Singleton** class. Lines 5 and 6 create private static properties to facilitate the creation of the singleton. The first contains the instance created from the class, and the second is a Boolean that allows or disallows instantiation, which is initialized as **false**.

Lines 9 through 13 contain the class constructor. Because you don't want multiple singletons, you want to avoid the use of the **new** keyword to instantiate an object. The constructor first checks to see if the regulating Boolean, **_okToCreate**, is **false**. This is the case because it has been initialized in line 6. Therefore, if the constructor is invoked first, a warning is given stating that the **getInstance()** method must be used to create the singleton.

NOTE

A singleton's instantiation method is sometimes placed before the constructor to grab the attention of those who may edit the class, but for consistency we'll observe the standards we've established in this book and include the constructor immediately after the property declarations.

Now let's skip ahead a bit to lines 15 through 22, which contain the method used to create the singleton. This method starts by checking to see if an instance of the class has already been created. If an instance does not already exist, the method first sets the **_okToCreate** Boolean to **true**. This step allows the constructor to proceed, and an instance of the class is created. Immediately thereafter, the regulating Boolean is set to **false**. Finally, the singleton instance is returned to the script that invoked the method.

Now take a look at what happens if an instance of the singleton already exists. If the constructor is invoked, the conditional in line 10 will again fail, and an error will be issued. If the correct method is used, the condition in line 16 fails, and the existing instance is automatically returned. This is what prevents more than one instance of the class from being created.

Singleton.as

```
1    package {
2
3        public class Singleton {
4
5            private static var _instance:Singleton;
6            private static var _okToCreate:Boolean = false;
7
8
9            public function Singleton() {
10               if (!_okToCreate) {
11                   throw new Error("Error: " + this + " is
                     a singleton and must be accessed with the
                     getInstance() method");
12               }
13           }
14
15           public static function getInstance():Singleton {
16               if (!Singleton._instance){
17                   _okToCreate = true;
18                   _instance = new Singleton();
19                   _okToCreate = false;
20               }
21               return _instance;
22           }
23       }
24   }
```

To see the class instantiated, look at this document class sample, **SingletonExample**, which shows the right and wrong way to create the object. Line 12 correctly invokes the **getInstance()** method, while line 16 errantly uses the **new** keyword. The former works, while the latter throws an error.

SingletonExample.as

```
1    package {
2
3        import flash.display.Sprite;
4
5        public class SingletonExample extends Sprite {
6
7            private var _singleton:Singleton;
8
9
10           public function SingletonExample() {
11               //create game score and give it a value
12               _singleton = Singleton.getInstance();
13
14
15               //accidentally try to use new
16               //singleton = new Singleton();
17           }
18       }
19   }
```

The pattern in action

Here's an example of the Singleton pattern used to maintain a game player's score (for which there must be only one value), as previously discussed. To the Singleton class, first replace empty line 7 with the following, which creates a private property called _score.

```
7                private var _score:int = 0;
```

Then, at the end of the class, replace the closing lines 23 and 24 with the following, which adds a getter/setter pair that returns the score when requested or sets the score to the new value passed to the method.

```
23
24               public function get score():int {
25                   return _score;
26               }
27
28               public function set score(val:int):void {
29                   _score = val;
30               }
31       }
32   }
```

Finally, in the **SingletonExample** class, put the singleton to work, replacing the constructor with the following new code. The first change adds line 13 to show the proper use of the singleton, passing a value of 100 to the **score** setter. Then, for demonstration purposes, the new code tries to create a second instance of the singleton with a new value in lines 19 and 20. In a real-world scenario, this would be attempted at some other point in your project when you, or a programmer colleague, might not be aware that an instance of the class already exists. For example, a bonus of some kind might require the score to be increased by 20, which is handled separately from the normal process of shooting spaceships or whatever is responsible for adding value to the player's score.

Without using the Singleton pattern, a new instance of the game score would be created errantly resulting in one score of 100 and another of 20, instead of adding 20 to the existing score to result in a final value of 120. However, with a singleton in use, you will see in lines 23 though 25 that only one score is maintained. Lines 23 and 24 will both trace 120. As an added measure, line 25 checks for *strict equality* (the triple-equal sign which, in this case, compares two object references to see if they refer to the same object, rather than just having the same values) and will trace **true**.

```
10               public function SingletonExample() {
11                   //create game score and update it
12                   _singleton = Singleton.getInstance();
13                   _singleton.score = 100;
14
15                   //accidentally try to use new
16                   //_singleton = new Singleton();
17
18                   //accidentally try to create another score
19                   _singleton2 = Singleton.getInstance()
20                   _singleton2.score += 20;
```

```
21
22          //confirm that only one score exists
23          trace(_singleton.score);
24          trace(_singleton2.score);
25          trace(_singleton === _singleton2);
26      }
```

Resources

We hope you've learned a great deal from this book, but it still only scratches the surface when it comes to the depth and breadth of ActionScript 3.0. Supplemental resources are essential to continue your learning. The first two resources, which we've stressed throughout this book, are its companion web site and Flash itself.

The web site has the most up-to-date information about this book, including possible errata, supplemental exercises, self quizzes, and more. The Flash Help menu provides access to a wealth of resources, not the least of which is the built-in help system. Also featured are many online resources such as the Flash Developer and Support centers, the Flash Exchange for enhancing Flash with extensions and related products, and Adobe's online forums.

The truly active exchange of information, however, comes from developers in the field. The Flash community is filled with talented and generous designers and developers who contribute regularly through forums and blogs. Add book and video training resources, as well as conferences that collect talent from all over the world, and you have a wide array of information at your disposal.

WARNING

We are guaranteed to have unintentionally overlooked valuable resources in this list—confined both by time of printing and limited space. Please check the companion web site for more information and send in any resources you enjoy.

Blogs

There are many dozens of blogs that add to the published material about Flash and ActionScript. What follows is a small list of some of the best resources of the blogging community, preceded by aggregators that monitor many, many blogs, collecting posts on related topics.

Aggregators

MXNA—*http://weblogs.macromedia.com/mxna/*

Full as a Goog—*http://www.fullasagoog.com*

Blogs

ActionScript Architect (Paul Spitzer)—
   http://www.actionscriptarchitect.com

Actionscript.com—*http://www.actionscript.com*

The Algorithmist (Jim Armstrong)—*http://algorithmist.wordpress.com*

Todd Anderson—*http://www.custardbelly.com/blog/*

Aral Balkan—*http://aralbalkan.com*

Bit-101 (Keith Peters)—*http://bit-101.com/blog/*

Brajeshwar Oinam—*http://www.brajeshwar.com*

Lee Brimelow—*http://www.theflashblog.com*

ByteArray (Thimbault Imbert)—*http://www.bytearray.org*

Mike Chambers—*http://www.mikechambers.com/blog/*

Martijn de Visser—*http://www.martijndevisser.com/blog/*

Brendan Dawes—*http://www.brendandawes.com*

John Dowdell—*http://weblogs.macromedia.com/jd/*

Mike Downey—*http://madowney.com/blog/*

[draw.logic] (Ryan Christensen)—*http://drawk.wordpress.com*

Josh Dura—*http://www.joshdura.com*

Joa Ebert—*http://blog.je2050.de*

Peter Elst—*http://www.peterelst.com/blog/*

Lee Felarca—*http://www.zeropointnine.com/blog/*

FlashGuru (Guy Watson)—*http://www.flashguru.co.uk*

FlashComGuru (Stefan Richter)—*http://www.flashcomguru.com*

John Grden—*http://www.rockonflash.com/blog/*

H1DD3N.R350URC3 (Sascha)—*http://blog.hexagonstar.com*

Kevin Hoyt—*http://blog.kevinhoyt.org*

Den Ivanov—*http://www.cleoag.ru*

Seb Lee-Delisle—*http://www.sebleedelisle.com*

Jobe Makar—*http://jobemakar.blogspot.com*

André Michelle—*http://blog.andre-michelle.com*

Colin Moock—*http://www.moock.org/blog/*

Paul Ortchanian—*http://reflektions.com/miniml/default.asp*

Sam Robbins—*http://blog.pixelconsumption.com*

Ted Patrick—*http://onflex.org*

Polygonal Labs (Michael Baczynski)—*http://lab.polygonal.de*

Quasimondo (Mario Klingemann)—*http://www.quasimondo.com/*

Darron Schall—*http://www.darronschall.c om/weblog/*

Senocular (Trevor McCauley)—*http://www.senocular.com*

Sephiroth (Alessandro Crugnola)—*http://www.sephiroth.it*

Grant Skinner—*http://www.gskinner.com/blog/*

Geoff Stearns—*http://blog.deconcept.com*

Jared Tarbell—*http://www.levitated.net*

Tink (Stephen Downs)—*http://www.tink.ws/blog/*

Josh Tynjala—*http://www.zeuslabs.us*

Carlos Ulloa—*http://blog.noventaynueve.com*

Unit Zero One (Ralph Hauwert)—*http://www.unitzeroone.com/blog/*

Tinic Uro—*http://www.kaourantin.net*

Forums

Here are some community forums, preceded by some ActionScript 3.0 tips by the always-fabulous Senocular, and hosted by the Kirupa forum.

ActionScript 3 Tip of the Day—
   http://www.kirupa.com/forum/showthread.php?t=223798

ActionScript.com—*http://www.actionscript.com/Forum/tabid/61/view/topics/forumid/8/Default.aspx*

ActionScript.org—
   http://www.actionscript.org/forums/forumdisplay.php3?f=75

Kirupa—
   http://www.kirupa.com/forum/forumdisplay.php?f=141

Books

Here is a handful of additonal ActionScript 3.0 books.

ActionScript 3.0 Bible—Roger Braunstein, Mims H. Wright, and Joshua J. Noble (Wiley)

ActionScript 3.0 Cookbook—Joey Lott, Darren Schall, Keith Peters (O'Reilly)

ActionScript 3.0 Design Patterns: Object-Oriented Programming Techniques—William Sanders and Chandima Cumaranatunge (O'Reilly)

Advanced ActionScript 3 with Design Patterns—Joey Lott and Danny Patterson (Adobe Press)

Essential ActionScript 3.0—Colin Moock (O'Reilly)

Foundation ActionScript 3.0 Animation: Making Things Move!—Keith Peters (Friends of ED)

Object-Oriented ActionScript 3.0—Todd Yard, Peter Elst, Sas Jacobs (Friends of ED)

Video Training

For some, video training is a good way to begin learning ActionScript because it teaches by actual demonstration rather than descriptive text. Here are a couple of great resources with materials related to Flash and ActionScript.

gotoAndLearn() (Lee Brimelow)—*http://www.gotoandlearn.com*

Lynda.com—*http://www.lynda.com*

Conferences

The initial explosion, and continued growth, of the Flash community was largely bolstered by conferences that focused on Flash and related technologies and gathered talented speakers from all over the world. If you get a chance to attend any of these conferences, you won't regret it.

Adobe MAX—*http://www.adobe.com/events/max/*

Flash in the Can—*http://www.flashinthecan.com*

Flash on the Beach—*http://www.flashonthebeach.com*

Flashbelt—*http://www.flashbelt.com*

FlashForward—*http://www.flashforwardconference.com*

Libraries

While using a precreated library of code is not typically common for beginner users, it's very helpful to know that these libraries exist as you begin work on new projects. Sometimes, it's worth investing a little time learning how to use a script library rather than reinventing the wheel. Libraries, when used in combination with knowing how to write your own scripts, can be powerful development assets. We've also included some ActionScript 3.0 documentation generators in this list. They're not exactly libraries, but they can be used to create documentation for your libraries.

Collections

Google Code (AS3 category search)—
  http://code.google.com/hosting/search?q=label:AS3

ActionScript 3 Libraries (Adobe corelib, eBay, FlexUnit, Flickr, Mappr, Syndication Library, Odeo, YouTube)—
  http://actionscript3libraries.riaforge.org/

Hexagon (see Games)

Yahoo! (search, weather, more)—*http://developer.yahoo.com/flash/*

OsFlash (open source Flash portal)—*http://www.osflash.org*

3D

ASCOLLADA (reading Collada files)—
http://code.google.com/p/ascollada/

Away3D—*http://www.away3d.com*

Papervision3D—*http://blog.papervision3d.org*

Sandy—*http://sandy.media-box.net/blog/*

Games

APE (ActionScript Physics Engine)—*http://www.cove.org/ape/*

as3cards (playing cards)—*http://as3cards.riaforge.org*

as3ds (Data Structure for Game Developers)—
http://code.google.com/p/as3ds/

Hexagon (collection)—*http://code.google.com/p/hexagon/*

MechEye (collection)—*http://code.google.com/p/mecheye-as3-libraries/*

WiiFlash (Windows only)—*http://www.wiiflash.org*

Media

YouTube, Odeo, Flickr—See "Collections"

Animated GIF player and encoder—*http://code.google.com/p/as3gif/*

as3soundeditorlib—*http://code.google.com/p/as3soundeditorlib/*

Popforge (audio synthesis, image processing, cubicVR)—
http://code.google.com/p/popforge/

Tweening

Animation Package—
http://www.alex-uhlmann.de/flash/animationpackage/

AS3 Animation System v. 2.0—*http://www.boostworthy.com/blog/?p=170*

asinmotion—*http://code.google.com/p/asinmotion/*

Go—*http://blog.mosessupposes.com/?cat=4*

Tween Lite, TweenFilterLite—*http://blog.greensock.com/tweenliteas3/*

Tweener—*http://code.google.com/p/tweener/*

Data/File Exchange

Alive PDF (PDF generation)—*http://www.alivepdf.org*

as3awss3lib (Amazon S3)—*http://code.google.com/p/as3awss3lib/*

As3Crypto (cryptography)—*http://crypto.hurlant.com*

asSQL (SQL access without middleware)—*http://maclema.com/assql/*

ASZip (Zip compression)—*http://code.google.com/p/aszip/*

FZip (Zip decompression)—*http://codeazur.com.br/lab/fzip/*

JSON (JavaScript Object Notation)—
http://www.darronschall.com/weblog/archives/000215.cfm

Lightweight Remoting—*http://as3lrf.riaforge.org*

SWX (SWF-based data exchange)—*http://swxformat.org*

Maps

MapQuest—*http://company.mapquest.com/mqbs/4a.html*

Yahoo Maps—See "Collections"

Social Networking

Digg—*http://code.google.com/p/diggflashdevkit/*

Facebook—*http://as3facebooklib.riaforge.org*

Flickr—See "Collections"

Last.fm—*http://code.google.com/p/lastfm-as3/*

Twitter—*http://twitter.com/blog/2006/10/twitter-api-for-flash-developers.html*

> ## Project Package
>
> The project package for this, our final chapter, includes our **Singleton** class. For more information about the companion web site project, see Chapter 6.

Documentation

ASDoc (part of the Flex distribution)—*http://www.adobe.com*

ZenDoc—*http://www.zendoc.org*

Don't forget to check the companion web site for updated resources and to contribute your own suggestions!

What's Next?

This edition of *Learning ActionScript 3.0* has come to an end. It's now time to put everything you've learned into practice. This book's companion web site, *http://www.learningactionscript3.com* contains a growing list of additional exercises and resources for you to explore. Included is a cumulative project that highlights most of the skills we've covered herein, and assembles an *AS3 Lab* to showcase your work. The end result is an object-oriented application that you can expand and use for your own experiments in the future.

Also coming to the web site are community resources, including a forum in which we will participate, and news about upcoming projects and future books. We hope you enjoyed this book, and we hope you visit the web site!

INDEX

URLRequest object, loading sound, 280
URLStream class, 292
URLVariables class, 281–282
useCapture parameter,
    addEventListener()
    method, 47
useHandCursor property
    MainMenu class, 113–114
UTF-8, encoding, 262

V

V-Model programming design
    methodology, 336, 338
variables
    data typing, 16–17
    declaring, 16
        mandatory in version 3.0, 17
    loading, 281–284
    local variables, 25
    naming, 16
var keyword, 16
vector drawing
    bitmap caching, 168–169
    color picker, 161–163
    CreateRoundRectButton class,
        163–165
    flash.geom package classes, 149–158
    Graphics class
        basics, 142–143
        curves, 144–145
        fills, gradient, 147–148, 161–163
        fills, solid, 145
        lines, 143–144
        shapes, 145–146
        shapes, skewing, 154–155
    Motion package classes, 158–159
    9-slice scaling, 159–161
    Pencil tool (Flash), simulating,
        148–149
    versus bitmap graphics, 168–169
vector quantities
    acceleration, 117, 126
    velocity, 117, 126
Vehicle class
    composition, 100–101
    encapsulation, 103–105
    inheritance, 95–99
velFriction() function,
    deceleration, 128

velocity, 126
    basics, 117–118
    example, 121–122
    vector quantities, 117
versioning code
    programming methodologies, 338
video
    captioning
        cue points, 264–268
        multiple languages, 268–271
        overview, 260–261
        Rehabilitation Act of 1973, 260
        Timed Text files, 261–263, 268–270
    encoding, 252–253
    FLVPlaybackCaptioning
        component, 256
        with FLV Playback component, 260
        Timed Text files, 264
    FLVPlayback component, 256–261
        advantages, 254–255
        with FLVPlaybackCaptioning, 260
        Timed Text files, 264
    H.264-encoded format support, 254
    loading, 280–281
        security, 292
    QuickTime movie format
        support, 254
    true full-screen video, 258–260
    web video distribution, 254
Video class, 52, 53
Video Encoder, 252–253
    deinterlacing support, 258–259
video player, creating, 272–276
VideoPlayer class, 276
video training, ActionScript/Flash
    resources, 348
virtual machines
    AVM1 and AVM2, 289–290
visible property, movie clips, 33
Visualization class, 240, 242, 244–249
visualizing sound data
    microphone sounds, 237–239
    playing in real time, 239
        SoundPlayBasic class, 239–244
        Visualization class, 244–249
    stereo channels, 234–236
volume controls, 223, 229–231
VP6 codec (On2), 252–253

W

W3C Timed Text format. See TT
Waterfall programming design
    methodology, 334–335, 338
    Fountain, 334, 335
    Spiral, 335, 336–337, 338
    V-Model, 336, 338
WAVE files, 224
waveform visualization, sound
    playing, 234, 239
    SoundPlayBasic class, 239–244
    Visualization class, 244–249
WC3 (World Wide Web Consortium)
    E4X, 297
weak references, addEventListener()
    method, 47, 63
web sites
    absolute versus relative addresses, 28
    security controls, 294
while loops, 22
width property, movie clips, 33
Windows, absolute versus relative
    addresses, 28
with statements
    methods, 142–143, 145
    objects, 142
    properties, 142–153
wordWrap property, 199
World Wide Web Consortium.
        See WC3
wrapOption parameter, cue points, 266

X

x coordinate property
    Motion class, 133
    movie clips, 33
XML (Extensible Markup Language)
    comments, 300–301
    communicating with servers
        send-and-load technique, 315–317
        sockets, 317–319
    declaration tags, 300
    deleting, 313–314